Acc

D1437346

LYLE PRICE GUIDE
ART DECO
CERAMICS

First published in 1999

1 3 5 7 9 10 8 6 4 2

Ebury Press
Random House, 20 Vauxhall Bridge Road, London SW1V 2SA

Random House Australia Pty Limited
20 Alfred Street, Milsons Point, Sydney, New South Wales 2061,
Australia

Random House New Zealand Limited
18 Poland Road, Glenfield, Auckland 10, New Zealand

Random House South Africa (Pty) Limited
Endulini. 5A Jubilee Road, Parktown 2193, South Africa

Random House UK Limited Reg. No. 954009

A CIP catalogue record for this book is available from the British
Library

ISBN 0091868343

Printed and bound in Great Britain by Butler & Tanner

LYLE PRICE GUIDE
ART DECO
CERAMICS

TONY CURTIS

The publishers wish to express their sincere thanks to the following for their involvement and assistance in the production of this volume.

TONY CURTIS (Editor)

EELIN McIVOR (Sub Editor)

ANNETTE CURTIS (Editorial)

CATRIONA DAY (Art Production)

ANGIE DEMARCO (Art Production)

NICKY FAIRBURN (Art Production)

PHILIP SPRINGTHORPE (Photography)

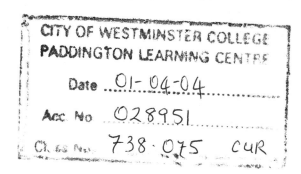

CONTENTS

While every care has been taken in the compiling of information contained in this volume, the publisher cannot accept liability for loss, financial of otherwise, incurred by reliance placed on the information herein.

All prices quoted in this book are obtained from a variety of auctions in various countries and are converted to dollars at the rate of exchange prevalent at the time of sale. The images and the accompanying text remain the copyright of the contributing auction houses.

ACKNOWLEDGEMENTS

Anderson & Garland, Marlborough House, Marlborough Crescent, Newcastle NE1 4EE

Auctionshaus Arnold, Bleichstr. 42, 6000 Frankfurt a/M, Germany

Bearne's, St Edmunds Court, Okehampton Street, Exeter EX4 1DU

Bonhams Chelsea, 65–69 Lots Road, London SW10 0RN

Bonhams West Country, Dowell Street, Honiton, Devon

Bristol Auction Rooms, St John Place, Apsley Road, Clifton, Bristol BS8 2ST

Butterfield & Butterfield, 220 San Bruno Avenue, San Francisco CA 94103, USA

Butterfield & Butterfield, 7601 Sunset Boulevard, Los Angeles CA 90046, USA

Canterbury Auction Galleries, 40 Station Road West, Canterbury CT2 8AN

Christie's (International) SA, 8 place de la Taconnerie, 1204 Genève, Switzerland

Christie's Monaco, S.A.M, Park Palace 98000 Monte Carlo, Monaco

Christie's Scotland, 164–166 Bath Street, Glasgow G2 4TG

Christie's South Kensington Ltd., 85 Old Brompton Road, London SW7 3LD

Christie's, 8 King Street, London SW1Y 6QT

Christie's East, 219 East 67th Street, New York, NY 10021, USA

Christie's, 502 Park Avenue, New York, NY10022, USA

Christie's, Cornelis Schuytstraat 57, 1071 JG Amsterdam, Netherlands

Christie's SA Roma, 114 Piazza Navona, 00186 Rome, Italy

Christie's Swire, 2804–6 Alexandra House, 16–20 Chater Road, Hong Kong

Christie's Australia Pty Ltd., 1 Darling Street, South Yarra, Victoria 3141, Australia

The Crested China Co., Station House, Driffield, E. Yorks YO25 7PY

Wiilliam Doyle Galleries, 175 East 87th Street, New York, NY 10128, USA

Dee, Atkinson & Harrison, The Exchange Saleroom, Driffield, Nth. Humberside YO25 7LJ

Du Mouchelles Art Galleries Co., 409 E. Jefferson Avenue, Detroit, Michigan 48226, USA

Eldred's, Box 796, E. Dennis, MA 02641, USA

Ewbanks, Burnt Common Auction Rooms, London Road, Send, Woking GU23 7LN

Finarte, 20121 Milano, Piazzetta Bossi 4, Italy

G A Key, Aylsham Saleroom, Palmers Lane, Aylsham, Norfolk, NR11 6EH

The Goss and Crested China Co., 62 Murray Road, Horndean, Hants PO8 9JL

Greenslade Hunt, Magdalene House, Church Square, Taunton, Somerset, TA1 1SB

Andrew Hartley Fine Arts, Victoria Hall, Little Lane, Ilkely

Muir Hewitt, Halifax Antiques Centre, Queens Road/Gibbet Street, Halifax HX1 4LR

ACKNOWLEDGEMENTS

Hobbs & Chambers, 'At the Sign of the Bell', Market Place, Cirencester, Glos

Hotel de Ventes Horta, 390 Chaussée de Waterloo (Ma Campagne), 1060 Bruxelles, Bel.

Jackson's, 2229 Lincoln Street, Cedar Falls, Iowa 50613, USA.

George Kidner, The Old School, The Square, Pennington, Lymington, Hants SO41 8GN

Kunsthaus am Museum, Drususgasse 1–5, 5000 Köln 1, Germany

Lawrence's Fine Art Auctioneers, Norfolk House, 80 High Street, Bletchingley, Surrey

David Lay, The Penzance Auction House, Alverton, Penzance, Cornwall TA18 4KE

Dave Lewis, 20 The Avenue, Starbeck, Harrogate, North Yorkshire HG1 4QD

Christopher Matthews, 23 Mount Street, Harrogate HG2 8DG

John Maxwell, 133a Woodford Road, Wilmslow, Cheshire

Outhwaite & Litherland, Kingsley Galleries, Fontenoy Street, Liverpool, Merseyside L3 2BE

Phillips Manchester, Trinity House, 114 Northenden Road, Sale, Manchester M33 3HD

Phillips West Two, 10 Salem Road, London W2 4BL

Phillips, 11 Bayle Parade, Folkestone, Kent CT20 1SQ

Phillips, 49 London Road, Sevenoaks, Kent TN13 1UU

Phillips, 65 George Street, Edinburgh EH2 2JL

Phillips, Blenstock House, 7 Blenheim Street, New Bond Street, London W1Y 0AS

Phillips Marleybone, Hayes Place, Lisson Grove, London NW1 6UA

Phillips, New House, 150 Christleton Road, Chester CH3 5TD

Riddetts, 26 Richmond Hill, Bournemouth

Russell, Baldwin & Bright, The Fine Art Saleroom, Ryelands Road, Leominster HR6 8JG

Skinner Inc., Bolton Gallery, Route 117, Bolton MA, USA

Sotheby's, 34–35 New Bond Street, London W1A 2AA

Sotheby's, 1334 York Avenue, New York NY 10021

Sotheby's, 112 George Street, Edinburgh EH2 2LH

Sotheby's, Summers Place, Billingshurst, West Sussex RH14 9AD

Sotheby's, Monaco, BP 45, 98001 Monte Carlo

Tennants, Harmby Road, Leyburn, Yorkshire

Sam Weller, Ash House, 28 Bure Way, Aylsham, North Norfolk NR11 6HJ

Peter Wilson, Victoria Gallery, Market Street, Nantwich, Cheshire CW5 5DG

Wintertons Ltd., Lichfield Auction Centre, Fradley Park, Lichfield, Staffs WS13 8NF

Woolley & Wallis, The Castle Auction Mart, Salisbury, Wilts SP1 3SU

ART DECO CERAMICS

Art Deco is essentially a phenomenon of the twentieth century. Indeed, it is inconceivable that it should have developed at any other time in history. When we look back at the aspiring arches of gothic, the clean simplicity of classicism, the florid exuberance of baroque and rococo, even the harmonious, flowing lines of Art Nouveau, we see how utterly different it was in concept from any of these. If we ask why, we may see that it was the product of a completely different world.

Underpinning all these other movements was an innate belief, whether religious or rational, in some essential order in the world. This confidence, like so much else, was to die in the carnage of the First World War. Thereafter, a traumatised world was to wake up to the fact that life was uncertain, that while it was there it should be lived and enjoyed to the full, that what mattered was sensation and experience. Art Deco, with its bright colours and its unusual, often jarring shapes, reflected this almost frenetic desire for something that would divert attention from the recollection of how fragile was the framework of life.

Of course, this was not the full story, and many of the seeds of the Art Deco movement were sown even before 1914.

The Wiener Werkstätte was established in Austria as early as 1903, and was followed in Germany by the Deutscher Bund, to be followed in turn in 1919 by the Bauhaus. All these organisations emphasised simplicity and functionalism of design, not only for furniture but also for architecture, metalwork, textiles and ceramics. Then, too, there is perhaps the most often quoted influence of Diaghilev's Ballets Russes, which came to Paris in 1909 and took the place by storm with their explosive mix of colour and sound. In art too, the groundwork had been laid in the work of the Cubists and the Fauves, who used vivid combinations of pure colour.

All sorts of other influences were also brought to bear by the way in which the world was opening up, in one case literally when the tomb of Tutankhamen had been discovered and opened in 1922. This occasioned tremendous interest in things Egyptian, and ancient Egyptian symbols were immensely popular copied onto jewellery, pottery and furniture. Things African, often funnelled through the craze for jazz and coloured entertainers, also captured the public imagination at this time, as did Central American Aztec designs, and oriental and East European motifs. The world in fact was shrinking fast with the advent of new communications media and faster means of travel. Art Deco was an eclectic movement which, sometimes indiscriminately, welcomed and adapted motifs from a wide variety of sources.

The name Art Deco itself derived from the Exposition Internationale des Arts Decoratifs et Industriels Modernes, which, after numerous delays caused by the international situation, was held in Paris in 1925. Its avowed aim was to demonstrate the very best of modern design, and put Paris back at the forefront of international style. This enormous and glittering event was intended to be international, as its name suggested, but in reality only France was fully represented. The USA and Germany made excuses, and many British exhibitors were reluctant to take part in a flag waving exercise, and preferred to participate in such domestic events as the British Empire Exhibition at Wembley in 1924.

Nevertheless, the British pottery industry adopted Art Deco styles with enthusiasm and an amazing range of items were made in the two succeeding decades, often by the most prosaic of factories. For this was essentially a people's movement. Education had improved by leaps and bounds and a whole new market of literate householders were now open to all the new marketing techniques which were now developing in the form of sophisticated sales literature, newspaper advertising and so on. Also, the Art Deco style was not confined to a few individually designed studio pots for the connoisseurs and the very rich. They appeared on all kinds of everyday items, teapots, vases, bowls, ornaments, mass produced and available in such stores as Woolworths. For this reason quality varies enormously, and is not always reflected in the value objects fetch today. Some of Clarice Cliff's pieces for example were intended to be sold cheaply and cheerfully, in some cases for about 6d. each. Today, they will often fetch into four figures. And in some cases, it seems the more kitsch the piece, the more it sells for.

Yet most Art Deco items have an undeniably endearing quality about them. Perhaps it is because they are so bright and bold and, in contemporary parlance, in-your-face. They do lift the spirits, which is possibly what the movement, consciously or not, set out to do. There is a huge range of styles to choose from, and, even better, many items are still very affordable for the average collector.

In this book we have attempted to cover the widest possible range of Art Deco items which will be regularly found at auction up and down the country. We have also included work by such studio potters as Lucie Rie and Hans Coper, which, while not strictly in the Art Deco idiom, are yet of the period, and are also highly collectable.

It is our hope that we have provided Art Deco enthusiasts with an indispensable reference work which will help them further their knowledge and buy and sell the pieces they deal with to their maximum advantage.

The United States have always had a strong ceramic tradition, from earliest Native American examples through the redware of the European settlers.

During the Art Deco period many existing potteries adapted their output to this style, sometimes borrowing heavily on their European counterparts, but as often developing their own distinctive version.

Such potters as Rockwell Kent, for example, would produce plates with geometric borders, but featuring stylised but instantly recognisable American skyscraper scenes in the well. The McCoy Pottery of Roseville, Ohio, specialised in cookie jars with bright glazes in the shape of lively figures, while Harlequin Pottery, manufactured by the Homer Laughlin Company was marketed exclusively at F.W. Woolworth stores. It was geometric in shape, with Art Deco style handles and bright colours, such as blue, red-orange and yellow, and has a wide following among Art Deco collectors.

Chelsea Keramic Art Works pillow vase, incised palm tree decoration under blue glaze, signed *H.C.R., Chelsea Keramic Art Works, Robertson & Sons,* 6½in. high. *(Skinner)* **£107 $172**

Five Rockwell Kent 'Salamina' ceramic plates, designed in 1939 for Vernon Kilns, Vernon and Los Angeles, brown stamp marks, 16¾ x 9½in. diameter. *(Skinner)* **£354 $575**

North Dakota Art pottery vase, dated 1953, in squat globular form with pink floral design, signed *Lebacken,* 7½in. high. *(Eldred's)* **£242 $395**

Art Pottery vase, dynamic iridescent and gold shimmering glaze on red clay, thumbprint in side, obscured marks, 7½in. high. 5½in. diameter. *(Skinner)* **£185 $300**

Chelsea Pottery U.S. Tulip on Raised Upside Down Dolphin plate, impressed *C.P.U.S.* mark, 10in. diameter. *(Skinner)* **£3,105 $5,175**

Chelsea Keramic Art vase, applied white flowers on crimpled squat-form with butterscotch glaze, 5in. wide.
(Skinner) **£400 $650**

Chelsea Keramic Art Works vase, Massachusetts, late 19th century, with relief decoration of squirrels and oak branches, 12in. wide.
(Skinner) **£800 $1,300**

A pair of Chelsea Keramic Art Works double handled vases, Massachusetts, circa 1885, blue-green and brown glaze, 6¼in. high. *(Skinner)* **£400 $650**

Important Devil's face jug, Javan or Davis Brown, circa 1940, stamped signature *Brown Pottery Arden, NC, Hand Made*, the jug of unglazed stoneware depicting a devil's face with applied facial features, horns, moustache, and beard, and porcelain teeth, inscribed *Graham's Furniture and Hardware Store, Bakersvlle. NC, 19in. high.*

This unusually large jug is one of two known advertising jugs made by Brown's pottery. It was commissioned for the opening of Graham's Hardware Store.
(Skinner) **£15,000 $24,150**

Exceptional Chelsea Keramic Art Works, Robertson & Sons ceramic tile with a copper covered relief of a figure holding two rearing stallions, 10½in. square.
(Skinner) **£3,640 $6000**

Chelsea Keramic Art works pottery vase, flat oval form, handles at sides, blue and brown glaze, impressed mark, 13in. high. *(Skinner)* **£200 $325**

A green-glazed grotesque jug, American, 20th century, the bulbous form with articulated ears flanking a human face, 16in. high. *(Christie's)* **£771 $1,150**

Pewabic Pottery vase, sloped base with flared neck to rounded lip, blue to green glazes, stamped *Pewabic Detroit*, 10¼in. high. *(Du Mouchelles)* **£1,115 $1,800**

Pewabic Pottery vase, circa 1920, baluster form with iridescent blue, green, lavender and brown glazes, stamped *Pewabic Detroit* in a circle, 11¾in. high. *(Du Mouchelles)* **£465 $750**

A fine pair of Chelsea Keramic art pottery vases with blue-green glossy glaze, circa 1885, 11¼in. high. *(Skinner)* **£850 $1,400**

Pewabic Pottery vase, Detroit, warty iridescent glaze in bronze and red, cream glazed interior, 15½in. high. *(Skinner)* **£2,683 $4,375**

Pewabic Pottery vase, late 1920s, globular form with upright neck, and flared lip, blue iridescent glaze, 8in. high. *(Du Mouchelles)* **£1,000 $1,600**

American Encaustic Tiling Co. Ltd., figural of a woman with urn, New York, W.J. Griffiths, inscribed artist's signature, 11¼in. high. *(Skinner)* **£500 $815**

Pewabic pottery vase, iridescent rose to blue to green glaze, tapering sides terminating in a foot, mid 20th century, 6in. high. *(Du Mouchelles)* **£575 $935**

Buffalo Pottery Deldare Ware pitcher, Buffalo, New York, J. Gerhardt, 1909, 'The Fallowfield Hunt', 6in. high. *(Skinner)* **£269 $403**

Chelsea Pottery U.S., Dolphin with Mask plate, possible H.C.R. signature in border, impressed *C.P.U.S.* mark, diameter 10in. *(Skinner)* **£3,795 $6,325**

Barbotine Pottery vase, portrait of a lady, creamy blue glaze, obscured artist name, 8¼in. high, 7in. wide. *(Skinner)* **£180 $300**

Vance faience vase with moulded mermaid decoration, Ohio, circa 1905, with repeating figures and fish, 12½in. high. *(Skinner)* **£190 $310**

Chelsea Pottery U.S., rabbit facing left pattern plate, raised design, impressed *C.P.U.S.* mark, initials, *F.S.* 10in. *(Skinner)* **£1,294 $2,070**

Chelsea Keramic Art Works ewer, mottled sea green glaze, impressed mark, 10in. high, 5½in. wide. *(Skinner)* **£500 $800**

The Amphora Porzellanfabrik was established at Turn-Teplitz in Bohemia to make earthenware and porcelain. Much of their porcelain figure output was exported.

The mark consists of three stars in a burst of rays over RSK (for the proprietors Reissner & Kessel).

Austrian Amphora mirror with stylised Art Nouveau figure, 1910, 13in. high.
(Muir Hewitt) **£300 $450**

An earthenware vase, by Amphora, circa 1900, squat form decorated with 'honeycomb' design applied with multicoloured glass cabochons, 6¼in. high., stamped on the base *Amphora Austria* in an oval and numbered *93, 3661, 52. (Christie's)* **£1,380 $2,208**

Amphora Pottery pitcher, Scottish Rose design in yellow, red, and blue on mottled ivory ground, 11½in. high.
(Skinner) **£245 $400**

Amphora centrepiece, with incised decoration and jewel style insets, 9¼in. high. *(Skinner)* **£218 $345**

An Amphora Turn-Teplitz bowl, designed by Reissner, Stellmacher & Kessel, painted on the obverse with the bust of a woman in pink, blues, green and purple, 10¼in. wide. *(Bonhams)* **£600 $900**

An Amphora oviform earthenware jardinière, painted with geese walking in a wooded landscape, 8½in. high. *(Christie's)* **£375 $600**

15

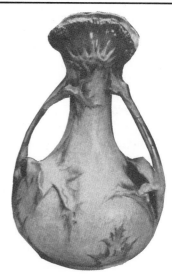

Pair of Amphora vases, cylindrical form with flared rim and foot, decorated with a carved relief landscape scene, 11¾in. high. *(Skinner)* **£436 $690**

Large Amphora floral vase, bulbous form with two handles, applied floral blooms in soft pink and green on a carved relief green ground, 18in. high. *(Skinner)* **£254 $402**

An exceptionally large gilt decorated and applied glazed earthenware vase, after the model by Reissner, manufactured by Amphora, circa 1900, modelled in full relief with a naked maiden kneeling beside a richly decorated vase with gilded neck pierced at the rim, the base with deep red glaze, decorated in relief with formalised flowers detailed in blue and gilding, the centres with applied brightly coloured ceramic roundels 17⁷/₈in. high. *(Christie's)* **£10,000 $16,000**

Important Amphora ceramic bust for the Paris Exposition 1900, swirling portrait of a finely detailed woman in a cream glaze, 10¾in. high. *(Skinner)* **£1,674 $2,645**

The Ashtead Pottery was established in 1923 by Sir Laurence and Lady Weaver to give employment to disabled ex-servicemen. It was immediately successful and by 1925 the original workforce of 14 had increased to 30. The pottery produced tableware, nursery novelties and figures, at first in white glazed earthenware. Painted landscape decoration and linear designs were introduced later, and the figures, usually in white glazed earthenware with touches of colour, are characterised by garlands of flowers painted in bright blue, yellow, maroon, light green. These are typical of the early 1930s, when they were produced.

The mark which was used between 1926 and 1936 comprised a printed tree and *Ashtead Potters.*

A pair of Ashtead Pottery bookends designed by Percy Metcalfe, each modelled as a seated cherub with doves at his feet, 18cm. high.
(Christie's) **£200 $320**

An Ashtead advertising plaque, for the Ideal Home magazine, moulded in relief with a ballet dancer, 6in. high.
(Christie's) **£150 $240**

Three of five Art Deco Ashtead Pottery wall plates,
(Phillips) **£300 $480**

'Wembley Lion', an Ashtead Pottery figure, modelled by Percy Metcalfe, covered in an orange glaze, 18cm. high.
(Christie's) **£138 $207**

An Ashtead lamp base of ovoid form, moulded in relief on each shoulder with the head of a gazelle, 11in. high.
(Christie's) **£250 $400**

AULT

William Ault (b. 1841) was an English potter who worked in Staffordshire before going into partnership with Henry Tooth in 1882 to open an art pottery at Church Gresley, Derbyshire. In 1887 he opened his own pottery near Burton-on-Trent, where he produced earthenware vases, pots, pedestals and grotesque jugs.

The painted decoration of flowers and butterflies was often executed by his daughter Clarissa. Between 1892-96 Christopher Dresser designed some vases for Ault, which he sometimes covered in his own aventurine glaze. Between 1923-37 the firm traded as Ault and Tunnicliffe and thereafter became Ault Potteries Ltd.

Marks include a tall fluted vase over *Ault* on a ribbon, or a monogrammed *APL*.

An Ault Pottery vase, designed by Christopher Dresser, the vessel of broad double-gourd form, glazed in streaked green and manganese brown, 27.5cm. high.
(Phillips) **£1,500 $2,265**

An unusual Ault Pottery pouring vessel, designed by Christopher Dresser, of compressed globular shape with two pouring spouts, 28cm. wide.
(Phillips) **£2,400 $3,850**

An Ault Pottery vase, possibly designed by Christopher Dresser, moulded on each side with a stylised fish face, 18cm. high.
(Sotheby's) **£410 $635**

An Ault Pottery bottle vase, designed by Dr. Christopher Dresser, the bulbous lobed base with slender neck, covered overall with an ox blood glaze, 9in. high.
(Bonhams) **£150 $240**

An Ault vase, designed by Dr. Christopher Dresser, with curling lip continuing to form two handles, streaked turquoise glaze over dark brown, 18cm.
(Christie's) **£1,000 $1,600**

While most people tend to think of Beswick as a product of the 1950s, it was in fact in 1894 that James Wright Beswick established his pottery at Longton, Stoke on Trent. By the 1920s they were producing tableware, glazed ornaments and a whole range of figurines and animals. In the 1930s, they decided to recruit a resident modelling team, and it is from this time that their move away from tableware to purely decorative items dates. Throughout the succeeding four decades they produced well-modelled, bright and affordable ornaments. Their range of horses are particularly well-known as are the legendary flying duck wall plaques, which have come to epitomise the style of the 50s. Almost from the beginning, Beswick was a collector's dream, appealing to adults and children alike, as they introduced ranges such as Beatrix Potter and Disney characters. In 1969, the company were taken over by Royal Doulton, and under Doulton's subsidiary Royal Albert, they are still in production today.

Beswick large model of a jay, (second version), model number 1219B, painted in colours, 6in.
(G.A. Key) **£200 $320**

Beswick wall mask of a flaxen haired girl with green ribbons.
(Muir Hewitt) **£300 $500**

Beswick Beatrix Potter figure of Benjamin Bunny, introduced 1948, gold oval back stamp, the first version with left arm and slipper held away from the body, 4in. high.
(Ewbank) **£280 $460**

Beswick, 15th century knight in armour on horse, no number, should be 1145, introduced 1949, withdrawn 1969.
(Peter Wilson) **£390 $608**

Beswick white vase of cornucopia design, 1950s. *(Muir Hewitt)* **£40 $65**

Beswick Ware Atlantic salmon, pattern No. 1233, 9in., English, 20th century. *(G.A. Key)* **£80 $130**

Beswick, graduated set of three seagull wall plaques, numbered *658/1/2/3*, introduced 1938, withdrawn 1967. *(Peter Wilson)* **£65 $101**

Beswick vase with geometric design, 9in. high, 1930s. *(Muir Hewitt)* **£80 $130**

Beswick Galleon wall plaque in brown, blue and cream, 1930s. *(Muir Hewitt)* **£200 $325**

Beswick model of a Cairn terrier with ball on left leg, decorated in beige with brown stripes and red ball, No. 1055A, 4in. long. *(G.A. Key)* **£32 $51**

A Beswick model of a swallow-tail butterfly, 5¼ x 3½in., impressed number *1492*, green mark.
(Anderson & Garland) **£120 $188**

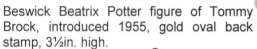

Beswick Beatrix Potter figure of Tommy Brock, introduced 1955, gold oval back stamp, 3½in. high.
(Ewbank) **£220 $365**

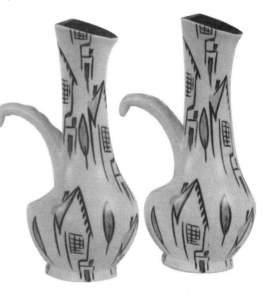

A pair of Beswick Art Deco style vases, 1950s. *(Muir Hewitt)* **£225 $370**

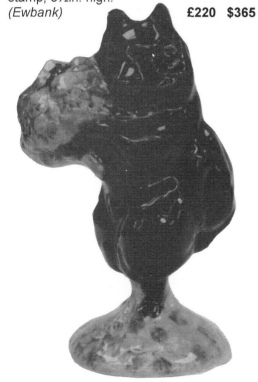

Duchess with Flowers, a rare figure, 1954-67.
(Phillips) **£1,600 $2,560**

Beswick 1930s Red Indian wall mask, 5in. high. *(Muir Hewitt)* **£120 $195**

A pair of Beswick Art Deco style vases, 1950s. *(Muir Hewitt)* **£200 $325**

Beswick dog wall mask with blue bow, 1930s. *(Muir Hewitt)* **£100 $160**

Beswick seagull, 8½in. wide, circa 1939. *(Muir Hewitt)* **£100 $160**

Beswick model of a large T'ang horse, No. 2205, mainly decorated in bronze with green detail, 13in. high. *(G.A. Key)* **£225 $362**

Beswick Beatrix Potter figure of Pigling Bland, first version with dark mauve jacket, 4¼in. high, introduced 1955 with gold round back stamp. *(Ewbank)* **£200 $332**

Jiminy Cricket, a Beswick
Walt Disney character,
1952-65.
(Phillips) **£260 $416**

Beswick model of a cougar,
pattern No. 1702, white
polychrome glazes, 12in.,
English, 20th century.
(G.A. Key) **£95 $154**

Large Beswick Dalmatian
dog, 14in.
(G.A. Key) **£110 $169**

Ginger Nutt, a Beswick
David Hand Animalland
figure, painted in colours,
10cm. high.
(Christie's) **£288 $461**

Frog Footman, and Fish
Footman, 1975-83.
(Phillips) **£320 $512**

A Beswick model of a
seated fox, number 2348,
(Fireside Series), impressed
marks, 12½in.
(G.A. Key) **£260 $416**

A Beswick Pinto horse, (tail
hanging loose), 6¼in. high.
(Dee, Atkinson & Harrison)
£20 $30

Tom Kitten, a rare Beswick
wall plaque, 1967-69.
(Phillips) **£1,350 $2,160**

A Beswick green
woodpecker, No. 1218,
8½in. high. *(Dee, Atkinson &
Harrison)* **£70 $107**

23

A Beswick Pottery teapot featuring Sairey Gamp, 5¾in. high, introduced 1939. *(Lyle)* **£100 $165**

Lady with Beads wall plaque by Beswick Pottery, 12in. high, introduced 1936. *(Lyle)* **£350 $570**

Basket of Flowers wall plaque by Beswick, 10½in. high, introduced 1937. *(Lyle)* **£160 $260**

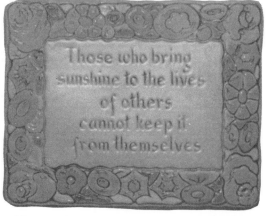

Beswick Beatrix Potter figure of Foxy Whiskered Gentleman, introduced 1954, gold oval back stamp. *(Ewbank)* **£280 $460**

'Those who bring sunshine' wall plaque by Beswick Pottery, 9½ x 7½in., introduced 1937. *(Lyle)* **£180 $300**

Barnaby Rudge character jug by Beswick Pottery, 4½in. high, introduced 1948. *(Lyle)* **£70 $115**

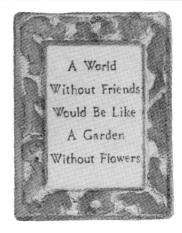

'A World without Friends' wall plaque by Beswick Pottery, 9½ x 7½in., introduced 1939. *(Lyle)* **£180 $300**

Kangaroo by Beswick Pottery, 5in. high, introduced 1970. *(Lyle)* **£135 $220**

Peggoty teapot by Beswick Pottery, 6in. high, introduced 1948. *(Lyle)* **£100 $165**

A Beswick Pottery child's tea service, comprising; teapot and cover, milk jug, sugar basin, two cups, saucers and plates, printed with scenes from various Walt Disney films. *(Bearne's)* **£420 $685**

Beswick Pottery model of a clouded yellow butterfly with impressed number 1490, 5¼in. wide, issued 1957. *(Lyle)* **£175 $285**

Girl with Beret, mark of Beswick, 6in. high, introduced 1934. *(Lyle)* **£150 $245**

Set of three Beswick Mallard wall plaques, the largest 10in. high, issued 1938 withdrawn 1973. *(Lyle)* **£175 $285**

'Jemima Puddleduck', a Beatrix Potter wall plaque, painted in shades of pale blue, pink, green, yellow and white, printed gilt marks, 15.1cm. high. *(Christie's)* **£552 $1,210**

'Pig-Wig', a Beatrix Potter figure, painted in colours, printed brown mark. *(Christie's)* **£241 $390**

Set of three Beswick Pottery swallows, the largest 6in. high, issued 1939 withdrawn 1973. *(Lyle)* **£100 $165**

Beswick model of a Red Setter lying down, 3in. high, issued 1946. *(Lyle)*   **£45 $75**

Beswick model of a terrier, 4in. high, issued 1946. *(Lyle)*   **£45 $75**

A rare Panda bear teapot, shape no.742, the reclining figure painted in black and white, circa 1930s, printed factory and painted marks, 15.1cm. high.
(Christie's)   **£300 $500**

Set of three Beswick Kingfisher wall plaques, the largest 7½in. high, issued 1939 withdrawn 1971. *(Lyle)*   **£115 $185**

Beswick Pottery figure of a comical dog, 4½in. high, issued 1946.
(Lyle)   **£70 $110**

Beswick model of a cat, 6½in. high, issued 1945. *(Lyle)*   **£55 $90**

27

Captain Cuttle character jug by Beswick, 4½in. high, introduced 1948. *(Lyle)* **£70 $115**

Beswick model of an equestrian huntsman, 7in. high. *(Lyle)* **£85 $140**

Boy with Red Hair, mark of Beswick, 7¼in. high, introduced 1938. *(Lyle)* **£225 $365**

Basket of Flowers wall plaque by Beswick Pottery, 10in. high, introduced 1937. *(Lyle)* **£150 $245**

Beswick character jug, moulded with Shakespearean figures within a castle, entitled on the base *Hamlet, Prince of Denmark,* 8in. high. *(G.A. Key)* **£60 $93**

Toby Philpot Toby jug by Beswick Pottery, 8in. high, introduced 1948. *(Lyle)* **£105 $170**

Toby jug depicting Midshipman Toby, by Beswick Pottery, 5¼in. high, introduced 1948. *(Lyle)* **£175 $285**

A Beswick Pottery wall mask modelled as the face of a young woman, 9½in. high. *(Lyle)* **£375 $600**

Beswick ware pottery ornament, made for Double Diamond, inscribed *A Double Diamond Works Wonders,* 8in. *(Lyle)* **£150 $245**

ARCADIAN

Arcadian has the distinction of being the largest producer of crested china over the longest period. The company was owned by Harold Taylor Robinson, who began as a traveller for Wiltshaw and Robinson in 1899. By 1903, he was able to start up his own manufactory, called Arkinstall & Son, and using the trade name Arcadian. During the succeeding years he managed to acquire a number of other companies, including Cauldon, Coalport and Goss. He ended up as a director of no less than 32 different firms. The Depression brought disaster, however, and Robinson was declared bankrupt in 1932.

Arcadian is now perhaps most associated with the souvenir china field. In 1925 the popular Black Cat series was introduced, but pieces were also made in an Art Deco style, as well as female figures, Arcadian ladies, and also some lustre ware.

BOOTH

Thomas G. Booth set up his pottery in 1872 in Tunstall to produce earthenware. The company remained in business until 1948, and it was also engaged in producing earthenware copies of Royal Worcester porcelain.

A variety of marks were used, with *Silicon China* from around 1906. The late mark of 1930-48 consists of a crown with three Bs and *England* under.

BRETBY

The Bretby pottery was founded in 1883 at Woodville, Derbyshire, by Henry Tooth and William Ault. They made jardinières, bowls, jugs, vases etc. first in earthenware decorated with coloured glazes and applied with flowers and insects in light coloured clay. Later decoration imitated hammered metals with applied ceramic jewels.

'Carved bamboo' and Clantha ware were further innovations.

BURMANTOFTS

The pottery of Wilcock & Co was established in 1858 in Leeds for the production of terracotta architectural ware. By 1880, they were producing buff-coloured, high temperature fired earthenware with a feldspathic glaze which came to be known as Burmantofts faience, for tiles. Between 1882 and 1904 art pottery was added to the range, the output consisting of vases, bowls, jardinières, pedestals and figures with coloured glazes. An alternative decorative style comprised underglaze designs trailed in slip, painted or incised, and copper and silver lustre could be used on dark red or blue colours.

After 1904, the main output once again reverted to terracotta, and the company later became known as the Leeds Fireclay Co.

Marks consisted of the full company name or a *BF* monogram.

CAULDON POTTERIES

Cauldon Potteries were born out of Brown, Westhead, Moore & Co. who had been operating at the Cauldon Place Works in Hanley since 1858. From 1904, they traded as Cauldon Ltd., and then, when granted the royal warrant in 1924, they became Royal Cauldon.

Their wide range of products included, during the Art Deco period, several tube-lined types, including their popular Poppy design by Edith Gater, which was used on a number of shapes.

Their trademark was a crown with *Royal Cauldon England Est 1774* below. The firm went out of business in 1962, following a takeover by Pountney & Co. of Bristol (subsequently the Pountney Cauldon Potteries of Redruth in Cornwall).

GEORGE CLEWS & CO. LTD

This factory opened at the Brownhills Factory in Tunstall in 1906, and survived until 1961. They are perhaps best known for their Chameleon Ware, their trademark in the 1930s comprising a picture of a little lizard in an inverted triangle with *Chameleon* above, and *Clews & Co. Ltd. Tunstall/Made in England below*. The choice of chameleon as a name may have to do with the distinctive variety of colours which they used to decorate their wares. While the range was not particularly extensive, blues, beiges, golds and browns, for example, they achieved striking effects. Shapes were also very eyecatching and sophisticated, as was the style of decoration, some of their all-over patterns recalling the influence of Eastern pottery.

Along with others such as Mintons and Wedgwood, Clews leased the cube teapot shape from the Cube Teapot Company of Leicester, realising its appeal to the hotel trade, where space or lack of it was often a crucial factor.

Their pieces are characterised by their sophistication, and are eagerly sought after by collectors.

GRIMWADES

The company started life as Grimwade Bros. in 1886 at the Winton Potteries in Hanley and the Elgin Potteries in Stoke, becoming Grimwades in 1900. They incorporated the Rubian Art Pottery in 1913 and later the Atlas China Co.

Throughout the 1920s, Grimwades produced hotel ware and brightly decorated tableware. Flowers were a major decorative theme, some being moulded as handles on cups, jugs and coffee and teapots. Lilies, roses or violas would be offset against plain pink, yellow or light green backgrounds, and the whole would be highly glazed. In contrast, Grimwades also produced handpainted ranges in vivid colours decorated with strongly Art Deco motifs, such as the Delhi range. Printed patterns were also used in their Chintz range.

A circular trademark was used on their Royal Winton floral range, with various variations of *Royal Winton, Grimwades England* and *Royal Winton Ivory England*. After 1950, however, the circular mark was phased out, and the same words were used horizontally.

THOMAS LAWRENCE (LONGTON) LTD

Thomas Lawrence established his pottery originally at Trent Bridge in 1885. It moved to the Falcon Works in Longton, from which the name of its wares, Falcon ware, was taken. In the early 1930s it was taken over by Lawrence's nephew, John Grundy. Unfortunately Grundy died only six months later, and his widow approached a relative by marriage, Richard Hull, to take over the plant. Hull was already heavily involved in

the management of Shaw & Copestake, and he asked a friend, Eric Dennis, to help with Thomas Lawrence, which at this point became a limited company.

This close connection with the SylvaC works meant that for a time some SylvaC wares carried the Falcon mark, while others were marked for both companies. For a period after the war they were run separately, but finally merged completely after the Falcon Works premises were sold to Beswick in 1957. The Lawrence side of the newly merged group was closed in 1964, while SylvaC continued until 1982.

To further complicate matters, a range of pottery called Falcon Ware was also produced by J.H. Weatherby of Hanley, but this always also bore the Weatherby trademark, while the output of the Lawrence factory carried only *Falcon Ware* in script or with the picture of a falcon or an artist's palette.

MAW & CO

This company started out as tile manufacturers who in 1850 bought premises on the site of the Flight, Barr & Barr Worcester porcelain works, before moving two years later to Broseley, Shropshire. The company developed rapidly, becoming the largest English tile manufacturer by the end of the decade.

They produced tiles in Hispano-Moresque and Italian styles, decorated with rich glazes and relief designs, and also began to make tessera for use in decorative mosaics.

Their decorative techniques included carving layers of clay so that the contrasting colour below could be seen, overglaze colours painted over slip decoration, and moulded relief designs for use against a contrasting background.

Relief decoration was also used on the majolica vases and dishes which they made, and some of these were decorated by Walter Crane, a close associate of William Morris. Many of his examples for Maw feature a rich ruby lustre.

The firm moved to Jackfield in Shropshire in 1883, where they continued until 1967. Marks include *MAW, Maw & Co/Benthall Works/ Broseley/Salop*, or the name *MAW* enclosed in a circular label *FLOREAT SALOPIA*.

MINTON

The Minton Pottery is perhaps better known for its delicate traditional bone china and its majolica rather than for strong Art Deco associations. It was begun by Thomas Minton, in partnership with William Pownal and Joseph Poulson in 1793, and was built up by his son, Herbert, who worked to attract designers and decorators from all over Europe.

Minton produced some exciting Art Nouveau designs, such as their Secessionist Ware, but showed little interest in following Art Deco trends until in 1930 a new Art Director, Reginald Haggar, applied some strikingly Modernist ideas to their tableware.

Mintons were taken over by Doulton in 1968, by which time they had abandoned earthenware for bone china.

PARAGON

The Paragon China Co. was established in Longton, Staffordshire, in 1920, for the manufacture of porcelain.

It held a royal warrant and produced much commemorative ware. A variety of marks were used, including royal arms and *Paragon*.

Paragon is now part of Allied English Potteries Ltd.

FREDERICK RHEAD

Perhaps now best remembered in some quarters as the father of Charlotte and Frederick Hurten, Frederick Albert Rhead (1856-1933), was himself a ceramic designer. He studied under Marc Solon at Mintons and also designed for Wedgwood before, in 1908, setting up with F.H. Barker at the Atlas Tile Works, where his daughter joined him.

This was a short-lived venture, however, and by 1913 he was Art Director at Wood & Son, where once again, Charlotte came to join him.

RIDGWAYS

This pottery was established in Hanley in the early 19th century to produce earthenware. Edward John Ridgway took over the Bedford Works in Shelton in 1866 and the firm flourished under various partnerships for the next 100 years. From 1920-52 the mark was *Ridgways* and/or *Bedford*. Thereafter it became *Ridgway & Adderley* in 1952, *Ridgway, Adderley, Booths & Colclough Ltd* in 1955 and (perhaps not surprisingly) this was simplified to the *Ridgway Potteries Ltd* in the same year. In 1952 they were part of Allied English Potteries, now the Royal Doulton Group.

RUBIAN ART POTTERY

The Rubian Art Pottery flourished between 1906 and 1933 in Fenton, Staffordshire, being taken over by Grimwade's in 1913. It produced earthenware which was called Rubay Art Ware, which was marked as such during the Art Deco period.

JAMES SADLER & SONS

This company was set up in 1899 in Burslem, and is best known for its novelty teapots. The 1930s racing car, for example, was available in a range of colours, with a lustre trim and the registration number OKT 42. There was a matching sugar basin in the form of a caravan, and these are now very rare. Other forms, Bunny, Doggie and Father Christmas, for example, are also very sought after. The factory closed in the late 1950s.

Until 1937, the mark was usually *England J.S.S.B.* in two lines and thereafter became *Sadler Burslem England* in three lines. After 1947, *Sadler* was printed on a ribbon beneath a crown with *Made in England* under.

TILL & SONS

Thomas Till & Sons produced earthenware in Burslem from circa 1850-1928. Between 1922-8 their wares were marked *Tillson ware*.

WADE, HEATH & CO. LTD

This factory started from humble beginnings in 1810, when Henry Hallam started making pottery fittings for textile machinery. It moved to Wellington Street, Burslem in the mid 19th century, and the firm was bought by George Wade in the early years of the 20th century. It traded under various names until the operation was divided in the 1920s, becoming Wade, Heath & Co., and A.J. Wade & Co.

Wade, Heath & Co. started producing their nursery ware, featuring Walt Disney characters, in the 1930s, and this is now very popular with collectors. At much the same time, their Flaxman range appeared, which falls very much into the Art Deco category. This had its own mark, *Flaxman Ware, Handmade Pottery,* with *Wadeheath, England,* below..

Both factories employed a number of talented designers, among them Jessie Van Allen, who designed a range of figurines for A.J. Wade.

The Wade trademark was a standing lion with *Wade* above, and *England* below, in the 1920s, with *Wadeheath* replacing the former in the 1930s.

J.H.WEATHERBY

This company established the Falcon Pottery in Hanley in 1891, and during the Art Deco period they produced robust tableware, which nevertheless had attractive details such as floral knobs and handles. They also made novelty items, such as flower jugs with bird handles, which could be very naturalistically modelled.

Their motto was 'Durability' and this appeared regularly on their trademarks, in the 1920s appearing with *Falcon Ware.* In the 1930s they often used a Union Jack and *J.H.W. & Sons Ltd., Hanley, England, Royal Falcon Ware,* and at this time too used the trademark *Weatherby Ware.*

WILLOW

This trademark was used by Hewitt & Leadbeater of Longton, who went into partnership in 1905 as manufacturers of 'artistic and useful specialities of great variety.' They produced flowerholders and vases, many in the form of open flowers, and their Hop ware and Vine ware was of very high quality.

The company also made considerable quantities of Heraldic ware and souvenir china, which saw them comfortably through the Great War. They also produced a range of coloured buildings, and by 1920 offered a range of 200 finely designed and coloured miniatures.

Leadbeater left the firm in 1919, and Hewitt took his brother into partnership. They were early victims of the Depression, however, and the company was taken over by Harold Robinson in 1925. He reformed it as Willow Potteries, producing Willow China alongside his own Arcadian ware.

ARTHUR WOOD & SON LTD

This company started out in 1884 in Longport as the partnership of Capper & Wood, making teapots, but Arthur Wood became sole proprietor in 1900.

By the 1920s, their range had extended to include eyecatching designs handpainted on transferware, with large floral patterns or gilded spiders' webs and lustre decorated wall pockets.

Shapes, too were bold and striking, such as the Garden Wall series of jugs and urns which feature a sunburst motif above a cottage garden and an impressed pattern of brickwork.

Most of the pottery of this period features a globe backstamp with *Arthur Wood* on a ribbon and *England* on a further ribbon below. A later variation is *Made in England* printed below the globe, without the ribbon.

WOOD & SONS LTD

In 1865 Thomas Francis Wood, a descendant of the three great 18th century Staffordshire potters, Ralph, Aaron and Moses Wood, opened Wood & Son in Burslem, producing earthenwares. In 1889 Harry Wood joined the firm, and he was to be instrumental in encouraging such ceramic artists as Charlotte Rhead and Susie Cooper. Charlotte's father Frederick joined the company as their Art Director in 1912, with Charlotte following him a year later and remaining until 1926. In 1920 Wood's bought the Crown Works to accommodate the expansion of the Art Pottery activities, and in 1921 bought the Ellgreave Works, where Charlotte could produce her Lottie Rhead Ware. In 1930 Harry Wood did the same for Susie Cooper, offering her facilities to design her own whiteware shapes.

Amusing dog-shaped pottery container. *(Muir Hewitt)* **£20 $32**

1930s honeypot with bee finial. *(Muir Hewitt)* **£20 $32**

'Mother Bunnykins' D6004, a Bunnykins figure, painted in colours, printed factory marks, 17.5cm. high. *(Christie's)* **£1,092 $1,775**

'Japanese Fan', a bowl and cover designed by H. Tittensor, the cover decorated with seated Japanese figure holding a fan, painted in shades of green, orange, black and pale purple on a pearl lustre ground, printed factory mark, 19.4cm. high. *(Christie's)* **£299 $485**

Dismal Desmond dog with red markings, 1930s. *(Muir Hewitt)* **£25 $40**

Myott flower vase complete with liner, 9in. wide on stepped base. *(Muir Hewitt)* **£70 $110**

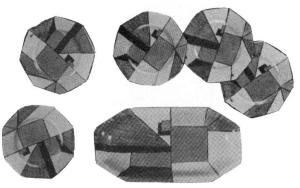

Myott flower jug with hand painted decoration, 7in. high, 1930s. *(Muir Hewitt)* **£50 $75**

A Bizarre octagonal sandwich set in the 'Cubist' pattern, comprising five sandwich plates and a tray, 29cm. wide. *(Christie's)* **£880 $1,346**

'Woman's Journal', a Bizarre Odilon tureen and cover, painted in colours, printed factory marks, 18cm. high. *(Christie's)* **£437 $710**

Dame Laura Knight, a Bizarre large platter, the well painted with a crowd of stylised naked women in pink and brown with a black background, the rim spiralling turquoise and brown streamers and orange stripes, printed factory marks, 46cm. diameter. *(Christie's)* **£6,325 $10,300**

Stylised porcelain dog, 1930s, 2½in. high. *(Christie's)* **£10 $16**

A Freeform vase, of flattened elliptical form, by Gwen Haskins, pattern X.PT, shape no.342, decorated with Butterflies in shades of green and mauve, printed factory mark and painted monogram, 19cm. high. *(Christie's)* **£230 $375**

A wall pocket in the form of a mask of Pan, covered in a mottled turquoise glaze over a green ground, 24cm. high. *(Christie's)* **£198 $320**

Dr Christopher Dresser, a Linthorpe Art Pottery jug, shape 341, incised with band of circled flowerheads, 17cm. *(Bristol)* **£185 $300**

'Estelle', a Royal Winton bedside set, printed in colours, 26cm. wide. *(Christie's)* **£805 $1,310**

A window display figure for Facchino Ice Cream, 20in. high. *(Dave Lewis)* **£175 $285**

Meltonian Shoe Cream & Dressings, counter display figure, 15½in. high. *(Dave Lewis)* **£100 $165**

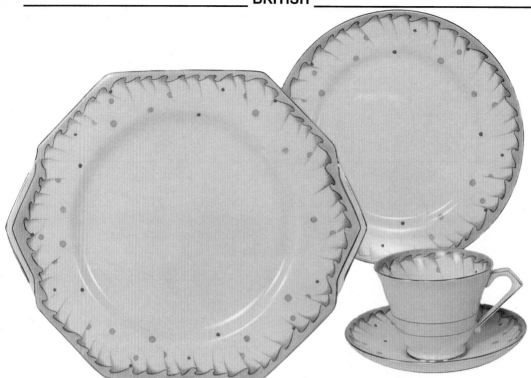

Paragon cup, saucer and plate together with a matching bread and butter plate, 1930s.
(Muir Hewitt)   **£60 $100**

Art Deco china tea service marked *St. Michael's*, a copy of Shelley design comprising 6 cups, saucers, plates, milk jug, sugar bowl and sandwich plate, 1930s.
(Muir Hewitt)   **£100 $160**

Art Deco floral cake plate with raffia covered handle. *(Muir Hewitt)* **£35 $60**

1930s orange dog ornament powder container. *(Muir Hewitt)* **£20 $32**

Jack and the Beanstalk jug, maker unknown, 1930s.
(Muir Hewitt) **£60 $100**

Wilkinson wall plaque 14in. diameter, decorated with stylised poppy design, circa 1925. *(Muir Hewitt)* **£200 $325**

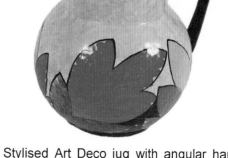

Art Deco plate with stylised tulip design, 8in. diameter, 1930s.
(Muir Hewitt) **£20 $32**

Stylised Art Deco jug with angular handle and leaf decoration, 1930s.
(Muir Hewitt) **£45 $75**

Sweet Pea, a Royal Winton 'Athena' teapot and cover, printed in colours and gilt, printed factory marks, 14.4cm. high; a stand, hot water pot and cover, milk-jug, sugar basin and toast rack.
(Christie's) **£1,265 $2,060**

Conical jug, 1930s, maker unknown, design, similar to a Thomas Forrester pattern, 13in. high.
(Muir Hewitt) **£75 $125**

A Wardle Pottery stickstand, tubeline decorated with stylised flowers and foliage on sinuous stems, in shades of brown and yellow, 56cm. high.
(Christie's) **£460 $690**

Marion, a Royal Winton tea set for six, printed in colours with gilt detailing to rims, comprising; 'Albans' teapot and cover 'Athena' milk-jug, sugar basin, six cups, saucers, side plates, two dishes and a twin-handled sandwich plate.
(Christie's) **£977 $1,590**

A Macintyre 'Claremont' pattern bowl, streaked blue and green ground with decoration of pink, green and blue mushrooms, circa 1903, 12cm. high.
(Christie's) **£825 $1,350**

A Carter tile, possibly from the Fishing Smacks series designed by Minnie McLeish, in typical colours, moulded *Carter 75*, painted *CD2*, 5in. diameter.
(Christie's) **£75 $125**

A pair of Brown-Westhead Moore & Co. porcelain square jardinières, moulded and gilt with masks and strapwork, mark for 1872, 10¾in. high.
(Christie's) **£1,092 $1,693**

A Macintyre 'Alhambra' vase, of low squat form, with four side handles, tube-lined, painted and gilt with tulips and other flowers, 14cm. high.
(Tennants) **£900 $1,450**

Susie Cooper vase with sgraffito decoration of squirrel, 9in. high.
(Muir Hewitt) **£250 $400**

A John Hassell 'Egg Man', modelled as a Policeman, Boy Scout and Country Yokel, 6in. high. *(Christie's)* **£200 $325**

1930s bluebell honeypot with bee finial, 5½in. high. *(Lyle)* **£30 $50**

Armchair pipe rest with stylised dogs, Continental, 1930s. *(Muir Hewitt)* **£35 $55**

Set of six 1950s liqueur bottles in the form of a jazz band. *(Muir Hewitt)* **£130 $210**

1930s green two handled pot with Dripware decoration. *(Lyle)* **£80 $130**

Willow Art china vase with enamelled American Indian design, 6in. high. *(Muir Hewitt)* **£90 $145**

1930s stylised cottage teapot and milk jug. *(Muir Hewitt)* **£70 $115**

Booths hors d'oeuvre dish decorated with a stylised country scene.
(Muir Hewitt)   **£180 $290**

Humpty Dumpty teapot, 1930s.
(Christie's)   **£110 $180**

A Keele Street Pottery teapot with moulded hunting scenes and a similar milk jug and cream jug. *(Lyle)*   **£50 $80**

1930s white china model of a dog with black markings. *(Muir Hewitt)* **£20 $32**

Deco jug with stylised floral decoration. *(Muir Hewitt)*   **£30 $50**

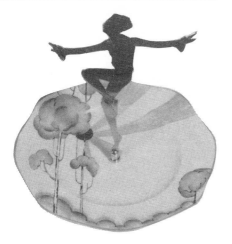

James Kent Sunrise design cake plate with chromium plate dancing lady handle. *(Muir Hewitt)* **£65 $105**

A Morrisware pottery vase, decorated with peonies in mauve, crimson and olive-green against a sea-ground, 16.5cm. high. *(Phillips)* **£300 $450**

Hollingshead and Kirkham plate with fruit decoration. *(Muir Hewitt)* **£50 $85**

A Brannam Pottery vase, by J. Dewdney, sgraffito decorated with large scaly fish, enhanced with green, yellow and brown coloured slips, having twin handles in the form of long-tailed beasts, 47.5cm. *(Phillips)* **£300 $490**

An Art Deco terracotta wall mask, modelled as a stylised girl with blue hair dressed with flowers, 9in. long. *(Christie's)* **£143 $280**

A globular green glazed bowl designed by Dr. C. Dresser, 14.5cm. high. *(Christie's)* **£1,000 $1,600**

British Art Pottery jardinière, decorated with flowers and foliage on yellow ground, circa 1920-6, 9¾in. high. *(G.A. Key)* **£110 $208**

Moorcroft pottery vase of bulbous form with the anemone pattern on a blue ground, 8in. high. *(Lyle)* **£175 $285**

Two Liberty & Co. terracotta jardinières, designed by Mrs F. G. Watts, after Archibald Knox. *(Bonhams)* **£1,000 $1,495**

Hancock's Butterfly dish in blue, black and mauve, 1930s. *(Muir Hewitt)* **£50 $85**

James Kent bowl with EPNS rim, 1930s. *(Muir Hewitt)* **£60 £100**

1940s green two handled planter, 13in. wide. *(Lyle)* **£30 $50**

Dog shaped vase by Flaxman, 1930s. *(Muir Hewitt)* **£20 $32**

Arcadian Ware baluster vase, in blue, cream and red, circa 1930. *(Muir Hewitt)* **£150 $245**

An interesting Staffordshire flower plate in red, green and black, 10in. diameter. *(Lyle)* **£85 $140**

Art Deco jug, maker unknown, with leaf decoration, 1930s. *(Muir Hewitt)* **£30 $50**

Art Deco Dripware vase marked *Gloria,* 7in. high. *(Lyle)* **£65 $105**

Biscuit barrel, 1930s, with floral decoration. *(Muir Hewitt)* **£50 $80**

1930s, galleon flower holder. *(Lyle)* **£25 $40**

1930s orange and green Dripware bulbous vase, 7in. high. *(Lyle)* **£100 $160**

1930s Staffordshire Art Deco yellow and black plant holder with floral decoration, 8in. high. *(Lyle)* **£75 $120**

Miniature vase with elf decoration. *(Muir Hewitt)* **£25 $40**

1930s budgie vase in green and fawn. *(Muir Hewitt)* **£45 $75**

Eleanor, a Royal Winton *Albans*, shape teapot, printed in colours and gilt, printed and painted marks, 15.1cm. high.
(Christie's) **£225 $365**

Floral Feast, a Royal Winton *Norman* shape teapot and cover, printed in colours, printed factory marks, 12.5cm. high.
(Christie's) **£253 $410**

Cheadle, a Royal Winton Bedside set, printed in colours, comprising; teapot and cover, milk-jug and sugar basin, one cup, toast rack and tray, printed and painted marks, 25.7cm. wide.
(Christie's) **£747 $1,210**

A decorated stoneware vase, attributed to Russell G. Crook, 1906-12, 9½in. high.
(Skinner) **£500 $800**

A Royal Staffordshire wall mirror, with printed and relief decorated gilt surround, printed in colours with flowers and birds, printed factory marks, 48cm. wide.
(Christie's) **£287 $465**

Art Deco Dripware jug, maker unknown, in green and orange, 1930s.
(Muir Hewitt) **£60 $100**

English Art Pottery vase, attributed to Watcombe, landscape scene, three applied handles, obscured impressed marks, 9½in. high. *(Skinner)* **£300 $500**

Two figures of jazz musicians, one with trumpet and the other with saxophone, painted in silver lustre, painted factory mark, 11½in. maximum. *(Christie's)* **£500 $800**

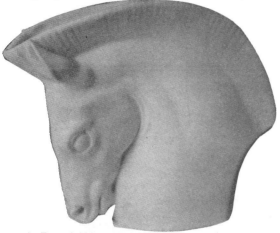

A Royal Worcester white porcelain vase, designed by Raoh Schorr, in the form of a Trojan Horse with well-sculpted features, 28.50cm. high. *(Phillips)* **£300 $490**

A rare Sabrina ware vase of pear shape, decorated with fish swimming among seaweed, 14cm., date code for 1931. *(Phillips)* **£200 $325**

After Privat Livemont, Johnson, Walker & Tolhurst Ltd, as retailers, large pot and cover with girl with yellow roses, *1901*, the cover with the head and shoulders of a young girl, stamped with maker's mark, 7.5cm. diameter. *(Sotheby's)* **£1,495 $2,400**

A Minton Secessionist jardinière, decorated in relief with large pink plant forms against a green ground with leaves and tendrils, 32cm. high. *(Phillips)* **£400 $650**

1930s cruet in the form of a stylised toucan. *(Muir Hewitt)* **£20 $32**

1930s green marbled bowl with incurved rim, 10in. diameter. *(Lyle)* **£40 $65**

1930s Dripware jug with splayed foot, 8in. high. *(Lyle)* **£35 $57**

China counter drinking figure *Guinness is good for you* by Wiltshaw & Robinson, 9¼in. high. *(Lyle)* **£160 $260**

20th century Staffordshire Rooster teapot. *(Lyle)* **£125 $200**

Art Deco vase with stylised decoration, 8in. high, 1930s. *(Muir Hewitt)* **£55 $90**

1930s green marbled two handled vase, 6in. high. *(Lyle)* **£20 $32**

Modernist jampot in red and black, 1950s. *(Muir Hewitt)* **£20 $32**

1930s Art Deco ewer with double loop handle, in brown and orange, 8½in. high. *(Lyle)* **£40 $65**

An Avonware handpainted teapot, sugar bowl and milk jug with leaf and fruit decoration. *(Lyle)* **£35 $57**

Colclough grey colourway Sabu teapot, circa 1939. *(Muir Hewitt)* **£180 $295**

Joyous pottery jug, 1930s. *(Muir Hewitt)* **£35 $60**

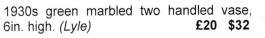

A David Sharp stoneware bust, modelled as a Norman figure with pointed beard, slender neck and medallion, painted in shades of brown on a buff ground, unmarked, 38cm. high.
(Christie's) **£402 $655**

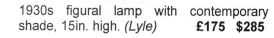

1930s figural lamp with contemporary shade, 15in. high. *(Lyle)* **£175 $285**

Invicta Underwear counter display figure by Harris & Sheldon, 22in. high.
(Sam Weller) **£225 $365**

'Japanese Fan', a bowl and cover designed by H. Tittensor, the cover decorated with seated Japanese figure holding a fan, painted in shades of yellow, green, black and purple on a pearl lustre ground, printed factory mark, 20.8cm. high.
(Christie's) **£598 $975**

A baluster vase decorated in the 'Eventide' pattern, in shades of ochre, pink, green and blue, 13in. high.
(Christie's)　£682　$1,216

Maling hand painted bowl, 10in. diameter, 1930s.
(Muir Hewitt)　£130　$195

A Susie Cooper wall mask modelled as the head of a woman with grey streaked black hair, 10¾in. long.
(Christie's)　£1,000　$1,500

A Gloria lustre waisted cylindrical vase painted in pink, lilac and gilt, painted Susie Cooper monogram, 12in. high.
(Christie's)　£700　$1,300

China dog money box in black and white with red collar, 1930s.
(Muir Hewitt)　£40　$65

A Phoebe Stabler plaster bust of a young girl with pigtails, painted yellow, inscribed Phoebe Stabler 1911, 15in. high.
(Christie's)　£275　$440

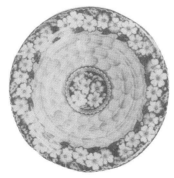

A Susie Cooper pottery jug, carved either side with a goat charging with its head lowered, 21.5cm. high, signed.
(Bearne's)　£145　$228

Maling decorative circular dish, the rim with lustre decoration of coloured rosettes, pattern no. 6450T, 10½in. diameter.
(G.A. Key)　£60　$93

'Fate', a Richard Garbe porcelain wall mask, edition limited to 100, No. 54, painted marks and impressed 848, 26.6cm. high. (Christie's)　£345　$560

Plichta Ware bunny with black eyes, 1930s. *(Muir Hewitt)* **£45 $75**

1940s trumpet shape wall vase. *(Muir Hewitt)* **£25 $40**

A Wileman & Co. 'Intarsio' vase, designed by Frederick Rhead, Celtic style foliate bands, the neck with flowers, 8¾in. high. *(Bonhams)* **£400 $650**

Prices blue duck with smiling countenance, 1930s. *(Muir Hewitt)* **£45 $75**

Unmarked blue bunny, possibly Price's, 1930s. *(Muir Hewitt)* **£45 $75**

Booth's baluster shape vase with flared lip, 1930, *(Muir Hewitt)* **£70 $115**

George Clews Chameleon Ware jug, 1930s, 8in. high. *(Muir Hewitt)* **£150 $245**

Price's stylised dog in turquoise, with wide grin, 1930s. *(Muir Hewitt)* **£40 $65**

Prices blue stylised cat with frightened expression, 1930s.
(Muir Hewitt) **£45 $75**

Dripware vase 1930s, in red and green, maker unknown, 7in. high.
(Muir Hewitt) **£40 $65**

1930s marbled green Art Deco vase.
(Muir Hewitt) **£30 $50**

Stylised dog, 1930s, decorated with red spots. *(Muir Hewitt)* **£35 $55**

An Aller Vale pottery model of a seated cat with an elongated neck and orange glass eyes, 29.3cm. high. *(Bearne's)* **£660 $1,075**

A Wade 5in. Disney model of Jock from Lady and the Tramp, 3½in. high. *(Anderson & Garland)* **£380 $610**

Vase, 1930s, maker unknown, with elaborate enamelled design. *(Muir Hewitt)* **£65 $105**

A single handled cylindrical vase, moulded with a circus artist jumping through a paper hoop, painted in colours, 22cm. high. *(Christie's)* **£528 $860**

'Skier', a Crown Works Nursery Ware Kestrel cocoa pot and cover, gazelle *SCP* mark, 5in. high. *(Christie's)* **£660 $1,220**

A Liberty vase, of tapering waisted cylindrical form, decorated in the 'Hazledene' pattern, in shades of blue and green printed factory marks, signed in green, 9in. high. *(Christie's)* **£748 $1,333**

Stylised elephant bottle, 1930s, 7½in. high. *(Muir Hewitt)* **£30 $50**

A cylindrical vase with inverted rim decorated with applied crescent motifs, incised signature, 7¾in. high. *(Christie's)* **£104 $195**

Pottery figurine, 1930s, 8in. high. *(Muir Hewitt)* **£35 $55**

A Bretby Pottery centrepiece in the style of Royal Dux modelled as a young maiden in flowing robes perched between conch shells, 15¼in. high. *(Christie's)* **£365 $547**

Window display figure for Facchino Ice Cream, 20in. high. (Dave Lewis) **£175 $285**

Maling plate with stylised Oriental decoration, 10in. diameter. *(Muir Hewitt)* **£200 $300**

Hobson's Choice Feet Plasters & Powders, counter display figure, 13in. high. *(Dave Lewis)* **£100 $165**

A Carved Ware baluster vase, with a continuous frieze of stylised leaves, incised signature and *592*, 9¼in. high. *(Christie's)* **£121 £225**

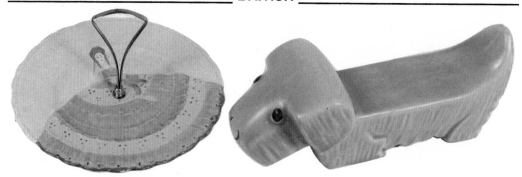

Crinoline lady cake plate with chromium plate handle, 8in. wide. *(Muir Hewitt)* **£50** **$85**

Art Deco stylised brown dog of elongated form, circa 1930. *(Muir Hewitt)* **£60** **$100**

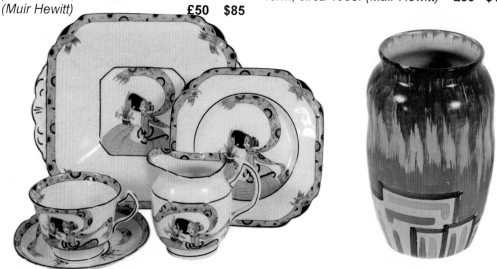

Dolly Varden tea service comprising six cups and saucers and plates, bread and butter plate, cream and sugar, 1930s. *(Muir Hewitt)* **£250** **$400**

Art Deco brown and orange vase, maker unknown, 1930s. *(Muir Hewitt)* **£35** **$60**

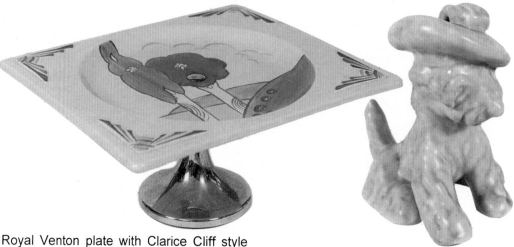

Royal Venton plate with Clarice Cliff style design, a copy of the Biarritz shape. *(Muir Hewitt)* **£120** **$195**

Art Deco Scottie dog with Tam o' Shanter, 1930s. *(Muir Hewitt)* **£20** **$32**

A comical unmarked white dog with black marking and blue eyes, circa 1930. *(Muir Hewitt)* **£30 $50**

Cake plate, 1930s, with chromium plate stand. *(Muir Hewitt)* **£20 $32**

Art Deco Dripware vase, maker unknown, in orange and green, 1930s. *(Muir Hewitt)* **£45 $75**

Crown Staffordshire tea set comprising six cups saucers and plates, cream, sugar and bread and butter plate, 1930s. *(Muir Hewitt)* **£120 $195**

Racing car teapot by Sadler & Co. in green and silver, 1930s. *(Muir Hewitt)* **£130 $210**

Staffordshire Rooster teapot, 1930s. *(Muir Hewitt)* **£75 $125**

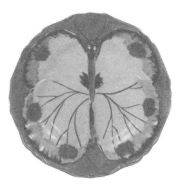

'Buster Boy', a pottery figure by Phoebe Stabler, of a putto with floral garland around his body, 7in. high. *(Christie's)* **£200 $320**

Hancock's butterfly plate, 1930's. *(Muir Hewitt)* **£65 $100**

A pair of Brown-Westhead Moore & Co. majolica vases, each modelled as cranes standing around bullrushes, circa 1880, 21cm. high. *(Christie's)* **£850 $1,350**

An Original Bizarre candlestick of tapering square form, stamped *Hand Painted by Clarice Cliff Newport England*, 7¾in. high. *(Christie's)* **£200 £320**

A pair of Liberty jardinières on pedestals, each with shallow hemispherical bowl decorated with entrelac border in relief, 80cm. high. **£2,100 $3,150**

An unusual Midwinter vase, designed by Jessie Tait, waisted cylindrical form painted with black linear motif on a white ground, 13.5cm. high. *(Christie's)* **£150 $243**

A David Sharp stoneware bust, modelled as a Norman knight in domed helmet, covered in a mottled brown and black glaze, 31cm. high. *(Christie's)* **£402 $655**

A pair of Compton Pottery stoneware bookends, each trefoil form with relief decoration of a butterfly, circa 1945, 12.2cm. high. *(Christie's)* **£110 $197**

A Gray's Pottery coffeepot and cover, designed by Susie Cooper, painted with pink bellflowers, 20.cm. high. *(Christie's)* **£125 $194**

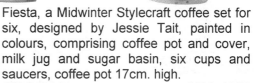

A ceramic chamber pot with everted rim, decorated with a design by Christopher Dresser, printed on black, brown, beige and green, 23cm. diameter.
(Phillips) **£375 $610**

Fiesta, a Midwinter Stylecraft coffee set for six, designed by Jessie Tait, painted in colours, comprising coffee pot and cover, milk jug and sugar basin, six cups and saucers, coffee pot 17cm. high.
(Christie's) **£200 $320**

'Dancers', a stylish Royal Worcester figure modelled by Doris Lindner, the man has a smart grey suit edged in blue, with blue shoes and hair, he holds his blonde female companion in long grey dress, close as they glide across the ballroom, 25cm. high.
(Phillips) **£400 $650**

A pair of Royal Doulton vases, waisted cylindrical form, modelled in relief with pendulous flowers and foliage in shades of blue and green, 33cm. high.
(Christie's) **£300 $486**

Flaxman running hare, 5in. wide, 1930s.
(Muir Hewitt) **£30 $45**

Pair of George Clews Chameleon Ware jugs, with tube lined decoration, 8in. high, 1930s.
(Muir Hewitt) **£250 $400**

A Till & Co cup, saucer and plate with floral decoration, 1930s.
(Muir Hewitt) **£60 $100**

1985 Midwinter reproduction Meiping shape vase in the Honolulu design, 14in. high. *(Muir Hewitt)* **£700 $1,150**

1940s pottery fruit bowl with floral decoration and chromium plated rim, 10in. diameter. *(Lyle)* **£35 $57**

An amusing 1930s china condiment set of two children seated in a basket, 4½in. wide. *(Lyle)* **£30 $50**

Jack and the Beanstalk jug, 9in. high. 1930s. *(Muir Hewitt)* **£65 $105**

Colclough bone china Sabu teapot in blue, circa 1939. *(Muir Hewitt)* **£200 $325**

A pair of Till & Co vases decorated with roses, 1930s. *(Muir Hewitt)* **£150 $245**

Art Deco wall mask of a hooded lady, maker unknown, 6in. high. *(Muir Hewitt)* **£150 $245**

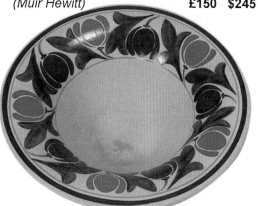

Dismal Desmond stylised dog, with mournful countenance, 1930s. *(Muir Hewitt)* **£25 $40**

Ridgways 1930s stoneware bowl with stylised floral border, 9in. diameter. *(Muir Hewitt)* **£60 $100**

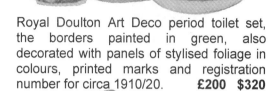

Royal Doulton Art Deco period toilet set, the borders painted in green, also decorated with panels of stylised foliage in colours, printed marks and registration number for circa 1910/20. **£200 $320**

Cissie, HN1809, designed for Doulton by L. Harradine, issued 1937-1993, colour variation, 5in. high. *(Lyle)* **£95 $152**

Sweet and Twenty (Style one) HN1549, designed for Doulton by L. Harradine, issued 1933-1949. colour variation, 6in. high. *(Lyle)* **£325 $520**

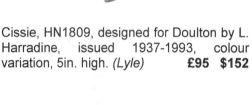

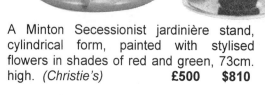

A Minton Secessionist jardinière stand, cylindrical form, painted with stylised flowers in shades of red and green, 73cm. high. *(Christie's)* **£500 $810**

A Royal Doulton 'Tango' pattern porcelain part coffee set, coffee pot, 20.75cm. high, c.m.l. & c., impressed dates *1.135* and *2.1.35. (Phillips)* **£500 $800**

A jug painted with vine leaves and purple grapes against a pink ground, c.m.l. & c., date letter for 1910, 8½in. high. **£780 $1,248**

A slip-cast vase of gourd-shape with projecting ribs and a mottled blue glaze, circa 1920, 5¾in. high. **£150 $240**

A late vase with stylised blue flowers and green leaves edged in white, c.m.& l., circa 1922, 7½in. high. **£195 $312**

A vase glazed in green, blue and brown with incised and raised borders, c.m. & l., circa 1925, 11¼in. high. **£390 $624**

Royal Doulton Art Deco period mug, with nursery rhyme scene, 5½in. high. *(G.A. Key)* **£35 $57**

'Hazledene', a Moorcroft waisted cylindrical vase, 20cm. high. **£920 $1,500** (Christie's)

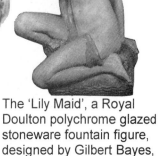

'Mary Bunnykin' D6002, a Bunnykins figure, painted in colours, printed factory marks, 16.5cm. high. (Christie's) **£1,265 $2,060**

Doulton Art Pottery jardinière with a blue ground and applied flowers, 8¾in. high. **£120 $192**

The 'Lily Maid', a Royal Doulton polychrome glazed stoneware fountain figure, designed by Gilbert Bayes, 61.5cm. high. *(Christie's)* **£15,000 $24,000**

A 1930s novelty three piece pottery tea set. *(Greenslades)* **£100 $160**

Royal Worcester figure of 'Friday's Child is loving and giving', 5in. high. *(Lyle)* **£110 $180**

Royal Worcester figure of August modelled by FC. Doughty, 4¼in. high. *(Lyle)* **£75 $120**

Cognac Martell Brandy advertising jug by Sanderson, Hanley, Staffordshire, 6½in. high. *(Lyle)* **£75 $120**

Art Deco stylised dog with pink collar, 1930s. *(Muir Hewitt)* **£20 $32**

1930s grey Bunny teapot.
(Muir Hewitt) **£125 $200**

Brannam Pottery orange glazed tall beaker
with handle. *(Lyle)* **£35 $60**

'Cheadle', a Royal Winton bedside set,
printed in colours with gilt detailing to rims,
comprising; teapot and cover, milk jug and
sugar basin, one cup, toast rack and tray,
printed and painted marks, width of tray
25.7cm. *(Christie's)* **£713 $1,160**

Dismal Desmond stylised dog container,
1930s. *(Muir Hewitt)* **£35 $60**

An unusual combined matchstriker and
ashtray entitled 'Chairman'.
(Lyle) **£200 $325**

Sweet Nancy, a Royal Winton Bedside set, printed in colours, printed and painted marks, 25.4cm. wide.
(Christie's)   £747 $1,210

Rosalynde, a James Kent teapot and stand, painted in colours and gilt, printed and painted marks, height of teapot 12.4cm. (Christie's)   £414 $675

A 1930s Scottish brown pottery Ziggaurat vase, 10in. high. (Lyle)   £25 $40

Eileen Soper, a very rare Worcester group of 'Take Cover' from the Wartime Series, showing a little girl, her brother beside her holding a puppy in his arms, both looking skywards in fear and apprehension, 15.5cm., date code for 1941.
(Phillips)   £400 $700

Clyde, a Royal Winton Bedside set, printed in colours, comprising; teapot and cover, milk-jug, sugar basin, one cup, toast rack and tray, printed and painted marks, 26cm. wide. (Christie's)   £483 $785

A Maling vase and cover, of baluster shape, decorated with a green dragon amidst peonies and other Oriental flowers on a purple lustre ground, printed castle mark, 1930s, 46cm. high.
(Tennants)   £4,950 $8,168

Summertime, a Royal Winton wall clock with Bentima movement, printed factory marks, 22.6cm. wide.
(Christie's) **£300 $490**

An earthenware oviform jug by Michael Cardew, impressed *MC* and Winchcombe Pottery seal, circa 1930, 22.6cm. high.
(Christie's) **£350 $570**

A Macintyre 'Alhambra' vase, of tapered form with bulbous knop, tube-lined, painted and gilt with tulips and other flowers, on a salmon pink and blue ground, 19.5cm. high. *(Tennants)* **£700 $1,140**

Sweet Pea, a Royal Winton Albans teapot and cover, hot-water pot and cover and shaped rectangular tray, printed factory marks, height of teapot 13cm.
(Christie's) **£897 $1,460**

Grimwades Cube lustre teapot, printed and painted with fairies, cobwebs and toadstools, printed factory mark, 4in. high.
(Christie's) **£150 $245**

A good Brown-Westhead & Moore porcelain urn vase, circa 1890, the squat globular body moulded with a foliate scrolled band, 10in. high.
(Bonhams) **£910 $1,410**

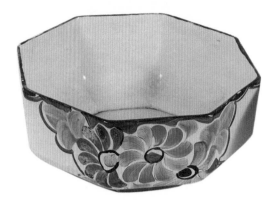

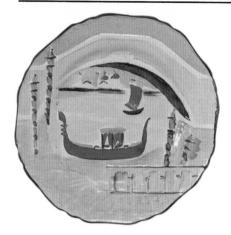

Art Deco bowl, maker unknown, with floral decoration, 1930s. *(Muir Hewitt)* **£20 $32**

Gondola plate with shaped edge, circa 1930. *(Muir Hewitt)* **£40 $65**

Woods charger, circa 1929, with galleon under sail, 17in. diameter. *(Muir Hewitt)* **£650 $1,060**

Art Deco black china bowl with stylised floral decoration, 1930s. *(Muir Hewitt)* **£100 $160**

Rubian Art Pottery bowl, 8in. diameter, circa 1930. *(Muir Hewitt)* **£50 $85**

Frederick Rhead design Amstel plate, 8in. diameter. *(Muir Hewitt)* **£140 $230**

1930s coffee pot set comprising six cups, saucers, coffee pot , cream jug and sugar bowl, with yellow body and floral embellishments. *(Muir Hewitt)* **£150 $245**

Art Deco fruit set comprising six dishes and serving bowl, 1930s.
(Muir Hewitt) **£40 $65**

1930s child's tea set with 6 cups, saucers and teaplates, sugar, cream jug and teapot. *(Muir Hewitt)* **£200 $325**

The Buffalo pottery was established in 1903 for the express purpose of making promotional free gifts for a soap firm in Buffalo, New York. They developed to produce also mail order gifts and then began to make advertising ware for other firms.

From there they progressed to tableware and in 1908 introduced a range with an olive green base, transfer printed and hand-decorated with hunting scenes, which was marketed as Deldareware.

Art Nouveau influence was apparent in Emerald Deldareware, which was introduced in 1911, decorated with Doctor Syntax subjects. Porcelain was also produced from 1915, *marked Buffalo China*. Most products were marked *Buffalo Pottery* and, until 1940, were also dated.

Buffalo Pottery Emerald Deldare vase, stylised foliate motif in shades of green and white on an olive ground, 8½in. high. *(Skinner)* **£500 $800**

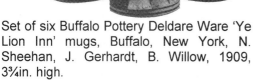

Set of six Buffalo Pottery Deldare Ware 'Ye Lion Inn' mugs, Buffalo, New York, N. Sheehan, J. Gerhardt, B. Willow, 1909, 3¾in. high.
(Skinner) **£306 $460**

Buffalo Pottery Deldare Ware jardinière and stand, Buffalo, New York, W. Foster and W. Forrester, 1908 and 1909, Ye Lion Inn, stamp marks, jardinière 9in. high.
(Skinner) **£2,110 $3,450**

Buffalo Pottery Deldare Ware water pitcher, 'Ye Old English Village', 10in. high.
(Eldred's) **£325 $523**

Two Buffalo Pottery Deldare Ware bisque plates, Buffalo, New York, 1909, 'Ye Olden Times', one with partial decoration, 9¼in. diameter.*(Skinner)* **£115 $172**

Burgess & Leigh evolved from the firm of Hulme & Booth in 1877, when the other partners retired. It moved to a new factory at Middleport, Burslem in 1889, and on the death of R.S. Burgess in 1912, passed entirely into the hands of the Leigh family, who still own it today.

They produced domestic and ornamental wares, many with underglaze prints, but some also hand painted, tube-lined, or lithographed.

Burgess & Leigh are perhaps best known for their 'flower' jugs of the 1930s, which appeared in various forms such as Squirrel, modelled by their young apprentice Ernest Bailey. A parrot, a dragon, a kingfisher and flamingo followed, and then Harvest - a rabbit on a stook of corn-, Highwayman, etc., the subject forming the handle, with appropriate decoration on the body. Many of these were designed by Charles Wilkes. Later additions to the range included Butterfly, Village Blacksmith, Coronation, Tally-ho and Sally in our Alley, and a range featuring sporting characters, such as a golfer, cricketer and tennis player, was also produced. They came in various sizes and colourways, some with matching plaques, and proved highly successful, so much so that by 1950 a quarter of a million had been produced.

Further series of Dickensian and Shakespearean toby jugs were made, as were bird jugs. Much of Burgess & Leigh's tableware featured strongly Art Deco decoration, while their lozenge vases are usually bright yellow with stylised fish, swans or galleons.

In 1926, Charlotte Rhead came to work for them, creating pieces decorated with stylised fruit, flowers and landscapes in the Art Deco style. She remained with Burgess & Leigh until 1932, when she moved to Richardsons.

The pre-war mark is usually a beehive with leaves around and *Burleigh Ware Made in England*. Post 1940 items have a smaller hive with no foliage and with *Burleigh Ware, Burgess & Leigh Ltd* above, and *Burslem England* below.

Burleigh ware lustre jug with squirrel handle, 8in. high, 1930s. *(Muir Hewitt)* **£70 $110**

A Burleigh ware bowl with fluted rim, pattern No. 4133, painted with stylised flowers and foliage, in shades of orange, yellow, green and blue on a white ground, printed and painted marks, 27cm. diameter. *(Christie's)* **£175 $271**

Burleigh ware Harvest jug, 8in. high, 1930s. *(Muir Hewitt)* **£55 $85**

A Burleigh ware character jug, modelled as Winston Churchill in naval dress, 13cm. high.
(*Christie's*)   **£210 $325**

Burleigh ware jug with parrot handle, 8in. high, 1930s.
(*Muir Hewitt*)   **£75 $115**

Burleigh Ware jug with squirrel handle, 8in. high, 1930s.(*Muir Hewitt*)   **£75 $125**

Burleigh Ware yellow galleon wall plaque with silver detail, 1930s.
(*Muir Hewitt*)   **£170 $275**

Burleigh Ware Galleon green wall plaque, 14in. diameter, circa 1930.
(*Muir Hewitt*)   **£140 $230**

Burleigh Ware 1930s Red Indian wall mask, 5in. high. (*Muir Hewitt*) **£140 $230**

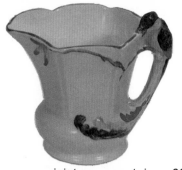

Burleigh ware miniature parrot jug, 3½in. high, 1930s.
(Muir Hewitt) **£55 $85**

Burleigh Ware flower arranger with squirrel decoration, 6in. high.
(Muir Hewitt) **£30 $50**

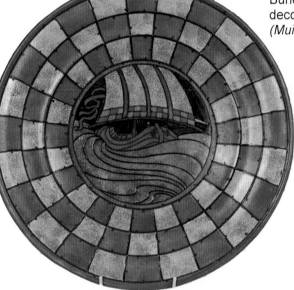

A rare Burleighware wall plaque with a design of a galleon in full sail by Charlotte Rhead. *(Michael Newman)* **£940 $1,530**

Burleigh Ware dragon jug, 1930s, 10in. high. *(Muir Hewitt)* **£175 $285**

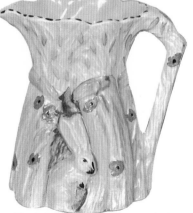

1930s Burleigh Ware Harvest jug, 8in. high. *(Lyle)* **£85 $140**

Burleigh Ware vase with stylised feather design, 1950s
(Muir Hewitt) **£40 $65**

A pair of Burleigh stylised fish design vases in red and black, 1950s.
(Muir Hewitt) **£125 $200**

Art Deco jug by Burgess and Leigh marked *Burleigh Ware*, 10in. high, 1930s.
(Lyle) **£120 $195**

Burleigh ware jug by Burgess & Leigh, in the Art Deco style, 1930s, 9in. high.
(Lyle) **£85 $140**

A Burleigh toby jug, modelled as Winston Churchill, in full riding attire, straddling a bulldog, 28cm. high.
(Christie's) **£840 $1,302**

Burleigh ware Pied Piper jug, 8in. high, 1930s.
(Muir Hewitt) **£130 $210**

This was a trademark of H.J. Wood & Sons Ltd., (q.v.), which came into use about 1930. Under Harry Wood, who joined the company in 1889, H.J. Wood was notable for fostering the talents of ceramic artists throughout the first half of the twentieth century. They were rewarded by being able to rely on the services of a number of talented designers under the trademark, including Frederick Rhead, (who became Art Director there in 1912) Dora Tennant, and, of course, most famous of all, Charlotte Rhead. She followed her father into Wood's employ in 1913, but it was not until her second period there, beginning in 1942, that she began to design under the Bursley Ware mark.

Charlotte Rhead produced over 100 designs for the trademark, with the backstamp *Bursley Ware* and *Charlotte Rhead* in script. After her death in 1947, these patterns continued in use until around 1960, a testament to the lasting appeal and versatility of her designs.

Charlotte Rhead plate with floral decoration, Bursley ware, 1940s, 12½in. diameter. *(Muir Hewitt)* **£280 $420**

Pair of Charlotte Rhead Bursley ware vases, circa 1925, 7in. high. *(Muir Hewitt)* **£465 $700**

A Bursley ware vase designed by Frederick Rhead, decorated in the 'Trellis' design, 31cm. high. *(Christie's)* **£165 $251**

Bursley Ware Art Deco bowl designed by Dora Tennant, circa 1929. *(Muir Hewitt)* **£100 $160**

James Cope established his pottery at the Wellington Works in Longton, Staffordshire in 1887. They produced everyday china in bright colours decorated with floral, landscape or geometric patterns. They also made, in the Art Deco period, a range of wall masks, which are very sought after today. Their wares are marked with backstamps, *JHC & Co,* being introduced circa 1900, *Wellington China* with a crown, around 1906, and *Wellington China*, with a profile of the Duke, from 1924-1947, when the factory closed. Many of the facemasks bear another mark *C & Co.*

J.H. Cope & Co. wall mask, 6in. high, 1930s. *(Muir Hewitt)*   **£100 $160**

C. & Co. wall mask of a young lady, 1930s, 5in. high. *(Muir Hewitt)*   **£100 $160**

C and Co. (J. H. Cope) wall mask of a young lady, English, 1930s. *(Muir Hewitt)*   **£150 $245**

C and Co. (J. H. Cope) wall mask of a young lady, English 1930s. *(Muir Hewitt)*   **£150 $245**

C. & Co. (J. H. Cope) wall mask of a young lady with a feathered hat, 1930s. *(Muir Hewitt)*   **£170 $275**

Carlton was born out of the partnership of J. F. Wiltshaw and H. T. Robinson, who got together in 1890 to operate out of the Carlton Works in Stoke on Trent. Robinson bowed out of the enterprise some twenty years later, and the firm then remained in the hands of the Wiltshaw family until the late 1960s, when it became part of Arthur Wood & Son (Longport). It finally ceased production in 1989.

From the first, Carlton ware was noted for the enormous range and versatility of its designs, from lustre items destined for the luxury end of the market, down to what can most kindly be described as kitsch.

At the top end, items were produced to the highest standards, with rich lustre glazes, fine gilding and stylised Jazz Age decorative motifs being applied to such classical shapes as footed bowls, ginger jars, and the like.

Carlton's embossed floral ware proved highly successful from the mid 1920s, and in 1928 print and enamel decorated china tableware was introduced, followed a year later by Ovenware - a great novelty at the time. In the 1930s Carlton undertook the production of advertising novelties for such companies as Guinness, and salad ware.

Carlton Ware wicker moulded honeycomb pot, decorated with bees. *(Lyle)* **£35 $57**

Carlton Ware Oak Tree design bulbous jug, with branch handle. *(Lyle)* **£150 $245**

'Fan', a cylindrical biscuit barrel and cover, pattern 3557, printed and painted in colours and gilt on a blue ground, printed script mark, 13.5cm. high. *(Christie's)* **£299 $485**

A twin-handled dish of ovoid form, printed and painted in colours and gilt on a dark blue ground with a bird of paradise flying past a tree and foliage, printed script mark, 31.9cm. high. *(Christie's)* **£287 $468**

Carltonware salad dish and strainer, 7in. wide, 1940s.
(Muir Hewitt) **£40 $65**

A Carltonware twin-handled boat shape bowl on splayed cylindrical column painted with an exotic bird of paradise, 23.5cm. high.
(Phillips) **£190 $285**

'Mikado', a shouldered vase and cover, the cover with lion finial, printed and painted in colours and gilt on a red lustre ground, printed script mark, 38cm. high.
(Christie's) **£200 $325**

A pair of Carltonware bookends, each modelled with a Britannia figure standing with shield and serpent against a triangular back, 18.5cm. high.
(Christie's) **£121 $184**

A Carltonware Keg Bitter advertising figure modelled as Shakespeare holding a quill and book, painted with naturalistic tones, 27.5 cm. high.
(Christie's) **£175 $280**

Carltonware vase with raised oak leaf decoration, 8½in. high.
(Muir Hewitt) **£75 $112**

A Carltonware plaque painted in gilt, orange, blue, green and white with wisteria and exotic plants, 15½in. diameter. *(Christie's)* **£250 $400**

Carltonware ceramic cruet set in the form of a mushroom with pepper, salt and mustard pot. *(Muir Hewitt)* **£50 $75**

Egyptianesque jardinière with frieze decoration and hieroglyphics on a blue ground, 16cm. high. **£1,000 $1,600**

A Carltonware service decorated in polychrome enamels, coffee pot 20.4cm. high. **£820 $1,230**

A Carltonware oviform ginger jar and cover, painted with clusters of stylised flowerheads and bold geometric bands, 31cm. high. *(Christie's)* **£1,250 $2,000**

Deep red jug with gold handle and sea-green interior, one of the famous Birds series, featuring fantastic and mythical birds, 29.5cm. high. **£225 $360**

'Paradise bird and tree' a hexagonal rimmed bowl, pattern no.3155, printed and painted in colours and gilt on a blue ground with trees, butterflies and birds of paradise, impressed script and painted marks, 24cm. wide. *(Christie's)* **£115 $185**

'Jazz Stitch', a shouldered, slender ovoid vase, pattern no.3655, printed and painted in colours and gilt on an orange ground, printed script mark, 26cm. high. *(Christie's)* **£575 $935**

A baluster vase and cover, the domed cover surmounted with lion finial, printed and painted in colours and gilt on a blue ground with cranes wading through rushes, printed script and painted mark, 39.8cm. high. *(Christie's)* **£552 $900**

A Handcraft twin-handled pedestal bowl, of quatrelobe form, pattern 3566, printed and painted in colours and gilt on a blue ground with Art Deco flowers and panels, printed script mark, 34cm. wide. *(Christie's)* **£207 $335**

'New Mikado', a twin-handled pedestal dish pattern no.2728, printed and painted in colours and gilt on a blue mottled ground with black interior, decorated with pagoda landscape, printed script and painted marks, 21.9cm. high. *(Christie's)* **£287 $465**

Carltonware shell cruet, 1930s. *(Muir Hewitt)* **£50 $75**

Carlton Ware crinoline lady napkin ring, 3½in. high. *(Muir Hewitt)* **£40 $65**

'Tutankhamen', a shouldered vase, pattern 2710, printed in gilt on a blue ground, printed bluebird mark and Tutankhamen mark, 21cm. high. *(Christie's)* **£345 $560**

'Lightning', a Handcraft rectangular box a cover, on four feet, pattern 3692, printed and painted in shades of orange and black on a white ground, printed script mark, 15.5cm. wide. *(Christie's)* **£207 $335**

'Rabbits at Dusk', a shouldered vase with everted rim, pattern 4249, printed and painted in colours on an orange lustre ground, printed script mark, 26.5cm.high. *(Christie's)* **£276 $450**

'Paradise bird and tree with cloud', a pedestal bowl, pattern no.3144, printed and painted in colours and gilt on a mottled light blue lustrous ground, decorated with a paradise bird flying over stylised landscape, printed script, painted marks and paper label, 13.6cm. diameter. *(Christie's)* **£575 $935**

'Prickly Pansy' a hexagonal baluster jar an cover, pattern 3449, printed and painted in colours and gilt on an orange ground, the cover with lion finial, printed script and painted marks, 30cm. high. *(Christie's)* **£600 $975**

Carltonware cheese dish, the sloping cover with crimped rim with gilt border and printed in colours, Chrysanthemum pattern, 9in. (G.A. Key) **£40 $63**

Carltonware twin-handled bowl, printed and painted in colours and gilt on a blue ground with stylised flowers and foliage, 31cm. wide. (*Christie's*) **£460 $736**

Carltonware lustre jug with gilt loop handle, the body painted and gilded with stylised floral and fan decoration, 5in. high. (*Phillips*) **£250 $400**

Carltonware Art Deco style conical baluster formed jug, gilt handle, decorated in green with 'handcraft' pattern, printed mark and impressed, 6½in. high. (G.A. Key) **£95 $153**

An hexagonal vase with chinoiserie decoration, 17.5cm. **£125 $200**

A Fine Carltonware scenic vase with shaped handles, 7in. high. **£55 $83**

A Carltonware orange ground bowl boldly decorated with flowers and multi-patterned quarter circle motifs, 9½in. diameter. *(Christie's)* **£150 $240**

A Carltonware 9¼in. circular bowl, the interior painted with a jardinière of flowers and shrubs, painted flowering boughs and insects on blue ground. *(Anderson & Garland)* **£200 $360**

A Carltonware ginger jar and cover, painted with stylised flowerheads and bellflowers against a mottled burgundy ground, 7½in. high. *(George Kidner)* **£280 $440**

Oviform vase with dark grey ground simulating nightfall, signed by E.F. Paul, with Kate Greenaway style fairies design, 230mm. high. **£600 $960**

Standard Carltonware vase of pale blue ground with tube lined floral decorations on primary colours, also blue inside the vase, 165mm. high. **£100 $160**

A large Carltonware two-handled punch bowl, moulded and painted on one side with King Henry VIII and Cardinal Wolsey on the other. *(Bearne's)* **£375 $600**

A bowl, pattern 3563, decorated with orange roof house and trees in shades of green, grey, blue, white, brown and orange on a blue ground and gilt rim, printed script and painted marks, 23.1cm. diameter. *(Christie's)* **£517 $840**

'Figurehead', a coffee set for four, pattern no.3684, painted in colours and gilt on a banded lemon yellow and mottled red ground with stylised figure handle, comprising tapered coffee pot and cover, sugar basin, milk jug, four cups and saucers, printed script and painted marks, height of coffeepot 15.9cm. high. *(Christie's)* **£920 $1,500**

'Forest Tree', a coffee set for six, decorated with tree and swallow pattern, printed and painted in colours and gilt on a blue ground, comprising; coffeepot and cover, milk jug, sugar bowl, six cups, and saucers, printed and painted marks *3279*, 22cm. high. *(Christie's)* **£1,035 $1,685**

'Tutankhamen', a twin-handled pedestal bowl of shaped rectangular section, printed and painted in colours and gilt on a blue ground with Egyptian figures and hieroglyphics to the well, printed bluebird mark, painted marks, 29.4cm. wide. *(Christie's)* **£1,380 $2,250**

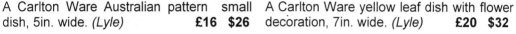

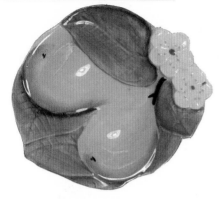

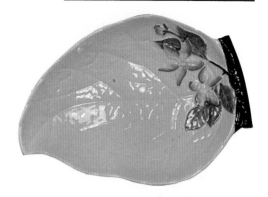

A Carlton Ware Australian pattern small dish, 5in. wide. *(Lyle)* **£16 $26**

A Carlton Ware yellow leaf dish with flower decoration, 7in. wide. *(Lyle)* **£20 $32**

'Barge', pattern no.2519, a twin-handled pedestal bowl of rectangular form, printed and painted in colours and gilt on a blue ground with oriental figures travelling in a barge, printed bluebird and painted marks, 30.5cm. long. *(Christie's)* **£402 $655**

A footed bowl and stand printed and painted in colours and gilt on a dark blue ground, the bowl decorated with pagoda landscape, printed script and painted mark, width of bowl, 25.2cm.
(Christie's) **£368 $600**

'Scimitar', a pedestal powder bowl and cover with flower bud finial, painted in colours with gilt detailing on a pale blue ground, the interior in pearl lustre, printed script and painted marks, 12.9cm. high.
(Christie's) **£862 $1,405**

A rectangular footed bowl with inverted rim, printed and painted in colours and gilt on a blue ground decorated to the well with pagoda and figural landscape, the rim with a band of chrysanthemums, printed script mark, 32.8cm. wide. *(Christie's)* **£287 $465**

'Leaf', a centrepiece of cylindrical body and disc shaped rim, pattern 3857, printed and painted in colours and gilt on a dark blue ground with leaves and flowers.
(Christie's) **£100 $165**

A twin-handled dish, with wavy rim, pattern no. 4284, printed and painted in colours and gilt on a dark blue ground with bird flying amongst trees and foliage, printed script and painted mark, 31.1cm. wide.
(Christie's) **£322 $525**

'Drayman', a Carlton ware Guinness advertising figure, painted in colours, printed factory marks, 13cm. wide.
(Christie's) **£500 $815**

A Carlton ware 6in. circular bowl, the interior and exterior painted butterflies and shrubs on stippled blue ground, printed marks and number *2071*.
(Anderson & Garland) **£95 $155**

'Rainbow Fan', a pottery vase, by Carlton ware, 1937, shape no.217, pattern no.3700, printed and painted in colours and gilt on a mottled mint green ground, printed script mark, impressed number, painted pattern number, original paper sticker, 8in. high.

The vogue for Egyptianesque designs caused by Howard Carter's excavation of Tutankhamen's tomb continued in the 1930s. Carlton ware produced a range printed and enamelled with designs from the tomb and also created new designs with bell flowers and fan motifs inspired by the newly exposed treasures.
(Christie's) **£5,000 $8,100**

A fine Carlton ware 'Rouge Royale' table cigarette lighter contained in 8¼in. Aladdin's Lamp pattern case with Chinese figure and foliage decoration.
(Anderson & Garland) **£100 $160**

A Carltonware ginger jar and cover, covered in a mottled blue glaze, with gilt and polychrome enamel decoration of a heron in flight, 26cm. high.
(Christie's) **£440 $766**

'Eastern Splendour', a fluted dish, printed and painted in colours and gilt on a red lustre ground with a sultan and his distant castle, printed script and painted marks, 22.1cm. wide.
(Christie's) **£184 $300**

'Floral Comets' , a Carlton ware coffee set for six, printed and painted in colours and gilt on a pale blue ground, comprising; coffee pot and cover, milk-jug and sugar basin, six cans and saucers, printed factory marks, coffee pot 16cm. high.
(Christie's) **£500 $815**

'Chinaland', a Carlton ware large ginger jar, pattern 2948, printed and painted in colours and gilt printed script and painted marks, 22cm. high.
(Christie's) **£400 $650**

'Mikado', pattern no.2364, a pair of vases of ovoid form with waisted neck and everted rim, printed and painted in colours and gilt on a blue mottled ground with pagoda landscape, printed bluebird mark, 26.7cm. high.
(Christie's) **£300 $490**

1930s marmalade dish in red and green by Carltonware. *(Muir Hewitt)* **£35 $60**

Carltonware bowl with leaf decoration, 1930s. *(Muir Hewitt)* **£150 $245**

Carlton Ware Oak tree design jug, 16in. high. *(Muir Hewitt)* **£250 $400**

Carltonware jug with leaf decoration, 1930s. *(Muir Hewitt)* **£175 $285**

Carlton Ware Oak tree bowl in brown and grey, 10in. wide, 1930s. *(Muir Hewitt)* **£95 $155**

Carlton Ware yellow and black stylised jug, 1930s. *(Muir Hewitt)* **£50 $85**

Carltonware jug with embossed decoration, 1930s. *(Muir Hewitt)* **£150 $245**

Carlton China coffee set comprising a cup and saucer, sugar bowl and jug, 1930s. *(Muir Hewitt)* **£125 $200**

Carlton Ware lustre jug, 1930s, with floral decoration, 8in. high. *(Muir Hewitt)* **£150 $245**

Carlton Ware Oak tree design jug in grey and brown, 16in. high. *(Muir Hewitt)* **£280 $450**

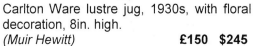

A Carlton ware 7¾in. circular bowl painted coloured flowers and foliage on orange ground, printed script mark and impressed number *276*.
(Anderson & Garland) **£100 $160**

Vibrant lustrous red 'Rouge Royale' leaf, one of a series introduced after 1930, 220mm. long. **£30 $48**

'Towering Castle', a footed ovoid vase with everted rim, pattern 3458, painted in colours on a mottled cream and brown ground decorated with a castle and trees, printed script factory marks, 24.3cm high.
(Christie's) **£300 $490**

A Carlton ware '3142' pattern Orange lustre part teaset, brightly enamelled with stylised trees beneath a band of flying swallows, comprising four cups, saucers and plates and sugar and cream.
(Bonhams) **£150 $245**

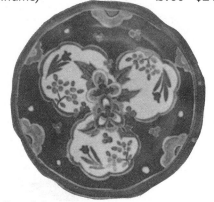

'Yellow Buttercup', a Carlton ware tea for two, modelled in relief, comprising; teapot and cover, milk-jug and sugar basin, two cups and saucers.
(Christie's) **£200 $325**

'Floribunda', a plate with wavy rim, pattern no.3236, decorated with stylised flower design and painted in shades of blue, purple, yellow, green and black, printed script and painted marks, 22.9cm. diameter. *(Christie's)* **£180 $290**

'Babylon', a Carlton ware single-handled dish, printed and painted in colours and gilt on a streaked yellow and green ground, printed factory marks 4125, 26cm. wide.
(Christie's)   **£300 $490**

A Carltonware ginger jar and cover, with gilt coloured chinoiserie decoration depicting temples and pagodas, 31cm. high.
(Phillips)   **£310 $465**

'Tubelined Flower', a bulbous jug with strap handle, painted in shades of turquoise, blue and yellow on a cream ground, printed script and painted marks, 17.3cm. high.
(Christie's)   **£225 $365**

Carltonware teapot, modelled as the 'Red Baron', printed mark, 8½in.
(G. A. Key)   **£58 $94**

'Spider's Web', an elliptical dish with wavy rim, printed and painted in colours and gilt on a blue ground with a spider weaving its web amongst foliage design, printed script and painted mark, 29.9cm. long.
(Christie's)   **£260 $425**

'Jazz', a Carlton ware compressed vase with cylindrical neck, painted in colours, highlighted in gilt on a mottled red ground, printed factory marks, 10cm. high.
(Christie's)   **£225 $365**

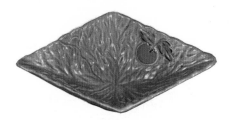

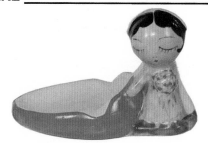

A small Carlton Ware green dish with strawberry decoration, 5in. wide.
(Lyle) **£12 $20**

Carltonware Bride ashtray with cartoon style Bride figure, 1930s.
(Muir Hewitt) **£60 $100**

A twin-handled footed bowl, of waisted form with fluted rim, printed and painted in colours and gilt on a dark blue ground with oriental figures sailing in a junk boat in a pagoda landscape, printed bluebird mark, 31cm. wide. *(Christie's)* **£250 $405**

'Prickly Pansy', a flaring bowl raised on three ball feet, pattern no.3449, printed and painted in colours and gilt on an orange lustrous ground with pansies, spikes and trees, printed script and painted marks, 27cm. diameter. *(Christie's)* **£299 $485**

'Fantasia' twin-handled pedestal dish, of rectangular section, pattern 3389, printed and painted in colours and gilt on a mauve ground, printed script mark, 31cm. wide. *(Christie's)* **£276 $450**

'Red Devil', a rare jug, of ovoid form printed and painted in enamels and gilt on a pale blue ground, printed and painted marks, 3767, 15cm. high. *(Christie's)* **£1,955 $3,185**

'Tutankhamen', a shallow bowl with inverted rim, the well decorated with Egyptian figures, in shades of pink, green, blue and gilt on a pearl ground, the exterior painted black with gilt detailing, printed script mark, 31.3cm. diameter. *(Christie's)* **£207 $335**

'Flower and Falling Leaf', a shouldered jug, pattern 3949, printed and painted in colours and gilt on a red lustre ground, printed script and painted marks, 19.5cm. high. *(Christie's)* **£690 $1,125**

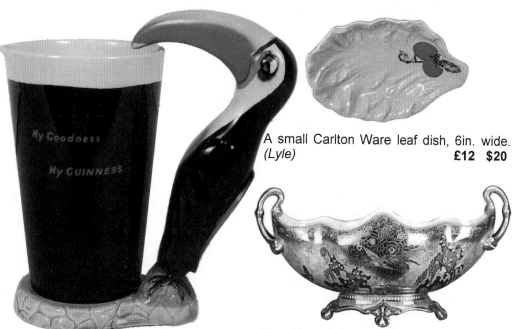

A small Carlton Ware leaf dish, 6in. wide. *(Lyle)* **£12 $20**

'My Goodness My Guinness', china counter display sign by Carltonware, Stoke on Trent. *(Lyle)* **£150 $245**

'Paradise Bird and Tree with cloud, a twin-handled pedestal bowl, pattern 3144, printed and painted in colours and gilt on a mottled blue lustre ground with a 'Paradise bird' flying past trees and foliage, printed and painted marks, 33cm. wide. *(Christie's)* **£437 $710**

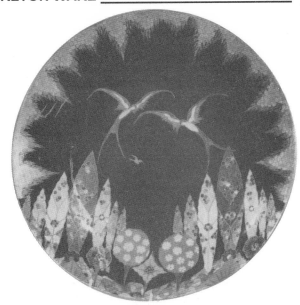

A Carlton ware ginger jar and cover with Chinese pagodas in gilt on a royal blue ground, the lid with Dog of Fo finial, 42cm. high. *(Phillips)* **£275 $450**

A Carlton ware lustre pottery charger, painted with exotic birds in flight over stylised flowering trees on a blue ground, with gilt embellishment, 15in. wide. *(Andrew Hartley)* **£1,750 $2,835**

'New Mikado', a Carlton ware smokers set, printed and painted in colours and gilt on a blue ground, comprising; vesta holder, pipe dish, ashtray, tapering cigarette holder and tobacco jar and cover, printed and painted marks 2728, tobacco jar 10.5cm. high. *(Christie's)* **£700 $1,140**

'Jazz', a pottery vase by Carlton ware, 1933, shape no.443, pattern no.3353, slender shouldered form, printed and painted in colours and gilt on a mottled orange lustre ground, printed script mark, impressed shape number, painted pattern numbers, 10.5cm. high. *(Christie's)* **£3,200 $5,184**

A Carltonware ginger jar decorated with flying birds in gilt clouds on a mottled blue ground, 8½in.
(*Russell, Baldwin & Bright*) **£75 $114**

A Rouge Royale twin-handled pedestal dish, of elliptical form with fluted rim, printed and painted in colours and gilt on a red lustre ground with pagoda scene, printed script and painted marks, 30.9cm. wide. (*Christie's*) **£275 $450**

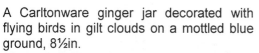

'Scimitar', a pottery pedestal dish by Carlton ware, circa 1935, twin-handled rectangular section, pattern no.3651, printed and painted in colours and gilt on a green, purple and blue ground printed and painted marks, 12in. wide.
(*Christie's*) **£3,200 $5,184**

A Carlton ware 8in. circular tapered vase richly painted a stork in flight with flowers and gilt trees on stippled blue ground.
(*Anderson & Garland*) **£340 $555**

A shouldered ovoid vase, with cylindrical neck, printed and painted in colours and gilt on a dark blue ground with a pheasant amongst foliage design and a stylised band of flowers to the rim, printed script mark, 14.8cm. high.
(*Christie's*) **£747 $1,210**

'Red Devil' a twin-handled pedestal bowl by Carlton ware, 1937, pattern no.3709, printed and painted in colours and gilt on a pale blue ground, printed script mark, painted pattern number, 12in. wide.
(*Christie's*) **£2,000 $3,240**

'Mikado', a hexagonal baluster jar and cover, pattern 2364 printed and painted in colours and gilt on a blue ground with a pagoda landscape, the cover with lion finial, printed bluebird mark and painted marks, 31cm. high. *(Christie's)* **£300 $490**

'Noire Royale', a gilt lined coffee set for four, pattern no.1562, printed in gilt and decorated with lily of the valley in shades of white and green, comprising; coffee pot and cover, milk jug, covered sugar basin, four cups and saucers, printed script and painted marks, coffeepot 19.4cm. high. *(Christie's)* **£747 $1,215**

'Cockerels', an ovoid baluster jar and cover, pattern 2250, printed and painted in colours and gilt on a blue ground with cockerel and foliage decoration, the cover with lion finial, printed script and painted marks, 36.6cm. high. *(Christie's)* **£287 $465**

A set of flying toucans produced for Guinness by Carltonware of Stoke on Trent, 1930s.
(Lyle) **£250 $400**

'Moonlight Cameo', a twin-handled pedestal bowl, rectangular form, pattern 2944, printed and painted in colours and gilt on an orange ground, printed bluebird mark, 30cm. wide. *(Christie's)* **£402 $655**

'Birds on Bough', a powder box and cover, pattern no.3394, printed and painted in colours and gilt on a pale blue ground, printed script mark, 14cm. wide. *(Christie's)* **£200 $325**

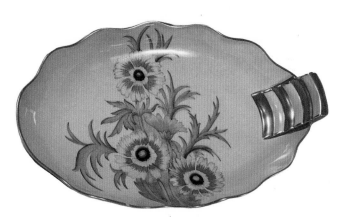

Carlton Ware crinoline lady napkin ring, 3½in. high. *(Muir Hewitt)* **£30 $50**

Carlton Ware dish with floral decoration, 1930s. *(Muir Hewitt)* **£60 $100**

A coffee set for six painted in polka-dot, pattern 1582, in shades of purple on a pale green ground with gilt lining and detailing, comprising; coffee pot and cover, milk jug, covered sugar basin, six cups and saucers, printed script and painted marks, height of coffee pot 19.2cm. *(Christie's)* **£322 $525**

'Paradise bird and tree and cloud', a powder box and cover, circular form, pattern 3144, printed and painted in colours and gilt on a pale blue lustre ground, printed script mark, remains of paper label, 14.5cm. diameter. *(Christie's)* **£207 $337**

'Persian', a small bowl, printed and painted in colours and gilt on a blue ground with a dancing figure amongst trees and foliage design to the well, the rim decorated with a band of stylised flowers and temple motif, printed bluebird and painted mark, 12.6cm. diameter. *(Christie's)* **£175 $285**

Fairy, a Carltonware vase and cover, printed and painted in colours and gilt on a blue lustre ground, 17cm. high. *(Christie's)* **£1,150 $1,840**

'Temple', an ovoid ginger jar, pattern no. 2880, printed and painted in colours and gilt on a terracotta ground with oriental figures in a temple garden, the base with a band of stylised foliage, printed bluebird mark, 17.2cm. high. *(Christie's)* **£260 $425**

A pair of Carlton ware vases, 21cm. high, and a tray, 25cm. wide. *(Christie's)* **£600 $960**

A Carlton ware ginger jar and cover with cranes amid exotic foliage in polychrome on a blue ground, 29cm. high. *(Phillips)* **£225 $370**

A Rouge Royale charger, printed and painted in colours and gilt on a red ground with a pagoda and foliage landscape, printed script mark, 32.5cm. diameter. *(Christie's)* **£218 $355**

A Carlton ware 'Hollyhocks' Handcraft preserve pot, cover and saucer.
(Christie's) **£125 $200**

A Carlton ware novelty box and cover, modelled as a Crinoline lady, wearing black top and orange lustre dress, printed factory marks, 14.5cm. high.
(Christie's) **£275 $450**

'Garden', a cylindrical vase with flared rim, pattern no.3478, painted in colours with hollyhocks in shades of blue, purple, yellow, red, black and green on an orange lustrous mottled ground with gilt detailing, printed script mark, 26cm. high.
(Christie's) **£391 $635**

'Diamond', a boxed gilt lined coffee set for six, pattern no.3546, decorated with diamond design in gilt on an off white and pale blue ground, comprising; six cups and saucers, printed script marks, cup 5.9cm. high. *(Christie's)* **£977 $1,600**

A Carlton ware Guinness advertising lampbase and shade, modelled as a sea lion balancing a globe shade, in colours, printed factory marks, 35cm. high.
(Christie's) **£400 $650**

A Handcraft shouldered ovoid vase, pattern 3509, decorated with tree design in shades of blue, brown and green on a bright green ground with gilt rim, printed script and painted marks, 19.3cm. high.
(Christie's) **£200 $325**

An unusual box and cover modelled as an eighteenth century lady in yellow and black gown, painted with black floral motif, printed bluebird mark, 14.5cm. high.
(Christie's) **£172 $280**

'Sketching Bird', a globular vase with everted rim, pattern no.3889, printed and painted in colours and gilt on a mottled red lustrous ground with a bird of paradise flying past trees and foliage, printed script and painted marks, 14.4cm. high.
(Christie's) **£552 $900**

'Rainbow Fan', a shouldered ovoid vase, pattern 3721, printed and painted in colours and gilt on a pale blue ground, printed script mark,19cm. high.
(Christie's) **£2,300 $3,750**

'Hollyhocks', a twin handled pedestal bowl with fluted rim, printed and painted in colours and gilt on a mottled pale blue and black ground with pearl interior, decorated with 'hollyhocks', printed script and painted marks, 33.1cm. long.
(Christie's) **£690 $1,125**

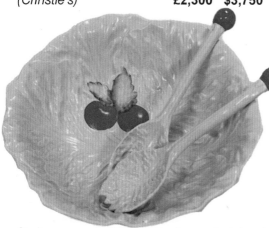

Carltonware Australian design salad bowl and servers, 8in. diameter.
(Muir Hewitt) **£50 $75**

A Carltonware stylised dog in shades of brown, with ribbed body, 1930s.
(Muir Hewitt) **£55 $83**

The history of this famous pottery began in 1873, when Jesse Carter set up in business in Poole, Dorset. He was joined by his sons Ernest, Charles and Owen, and they engaged the services of the distinguished designer, James Radley Young, in the early 1900s. It was Young who developed the glazes which have come to characterise the output of this factory. These are in the delft style, the glaze and decoration being fired on to the biscuit body, the result being a matt, silken effect.

In 1913 the silversmith, Harold Stabler, and his wife Phoebe, joined the company, which by now was supplying Heal's, Liberty and an eager American market. John Adams and his wife Truda completed the team in 1921, on their return from South Africa.

At this time the pottery was hand thrown and hand decorated, and included earthenware in simple shapes for table use and stoneware painted boldly and sketchily in clear, fresh colours. Many of their painted designs were by Truda Adams, and featured floral motifs based on Jacobean and peasant embroidery patterns, presented in a highly stylised form. They also produced strongly Art Deco designs throughout the 20s and 30s. The company kept going with a skeleton staff during the war, and business built up again in the subsequent period. From 1963 it was known officially as the Poole Pottery, and was taken over in 1971 as a unit within the Thomas Tilling group.

A Carter, Stabler, Adams pedestal bowl, by Ruth Pavely, pattern UE, shape no. 464, painted with geometric foliage in blue, mauve, yellow, green, grey and black on a white ground, impressed *CSA* marks, painted marks, 21.3cm. diameter. *(Christie's)* **£460 $750**

'Poole Pottery', a shaped rectangular advertising plaque, designed by Ann Read, resist decorated with silhouetted Freeform, Contemporary and tableware designs, in shades of grey, blue and brown on a white ground, printed factory marks, 35cm. wide. *(Christie's)* **£920 $1,500**

A Carter, Stabler, Adams bowl, with everted rim by Mary Brown, pattern XC, shape no. 383, painted with geometric flowers in blue, yellow, white and black on a white ground, 1926-1934, impressed factory marks, painted marks, 24.3cm. high. *(Christie's)* **£322 $525**

A Carter, Stabler, Adams twin-handled jardinière by Anne Hatchard, pattern CO, shape no.676, painted with stylised flowers and foliage in blue, mauve, yellow, red, green and black on a white ground, 1924-1934, impressed CSA marks, painted marks, 16cm. high. *(Christie's)* **£350 $570**

A terracotta sculpture of a fully rigged galleon modelled by Harry Stabler, glazed in shades of blue, green, yellow and white, 20½in. high. *(Christie's)* **£775 $1,250**

A Poole Pottery jug by Eileen Prangnell, painted with stylised flowers and foliage in colours belwo geometric banding, 19.5cm. high, *(Christie's)* **£253 $405**

A Poole Pottery twin-handled vase, shouldered form, by Phyllis Allen, painted with geometric flowers and foliage in colours on a white ground, 13cm. high. *(Christie's)* **£172 $275**

A terracotta plate painted by Anne Hatchard with a green spotted leaping gazelle amongst fruiting vines, impressed *CSA* mark, 12in. diameter. *(Christie's)* **£900 $1,440**

A Poole Pottery deep dish, made to commemorate the sail ship, drawn by Arthur Bradbury, painted by Ruth Pavely, impressed mark and *528*, 15in. diameter. *(Woolley & Wallis)* **£220 $433**

A terracotta two-handled oviform vase shape No. 973, painted with flowers and foliage below geometric border, impressed *CSA Ltd.* mark, 7in. high. *(Christie's)* **£450 $720**

A pair of pottery doves designed by John Adams and modelled by Harry Brown, impressed *Poole England*, 8¼in. high.
(Christie's) **£300 $480**

A pottery charger painted by Nellie Blackmore with a view of the ship the Harry Paye, by Arthur Bradbury, 15in. diameter.
(Christie's) **£625 $1,000**

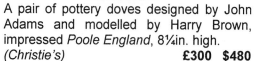

A terracotta shallow bowl, decorated by Anne Hatchard painted with a deer in an open landscape, impressed *CSA* mark, painted insignia and *RG*, 9½in. diameter.
(Christie's) **£250 $400**

Poole Carter Stabler & Adams two handled baluster vase, rim decorated in typical colours with flying birds, stylised clouds and foliage, decorator's initials P.N., dated 1929, moulded mark, 7in.
(G.A. Key) **£130 $208**

A terracotta twin-handled oviform vase painted by Ruth Pavely with bluebirds and foliage between contrasting borders, impressed *CSA Ltd.* mark, 6½in. high.
(Christie's) **£700 $1,120**

A Phoebe Stabler 'Piping Faun' roundel, modelled as a young faun with pan pipes tripping through a circular garland of flowers and reeds, 40cm. diameter.
(Phillips) **£520 $780**

Poole Pottery cruet set comprising a mustard pot, salt dish and pepper, 1950s. *(Muir Hewitt)* **£60 $100**

Poole Pottery vase with stylised decoration in orange, yellow and black, 1930s. *(Muir Hewitt)* **£125 $200**

Poole Pottery hors d'oeuvres dish with six compartments. *(Muir Hewitt)* **£50 $85**

Poole Pottery jug with stylised flower decoration, 1930s, 8in. high. *(Muir Hewitt)* **£200 $325**

Poole Pottery seafood entrée dish with scroll over handles, 7in. long, 1950s. *(Muir Hewitt)* **£30 $50**

Poole Pottery biscuit barrel, with wickerwork handle and floral decoration, 1930s. *(Muir Hewitt)* **£100 $160**

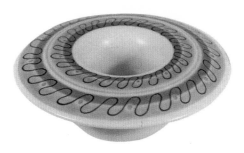

Poole Pottery free form dish, 6in. diameter with spiral decoration, 1950s.
(Muir Hewitt) **£40 $65**

Poole Pottery posy dish with leaf and flower decoration, 1950s.
(Muir Hewitt) **£20 $32**

Poole Pottery candelabra moulded with fruit and foliage, 8½in. high.
(Muir Hewitt) **£150 $245**

Poole Pottery jug with geometric design, 1930s, 8in. high.
(Muir Hewitt) **£200 $325**

Poole Pottery butter dish with floral decoration, 1930s.
(Muir Hewitt) **£80 $130**

Poole Pottery entrée dish with floral decoration, 1930s.
(Muir Hewitt) **£20 $32**

A Poole Pottery baluster vase painted with flowers in purple, yellow, green and blue within purple, green and yellow banding, 5¾in. high. *(Andrew Hartley)* **£60 $96**

Poole Pottery jug, cream with geometric decoration, 4in. high. *(Muir Hewitt)* **£100 $160**

The Bull, a pottery group designed by Phoebe and Harold Stabler, modelled as two infants astride a bull in ceremonial trappings of swags and garlands, impressed *CSA* mark, 13 in. high. *(Christie's)* **£2,500 $4,000**

A pair of Pheobe Stabler earthenware figures modelled as a boy and girl, each draped with a garland of flowers, impressed *Hammersmith Bridge* mark, 7in. high. *(Christie's)* **£575 $920**

A Poole Pottery jug, by Eileen Prangnell, pattern CO, painted with stylised flowers and foliage in colours below geometric banding, 19.5cm. high. *(Christie's)* **£253 $410**

A small ovoid vase with collar rim, by Marian Heath, pattern YI, shape no. 442, decorated with stylised flower and foliage design, painted in shades of pink, grey, blue, green and black, impressed factory mark, 16.2cm. high. *(Christie's)* **£483 $785**

Poole Pottery jam pot with stylised floral decoration, circa 1950. *(Muir Hewitt)* **£60 $100**

A pottery wall decoration modelled as a yacht in full sail, glazed in yellow on grey base, impressed *Poole England* mark, 4in. high. *(Christie's)* **£50 $80**

A pair of pottery bookends each modelled in full relief as leaping gazelles, impressed *Poole* and incised *831*, 8in. high. *(Christie's)* **£450 $720**

A pottery candelabra, moulded with fruit and foliage and covered in a light blue glaze, impressed *Poole England* mark, 8½in. high. *(Christie's)* **£75 $120**

A pottery nursery rhyme jug, designed by Dora Batty and painted by Ruth Pavely, depicting a scene from 'Ride a Cock Horse to Banbury Cross', impressed *Poole England* mark, 7½in. high. *(Christie's)* **£90 $145**

A Carter Stabler Adams pottery dish, possibly a design by Erna Manners, painted in mauve, green and blue with stylised leaves and scrolling tendrils, 37.8cm. diameter. *(Phillips)* **£190 $285**

A Carter, Stabler, Adams shouldered vase, of slightly waisted form, painted by Anne Hatchard pattern EB, decorated with stylised foliage and zig-zag band in shades of green, purple, yellow, black and pink on a white ground, impressed *CSA* mark and painted monogram, 16.7cm. high.
(Christie's) **£287 $465**

A large charger by Ruth Pavely, pattern HX, the well decorated with stylised flowers, the rim with repeated flower design and bands in shades of purple, black, yellow, green, mushroom, grey and pink on a white ground, impressed factory mark and painted monogram, 37.4cm. diameter.
(Christie's) **£2,760 $4,500**

A Carter, Stabler, Adams vase, by Marian Heath, pattern DP, shape no. 486, painted with stylised flowers and foliage in blue, mauve, yellow, green and black on a white ground, 1925-1934, impressed factory marks, painted marks, 15cm. high.
(Christie's) **£200 $325**

A twin-handled ovoid vase by Gladys Hallett, pattern CU, shape no. 462, decorated with stylised floral design in shades of blue, green, mushroom, grey and black on a white ground, impressed factory mark and painted monogram, 19cm. high. *(Christie's)* **£402 $655**

A Carter, Stabler, Adams bulbous jardinière painted by Mary Brown, pattern EP, shape no.924, decorated with a geometric floral design and zig-zag banded neck, painted in shades of mushroom, pink, purple, blue, grey, green, yellow and black on white ground, impressed CSA mark and painted monogram, 18.1cm. high. *(Christie's)* **£782 $1,275**

'Persian Deer', a large ovoid vase with everted rim, painted by Susan Russell, pattern SK, painted in colours on a white ground, printed and painted marks, 33.1cm. high. *(Christie's)* **£460 $750**

An ovoid vase, with tapering neck, painted by Rene Haynes, pattern .V, shape no.337, decorated with stylised flowers and foliage between bands and zig-zag design, painted in shades of green, blue, black, purple, yellow and pink on an off white ground, impressed factory mark and painted monogram, 24.7cm. high. *(Christie's)* **£391 $635**

A Carter, Stabler, Adams tapered jug, with strap handle and pulled lip, painted by Anne Hatchard, pattern AY, shape no. 316, decorated with stylised flowers and foliage in shades of mint green, brown, grey and black, impressed *CSA* mark and painted monogram, 17.3cm. high. *(Christie's)* **£230 $375**

A bulbous vase, with tapered neck, painted by Marjorie Batt pattern GPA, shape no. 443, decorated with stylised foliage design in shades of green, grey and black on a white ground, impressed factory mark and painted monogram, 17.1cm. high. *(Christie's)* **£322 $525**

A Carter, Stabler, Adams shouldered ovoid vase, pattern ZW, shape no. 429, decorated with flowers and foliage in shades of blue, pink, purple, mushroom, yellow and black, impressed *CSA* mark, painted monogram and *Kirk & Co Montpellier Parade Harrogate* label, 25.5cm. high. *(Christie's)* **£207 $335**

Poole Pottery jug with stylised floral decoration, 1930s.
(Muir Hewitt)   **£100 $160**

An ovoid vase, by Marian Heath, pattern TZ, shape no. 336, decorated with leaping gazelle amongst stylised foliage in shades of yellow, blue, black, green, pink and purple on a white ground, impressed mark and painted monogram, 18.3cm. high.
(Christie's)   **£460 $750**

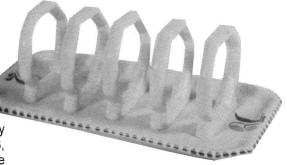

An ovoid vase with cylindrical neck, by Hilda Hampton, pattern FH, shape no. 203, painted with stylised flowers and foliage between bands in shades of blue, purple, yellow, black, brown, and green on a white ground, impressed factory mark and monogram, 20.5cm. high.
(Christie's)   **£299 $485**

Poole Pottery toast rack with dotted border, 1950s. *(Muir Hewitt)*   **£20 $32**

A Poole pottery twin-handled vase, shouldered form, by Phyllis Allen, painted with geometric flowers and foliage in colours on a white ground, 13cm. high.
(Christie's)   **£172 $280**

An ovoid vase, of tapering neck by Eileen Prangnell, pattern .ZW, shape no.337, decorated with stylised foliage and bands in shades of yellow, brown, black, purple, pink and green, circa 1934-37, impressed and painted factory marks, 25.1cm. high.
(Christie's)   **£350 $570**

Poole Pottery circular large vase of conical baluster form, densely decorated with stylised flowers, 10in.*(G.A. Key)* **£360 $547**

'Persian Deer', an ovoid ginger jar and cover, painted by Donna Ridout, pattern SK, painted in colours on a white ground, printed and painted marks, 30.5cm. high. *(Christie's)* **£287 $465**

A Carters Poole tile panel, comprising four six inch tiles, with a girl and boy, a cockerel, a pig and two sheep. *(Phillips)* **£500 $800**

A large ovoid vase, with everted rim, painted by K Hickisson, shape no. 660, decorated with stylised flower design in shades of pink, purple, blue, green and yellow on a white ground, impressed factory mark and painted monogram, 33.1cm. high. *(Christie's)* **£345 $560**

A pottery oviform jug, shape No. 304, painted by Marjorie Batt with bluebirds and foliage in typical colours, impressed *CSA Ltd* mark, 5in. high. *(Christie's)* **£250 $400**

A Carter, Stabler, Adams globular vase, by Marian Heath pattern .PN, shape no.202, applied with two strap handles, painted in the 'Bluebird' pattern, in shades of blue, purple, green and yellow, impressed *CSA* mark and painted monogram, 17.5cm. high. *(Christie's)* **£250 $405**

A Carter, Stabler, Adams shouldered vase, of slightly waisted body, by Marian Heath, pattern CR, 16.8cm. high.
(Christie's) **£276 $450**

A pair of candlesticks, by Eileen Prangnell, pattern JY, shape no.269, decorated with geometric design and bands in shades of blue, mushroom and grey, impressed factory marks and painted monograms, 24.7cm. high. *(Christie's)* **£400 $650**

A Carter, Stabler, Adams twin-handled ovoid jug, by Anne Hatchard, pattern EJ, shape no. 462, decorated with a band of flowers and foliage in shades of yellow, blue, purple, green, black and mushroom, impressed *CSA* mark and painted monogram, 18.3cm. high.
(Christie's) **£345 $560**

A Carter, Stabler, Adams shouldered ovoid jug, with strap handle, by Mary Brown, pattern AX, shape no.309, decorated with geometric flower design in shades of mushroom, blue and brownish grey, impressed *CSA* mark and painted monogram, 19.9cm. high.
(Christie's) **£300 $490**

Poole Pottery vase with stylised floral declaration, 6½in. high.
(Lyle) **£200 $325**

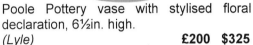

A shouldered ovoid vase, by Vera Bridle, pattern TZ, painted with leaping gazelle amongst foliage, in shades of blue, mushroom, green, purple, yellow and black, printed factory and painted marks, 11.2cm. high. *(Christie's)* **£287 $465**

A Carter, Stabler, Adams vase of ovoid shouldered form by Ruth Pavely, pattern AX, shape no. 966 painted with geometric flowers and foliage in mushroom, blue and grey on a white ground, impressed factory marks, painted marks, 24.6cm. high.
(Christie's) **£2,070 $3,375**

A Carter, Stabler, Adams twin-handled ovoid vase, by Anne Hatchard, pattern NO, shape no. 973, decorated with leaping gazelle amongst stylised foliage in shades of mushroom, yellow, grey and black on a white ground, impressed CSA mark and painted monogram, 18cm. high.
(Christie's) **£862 $1,405**

A twin-handled ovoid vase by Barbara Meades, pattern .AP, shape no.462, painted with flowers and foliage between bands in shades of pink, purple, mushroom, green, blue, yellow and black on a white ground, impressed factory marks and painted monogram, 18.8cm. high. *(Christie's)* **£446 $750**

Poole Pottery jug with geometric decoration, 1930s.
(Muir Hewitt) **£100 $160**

A pottery biscuit barrel and cover with wicker handle painted by Sylvia Penney, with stylised flowers and foliage, impressed *Poole*, 5½in. high. *(Christie's)* **£140 $225**

A Carter, Stabler, Adams vase of ovoid form with everted rim, by Marian Heath, pattern YW, shape no. 619, decorated with geometric flowers and foliage in blue, mauve, red, yellow, green and black on a white ground, 1937-1938, impressed *CSA* mark, painted mark, 18.1cm. high.
(Christie's) **£402 $655**

Poole Pottery entrée dish, 1950s, with stylised seafood compartments.
(Muir Hewitt) **£40 $65**

Poole Pottery jug, with stylised floral band, 7½in. high, 1930s.
(Muir Hewitt) **£125 $200**

Poole Pottery vase with geometric design shoulder, 4in. high, 1930s.
(Muir Hewitt) **£50 $85**

Poole Pottery jam pot with stylised floral decoration, circa 1950.
(Muir Hewitt) **£60 $100**

Poole Pottery large baluster jug, with grey speckled rim, decorated with panels of stylised foliage, flowers etc, by Ruth Pavely, 11½in. (G.A.Key) **£180 $288**

A Carters Poole Art Deco tile panel, comprising four tiles, block printed with a lady golfer teeing off, 30.2cm. square.
(Phillips) **£1,000 $1,600**

A shouldered cylindrical vase by Eileen Prangnell, pattern .V, shape no.599, with stylised foliate decoration between bands and zig-zag design, painted in shades of purple, blue, yellow, green, brown and black, impressed, incised and painted factory marks, 20.8cm. high.
(Christie's) **£368 $600**

A pottery vase, decorated with scrolling flowers and foliage, in typical colours on a white ground, impressed *CSA Ltd.* mark, 7in. high. (Christie's) **£150 $240**

A pottery vase, shape No. 466, painted by Rene Hayes with a band of geometric pattern in typical colours on a white ground, impressed *CSA Ltd* mark and painted insignia, 5½in. high.
(Christie's) **£100 $160**

Charlotte Rhead, who, with Clarice Cliff and Susie Cooper, is one of the famous 'Pottery Ladies', was a gentle, unassuming soul who was taught to draw and paint at home by her father, Frederick Rhead. Her childhood was dogged by ill-health, but she was able to attend the Fenton Art School with her younger sister Dollie. Thereafter she worked for various factories as a tube-liner and enameller, until her father set up his own business at the Atlas Tile Works, and both girls joined the family firm.

This venture was sadly short-lived and in 1913 Charlotte moved with her father to Wood & Sons, where he had been appointed Art Director. The vividly coloured pieces which she produced for them are sometimes marked *Lottie Rhead Ware.*

In 1926 she moved to Burgess & Leigh, where she introduced tube-lining, a tricky process whereby liquid clay or 'slip' is squeezed from a rubber bag through a glass nozzle on to the surface of an item, rather as icing is piped onto a cake. She produced many designs for Burgess & Leigh, such as Florentine, Sylvan, Garland and Laurel Band, her favourite motifs remaining fruit and flowers, still effected in bright colours but in rather more subtle juxtapositions. In 1931, she moved to A.G. Richardson at Tunstall, where she produced such superb designs as Rhodian, Byzantine, Persian Rose and Golden Leaves, all marked with a tube-lined *C. Rhead* on the base, together with the Crown Ducal trademark.

She returned to Woods in 1942, where, despite failing health, she produced over a hundred new designs before her death in 1947. These have a Bursley ware trademark, with *Charlotte Rhead* in script. It says much for the popularity and durability of her work that her designs remained in production until 1960.

Sometimes the tube lined signature is missing from her pottery, but her pieces can usually be easily identified from the patterns alone, which are very well documented.

Charlotte Rhead Vine Fruits octagonal bowl, circa 1926. *(Muir Hewitt)* **£250 $400**

Charlotte Rhead jug in green, orange and silver design, 1930s.
(Muir Hewitt) **£125 $200**

Charlotte Rhead Crown Ducal 'Manchu' design vase. *(Muir Hewitt)* **£120 $195**

Charlotte Rhead dish in green, orange and silver design, 1930s. *(Muir Hewitt)* **£60 $100**

Charlotte Rhead jug in brown, orange and black, 9in. high. *(Muir Hewitt)* **£125 $200**

Pair of Charlotte Rhead candlesticks, 2in. high. *(Muir Hewitt)* **£140 $230**

Charlotte Rhead Crown Ducal Golden Leaves charger, 18in. diameter. *(Muir Hewitt)* **£450 $735**

Charlotte Rhead, Burgess and Leigh, Burleigh Ware charger with *L. Rhead* signature, circa 1929. *(Muir Hewitt)* **£675 $1,100**

Charlotte Rhead floral design vase, 10in. high. *(Muir Hewitt)* **£300 $500**

Charlotte Rhead vase, Crown Ducal in stepped Aztec design, 7in. high. *(Muir Hewitt)* **£200 $300**

Charlotte Rhead Art Deco vase, 5½in. high. *(Muir Hewitt)* **£200 $320**

Charlotte Rhead Stitch pattern jug, 9in. high. *(Muir Hewitt)* **£80 $130**

Charlotte Rhead plaque by Crown Ducal, 14in. diameter. *(Muir Hewitt)* **£350 $570**

Charlotte Rhead Bursley Ware vase with floral design, 8in. high. *(Muir Hewitt)* **£200 $325**

Crown Ducal Charlotte Rhead jug, signed *C. Rhead,* 1930s, 9in. high. *(Muir Hewitt)* **£200 $320**

Charlotte Rhead Crown Ducal wall plaque by A. G. Richardson, 14in. diameter. *(Muir Hewitt)* **£300 $500**

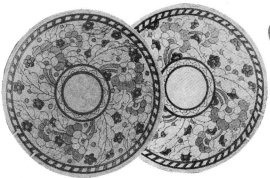

A pair of Charlotte Rhead Crown Ducal pottery wall plaques, tubelined in brown and decorated with orange flowers and scattered blue and red flower heads, 14in. diameter. *(Spencers)* **£200 $320**

Charlotte Rhead vase, 1930s, Bursley ware, 8in. high. *(Muir Hewitt)* **£300 $480**

Charlotte Rhead Golden Leaves vase, 9in. high. *(Muir Hewitt)* **£150 $245**

Charlotte Rhead Arabesque Daisies dish, 7in. wide. *(Muir Hewitt)* **£140 $230**

Charlotte Rhead jug in green, fawn and orange, 9in. high. *(Muir Hewitt)* **£80 $130**

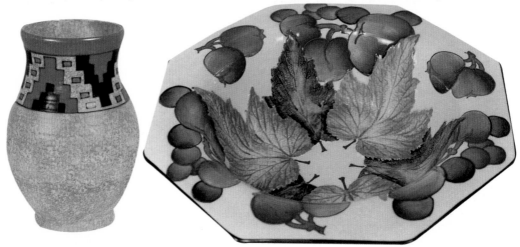

Charlotte Rhead Aztec design vase in brown, orange and black, 9in. high. *(Muir Hewitt)* **£130 $210**

Charlotte Rhead Bursley Ware fruit serving dish, 8in. wide. *(Muir Hewitt)* **£250 $400**

Charlotte Rhead Bursley Ware Vine Fruits pattern bowl signed *L. Rhead* (Lottie Rhead), circa 1926. *(Muir Hewitt)* **£200 $325**

Charlotte Rhead Crown Ducal vase with floral decoration, 7in. high. *(Muir Hewitt)* **£100 $160**

Charlotte Rhead Crown Ducal floral design vase. *(Muir Hewitt)* **£150 $245**

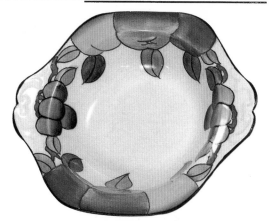

Charlotte Rhead Vine Fruits dish. *(Muir Hewitt)* **£35 $60**

Charlotte Rhead Burleigh Ware bowl by Burgess and Leigh, 9½in. diameter. *(Muir Hewitt)* **£300 $500**

Crown Ducal vase, 1930s, possibly designed by Charlotte Rhead, 8in. high. *(Muir Hewitt)* **£150 $245**

Charlotte Rhead design jug by Crown Ducal, with floral decoration, 1930s. *(Muir Hewitt)* **£150 $245**

Charlotte Rhead Persian Rose design charger, 17in. diameter. *(Muir Hewitt)* **£400 $650**

Charlotte Rhead Crown Ducal pottery charger, decorated with flowers and foliage, on speckled brown ground, green rim, 14½in. diameter. *(G.A Key)* **£325 $530**

A rare Burleigh Ware charger, designed by Charlotte Rhead, pattern 4012, painted to the well with a pheasant perched on a fruiting bough of pomegranates, the rim with panels of pomegranates and overlapping foliage, 36in. diameter. *(Christie's)* **£1,200 $1,950**

Charlotte Rhead Rhodian bowl, 1930s, 17in. diameter. *(Muir Hewitt)* **£180 $295**

Arabesque, a Charlotte Rhead spherical pottery lamp base decorated in a Chinese style pattern of peonies in foliate roundels, 6in. high. *(Christie's)* **£275 $450**

Charlotte Rhead plaque green, orange and silver design, 1930s. *(Muir Hewitt)* **£250 $400**

Bursley Ware balustered ewer, elaborately decorated with stylised flowers in colours, by Charlotte Rhead, printed marks and No. TL71, 8½in. high. *(G.A. Key)* **£120 $192**

Crown Ducal Art Deco period baluster formed ewer, elaborately decorated and painted in colours with stylised flowers, by Charlotte Rhead, 10in. high.
(G.A. Key) **£225 $360**

A Burslem ware ceramic wall plaque, the design attributed to Charlotte Rhead, decorated with stylised brown, and cream chrysanthemums with blue leaves and berries, 41cm. diameter.
(Phillips) **£400 $650**

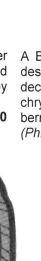

Charlotte Rhead Golden Leaves plate by Crown Ducal, 8in. diameter.
(Muir Hewitt) **£150 $245**

Charlotte Rhead vase with stylised tube lined floral decoration, 1930s, 12½in. high.
(Muir Hewitt) **£360 $540**

Charlotte Rhead Persian rose, orange, brown and green colourway jug, 8in.
(Muir Hewitt) **£175 $285**

A Crown Ducal 'Manchu' pattern bowl, designed by Charlotte Rhead, 25.5cm. diameter. *(Phillips)* **£250 $400**

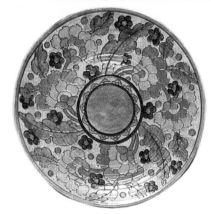

Charlotte Rhead Trellis design vase, 7in. high. *(Muir Hewitt)* **£130 $210**

Charlotte Rhead Crown Ducal charger, 16in. diameter. *(Muir Hewitt)* **£400 $650**

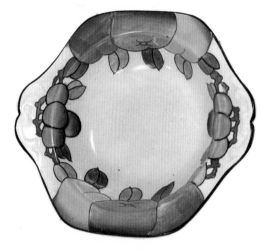

Charlotte Rhead small Vine Fruits dish. *(Muir Hewitt)* **£35 $60**

Charlotte Rhead Edward VIII jug, 9in. high. *(Muir Hewitt)* **£275 $450**

Charlotte Rhead Stitch pattern Crown Ducal vase, 8in. high. *(Muir Hewitt)* **£75 $125**

Charlotte Rhead Bursley Ware charger with floral decoration, 17in. diameter. *(Muir Hewitt)* **£475 $775**

The legendary Clarice Cliff was born in 1899 in, perhaps inevitably, Staffordshire, where she started work at 13 in one of the local potteries, painting freehand onto pottery.

Her formal training comprised a year, when she was 16, at the Burslem School of Art, and a later year at the Royal College of Art, where she studied sculpture. (It is interesting to note that while at Burslem she signally failed to impress the Director there, Gordon Forsyth, who was himself a brilliant ceramic designer, but who considered her work as trivial and lacking in depth.)

At 17, she had gone to work for the firm of A.J. Wilkinson & Co, and she remained with them, and their subsidiary, the Newport Pottery, for the next two decades, ending up as Art Director, and marrying the boss, Colley Shorter, at the age of forty.

During the 1920s she painted Tibetan ware, large jars painted with floral designs in bright colours and gold, and she also transferred onto pottery designs by such distinguished artists as Paul Nash and Dame Laura Knight.

In 1928, however, she painted 60 dozen pieces of her own design to test the market at a trade fair, These proved to be so popular that by 1929 the whole factory was switched to producing her Bizarre ware.

Cliff's style is characterised by combinations of bright colours, such as orange, blue, purple and green, or black, yellow, orange and red. Her pieces are often angular in shape and strongly Art Deco in style. Major ranges include, besides Bizarre, Crocus, Fantasque, Biarritz and Farmhouse. In all, she designed over fifty different landscapes, as well as more than forty geometric patterns and flower motifs. These patterns were applied to all sorts of objects, from tea and coffee sets, plates and bowls, to vases, which were in turn produced in many different shapes.

At the beginning of the Second World War, the factory was commandeered by the Ministry of Supply, and Wilkinson produced only a few white pieces.

Clarice Cliff Bizarre Gayday design cake stand, 8in. wide. *(Muir Hewitt)* **£300 $500**

'Original Bizarre', an octagonal tray, painted with a radiating design of arrowheads, in shades of blue, orange and yellow outlined in brown, inside green border, printed factory marks, 29.5cm. wide *(Christie's)* **£300 $490**

Nemesia Stamford shape tureen by Clarice Cliff, circa 1934. *(Muir Hewitt)* **£175 $285**

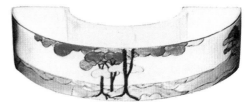

'Blue Firs', a Bizarre centrepiece, shape no.659, curved form painted in colours, printed factory marks, 25cm. wide. *(Christie's)* **£747 $1,210**

'Alton', a Fantasque Bizarre cube inkwell and cover, shape no.458, painted in colours, printed factory marks, 7.5cm. high. *(Christie's)* **£575 $935**

A novelty pencil holder, modelled as a Golly seated on a cushion beside a pot, painted in colours, printed factory marks, 15cm. high. *(Christie's)* **£977 $1,590**

'Propellor', an unusual Bizarre lampbase, swollen cylindrical form on broad circular foot, painted n colours between orange and black bands, printed factory marks, 18cm. high.

This is the first example recorded of this shape, previously only known from the shape sheets where it was decorated in a simple banded design.
(Christie's) **£805 $1,310**

A 'Circus' pattern set of three graduated oval serving plates, designed by Dame Laura Knight, the centres decorated with the entrance of the circus horses featuring two girl riders, a ringmaster and clown, the largest 16¾in. diameter, the medium 14½in. diameter, the smallest 12½in. diameter. *(Bonhams)* **£2,200 $3,585**

'Blue Crocus', a Bizarre clog, painted in colours, printed factory marks, 14.5cm. wide. *(Christie's)* **£253 $410**

A Bizarre model of a laughing cat, after a design by Louis Wain, the orange body with black spots, and green bow tie, 6in. high. *(Christie's)* **£825 $1,525**

A Clarice Cliff 'Age of Jazz', two sided plaque, 17.5cm. high. *(Phillips)* **£4,000 $6,520**

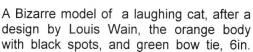

'Broth', a Fantasque Bizarre duck egg cruet set, comprising tray with central duck handle, and five egg cups, painted in colours, printed factory marks, 13cm. high. *(Christie's)* **£575 $935**

'Age of Jazz', a Bizarre table decoration modelled as two musicians in evening dress, rubber stamp mark, 6in. high. *(Christie's)* **£2,420 $4,475**

'Umbrellas and Rain', a Fantasque Bizarre lampbase, shape no. 124, painted in colours between orange, yellow and blue bands, with modern shade, printed factory marks, 22cm. high. *(Christie's)* **£920 $1,499**

'Sunray', a Bizarre clog, painted in colours printed factory marks, 13cm. high.
(Christie's) **£805 $1,310**

A 'Crocus' mustard pot and cover.
(Christie's) **£80 $130**

Dame Laura Knight, a set of six Bizarre plates, each painted to the well with a crowd of naked women in pink and brown on a black ground, the rim with spiralling turquoise and brown streamers and orange stripes, printed factory marks, 18cm. diameter. *(Christie's)* **£2,300 $3,750**

Clarice Cliff love birds wall pocket, 1930s.
(Muir Hewitt) **£450 $735**

Clarice Cliff wall pocket with Swallow decoration, 1930s.
(Muir Hewitt) **£250 $400**

'Original Bizarre', a sandwich set, painted with radiating star motif in shades of blue, purple and red outline in green, inside blue band, comprising; octagonal tray and six shaped side plates, printed factory marks, tray 29cm. wide. *(Christie's)* **£1,150 $1,875**

'Alton', a Bizarre clog, painted in colours, printed factory marks, 14cm. wide. *(Christie's)* **£300 $410**

A model of a Fox covered in a streaked beige glaze, printed factory marks, 24cm. wide; and a Wilkinson model of a fish. *(Christie's)* **£299 $485**

Dame Laura Knight, a Bizarre cruet set, comprising; salt and pepper pots and a mustard pot and cover, the mustard pot cover painted with a naked female bust in shades of brown and pink, the pots with turquoise and brown steamers and orange stripes, printed factory marks, salt and pepper, 8.5cm. high. *(Christie's)* **£345 $560**

A Fantasque Bizarre ginger jar and cover decorated in the 'Blue Autumn' pattern, painted in colours with contrasting banding, 7¾in. high. *(Christie's)* **£1,000 $1,600**

Dame Laura Knight, a Bizarre beer pitcher and six tankards, each painted with a crowd of naked women in shades of pink and brown on a black ground with a border of turquoise and brown spiralling streamers and orange stripes, printed factory marks, pitcher 28.5cm. high. *(Christie's)* **£2,300 $3,750**

'Fruitburst', a Fantasque Bizarre cigarette holder and ashtray, painted in colours, printed factory marks, 8cm. high.
(Christie's) **£437 $710**

'Red Roofs', a Fantasque Bizarre smoker's set, painted in colours, comprising; cigarette box and cover, match pot, two ashtrays and a tray, printed factory marks, tray 19cm. wide.

The shape 467 Smoker's set is one of the most intricately conceived sets Clarice produced. As earthenware suffers shrinkage during firing, the way the pieces neatly fit onto the tray was technically very advanced. Sadly few complete sets survive so this set with two of the original six ashtrays is still a rarity.
(Christie's) **£1,380 $2,250**

'Age of Jazz' a Bizarre table decoration of two musicians in full evening dress playing piano and banjo, naturalistically painted, on rectangular base, 14.5cm. high.
(Christie's) **£4,620 $7,069**

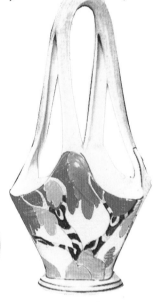

Dore Dore Clarice Cliff chamber pot made for Harrods, 11in. diameter.
(Muir Hewitt) **£600 $975**

'Honolulu', a Fantasque Bizarre flower basket and rose, painted in colours, printed factory marks, 32cm. high.

Clarice designed this shape in 1927. Its was popular for quite a few years and still in production in 1933 when it was issued in this design. This example still has the original flower block inside.
(Christie's) **£977 $1,600**

'Nemesia' Bizarre Stamford shape gravy boat, by Clarice Cliff.
(Muir Hewitt) **£250 $400**

A 'Gibraltar' pattern Viking Long Boat with flower holder, 15½in. long, 9¾in. high, lithograph mark *Fantasque Hand Painted Bizarre by Clarice Cliff Newport Pottery England.* (Bonhams) **£2,300 $3,750**

An important table lamp, designed by Dame Laura Knight, composed of clowns forming a human tower in support of five female acrobats with arms raised and hands joined beneath a cylindrical top hung with pendant garlands of puce outlined in gilt and all upon a triple stepped base of square section, 19in. high overall.
(Bonhams) **£6,000 $9,780**

A Clarice Cliff duck egg stand, in 'Melon' pattern, with three cups, stand unmarked except *Registration Applied for*, cups fully marked. *(Bristol Auction Rooms)* **£180 $265**

A Fantasque Bizarre cylindrical biscuit barrel and cover decorated in the 'Blue Autumn' pattern, 6¼in. high. *(Christie's)* **£350 $560**

Clarice Cliff biscuit barrel with cane handle, 7in. high, with geometric design. *(Muir Hewitt)* **£400 $650**

'Oranges and Lemons', a Bizarre biscuit barrel and cover, shape no.335, painted in colours, printed factory marks, 15cm. high. *(Christie's)* **£1,265 $2,060**

'May Avenue', a Fantasque Bizarre cylindrical biscuit barrel and cover, painted in colours, printed factory marks, 15cm. high. *(Christie's)* **£805 $1,310**

A 'Broth' pattern biscuit barrel and cover, with wicker handle, shape 335, 6in. high, large rubber stamp mark *Fantasque Hand Painted Bizarre by Clarice Cliff Newport Pottery England. (Bonhams)* **£400 $650**

'Autumn', a Fantasque Bizarre biscuit barrel and cover, shape no.335, painted in colours between yellow bands, printed factory marks, 16cm. high. *(Christie's)* **£690 $1,125**

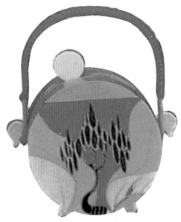

A Bizarre Bonjour biscuit barrel and cover with wicker handle, decorated in the 'Windbells' pattern, 6in. high.
(Christie's)   **£275 $450**

A Fantasque biscuit barrel by Clarice Cliff.
(Hobbs & Chambers)   **£300 $500**

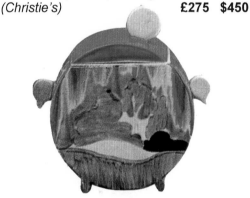

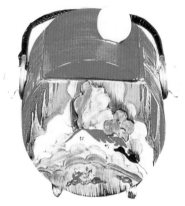

A 'Forest Glen' pattern Bon Jour biscuit barrel and cover, 6¼in. high overall, rubber stamp mark *Fantasque Hand Painted Bizarre by Clarice Cliff Newport Pottery England. (Bonhams)*   **£400 $650**

'Forest Glen', a Bizarre Bonjour biscuit barrel and cover, painted in colours, printed factory marks, 15cm. high.
(Christie's)   **£550 $900**

'Honolulu', a Fantasque Bizarre biscuit barrel, shape no.535, painted in colours, printed factory marks, 12cm. high.
(Christie's)   **£250 $405**

'Red Trees and House', a Fantasque Bizarre biscuit barrel and cover, shape no. 336, painted in colours, printed factory marks, 16cm. high. *(Christie's)* **£400 $650**

'Secrets', a Fantasque Bizarre biscuit barrel, shape no. 335, painted in colours, printed factory marks, 12cm. high. *(Christie's)* **£300 $500**

'Crocus', a Bizarre biscuit barrel, shape no. 422, painted in colours, printed factory marks, 13cm. high. *(Christie's)* **£300 $500**

'Kelverne', a Bizarre biscuit barrel and cover, shape no.335, painted in colours, printed factory marks, 12cm. high. *(Christie's)* **£300 $500**

'Autumn', a Fantasque Bizarre biscuit barrel and cover, shape no.335, painted in colours, printed factory marks, 14cm. high. *(Christie's)* **£300 $500**

'Feather and Leaves', a Fantasque Bizarre cylindrical biscuit barrel and cover, painted in colours above yellow band, printed factory marks, 13cm. high. *(Christie's)* **£450 $735**

A Bizarre biscuit barrel with electroplated mount and cover, on four feet, painted with abstract foliage, in colours, printed factory marks, 14cm. high. *(Christie's)* **£250 $405**

'Autumn', a Fantasque Bizarre cylindrical biscuit barrel, painted in colours between blue bands, printed factory marks, 13.5cm. high. *(Christie's)* **£250 $405**

'Crocus', a Bizarre biscuit barrel and cover, shape no.335, painted in colours, printed factory marks, 16cm. high. *(Christie's)* **£200 $325**

A pair of Bizarre bookends, shape no.406 decorated in the 'Honolulu pattern, painted in colours, 6in. high.
(Christie's) **£525 $840**

A pair of 'Bizarre' bookends, modelled as a pair of parakeets with green plumage on chequered base, 7in. high.
(Christie's) **£925 $1,480**

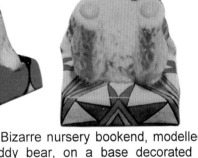

A pair of Clarice Cliff teddy bear book ends decorated in the 'Red Flower' pattern, painted in colours, 6in. high.
(Christie's) **£4,250 $6,800**

A Bizarre nursery bookend, modelled as a teddy bear, on a base decorated in the 'Sunburst' pattern, painted in colours, 15.5cm. high. *(Christie's)* **£495 $757**

A pair of Bizarre cottage book ends painted with orange roof to cottage, green and yellow base, 5½in. high.
(Christie's) **£1,650 $2,603**

A pair of 'Inspiration' moulded bookends, 6¼in. high, black printed mark *Inspiration* and painted *Floreat* in brown.
(Bonhams) **£700 $1,140**

A 'Marigold' pattern circular footed bowl with flared rim, 8³/₈in. diameter, rubber stamp mark *Hand Painted Bizarre by Clarice Cliff Newport Pottery England* and hand painted *Marigold.*
(Bonhams) **£300 $490**

An 'Inspiration Persian' Isnik rose bowl, shape 400, 6in. high, rubber stamp mark *Hand Painted Bizarre by Clarice Cliff Newport Pottery England,* and painted in decoration *Clarice Cliff.*
(Bonhams) **£850 $1,385**

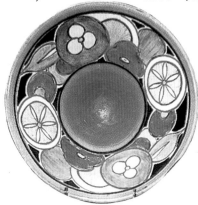

'Sliced Fruit', a Bizarre conical bowl on four square feet, painted in colours inside blue band, printed factory marks, 24cm. diameter. *(Christie's)* **£1,035 $1,685**

'Pastel Melon', Bizarre Daffodil bowl, painted in colours, printed factory marks, 32cm. diameter.
The 'Daffodil' range of tea and coffeeware proved popular so Clarice also designed several bowls and vases. This impressive bowl was certainly meant to be decorative rather than functional, having a full design on the well. 'Pastel Melon' was an adaption of the original 1930 'Melon' design in softer colours with the 'contour-line' removed. *(Christie's)* **£690 $1,125**

'Melon', a Fantasque Bizarre Hiawatha bowl, painted in colours, printed factory marks, 25cm. diameter.
(Christie's) **£253 $410**

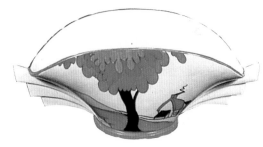

'House and Bridge', a Fantasque Bizarre Daffodil bowl, painted in colours, printed factory marks, 33.5cm. wide.
(Christie's) **£862 $1,400**

'Appliqué Lucerne', a Bizarre bowl, painted in colours, printed factory marks, 21cm. diameter. *(Christie's)* **£1,200 $1,950**

'Double V', a Bizarre bowl, painted in colours, printed factory marks, 9cm. diameter. *(Christie's* **£161 $260**

'Melon', a Fantasque Bizarre bowl, painted in colours between orange bands, printed factory marks, 22cm. diameter. *(Christie's)* **£218 $355**

'Fruit', a Fantasque Bizarre' bowl, painted in colours above orange band, printed factory marks, 24cm. diameter. *(Christie's)* **£368 $600**

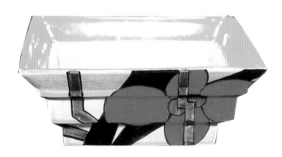

'Red Flower', a Bizarre stepped bowl, shape no.394, painted in colours, printed factory marks, 24cm. wide. *(Christie's)* **£1,725 $2,800**

'Coral Firs', a Bizarre stepped bowl, shape no.419, painted in colours, printed factory marks, 17cm. diameter. *(Christie's)* **£402 $655**

'Autumn', a Bizarre bowl, painted in colours, printed factory marks, 22cm. diameter. *(Christie's)* **£207 $335**

'Original Bizarre', a bowl, painted with a band of triangles, 21.5cm. diameter. *(Christie's)* **£322 $525**

Clarice Cliff bowl with geometric design, Newport Pottery Co., 8in. diameter. *(Lyle)* **£110 $180**

'Forest Glen', a rose bowl, shape no.450, painted in colours, printed factory marks, 33cm. wide. *(Christie's)* **£600 $975**

Clarice Cliff Crocus design bowl, circa 1928, 8½in. diameter. *(Muir Hewitt)* **£200 $325**

Clarice Cliff Gayday design conical shape bowl, 8in. diameter. *(Muir Hewitt)* **£650 $1,060**

Clarice Cliff Bizarre circles and squares bowl, 9in. diameter. *(Muir Hewitt)* **£350 $570**

Liberty design bowl by Clarice Cliff, 8in. diameter. *(Muir Hewitt)* **£450 $735**

Clarice Cliff Gayday bowl, 8in. diameter.
(Muir Hewitt) **£400 $650**

Clarice Cliff Rhodanthe design bowl in
orange, yellow and brown, 7in. diameter.
(Muir Hewitt) **£300 $500**

Clarice Cliff Trees and House bowl with
unusual banding of yellow and green.
(Muir Hewitt) **£400 $650**

Clarice Cliff bowl with leaf decoration,
8½in. diameter.*(Muir Hewitt)* **£250 $400**

Clarice Cliff style bowl, with orange and
black geometric design, unmarked, 1930.
(Muir Hewitt) **£120 $195**

Clarice Cliff Havre shape bowl, Green
Hydrangea design, 8in. diameter.
(Muir Hewitt) **£300 $500**

'Moonflower', a Bizarre bowl, painted in colours, printed factory marks, 22cm. diameter. *(Christie's)*   **£287 $465**

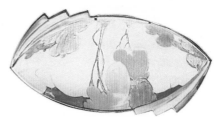

'Pastel Autumn', a Bizarre Daffodil bowl, painted in colours, printed factory marks, 33cm. wide. *(Christie's)*   **£805 $1,300**

A 'Tennis' pattern bowl, shape 441, 7³/₈in. diameter, rubber stamp *Hand Painted Bizarre by Clarice Cliff Newport Pottery England.*
(Bonhams)   **£600 $975**

An 'Orange V' pattern 'Holborn Bowl' bowl, 9³/₈in. diameter, small rubber stamp mark *Hand Painted Bizarre by Clarice Cliff Newport Pottery England.*
(Bonhams)   **£340 $555**

An Appliqué 'Blue Lucerne' conical bowl on four feet, shape 383, 7⁵/₈in. diameter, 4in. high, rubber stamp mark *Hand Painted Bizarre by Clarice Cliff, Newport Pottery, England. (Bonhams)*   **£1,000 $1,600**

A geometric design conical bowl, shape 383, 9¼in. diameter, 4¾in. high, rubber stamp mark *Bizarre Clarice Cliff Hand Painted Newport Pottery England.*
(Bonhams)   **£550 $900**

'Football', a Bizarre conical bowl on four square feet, painted in colours, printed factory marks, 9cm. diameter.
(Christie's)   **£575 $935**

'Sunrise', a Fantasque Bizarre octagonal bowl, painted in colours above an orange band, printed factory marks, 18cm. diameter. *(Christie's)*   **£345 $560**

'Orange Luxor, a Bizarre bowl, painted with band in colours above an orange band, printed factory marks, 22cm. diameter. *(Christie's)* **£402 $655**

'Gibraltar', a Fantasque Bizarre bowl shape no.498, painted in colours, printed factory marks, 15cm. diameter. *(Christie's)* **£402 $655**

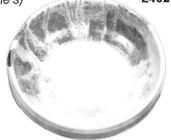

'Inspiration', a Bizarre bowl on three shallow feet, painted with abstract motif in shades of blue and buff on a turquoise ground, printed and painted marks, 18cm. diameter. *(Christie's)* **£345 $560**

An 'Orange Diamond Panel' design Havre bowl, 8in. diameter, large rubber stamp mark *Hand Painted Bizarre by Clarice Cliff Newport Pottery England.* *(Bonhams)* **£180 $295**

A geometric design conical bowl, shape 382, 9¼in. diameter, 5in. high, large rubber stamp mark *Hand painted Bizarre by Clarice Cliff, Newport Pottery England.* *(Bonhams)* **£950 $1,550**

A 'Latona Tree' pattern conical bowl, shape 383, 9¼in. diameter, 4½in. high, rubber stamp mark *Clarice Cliff Bizarre Newport England,* hand painted on lower body of bowl. *(Bonhams)* **£700 $1,140**

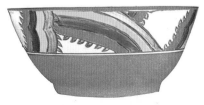

A 'May Avenue' pattern Havre bowl, 8½in. diameter, lithograph mark *Hand painted Bizarre by Clarice Cliff, Newport Pottery England. (Bonhams)* **£1,600 $2,600**

A 'Sharks Teeth' pattern Havre Bowl, 8¾in. diameter, small rubber stamp mark *Hand Painted Bizarre by Clarice Cliff Newport Pottery England. (Bonhams)* **£280 $455**

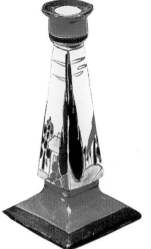

A 'Rudyard' pattern conical candlestick, shape 384, 4½ in. diameter, 2in. high, rubber stamp mark *Hand Painted Bizarre by Clarice Cliff Newport Pottery England.* (Bonhams) **£280 $455**

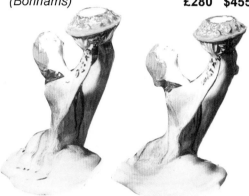

'Red Trees and House', a Fantasque Bizarre octagonal candlestick, painted in colours between red and black bands, printed factory marks, 21cm. high.
(Christie's) **£299 $485**

A pair of Bizarre candlesticks, modelled as a maiden offering up a bouquet of flowers, painted in colours, printed factory marks, 18.5cm. high. (Christie's) **£552 $900**

'Sun-Gay', a pair of Bizarre candlesticks, shape no.331, painted in colours, printed factory marks, 6cm. high.
(Christie's) **£345 $560**

'Umbrellas', a Fantasque Bizarre octagon candlestick, painted in colours, printed factory marks, 31cm. high.

This was originally put into production before Clarice Cliff was in charge of shape origination at Newport pottery. She adapted the candlestick to be a lampbase by drilling the piece. This is an early example in 'Umbrellas' from which evolved Clarice's 'Umbrellas & Rain' pattern.
(Christie's) **£690 $1,125**

'Rhodanthe', a Bizarre cube candlestick, shape no.658, painted in colours, printed factory marks, 6cm. high.
(Christie's) **£207 $335**

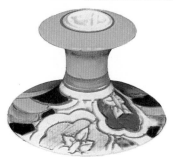

'Orange Gardenia', a Fantasque Bizarre candlestick, shape no.310, painted in colours, printed factory marks, 11.5cm. diameter. *(Christie's)* **£299 $487**

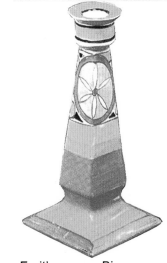

'Sliced Fruit', a Bizarre octagon candlestick, painted in colours between yellow and orange bands, printed factory marks, 20.5cm. high. *(Christie's)* **£402 $655**

Clarice Cliff Sunrise design candlestick on square base. *(Muir Hewitt)* **£400 $650**

A Bizarre double Bon Jour candlestick in the 'Green Bridgewater' pattern, painted in colours, 5in. high. *(Christie's)* **£550 $868**

An 'Inspiration' Caprice candlestick, of octagonal shape, 8in. high, brown painted mark *Inspiration Bizarre by Clarice Cliff Newport Pottery England.* *(Bonhams)* **£440 $720**

'Original Bizarre', an octagon candlestick, painted with a band of triangles in shades of yellow, blue and red, outlined in green, between red and blue bands, printed factory marks, 20cm. high. *(Christie's)* **£299 $485**

A ribbed charger in the 'Clovelly' pattern, painted in colours, 46cm. diameter. *(Christie's)* **£880 $1,346**

'Clouvre', a Bizarre charger, painted in colours, printed and painted marks, 45cm. diameter. *(Christie's)* **£2,500 $4,075**

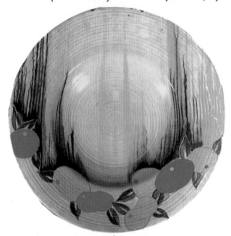

Clarice Cliff Coral Firs 13in. charger. *(Muir Hewitt)* **£1,800 $2,900**

'Delecia Citrus', a Bizarre charger, painted in colours, printed factory marks, 46cm. diameter. *(Christie's)* **£1,800 $2,935**

'Latona Tree', a Bizarre charger, painted in colours on a Latona white ground, printed and painted marks, 46cm. diameter. *(Christie's)* **£2,000 $2,935**

'Floreat', a Fantasque Bizarre charger, painted in colours inside an orange band, printed factory marks, 46cm. diameter. *(Christie's)* **£4,600 $7,500**

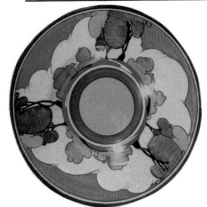

'Alton', a Fantasque Bizarre charger, painted in colours inside green band, printed factory marks, 32cm. diameter. *(Christie's)* **£920 $1,500**

A Fantasque Bizarre large ribbed wall charger, decorated in the 'Blue Autumn' pattern, painted in colours, 45.5cm. diameter. *(Christie's)* **£1,980 $3,029**

'Inspiration Knight Errant', a Bizarre charger, painted in shades of blue and ochre on a turquoise ground, printed factory marks, 46cm. diameter. *(Christie's)* **£5,000 $8,150**

'Latona Tree', a Bizarre charger, painted in colours on a Latona white ground, printed and painted marks, 46cm. diameter. *(Christie's)* **£2,000 $3,260**

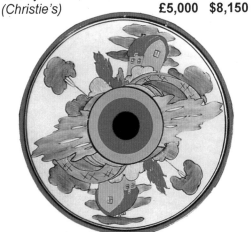

'Orange Roof Cottage', a Bizarre charger, painted in colours inside black and orange bands, printed factory marks, 34cm. diameter. *(Christie's)* **£1,840 $3,100**

'Floreat', a Bizarre wall charger, painted in colours inside green and orange bands, printed factory marks, 42cm. diameter. *(Christie's)* **£2,300 $3,750**

A 'Blue Chintz' pattern charger, 18in. diameter, lithograph mark *Fantasque Hand Painted Bizarre by Clarice Cliff Newport Pottery England. (Bonhams)* **£900 $1,465**

'Orange Roof Cottage', a Bizarre charger, painted in colours inside yellow, orange and black bands, printed factory marks, 42cm. diameter.

The thirteen inch plaque and unusual large charger show how Clarice's paintresses were able to use her designs as simple full height landscapes, and also radially to give a totally different effect. *(Christie's)* **£5,000 $8,150**

A 'Mountain' pattern charger, 13in. diameter, lithograph mark *Hand Painted Bizarre by Clarice Cliff Newport Pottery England. (Bonhams)* **£3,800 $6,200**

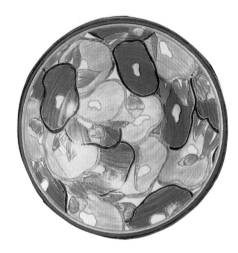

'Blue Chintz', a Fantasque Bizarre charger, painted in colours, printed factory marks, 46cm. diameter.

Clarice Cliff's largest wall ornaments were the eighteen-inch chargers and plaques. The chargers were cast, the plaques were pressed. She intended them as a prestige decorative piece to be used alongside her tea and coffee sets in the same design. *(Christie's)* **£1,265 $2,060**

A Fantasque Bizarre charger in the 'Farmhouse' pattern, painted in colours, 13in. diameter. *(Christie's)* **£550 $900**

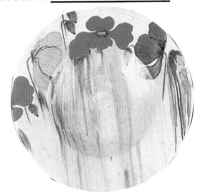

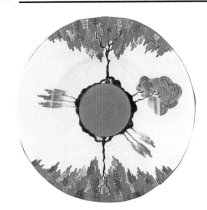

A 'Delecia Poppy' pattern charger, 18in. diameter, rubber stamp mark *Delecia Hand Painted Bizarre by Clarice Cliff Newport Pottery England, Provisional Patent No. 23585.* (Bonhams) **£750 $1,225**

A 'Latona Tree' pattern charger, 18in diameter, rubber stamp mark *Hand Painted Bizarre by Clarice Cliff Newport Pottery England.* (Bonhams) **£2,000 $3,260**

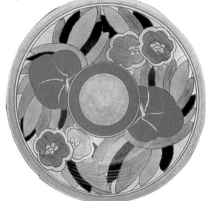

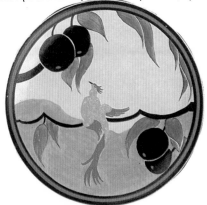

A 'Gardenia Red' wall charger, 18in. diameter, rubber stamp mark *Fantasque Hand Painted Bizarre by Clarice Cliff Newport Pottery England.* (Bonhams) **£3,800 $6,200**

An Appliqué Bird of Paradise charger, 13in. diameter, rubber stamp mark *Hand Painted Bizarre by Clarice Cliff Newport Pottery England* and hand painted *Appliqué* (Bonhams) **£2,700 $4,400**

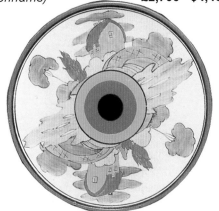

'Sunray', a Bizarre charger, painted in colours between yellow and green bands, printed factory marks, 48cm. diameter. (Christie's) **£747 $1,215**

'Orange Roof Cottage', a Bizarre charger, painted in colours inside black and orange bands, printed factory marks, 34cm. diameter. (Christie's) **£3,000 $4,890**

'Melon', a Fantasque Bizarre conical coffee pot and cover, painted in colours between orange bands, printed factory marks, 19.5cm. high. *(Christie's)* **£805 $1,310**

'Crocus', a Bizarre coffee pot and cover, painted in colours between orange and yellow bands, 19cm. high. *(Christie's)* **£402 $655**

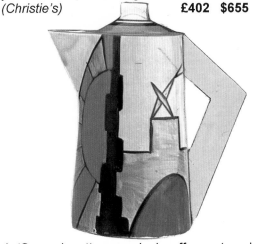

'Secrets', a Bizarre Bon Jour coffee pot and cover, painted in colours, printed factory marks, 19cm. high. *(Christie's)* **£575 $935**

A 'Sunray' pattern conical coffee pot and cover, 7½in. high, large mark *Hand Painted Bizarre by Clarice Cliff Newport Pottery England. (Bonhams)* **£900 $1,460**

'Spring Crocus', a Windsor shape coffee pot and cover, painted in colours between green bands, printed factory marks, 21cm. high. *(Christie's)* **£437 $710**

'Nasturtium', a Lynton coffee pot and cover, painted in colours, printed factory marks, 19.5cm. high. *(Christie's)* **£402 $655**

'Orange' Picasso Flower', a Bizarre globe teacup and saucer, printed factory marks, 8cm. high. *(Christie's)* **£391 $637**

'Orange Roof Cottage', a Bizarre conical cup and saucer and a Stamford sugar basin, painted in colours, printed factory marks, cup 6.5cm. high. *(Christie's)* **£575 $935**

'Tennis', a Bizarre conical cup, saucer and side plate, printed factory marks, Brice Rogers mark, plate 17.5cm. diameter. *(Christie's)* **£1,150 $1,875**

'Gibralter', a Bizarre conical Early Morning pair of cups and saucers with printed factory marks, cup 6.5cm. high. *(Christie's)* **£900 $1,460**

'Broth', a Bizarre cup, saucer and side plate, painted in colours inside orange bands, printed marks, side plate 17.5cm. diameter. *(Christie's)* **£345 $560**

A 'Red Gardenia' pattern coffee can and saucer, 4in. diameter of saucer, rubber stamp marks *Bizarre Hand Painted Fantasque by Clarice Cliff, Wilkinson Ltd. England. (Bonhams)* **£180 $290**

Clarice Cliff dish in 'House and Bridge' design, 10in. diameter.
(Muir Hewitt) **£620 $930**

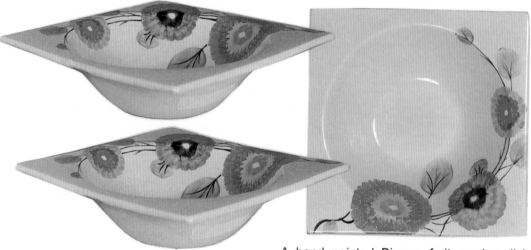

A hand painted Bizarre fruit serving dish and four bowls by Clarice Cliff.
(Lyle) **£80 $130**

GINGER JARS

A 'Pastel Comets' pattern ginger jar and cover, shape 132, 8¾in. high.
(Bonhams) **£2,700 $4,400**

'Sliced Fruit', a Bizarre ginger jar and cover, painted in colours between purple and blue bands, printed factory marks, 22cm. high. *(Christie's)* **£1,500 $2,445**

'Crocus', a Bizarre Beehive honeypot and cover, painted in colours, printed factory marks, 10cm. high.
(Christie's)　　**£253　$410**

'Nasturtium', a Bizarre Beehive honeypot and cover, painted in colours, printed factory marks, 7cm. high.
(Christie's)　　**£368　$600**

'Crocus', a Beehive preserve pot and cover, painted in colours, printed factory marks, 9.5cm. high.
(Christie's)　　**£414　$675**

'House and Bridge', a Bizarre Beehive honeypot and cover, painted in colours, printed factory marks, 9cm. high.
(Christie's)　　**£345　$560**

A Fantasque Bizarre beehive honey pot and cover in the 'Trees and House' pattern, painted in colours, 9cm. high.
(Christie's)　　**£209　$320**

'Orange Roof Cottage', a Bizarre Beehive honeypot and cover, painted in colours, printed factory marks, 9.5cm. high.
(Christie's) **£920　$1,500**

'Blue Japan', a Bizarre beehive honey pot cover, painted in colours, printed factory marks, 9.5cm. high.
(Christie's)　　**£345　$560**

'Secrets', a Fantasque Bizarre Beehive honeypot and cover, painted in colours, printed factory marks, 9.5cm. high.
(Christie's)　　**£322　$525**

'Crocus', a Bizarre beehive honeypot and cover, painted in colours, printed factory marks, 10cm. high.
(Christie's)　　**£299　$487**

Clarice Cliff jardinière in Canterbury bells design. *(Muir Hewitt)* **£680 $1,100**

Clarice Cliff Bizarre early geometric design pot, 7in. high, circa 1929. *(Muir Hewitt)* **£580 $945**

'Original Bizarre', a Dover jardinière, painted with a band of triangles in shades of blue, orange and yellow, outlined in green between blue and orange bands, printed factory marks, 15cm. high. *(Christie's)* **£368 $600**

An 'Inspiration Persian' Isnik design jardinière, shape 356, 6¾in. high, large underglaze blue mark and brown painted overglaze mark *Persian* and hand painted *P.* *(Bonhams)* **£800 $1,300**

'Orange House', a Fantasque Bizarre Dover jardinière, painted in colours between orange and yellow bands, printed factory marks. *(Christie's)* **£1,380 $2,250**

A Bizarre Dover jardinière, painted in colours between orange bands, printed factory marks, 16cm. high. *(Christie's)* **£483 $785**

A Fantasque Bizarre Dover jardinière decorated in the 'Trees and House' pattern, rubber stamp mark, 8in. high. *(Christie's)* **£1,300 $2,080**

'Alton', a Bizarre Dover jardinière, painted in colours, printed factory marks, 17cm. high. *(Christie's)* **£437 $712**

A 'Windbells' pattern jardinière, shape 356, 6¾in. lithograph mark *Hand Painted Bizarre by Clarice Cliff Newport Pottery England* and impressed shape number 356. *(Bonhams)* **£480 $780**

'Original Bizarre, a Dover jardinière, painted with a band of orange, black, yellow and blue triangles, outlined in green between orange and yellow, printed factory marks, 17.5cm. high. *(Christie's)* **£345 $560**

A Bizarre Dover jardinière in the 'Summerhouse' pattern, painted in colours, 20cm. diameter. *(Christie's)* **£1,045 $1,599**

A Bizarre Chippendale jardinière in the 'Crocus' pattern, painted in colours, 9¼in. diameter. *(Christie's)* **£264 $416**

'Melon' a Bizarre Chester fern pot, painted in colours, printed factory marks, 9cm. high. *(Christie's)*   **£437 $710**

'Gibraltar', a Fantasque Bizarre Chester fern pot, painted in colours, printed factory marks, 9.5cm. high. *(Christie's)* **£552 $900**

'Summerhouse', a Bizarre Dover jardinière, painted in colours between orange bands, printed factory marks, 21.5cm. high.

Summerhouse was initially outlined by the boy decorators Clarice employed from the Burslem School of Art. However the outlining on this Doverpot features trees painted rather differently to the original design, being more linear. It is perhaps the work of one of the female outliners, Sadie Maskrey or Ellen Browne.
(Christie's)   **£1,437 $2,340**

'Orange House', a Fantasque Bizarre pot, shape no.481, painted in colours, printed factory marks, 12cm. diameter.

Clarice was so amazingly productive in creating endless new shapes in the late twenties and early thirties that we are still recording previously unseen shapes. This 481 bowl is of Stamford shape and clearly followed on from her shape 460 Stamford vase which featured the same square section fins. *(Christie's)*   **£632 $1,030**

A 'Picasso Flower' (orange colourway) pattern Stamford jardinière, shape 479, 4⁷/₈in. high, lithograph mark *Hand painted Bizarre by Clarice Cliff, Newport Pottery England.* (Bonhams)   **£320 $520**

Clarice Cliff Broth Dover pot, 9in. high, with orange rim, 1930.
(Muir Hewitt)   **£1,000 $1,600**

154

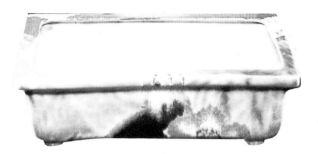

'Inspiration', a Bizarre rectangular planter, on four feet, painted with stylised flowerheads in shades of pink, blue and purple on a turquoise ground, printed and painted marks, 28cm. wide. *(Christie's)* **£345 $560**

'Autumn' a Bizarre Chester fern pot, painted in colours, printed factory marks, 9cm. high. *(Christie's)* **£402 $655**

A Bizarre Chester fern pot in the 'Swirls' pattern, painted in colours, 4in. diameter. *(Christie's)* **£264 $416**

'Inspiration Caprice', a Bizarre Dover jardinière, painted in shades of blue, purple and mushroom on a turquoise ground, printed and painted marks, 21cm. high. *(Christie's)* **£920 $1,450**

Clarice Cliff love birds planter, 4in. high, 10in. wide, circa 1939. *(Muir Hewitt)* **£180 $295**

'Crocus', a Bizarre stepped jardinière, painted in colours between yellow and brown bands, printed factory marks, 13cm. high. *(Christie's)* **£299 $485**

'Jonquil', a Bizarre single-handled Lotus jug, painted in colours, printed factory marks, 30cm. high.
(Christie's)   **£483 $785**

'Viscaria', a Bizarre single-handled Lotus jug, painted in colours, printed factory marks, 30cm. high.
(Christie's)   **£862 $1,400**

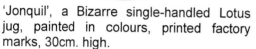

'Branch and Squares', a Bizarre single-handled Lotus jug, painted in colours between orange bands, printed factory marks, 30cm. high.
(Christie's)   **£1,500 $2,445**

'Autumn', a Fantasque Bizarre twin-handled Lotus jug, painted in colours between orange bands, printed factory marks, 29cm. high.
(Christie's)   **£1,840 $3,000**

'Blue Japan', a Bizarre single-handled Lotus jug, painted in colours, printed factory marks, 29cm. high.
(Christie's)   **£1,725 $2,800**

'Rudyard', a Bizarre single-handled Lotus jug, painted in colours, printed factory marks, 30cm. high.
(Christie's)   **£1,495 $2,435**

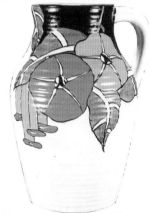

'Latona Flowerheads', a Bizarre single-handled Lotus jug, painted in colours on a Latona ground, printed and painted marks, 30cm. high. *(Christie's)* **£600 $975**

'Sunray', a Bizarre single-handled Isis jug, painted in colours between yellow and orange bands, printed factory marks, 25cm. high. *(Christie's)* **£2,070 $3,375**

'Sliced Fruit', a Bizarre single-handled Lotus jug, painted in colours between orange and black bands, printed factory marks, 30cm. high.
(Christie's) **£1,200 $1,950**

'Melon', a Fantasque Bizarre single-handled Lotus jug, painted in colours between orange bands, printed factory marks, 30cm. high.
(Christie's) **£1,955 $3,185**

'House and Bridge', a Fantasque Bizarre single-handled Lotus jug, painted in colours, printed factory marks, 30cm. high. *(Christie's)* **£2,300 $3,750**

'Inspiration Persian', a Bizarre twin-handled Lotus jug, painted in shades of blue, turquoise and buff, printed factory marks, 30cm. high. *(Christie's)* **£1,840 $3,000**

An Inspiration Bizarre single-handled Lotus vase, decorated in the 'Persian' pattern, in shades of blue, turquoise and beige, 30cm. high. *(Christie's)* **£1,980 $3,029**

'Melon', a Fantasque single-handled Lotus jug, painted in colours between orange bands, printed factory marks, 30cm. high. *(Christie's)* **£2,070 $3,375**

'Inspiration Caprice', a Bizarre twin-handled Lotus jug, painted in shades of blue, black and ochre on a turquoise ground, printed and painted marks, 30cm. high. *(Christie's)* **£2,185 $3,560**

'Fruitburst', a Fantasque Bizarre twin-handled Lotus jug, pained in colours between orange, yellow and green bands, printed factory marks, 30cm. high. *(Christie's)* **£1,150 $1,875**

'Pastel Autumn', a Fantasque Bizarre single-handled Lotus jug, painted in colours, printed factory marks, 30cm. high. *(Christie's)* **£1,000 $1,600**

'Appliqué Avignon', a Fantasque Bizarre single-handled Lotus jug, painted in colours, printed and painted marks, 30cm. high. *(Christie's)* **£2,300 $3,750**

'Windbells', a Fantasque Bizarre twin-handled Lotus jug, painted in colours, printed factory marks, 30cm. high.
(Christie's) **£1,380 $2,250**

A Fantasque Bizarre single-handled Lotus jug in the 'Orange Autumn' pattern, painted in colours, 30cm. high.
(Christie's) **£825 $1,262**

'Melon', a Fantasque Bizarre twin-handled Lotus jug, painted in colours between orange bands, printed factory marks, 29.5cm. high.
(Christie's) **£1,265 $2,060**

'Inspiration Persian', a Bizarre twin-handled Lotus jug, painted in shades of blue, turquoise and ochre, printed and painted marks, 29.5cm. high.
(Christie's) **£1,265 $2,060**

'Diamonds', a Bizarre twin-handled Lotus jug, painted in colours between orange and blue bands, printed factory marks, 30cm. high. *(Christie's)* **£2,530 $4,125**

'Football' a Bizarre single-handled Lotus jug, painted in colours between jade green bands, printed factory marks, 30cm. high. *(Christie's)* **£2,990 $4,875**

An 'Inspiration Persian' Isnik single handled Isis jug, 9½in. high, black printed mark *Persian. (Bonhams)* **£750 $1,220**

Clarice Cliff Lotus jug in Coral Firs design, 1930s. *(Muir Hewitt)* **£1,850 $3,000**

An 'Inspiration' Persian design two handled Lotus jug, 11¾in. high, hand painted brown mark *Inspiration Bizarre by Clarice Cliff Newport Pottery Burslem England.* *(Bonhams)* **£3,200 $5,200**

A 'Tennis' pattern single handled Lotus jug, 11¾in. high, rubber stamp mark *Hand Painted Bizarre by Clarice Cliff Newport Pottery England.(Bonhams)* **£2,000 $3,200**

Clarice Cliff Sunray Lotus jug, 1930s, 11½in. high. *(Muir Hewitt)* **£1,900 $3,000**

An Appliqué 'Avignon' pattern single handled Isis jug, 10in. high, rubber stamp mark *Hand Painted Bizarre by Clarice Cliff Newport Pottery England*, and impressed *Isis. (Bonhams)* **£1,900** **$3,100**

A Bizarre single-handled Lotus jug decorated in the 'Lightning' pattern, painted in colours between orange borders, 11½in. high. *(Christie's)* **£2,750** **$4,400**

An 'Inspiration' Clouvre Tulip design single handled Lotus jug, 11½in. high, rubber stamp mark *Hand Painted Bizarre by Clarice Cliff Newport Pottery England* and painted in brown *Clouvre.* *(Bonhams)* **£1,000** **$1,600**

An Appliqué 'Blue Lugano' single handled Lotus jug, 11¾in. high, hand painted *Appliqué* and small rubber stamp mark *Hand Painted Bizarre by Clarice Cliff Newport Pottery England.* *(Bonhams)* **£4,200** **$6,850**

A 'Honolulu' pattern single-handled Lotus jug, 11½in. high., lithograph mark *Hand Painted Bizarre by Clarice Cliff Newport Pottery England.* *(Bonhams)* **£1,700** **$2,770**

A 'Cubist' pattern single handled Lotus jug, 11¾in. high, large rubber stamp mark *Hand Painted Bizarre by Clarice Cliff Newport Pottery England* and impressed *Lotus. (Bonhams)* **£1,500** **$2,450**

Twin handled Isis jug by Clarice Cliff, 10½in. high. *(Muir Hewitt)* **£1,250 $1,875**

Clarice Cliff Lotus jug, 'Secrets' design from the Bizarre range, 12in. high, 1930s. *(Muir Hewitt)* **£1,900 $2,850**

'Orange Roof Cottage', a Fantasque Bizarre' single-handled Lotus jug, painted in colours between black, yellow and orange bands, printed factory marks, 29cm. high. *(Christie's)* **£1,150 $1,875**

'Blue W', a Fantasque Bizarre single-handled Lotus jug, painted in colours between orange and yellow bands, printed factory marks, 30cm. high. *(Christie's)* **£2,760 $4,500**

A Bizarre single-handled Lotus jug in the 'Luxor' pattern, painted in orange, green, lavender and blue between yellow borders, 30cm. high. *(Christie's)* **£1,320 $2,020**

An 'Acorn' pattern single handled Isis jug, 9¾in. high, small rubber stamp mark *Hand Painted Bizarre by Clarice Cliff Newport Pottery England.* (Bonhams) **£280 $455**

Clarice Cliff Bizarre Aurea design Lotus jug, 12in. high. *(Muir Hewitt)* **£800 $1,300**

A 'Café-au-lait Fruitburst' pattern, single handled Lotus jug, 11½in. high. *(Bonhams)* **£750 $1,220**

'Orange Trees and House', a Fantasque Bizarre single-handled Isis vase, painted in colours between black and orange bands, printed factory marks. 25cm. high. *(Christie's)* **£1,092 $1,780**

An 'Orange Luxor' pattern single handled Lotus jug, 11¾in. high, rubber stamp mark *Hand Painted Bizarre by Clarice Cliff Newport Pottery England.* *(Bonhams)* **£1,900 $3,100**

'Farmhouse', a Fantasque Bizarre single-handled Lotus jug, painted in colours, printed factory marks, 30cm. high. *(Christie's)* **£2,070 $3,375**

'Crocus', a Bizarre single handled Lotus jug, painted in colours, printed factory marks, 30cm. high. *(Christie's)* **£1,265 $2,060**

A 'Swirls' pattern single handled Lotus jug, 11¾in. high, small rubber stamp mark *Hand Painted Bizarre by Clarice Cliff Newport Pottery England.* (Bonhams) **£1,500 $2,450**

A 'Diamonds' pattern single handled Lotus jug, 11½in. high, large rubber stamp mark *Hand Painted Bizarre by Clarice Cliff Newport Pottery England.* (Bonhams) **£1,500 $2,450**

A 'Melon' pattern two handled Lotus jug, 11½in. high, rubber stamp mark *Fantasque Hand Painted Bizarre by Clarice Cliff Newport Pottery England.* (Bonhams) **£950 $1,550**

A 'Castellated Circle' pattern two handled Lotus jug, 11½in. high, large rubber stamp mark *Hand Painted Bizarre by Clarice Cliff Newport Pottery England.* (Bonhams) **£2,700 $4,400**

A 'Farmhouse' pattern single handled Lotus jug, 11½in. high, 11½in. high, lithograph mark *Fantasque Hand Painted Bizarre by Clarice Cliff Newport Pottery England.* (Bonhams) **£950 $1,550**

A 'Floreat' pattern single handled Lotus jug, 11½in. high, small rubber stamp *Fantasque Hand Painted Bizarre by Clarice Cliff Newport Pottery England.* (Bonhams) **£800 $1,300**

A 'Melon' pattern single handled Lotus jug, 11½in. high, lithographic mark *Fantasque Hand Painted Bizarre by Clarice Cliff Newport Pottery England.*
(Bonhams) **£1,000 $1,600**

A 'Picasso Flower' pattern single handled Lotus jug, 11½in. high, small rubber stamp mark *Hand Painted Bizarre by Clarice Cliff Newport Pottery England,* and impressed *Lotus.* (Bonhams) **£1,000 $1,600**

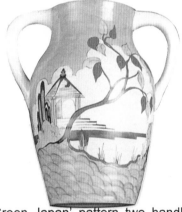

A 'Green Japan' pattern two handled Isis jug, 10in. high, lithographic mark *Hand Painted Bizarre by Clarice Cliff Newport Pottery England* and relief moulded *Isis.*
(Bonhams) **£950 $1,550**

A 'Mondrian' pattern single handled Lotus jug, 11¾in. high, large rubber stamp mark *Hand Painted Bizarre by Clarice Cliff Newport Pottery England.*
(Bonhams) **£1,800 $2,950**

A 'Butterfly' pattern single handled Isis jug, 9½in. high, rubber stamp mark *Fantasque Hand Painted Bizarre by Clarice Cliff Newport Pottery England* and impressed *Isis.* (Bonhams) **£1,300 $2,120**

A 'Latona Bouquet' single handled Isis jug, 9¾in. high, small rubber stamp mark *Hand Painted Bizarre by Clarice Cliff Newport Pottery England,* and hand painted *Latona.*
(Bonhams) **£950 $1,550**

A Bizarre twin-handled Lotus jug, in 'Autumn Crocus' pattern, 29cm. high. *(Allen & Harris)* **£250 $460**

'Orange Trees and House', a Fantasque Bizarre single-handled Isis vase, painted in colours between black and orange bands, printed factory marks, 25cm. high. *(Christie's)* **£1,500 $2,450**

'Original Bizarre', a single-handled Lotus jug, painted with a band of triangles, in shades of yellow, blue, orange and brown, outlined in green between orange bands, printed factory marks, 30cm. high. *(Christie's)* **£977 $1,590**

'Double V', a single handled Lotus jug, painted in colours, between brown, red and orange bands, impressed factory marks, 29cm. high.

This is the first example noted of the variably executed design in a rust, orange, yellow and brown colourway. Being on an unmarked Lotus jug it was perhaps a sample done just for display in the factory showroom. *(Christie's)* **£900 $1,465**

'Appliqué Orange Lucerne', a Bizarre single-handled Lotus jug, painted in colours, printed and painted marks, 30cm. high.

Appliqué designs took a great deal longer to decorate than the 'Fantasque' or 'Bizarre' ones so the range was more expensive. This example in Lucerne dates from the middle of the 1930s when Clarice adapted the original blue sky to orange, and it also has an unusually large image. *(Christie's)* **£6,325 $10,300**

A Fantasque double-handled Lotus jug in the 'Melon' pattern, painted in colours, 30cm. high. *(Christie's)* **£1,045 $1,599**

'Honolulu', a Bizarre single-handled Lotus jug, painted in colours between green bands, printed factory marks, 30cm. high.

The banding style used in Honolulu and also the Bridgewater, Killarney and Sungold designs featured a pale broad band with full lining overlaid onto it, and showed how skillful the banders were by 1933 when the design was introduced. *(Christie's)* **£3,220 $5,250**

'Inspiration Persian', a Bizarre single-handled Lotus jug, painted in shades of blue, ochre and turquoise printed and painted marks, 30cm. high. *(Christie's)* **£2,000 $3,250**

'Appliqué Blue Lugano', a Bizarre twin-handled Lotus jug, painted in colours, printed factory marks, 30cm. high.

Clarice issued various shapes with added handles as these were classed as functional rather than decorative items for tax purposes. The single-handled Lotus jug which had been a water jug and bowl set in 1919 was given two handles to make it more symmetrical, and sold as a flower holder. Very few examples are known of the shape in 'Appliqué Lugano'. *(Christie's)* **£4,600 $7,500**

'Orange Roof Cottage', a Fantasque Bizarre single-handled Lotus jug, painted in colours, between yellow, orange and black bands, printed factory marks, 29cm. high. *(Christie's)* **£2,760 $4,500**

'Football', a Bizarre large conical milk-jug, painted in colours, printed factory marks, 10cm. high. (Christie's) **£690 $1,125**

'Canterbury Bells', a Bizarre conical jug, painted in colours, printed factory marks, 15cm. high; and a Latona Tree conical sugar basin. (Christie's) **£207 $335**

Clarice Cliff Daffodil shape jug in the Alton design. (Muir Hewitt) **£200 $325**

Clarice Cliff Owl design jug, circa 1939, 8½in. high. (Muir Hewitt) **£280 $450**

Clarice Cliff, George shape jug, in the 'Blue Chintz' design, 8in. high. (Muir Hewitt) **£680 $1,100**

A Fantasque Bizarre Athens jug decorated in the 'Autumn' pattern, painted in colours, 20cm. high. (Christie's) **£187 $286**

Clarice Cliff Swirls design jug, 1930s, 4in. high. *(Muir Hewitt)* **£200 $325**

Clarice Cliff Bizarre Citrus Delecia Athens jug, 7in. high. *(Muir Hewitt)* **£300 $500**

Clarice Cliff Athens jug, in Petunia design, 8in. high. *(Muir Hewitt)* **£350 $520**

Clarice Cliff Bizarre Pure Delecia design jug, circa 1931, 8in. high. *(Muir Hewitt)* **£200 $325**

Clarice Cliff Athens shape Orange House design jug, 8in. high. *(Muir Hewitt)* **£600 $975**

An Athens jug in the 'Forest Glen' pattern, painted in colours, 16cm. high. *(Christie's)* **£418 $646**

'Forest Glen', an Athens jug, shape no.42, painted in colours, printed factory marks, 15.5cm. high. *(Christie's)* **£483 $785**

'Blue Chintz', a Fantasque Bizarre Athens jug, number 42, painted in colours, printed factory marks, 15cm. high. *(Christie's)* **£276 $450**

A Bizarre single-handled jug, shape no.342, in the 'Pastel Autumn' pattern, painted in colours, 25cm. high. *(Christie's)* **£715 $1,094**

Celtic Harvest jug by Clarice Cliff, circa 1939, 7½in. high. *(Muir Hewitt)* **£150 $245**

'Circle Tree', a Fantasque Bizarre coronet jug, painted in colours between yellow and orange bands, printed factory marks, 19cm. high. *(Christie's)* **£345 $560**

'Orange Trees and House', a Fantasque Bizarre conical jug, painted in colours between orange and black bands, printed factory marks, 16.5cm. high. *(Christie's)* **£517 $840**

'Original Bizarre', a Perth jug, painted with a band of green, orange and blue triangles, outlined in black, printed factory marks, 9cm. high. *(Christie's)* **£287 $470**

'Melon', a Fantasque Bizarre Bon Jour jug, painted in colours, printed factory marks, 17cm. high. *(Christie's)* **£977 $1,600**

'May Avenue', a Fantasque Bizarre, Athens jug, painted in colours, printed factory marks, 15cm. high.

The Athens shape jug was issued as both a functional item in simple designs and as a Flower jug when it was painted all over patterns such as May Avenue. Having a handle a jug attracted less tax than a vase, as it was classified as a functional item. *(Christie's)* **£1,265 $2,060**

'Umbrellas and Rain', a Fantasque Bizarre Athens jug, painted in colours between orange and blue bands, printed factory marks, 18cm. high.
(Christie's) **£299 $485**

'Sunburst', a Bizarre Crown jug, painted in colours above orange and black bands, printed factory marks, 9cm. high.
(Christie's) **£172 $280**

'Original Bizarre', a Bizarre coronet jug, painted with triangles in shades of red, blue, yellow outlined in green, printed factory marks, 17cm. high.
(Christie's) **£322 $525**

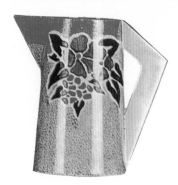

A novelty jug modelled as a tree trunk, two owls perched on a branch, the handle moulded with acorns, printed factory marks, 19.5cm. high.*(Christie's)* **£150 $245**

'Floral Nuage', a Bizarre conical jug, painted in colours, printed factory marks, 18cm. high. *(Christie's)* **£350 $575**

A 'Patina Tree' pattern Lotus jug, decorated in the blue colourway, 12in. high, lithograph mark *Patina Hand Painted Bizarre by Clarice Cliff Newport Pottery England and rubber Stamp Provisional patent No. 23385.* (Bonhams) **£460 $750**

'Crocus', four Bizarre graduated Athens jugs, painted in colours, printed factory marks, largest 8cm. high. *(Christie's)* **£460 $750**

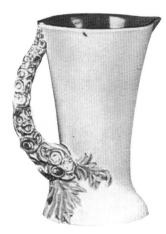

'Umbrellas and Rain', a Fantasque Bizarre Athens jug, size no.24, painted in colours, printed factory marks, 20cm. high. *(Christie's)* **£300 $500**

A Clarice Cliff jug, the handle moulded in relief with flowers, 22cm. high. *(Christie's)* **£100 $160**

'Acorn', a Bizarre single-handled jug, shape no.635, painted in colours, printed factory marks, 17cm. high. *(Christie's)* **£300 $500**

'Tennis', a Bizarre conical jug, painted in colours, printed factory marks, 16.5cm. high. *(Christie's)* **£1,100 $1,800**

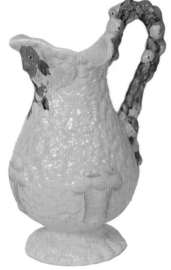

Clarice Cliff Celtic Harvest jug, 8in. high. *(Muir Hewitt)* **£120 $195**

'Blue Crocus', a Bizarre Bon Jour jug, painted in colours, printed factory marks, 15cm. high. *(Christie's)* **£368 $600**

A single-handled vase, shape no.850, moulded in relief with a budgerigar perched on a branch, painted in shades of blue, green and brown, printed factory marks, 22cm. high. *(Christie's)* **£150 $245**

An Appliqué 'Blue Lugano' conical jug, 7in. high, hand painted *Appliqué* and rubber stamp mark *Hand Painted Bizarre by Clarice Cliff Newport Pottery England.* *(Bonhams)* **£1,600 $2,600**

'Marlene', a Bizarre wall mask, painted in colours, printed factory, 17.5cm. high. *(Christie's)* **£368 $600**

'Flora', a Bizarre wall mask, modelled as a young lady with flowers and foliage in hair, painted in shades of orange, brown, yellow and green, 14⁵/₈in. high. *(Bonhams)* **£550 $900**

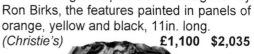

A Bizarre grotesque mask designed by Ron Birks, the features painted in panels of orange, yellow and black, 11in. long. *(Christie's)* **£1,100 $2,035**

Clarice Cliff Flora wall mask, large size 17in. high. *(Muir Hewitt)* **£1,700 $2,750**

'Marlene', a Bizarre wall mask, painted in colours, printed factory marks (hairline to rim), 17.5cm. high. *(Christie's)* **£299 $485**

A Bizarre wall mask modelled as the head of an exotic woman with blue ringlets and a cap of green foliage, 9in. long. *(Christie's)* **£330 $521**

174

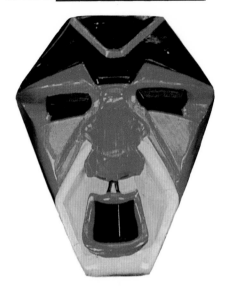

A Bizarre wallmask modelled as the head of a young girl wearing a green beret, painted in colours, 22.5cm. high.
(Christie's) **£748 $1,144**

A Bizarre grotesque mask designed by Ron Birks, painted in orange, red, yellow and black, 30cm. long.
(Christie's) **£1,210 $1,851**

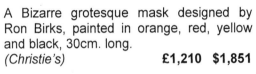

'Flora', a Bizarre wall mask, moulded in relief, painted in shades of green, orange and brown, printed factory marks, 36cm. high. *(Christie's)* **£1,100 $1,790**

'Chahar', a rare Bizarre wall mask, painted in shades of red, yellow and black, printed factory marks, original Wilkinson paper label, 25cm. high.

This was one of the earliest Clarice Cliff facemasks, modelled around the same time as the Archaic series of vases. Like them it was clearly based on an Egyptian influenced theme, after designs in 'Grammar of Ornament' which had been published in 1856.
(Christie's) **£1,150 $1,875**

'Marlene', a Bizarre wall mask, painted in colours, with printed factory marks, 17.5cm. high. *(Muir Hewitt)* **£400 $650**

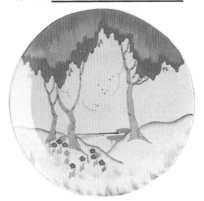

'Taormina', a wall plaque, painted in colours, printed factory marks, 34cm. diameter. *(Christie's)* **£402 $655**

'Canterbury Bells', a Bizarre wall plaque, painted in colours, printed and painted marks, 34cm. diameter.
(Christie's) **£575 $935**

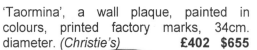

A 'Marigold' pattern wall plaque, 13in. diameter, rubber stamp mark *Hand Painted Bizarre by Clarice Cliff Newport Pottery England. (Bonhams)* **£1,000 $1,600**

Clarice Cliff wall plaque with floral decoration, 15in. diameter, circa 1930. *(Muir Hewitt)* **£750 $1,225**

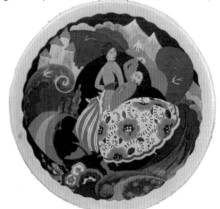

A superb wall plaque by Clarice Cliff painted with a scene inspired by Diaghilev's costume design for The Ballet Russe. *(Christie's)* **£8,500 $13,600**

'Latona Dahlia', a Bizarre wall plaque, painted in colours on a Latona white ground, printed and painted marks, 33cm. diameter. *(Christie's)* **£1,500 $2,445**

'Jonquil', a Bizarre wall plaque, painted in colours, printed factory marks, 34cm. diameter. *(Christie's)* **£500 $815**

Clarice Cliff plaque with embossed design of flower basket, 13in. diameter. *(Muir Hewitt)* **£280 $450**

A ribbed plaque in the 'Clovelly' pattern, painted in colours, 46cm. diameter. *(Christie's)* **£880 $1,435**

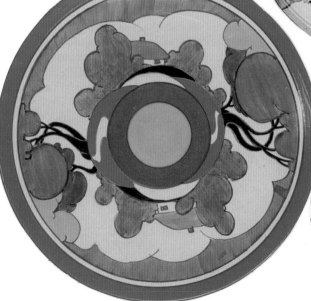

Clarice Cliff Blue Autumn plaque, 13in. diameter, 1930s. *(Muir Hewitt)* **£1,800 $2,950**

'Latona' Red Roses', a Bizarre wall plaque, painted in shades of red and black, 33cm. diameter. *(Christie's)* **£1,200 $1,950**

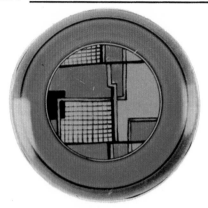

'Appliqué Idyll', a bizarre cake plate, painted in colours, printed factory marks, 23cm. diameter. *(Christie's)* **£253 $410**

A Fantasque plate decorated in the 'Football' pattern, painted in colours, 22cm diameter. *(Christie's)* **£308 $471**

'Original Bizarre', a plate, painted with radiating star motif, in shades of red, yellow, blue and purple, outlined in green, printed factory marks, 25cm. diameter. *(Christie's)* **£230 $375**

'Original Bizarre', a plate, painted with a radiating star design in shades of yellow, blue, orange and green, outlined in black inside orange band, printed factory marks, 25.5cm. diameter. *(Christie's)* **£460 $750**

A Fantasque plate in the 'Gardenia' pattern, painted in colours within yellow banding, 22.5cm. diameter. *(Christie's)* **£286 $438**

'Gloria', an unusual Bizarre plate, painted with radiating flowers in matt colours on a white ground, printed and painted marks, 23cm. diameter. *(Christie's)* **£200 $325**

'Tennis', a Bizarre plate, painted in colours, printed factory marks, 25cm. diameter. *(Christie's)* **£800 $1,300**

'Persian', a Bizarre plate, painted in colours, painted factory marks, 23cm. diameter. *(Christie's)* **£747 $1,220**

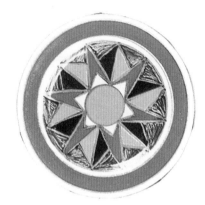

'Original Bizarre', a plate, painted with radiating star motif, in shades of blue, red, purple and yellow, outlined in green inside red band, printed factory marks, 25cm. diameter. *(Christie's)* **£368 $600**

'Apples', a Fantasque Bizarre cake plate with fluted rim, painted in colours inside black, yellow and orange bands, printed factory marks, 20.5cm. diameter. *(Christie's)* **£517 $840**

'Rudyard', a Bizarre octagonal plate, painted in colours inside green and blue bands, printed factory marks, 22cm. diameter. *(Christie's)* **£690 $1,125**

'Sunrise', a Fantasque Bizarre plate, painted in colours inside yellow and orange bands, printed factory marks, 25.5cm. diameter. *(Christie's)* **£437 $710**

Clarice Cliff plate painted in orange, yellow, blue, black and green, circa 1930.
(Muir Hewitt) **£200 $320**

'Brookfields', a plate, painted in colours, printed factory marks, 25cm. diameter. *(Christie's)* **£500 $815**

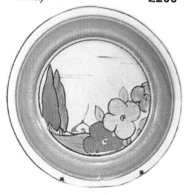

'Poplar', a Bizarre plate, painted in colours inside a green band, printed factory marks, 22.5cm. diameter. *(Christie's)* **£230 $375**

'Honolulu', a Bizarre plate, painted in colours to the well and rim, printed factory marks, 23cm. diameter.
(Christie's) **£977 $1,590**

'Farmhouse', a Fantasque Bizarre plate, painted in colours, inside yellow, orange and blacks, printed factory marks, 25cm. diameter. *(Christie's)* **£460 $750**

'Windbells', a Fantasque Bizarre plate, painted in colours inside green, yellow and orange bands, printed factory marks, 25cm. diameter. *(Christie's)* **£747 $1,215**

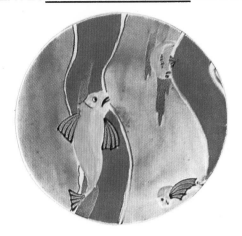

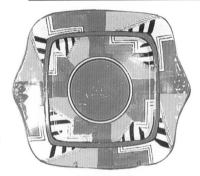

'Line Jazz', a 'Bizarre' sandwich plate, painted in colours, printed factory marks, 27cm. wide. *(Christie's)* **£207 $335**

'Tahiti', a Bizarre plate, painted with stylised leaping fish, in shades of green and blue highlighted in gilt, printed and painted marks, 22.5cm. diameter.

'Tahiti' was the name of a design range featuring both landscapes and subjects such as this, designed by Clarice's former supervisor John Butler. His work was issued alongside Clarice's for the first few years of 'Bizarre' ware.

(Christie's) **£230 $375**

'Keyhole', a Bizarre plate, painted in colours inside yellow and black bands, printed factory marks, 25cm. diameter.

The Keyhole design was an early variation on Original Bizarre, in 1928 when colourways were numerous. It was sometimes executed just in orange and black, and this example in orange, black and yellow is quite rare.

(Christie's) **£437 $710**

A 'Circus' pattern sandwich plate, designed by Dame Laura Knight, the centre decorated with circus horses adorned with exotic plumes and the rim with gilt dentil, puce printed marks *Designed by Laura Knight A.R.A. Produced in Bizarre by Clarice Cliff Wilkinson Ltd. England. Copyright Reserved First Edition 1934.*

(Bonhams) **£200 $325**

'House and Bridge', a Fantasque Bizarre plate, painted in colours inside yellow, orange and black, printed factory marks, 23cm. diameter. *(Christie's)* **£862 $1,405**

'Secrets', a Bizarre octagonal plate, painted in colours inside yellow and green bands, printed factory marks, 22cm. diameter. *(Christie's)* **£402 $655**

A Bizarre plate in the 'Sunray' pattern, painted in colours with orange and green banding, 25cm. diameter. *(Christie's)* **£605 $926**

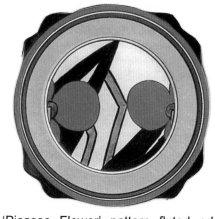

A 'Latona Blossom' plate, 9¹/₈in. diameter, rubber stamp mark *Hand Painted Bizarre by Clarice Cliff Newport Pottery England* and painted *Latona*. *(Bonhams)* **£1,200 $1,950**

A 'Picasso Flower' pattern fluted edged sandwich plate, 10½in. maximum diameter, lithograph mark *Hand Painted Bizarre by Clarice Cliff Newport Pottery England* and impressed *5/30*. *(Bonhams)* **£400 $650**

A 'Coral Firs' pattern foliate rimmed plate, maximum diameter 9¾in., lithograph marks *Hand Painted Bizarre by Clarice Cliff Newport Pottery England* and green Royal Staffordshire mark. *(Bonhams)* **£160 $260**

A Bizarre plate in the 'Lightning' pattern, painted in colours with orange and yellow banding, 25cm. diameter. *(Christie's)* **£1,100 $1,683**

'Blue W', a Bizarre plate, painted in colours inside orange band, printed factory marks, 25cm. diameter. *(Christie's)* **£1,495 $2,435**

'Pastel Autumn', a Fantasque Bizarre plate, painted in colours, printed factory marks, 22.5cm. diameter. *(Christie's)* **£460 $750**

A 'Blue W' pattern fluted sandwich plate, 9⁵/8in. diameter, rubber stamp mark *Hand Painted Bizarre by Clarice Cliff Newport Pottery England* and green stamp mark for *Royal Staffordshire Pottery Eng.*
(Bonhams) **£700 $1,140**

'Latona Tree', a Bizarre plate, painted in colours on a pink ground, printed · and painted marks, 26cm. diameter.

This example of Latona Tree is on a rare creamy brown coloured variant of the milky Latona glaze, produced briefly in 1929. *(Christie's)* **£575 $935**

'Café au Lait Zap', a Bizarre plate, painted in colours on a mottled green ground, printed factory marks, 25cm. diameter. *(Christie's)* **£460 $750**

'Appliqué Lugano', Bizarre octagonal side plate, painted in colours, printed factory marks, 14.5cm. diameter. *(Christie's)* **£1,265 $2,060**

Clarice Cliff Secrets design Bizarre plate, 8in. diameter. *(Muir Hewitt)* **£600 $975**

Clarice Cliff plate with leaf decoration, 7in. diameter. *(Muir Hewitt)* **£100 $160**

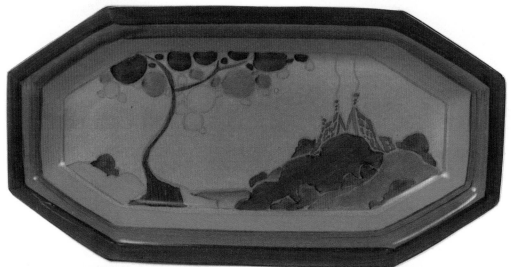

Clarice Cliff Secrets design cake plate, 1930s. *(Muir Hewitt)* **£350 $570**

A Latona Bizarre wall plate, decorated in the 'Red Roses' pattern, painted in red and black, 33.5cm. diameter.
(Christie's) **£770 $1,178**

'Xanthic', a Bizarre plate, painted in colours inside yellow and orange bands, printed factory marks, 22.5cm. diameter.
(Christie's) **£437 $710**

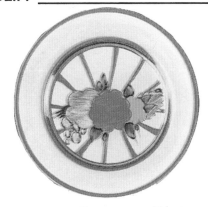

A Bizarre octagonal plate in the 'Tralee' pattern, painted in colours, 22cm. diameter. *(Christie's)* **£286 $438**

'Fruitburst', a Fantasque Bizarre plate, painted in colours, printed factory marks, 25.5cm. diameter. *(Christie's)* **£460 $750**

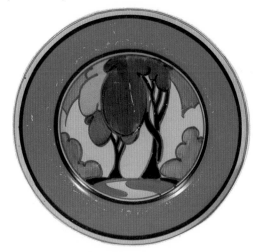

'Blue Autumn' pattern Clarice Cliff tea plate, 7in. diameter. *(Muir Hewitt)* **£300 $500**

Clarice Cliff Bizarre Farmhouse pattern octagonal plate, 9in. diameter. *(Lyle)* **£300 $490**

'Appliqué Idyll', a Bizarre plate, painted in colours inside yellow, black and red bands, printed factory marks, 25cm. diameter. *(Christie's)* **£575 $935**

'Moonlight', a Bizarre plate, painted in colours inside green and yellow bands, printed factory marks, 23cm. diameter. *(Christie's)* **£460 $750**

A Fantasque plate decorated in the 'Flora' pattern, painted in orange, yellow, green and black. *(Christie's)* **£225 $360**

A 'Bizarre' large meat platter, designed by Paul Nash, oval, painted with stylised acorn and foliage sprays, in colours, printed factory marks, 47cm. wide. *(Christie's)* **£322 $525**

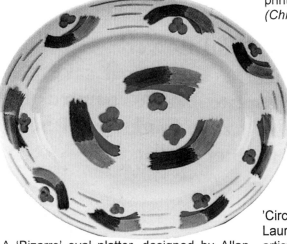

A 'Bizarre' oval platter, designed by Allan Walters, painted with stylised scrolling foliage in shades of green, brown and white, printed factory marks, 37cm. wide. *(Christie's)* **£172 $280**

'Circus', a Bizarre plate designed by Dame Laura Knight, printed and painted with an artist resting on the back of a performing horse, the rim a big top audience, in colours highlighted in gilt, printed factory marks, 25cm. diameter. *(Christie's)* **£690 $1,125**

'Avon', a Bizarre plate, painted in colours on a pale green ground, printed factory marks, 21.5cm. diameter. *(Christie's)* **£345 $560**

'Secrets', a Bizarre octagonal plate, painted in colours inside yellow and green bands, printed factory marks, 19cm. diameter. *(Christie's)* **£402 $655**

'Tennis', a Bizarre side plate, painted in colours, printed factory marks, 17cm. diameter. *(Christie's)* **£517 $842**

A Fantasque Bizarre plate in the 'Farmhouse' pattern, painted in colours, 9in. diameter. *(Christie's)* **£330 $521**

A 'Marigold' pattern small octagonal plate, 5½in. diameter, small rubber stamp mark *Hand Painted Bizarre by Clarice Cliff Newport Pottery England*, and hand painted *Marigold. (Bonhams)* **£400 $650**

'Rhodanthe', an octagonal plate, painted in colours, printed factory marks, 22cm diameter; two Biarritz side plates, a grapefruit dish and a single-handled dish in the same pattern. *(Christie's)* **£368 $600**

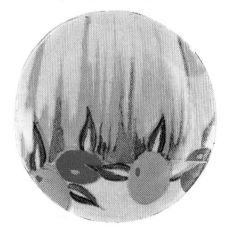

'Delecia Citrus', a plate, painted in colours, printed factory marks, 20cm. diameter. *(Christie's)* **£195 $320**

A Bizarre wall plate decorated in the 'Newlyn' pattern, painted in colours, 33.5cm. diameter. *(Christie's)* **£352 $539**

'House and Bridge', a Fantasque Bizarre low cylindrical preserve pot and cover, painted in colours, printed factory marks, 10cm. diameter. *(Christie's)* **£747 $1,210**

'Pastel Melon', a Bizarre preserve pot and cover, painted in colours, printed factory marks, 10cm. diameter. *(Christie's)* **£437 $710**

'Gibraltar', a Fantasque Bizarre cylindrical preserve pot and cover, painted in colours, printed factory marks, 9cm. high. *(Christie's)* **£400 $650**

'Tulip', a Bizarre preserve pot and cover, compressed form, painted in colours inside green bands, printed factory marks, 11cm. diameter. *(Christie's)* **£276 $450**

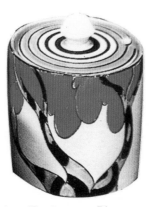

'Nasturtium', a Bizarre Bon Jour preserve pot and cover, painted in colours, printed factory marks, 10cm. high. *(Christie's)* **£575 $935**

'Honolulu', a Fantasque Bizarre cylindrical preserve pot and cover, painted in colours, printed factory marks, 9cm. high. *(Christie's)* **£575 $935**

'Crocus', a Bizarre Bon Jour preserve pot and cover, painted in colours, printed factory marks, 11cm. high.
(Christie's) **£253 $410**

'Gibraltar', a Fantasque Bizarre cylindrical preserve pot, painted in colours, printed factory marks, 8cm. high.
(Christie's) **£805 $1,310**

Clarice Cliff Bon Jour shape preserve pot, Rhodanthe design, 5in. high.
(Muir Hewitt) **£400 $650**

Clarice Cliff Crocus pattern preserve pot and cover, 4in. high.
(Muir Hewitt) **£250 $400**

'Killarney', a Bizarre low cylindrical preserve pot and cover, painted in colours, printed factory marks, 11cm. wide.
(Christie's) **£368 $600**

'Sunray Leaves', a Fantasque Bizarre cylindrical preserve pot and cover, painted in colours, printed factory marks, 8.5cm. high. *(Christie's)* **£322 $525**

An 'Acorn' pattern preserve pot and cover, 4in. high, rubber stamp mark *Hand Painted Bizarre by Clarice Cliff, Wilkinson Ltd. England. (Bonhams)* **£260 $425**

'Crocus', a Bizarre orange preserve pot and cover, painted in colours, printed factory marks. *(Christie's)* **£200 $325**

'Delecia Citrus', a Bizarre preserve pot on tripod foot with electroplated cover, painted in colours, printed factory marks, 11cm. high. *(Christie's)* **£400 $650**

'Crocus', a Bizarre cylindrical preserve pot and cover, painted in colours, printed factory marks, 9cm. high. *(Christie's)* **£250 $400**

'Canterbury Bells', a Bizarre cylindrical preserve pot and cover, painted in colours, printed factory marks, 10cm. high. *(Christie's)* **£300 $490**

'Crocus', a Bizarre apple shape preserve pot and cover, painted in colours, printed factory marks, 8.5cm. high. *(Christie's)* **£200 $325**

'Crocus', a Bizarre preserve pot and cover, shape no.230, painted in colours, printed factory marks, 8cm. high. *(Christie's)* **£120 $195**

'Broth', a Fantasque Bizarre cylindrical preserve pot with later electroplated cover, painted in colours, printed factory marks, 8cm. high. *(Christie's)* **£250 $400**

'Sunrise', a Fantasque Bizarre preserve pot with electroplated cover, shouldered square form, painted in colours, printed factory marks, 10cm. high. *(Christie's)* **£287 $465**

'Idyll', a preserve pot on tripod foot, with electroplated cover, painted in colours, printed factory marks, 11cm. high. *(Christie's)* **£253 $410**

'Double V', a Bizarre cylindrical preserve pot and cover, painted in colours, printed factory marks, 8cm. high. *(Christie's)* **£300 $490**

'Summerhouse', a Fantasque Bizarre preserve pot and cover, shape no.230, painted in colours, printed factory marks, 8.5cm. high. *(Christie's)* **£250 $400**

Clarice Cliff Bon Jour tea for two set, in the Orange Hydrangea design. *(Muir Hewitt)*   **£1,750 $2,850**

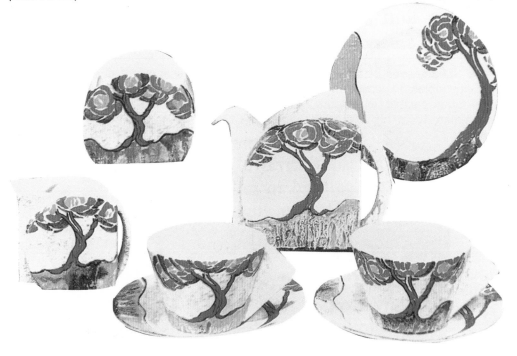

'Patina Tree', a Bizarre Stamford tea for two, painted in colours, comprising; teapot and cover, milk jug and sugar basin, two cups, saucers and a side plate, printed factory marks, teapot 13cm. high. *(Christie's)*   **£1,610 $2,625**

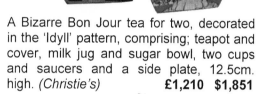

A Bizarre Bon Jour tea for two, decorated in the 'Idyll' pattern, comprising; teapot and cover, milk jug and sugar bowl, two cups and saucers and a side plate, 12.5cm. high. *(Christie's)* **£1,210 $1,851**

Clarice Cliff Marguerite design tea ware, circa 1930. *(Muir Hewitt)* **£85 $140**

Clarice Cliff Pastel Melon conical coffee service comprising coffeepot, six cups and saucers, cream and sugar. *(Muir Hewitt)* **£1,750 $2,850**

'Original Bizarre', a globe teapot, with electroplated cover, milk-jug and sugar basin, painted with a band of swags, in shades of yellow, blue and purple outlined in red between brown bands, printed factory marks, teapot 12cm. high. *(Christie's)* **£253 $410**

A 'Summerhouse' pattern conical coffee service, comprising; coffee pot and cover, six coffee cans and saucers, milk jug and matched sugar bowl, rubber stamp mark *Fantasque Hand Painted Bizarre by Clarice Cliff Newport Pottery England.* *(Bonhams)* **£1.800 $2,930**

'Tennis', a Bizarre Stamford Early Morning set, painted in colours, comprising; teapot and cover, milk jug and sugar basin, two cups, saucers and side plate, printed factory marks, teapot 12cm. high. *(Christie's)* **£3,450 $5,625**

'Cabbage Flower', a Bizarre Bon Jour coffee set, painted in colours, comprising; coffee pot and cover, milk jug and sugar basin, nine cups and ten saucers, printed factory marks, coffee pot 19.5cm. high.
(Christie's) **£2,300 $3,750**

'Windbells', a Fantasque Bizarre' Bon Jour coffee set for six, painted in colours, comprising; Bon Jour coffee pot and cover, milk jug and sugar basin and six conical cups and saucers, coffee pot 19.5cm. high.
(Christie's) **£3,910 $6,375**

'Idyll', a Bizarre Bon Jour tea for two, painted in colours, comprising; teapot and cover, milk jug and sugar basin, two cups, saucers and a side plate, printed factory marks, teapot 14cm. high.
(Christie's) **£2,530 $4,125**

'Crocus', a Bizarre coffee set for six, painted in colours, comprising; tankard coffee pot and cover, milk-jug and sugar basin, six cans and saucers, printed factory marks, coffee pot 19cm. high.
(Christie's) **£1,092 $1,780**

A Bizarre Stamford trio in the 'Tennis' pattern, painted in colours with red banding, height of teapot 4½in. high.
(Christie's) **£2,420 $4,475**

A Bizarre Stamford Early Morning set, painted with stylised flower sprays, painted in colours, comprising; teapot and cover, milk jug and sugar basin, two cups, saucers and side plates, printed factory marks, teapot 14cm. high.
(Christie's) **£483 $785**

'Original Bizarre', a teapot with electroplated cover, milk jug and sugar basin, painted with swag motif in shades of yellow, purple and blue outlined in red between green and brown bands, printed factory marks, teapot 10cm. high.
(Christie's) **£500 $815**

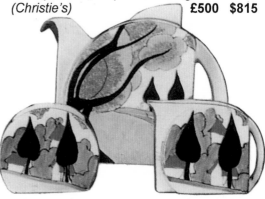

'Nasturtium', a Bizarre Stamford Early Morning set, painted in colours, comprising; teapot and cover, milk jug and sugar basin, two cups, saucers and a side plate, printed factory marks, 12cm. high.
(Christie's) **£1,495 $2,450**

A Clarice Cliff Fantasque Bizarre Stamford trio decorated in the 'May Avenue' pattern, painted in colours, height of teapot 4½in.
(Christie's) **£2,500 $4,000**

'Windbells', a Fantasque Bizarre tankard coffee set for six, painted in colours, comprising; coffee pot and cover, milk jug and sugar basin, six cups and saucers, printed factory marks, coffee pot 19cm. high. *(Christie's)* **£2,530 $4,125**

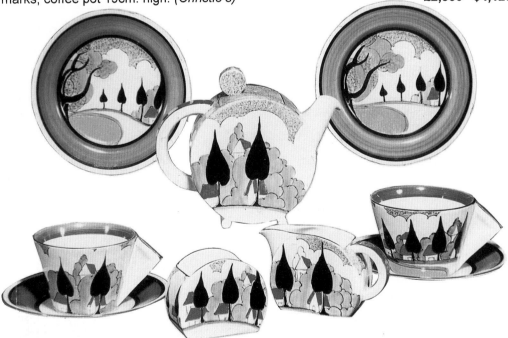

'May Avenue', a Bizarre Bon Jour Early Morning set, painted in colours, comprising; teapot and cover, milk jug and sugar basin, two cups, saucers and side plates, printed factory marks, 11cm. high.

This set has two plates, which confuses collectors. We know from original advertising the 'Early Morning sets' were normally sold with one plate, but customers were able to order any configuration they wanted, which is why this set has two.
(Christie's) **£13,570 $22,120**

'Patina Coastal', a Bizarre Stamford tea for two, painted in colours over mottled blue, comprising; teapot and cover, milk jug and sugar basin, two cups and saucers, printed factory marks, teapot 12.5cm. high. *(Christie's)*   **£862 $1,400**

'Oranges', a Fantasque Bizarre Stamford Early Morning set, painted in colours, comprising; teapot and cover, milk jug and sugar basin, two cups, saucers and a side plate, printed factory marks, teapot 12cm. high. *(Christie's)*   **£1,610 $2,665**

'Appliqué Avignon', a Bizarre coffee set for six, painted in colours, comprising; coffee pot and cover, milk-jug and sugar basin, six cups and saucers, printed factory marks, coffee pot 18cm. high.

This design was one of the first issued on Clarice's complete Conical coffee set. The pot had appeared briefly late in 1929 with a very impractical solid handle. By March 1930 it had been given an open handle and Clarice created the coffee cans with solid handles to complement it. (Christie's) **£6,325 $10,300**

'Orange Roof Cottage', a Bizarre Stamford trio, painted in colours, comprising; teapot and cover, milk jug and sugar basin, printed factory marks, teapot 12.5cm. high.
(Christie's) **£1,725 $2,810**

'Orange Chintz', a Fantasque Bizarre conical trio, painted in colours, comprising; teapot and cover, milk jug and sugar basin, printed factory marks, teapot 12cm high. *(Christie's)* **£1,495 $2,450**

'Blue Chintz', a Bizarre Stamford part Early Morning set, painted in colours, comprising; teapot and cover, milk jug and sugar basin, two cups, one saucer and a side plate, printed factory marks, teapot 14cm. high. *(Christie's)* **£1,495 $2,450**

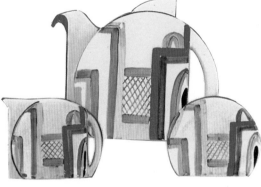

A 'Tennis' pattern tea for one, comprising; Stamford teapot and lid with modified spout, milk jug, sugar bowl, cup, saucer and side plate, lithograph marks *Hand Painted Bizarre by Clarice Cliff Newport Pottery England.* *(Bonhams)* **£2,000 $3,200**

'Orange Trees and House', a Fantasque Bizarre conical teapot and cover, milk jug and sugar basin, painted in colours, printed factory marks, teapot 13cm. high. *(Christie's)* **£1,150 $1,875**

A Fantasque Bizarre Stamford tea for two in the 'Trees and House' pattern, comprising: teapot and cover, two cups and saucers (one replacement), side plate, milk-jug and sugar bowl, height of teapot 11.5cm. *(Christie's)* **£1,210 $1,851**

'Rudyard', a Bizarre Stamford tea for two, painted in colours, comprising; teapot and cover, milk jug and sugar basin, two cups, saucers and a side plate, printed factory marks, teapot 12cm. high.

Stamford early morning sets were issued from September 1930 until 1936, but from 1933 onwards fewer were produced so examples such as this Rudyard set are quite rare.

(Christie's)   **£6,900 $11,250**

'Moonflower', a Bizarre conical coffee set for six, painted in colours, comprising; coffee pot and cover, milk-jug and sugar basin, six cans and saucers, printed factory marks, coffee pot 17.5cm. high.

(Christie's)   **£2,300 $3,750**

A 'Gibraltar' pattern conical tea for two, comprising; teapot and cover, sugar bowl, milk jug, two cups and two saucers and one cake plate 4¾in., height of teapot 4¾in, lithograph marks *Fantasque Hand Painted Bizarre by Clarice Cliff Newport Pottery England* and teapot impressed with no. *42. (Bonhams)*   **£2,200 $3,580**

'Delecia Citrus', a Bizarre Stamford tea for two, painted in colours, comprising teapot and cover, milk jug and sugar basin, two cups and a saucer, printed factory marks, teapot 12cm. high.
(Christie's) **£1,000 $1,600**

'Sunrise', a Fantasque Bizarre conical bachelor tea set, painted in colours, comprising; teapot and cover, milk jug and sugar basin, one cup, saucer and side plate, printed factory marks, 12cm. high.
(Christie's) **£1,500 $2,450**

'Sun-Gay', a Bizarre part teaset, painted in colours, comprising; teapot and stand, size 24, milk jug, cylindrical preserve pot and cover, five various cups and saucers and six side plates, printed factory marks, teapot, 12.5cm. high.
(Christie's) **£1,035 $1,685**

'Orange Trees and House', a Fantasque Bizarre Stamford bachelor tea set, painted in colours, comprising teapot and cover, milk jug, and sugar basin, one cup, saucer and side plate, printed factory marks, teapot 12cm. high.
(Christie's) **£1,725 $2,810**

'Blue Firs', a conical sugar sifter, painted in colours between blue and green bands, printed factory marks, Brown's original paper label, 14cm. high.

This piece unusually still has the original retailer's label from Browns of Sauchiehall Street in Glasgow.
(Christie's) **£1,955 $3,185**

'Red Roofs', a Fantasque Bizarre conical sugar sifter, painted in colours below black, blue and orange bands, printed factory marks, 14.5cm. high.
(Christie's) **£2,070 $3,375**

'Coral Firs', a Bizarre sugar sifter, painted in colours between brown, grey and yellow bands, printed factory marks, 14cm. high.
(Christie's)   **£632 $1,030**

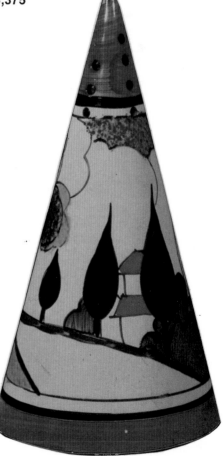

'Orange Roof Cottage', a Bon Jour sugar sifter, painted in colours, printed factory marks, 12.5cm. high.

The 'Bon Jour' dredger was issued in 1933 so is not found in many designs issued before then, so this example in 'Orange Roof Cottage' is a rarity, and is the first example recorded.
(Christie's) **£1,840 $3,000**

'Orange Erin', a Bon Jour sugar sifter, painted in colours, printed factory marks, 13cm. high.

Erin was the mythological name for Ireland so the fact that the Erin design was produced in green and orange colourways is rather significant.
(Christie's)   **£1,610 $2,625**

'May Avenue', a Bizarre conical sugar sifter, painted in colours between blue bands, printed factory marks, 14cm. high.
(Christie's)   **£5,750 $9,375**

'Secrets', a Fantasque Bizarre' conical sugar sifter, painted in colours, printed factory marks, 14cm. high. *(Christie's)* **£690 $1,125**

'Nasturtium', a Bizarre conical sugar sifter, painted in colours, printed factory marks, 14cm. high. *(Christie's)* **£460 $750**

'Sungold', a Bizarre conical sugar sifter painted in colours, printed factory marks, 14cm. high. *(Christie's)* **£862 $1,405**

'Orange Trees and House', a Fantasque Bizarre conical sugar sifter, painted in colours between green and orange bands, printed factory marks, 14cm. high. *(Christie's)* **£1,840 $3,000**

'Pastel Melon', a Fantasque Bizarre, conical sugar sifter, painted in colours between blue, pink and green bands, printed factory marks, 14cm. high. *(Christie's)* **£805 $1,310**

'Honolulu', a Fantasque Bizarre, conical sugar sifter, painted in colours between black and green bands, printed factory marks, 14cm. high. *(Christie's)* **£2,530 $4,125**

'Pastel Autumn', Fantasque Bizarre conical sugar sifter, painted in colours, printed factory marks, 14cm. high. *(Christie's)* **£920 $1,500**

Clarice Cliff 'Honeydew' sugar dredger with floral decoration. *(Muir Hewitt)* **£300 $500**

'Tiger Tree', a conical sugar sifter, painted in colours, printed factory marks, 14cm. high. *(Christie's)* **£632 $1,030**

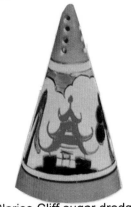

'Rhodanthe', a Bizarre conical sugar sifter, painted in colours, printed factory marks, 14cm. high.
(Christie's) **£299 $485**

Clarice Cliff sugar dredger with floral design.
(Muir Hewitt) **£400 $650**

'Crocus', a Bizarre conical sugar sifter, painted in colours, printed factory marks, 14.5cm. high.
(Christie's) **£345 $560**

'Orange Autumn', a Fantasque Bizarre conical sugar sifter, painted in colours, printed factory marks, 14cm. high.
(Christie's) **£1,092 $1,775**

'Orange Autumn', a conical sugar sifter, painted in colours between yellow bands, printed factory marks, 14cm. high.
(Christie's) **£632 $1,030**

'Autumn', a conical sugar sifter, painted in colours between orange bands, printed factory marks, 14cm. high.
(Christie's) **£862 $1,405**

A Bizarre conical sugar sifter decorated in the 'Kew' pattern, painted in colours, 13.5cm. high.
(Christie's) **£935 $1,431**

'Coral Firs', a Bizarre conical sugar sifter, painted in colours between brown and yellow bands, printed factory marks, 14cm. high.
(Christie's) **£747 $1,210**

'Autumn', a Fantasque Bizarre conical sugar sifter, painted in colours, printed factory marks, 14.5cm. high.
(Christie's) **£1,000 $1,600**

'Limberlost', a Bizarre conical sugar sifter, painted in colours, printed factory marks, 14cm. high.
(Christie's) **£977 $1,590**

'Blue Crocus', a Bizarre Lynton sugar sifter, painted in colours, printed factory marks, 13cm. high.
(Christie's)   **£437 $710**

'Poplar', a Fantasque Bizarre conical sugar sifter, painted in colours, printed factory marks, 14.5cm. high.
(Christie's) **£1,035 $1,685**

'Berries', a Fantasque Bizarre conical sugar sifter, painted in colours, printed factory marks, 14cm. high.
(Christie's) **£1,265 $2,060**

'Blue Firs', a Bizarre conical sugar sifter, painted in colours, printed factory marks, 12.5cm. high.
(Christie's) **£1,840 $3,000**

'Cornwall', a Bizarre conical sugar sifter, painted in colours, printed factory marks, 14cm. high.
(Christie's)   **£575 $935**

'Coral Firs', a Bizarre conical sugar sifter, painted in colours, printed factory marks, 14cm. high.
(Christie's)   **£920 $1,500**

'Coral Firs', a Bon Jour sugar sifter, painted in colours, printed factory marks, 12.5cm. high.
(Christie's)
   £1,035 $1,685

'Orange Roof Cottage', Bizarre conical sugar sifter, painted in colours, printed factory marks, 14cm. high.
(Christie's) **£1,667 $2,700**

'Orange Roof Cottage', a Bizarre conical sugar sifter, painted in colours, printed factory marks, 14cm. high. *(Christie's)* **£1,955 $3,185**

'Newlyn', a Lynton sugar sifter, painted in colours, 12.5cm. high. *(Christie's)* **£402 $655**

'Blue Firs', a Bizarre conical sugar sifter, painted in colours, printed factory marks, 14.5cm. high. *(Christie's)* **£1,610 $2,625**

'Rudyard', a Bizarre conical sifter, painted in colours, printed factory marks, 14cm. high. *(Christie's)* **£1,322 $2,150**

'Kelverne', a Bizarre Lynton sugar sifter, painted in colours, printed factory marks, 12.5cm. high. *(Christie's)* **£345 $560**

'Apples', a Fantasque Bizarre conical sugar sifter, painted in colours, printed factory marks, 14cm. high. *(Christie's)* **£1,955 $3,185**

'Mountain', a Bizarre conical sugar sifter, painted in colours, printed factory marks, 14cm. high. *(Christie's)* **£2,185 $3,560**

'Newlyn', a Bizarre Lynton sugar sifter, painted in colours, printed factory marks, 13cm. high. *(Christie's)* **£460 $750**

'Honolulu', Fantasque Bizarre conical sugar sifter, painted in colours, printed factory marks, 14cm. high. *(Christie's)* **£2,070 $3,375**

'Orange Trees and House', a conical teapot and cover, no.30, painted in colours, printed factory marks, 14cm. high. *(Christie's)* **£632 $1,030**

'Pastel Melon', a Fantasque Bizarre, conical teapot and cover, painted in colours, printed factory marks, 14cm. high. *(Christie's)* **£517 $840**

A Bizarre Bon Jour teapot and cover, painted in bright colours on a yellow ground with scenes of a Slavonic peasant couple, 5in. high. *(Christie's)* **£880 $1,625**

'Original Bizarre', a Fantasque Bizarre conical teapot and cover, painted with geometric motif in shades of yellow and orange outlined in black, printed factory marks, 10cm. high. *(Christie's)* **£700 $1,140**

'Delecia Pansies', a Bizarre Globe teapot and cover, painted in colours, printed factory marks, 13cm. high. *(Christie's)* **£632 $1,030**

'Rhodanthe', a Bizarre Athens teapot and cover, painted in colours, printed factory marks, 16cm. high. *(Christie's)* **£437 $710**

'Glendale', a small Windsor teapot and cover, painted in colours, printed factory marks, 12cm. high. *(Christie's)* **£250 $405**

'Orange Trees and House', a Fantasque Bizarre Athens teapot and cover, painted in colours, printed factory marks, 16.5cm. high. *(Christie's)* **£600 $975**

Clarice Cliff 1951 Teepee teapot with *Greetings from Canada* on underside. *(Muir Hewitt)* **£760 $1,140**

A 'Sunray' pattern conical teapot and cover, 5¾in. high, rubber stamp *Hand Painted Bizarre by Clarice Cliff Newport Pottery England* and *Registration Applied For. (Bonhams)* **£1,200 $1,950**

'House and Bridge', a Bizarre conical teapot and cover, shape no.42, painted in colours, printed factory marks, 12cm. high. *(Christie's)* **£1,150 $1,875**

'Orange Lily', a Fantasque Bizarre Athens teapot and cover, painted in colours, printed factory marks, 14cm. high. *(Christie's)* **£264 $430**

'Patina Coral Firs', a rare conical teapot and cover, painted in colours, printed factory mark, 10cm. high.
(Christie's)   **£920 $1,500**

'Orange Roof Cottage', a Bizarre Stamford teapot, painted in colours, with printed factory mark, 12.5cm. high.
(Christie's)   **£1,150 $1,875**

'Crocus', a Bizarre Stamford teapot and cover, painted in colours, with printed factory mark, 12cm. high.
(Christie's)   **£385 $625**

'Blue Firs', a Bizarre Stamford teapot and cover, painted in colours with printed factory marks, 12cm. high.
(Christie's)   **£2,420 $3,950**

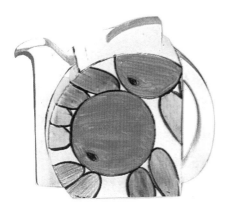

'Oranges', a Fantasque Bizarre Stamford teapot and cover, painted in colours with printed factory mark, 12cm. high.
(Christie's)   **£1,150 $1,875**

'Orange Chintz', a Fantasque Bizarre teapot and cover painted in colours, with printed factory mark, 12cm. high.
(Christie's)   **£920 $1,500**

A Bizarre conical vase, decorated in the 'Honolulu' pattern, painted in colours, 6in. high. *(Christie's)* **£1,210 $1,975**

'Gay Day', a Bizarre Isis vase, painted in colours, printed factory marks, 26cm. high. *(Christie's)* **£200 $325**

A Patina Bizarre spherical vase painted with red tree bearing blue and green foliage, under blue spattered slip, 6in. high. *(Christie's)* **£825 $1,350**

'Rhodanthe', a Bizarre Isis vase, painted in colours, printed factory marks, 24.5cm. high. *(Christie's)* **£400 $650**

'Farmhouse', a Fantasque Bizarre vase, shape no.465, painted in colours, printed factory marks, 18cm. high.

The shape 465 vase, and 464 vase which has just one tube, are examples of Clarice's most extremely Art Deco shape designs. They were issued in 1931 and produced until at least 1936 but in small quantities as they were difficult to manufacture. *(Christie's)* **£2,070 $3,375**

'Melon', a pair of Fantasque Bizarre vases, shape no.268, painted in colours between orange bands, printed factory marks, 20.5cm. high. *(Christie's)* **£1,610 $2,625**

A 'Lily' pattern Archaic series vase, shape 374, 12in. high, large rubber stamp mark *Fantasque. (Bonhams)* **£1,400 $2,280**

'Broth', a Bizarre Globe vase, shape no.370, painted in colours between blue bands, printed factory marks, 15cm. high.

This early 'Fantasque' design is not usually found with blue banding. As this example has a 'Bizarre' backstamp it was clearly not a standard production piece but perhaps painted to special order. *(Christie's)* **£1,725 $2,800**

'Secrets', a pair of Bizarre Meiping vases, painted in colours between green, yellow and brown bands, printed factory marks, 16cm. high. *(Christie's)* **£747 $1,210**

Clarice Cliff Rhodanthe design vase, 14in. high. *(Muir Hewitt)* **£850 $1,385**

A Bizarre Isis vase in the 'Diamonds' pattern, painted in colours between contrasting striped borders, 9¾in. high. *(Christie's)* **£1,210 $1,909**

'Orange Trees and House', a Fantasque Bizarre vase, shape no.386, painted in colours between orange bands, printed factory marks, 31cm. high.

Clarice designed this vase in 1929 to hold flowers perfectly. Strangely it proved less popular than the Lotus jug as a flower holder, but it was also used by the Shorter & Sons factory where it was produced in designs by Mabel Leigh.
(Christie's) **£1,610 $2,625**

'Rudyard', a pair of Fantasque Bizarre miniature vases, ovoid with everted rim, painted in colours between bands, printed factory marks to one, 6.5cm. high. *(Christie's)* **£1,150 $1,875**

'Blue Firs', a Bizarre Isis vase, painted in colours, with red roof cottage, between blue bands, printed factory marks, 24cm. high.

This example of 'Blue Firs' from 1934 is believed to be the first found on a 10in. Isis vase. *(Christie's)* **£5,175 $8,450**

'Castellated Circle', a Bizarre vase, shape no.361, painted in shades of red, blue yellow and black, printed factory marks, 21cm. high.

'Castellated Circle' was an early example of the designs that evolved from Clarice's Original Bizarre in 1929. This piece is in a new colourway, more vibrantly coloured than the standard versions, being in coral red and blue.
(Christie's) **£2,500 $4,075**

'Orange Picasso Flower', a Bizarre vase, shape no.361, painted in colours between yellow and orange bands, printed factory marks, 21cm. high.
(Christie's) **£862 $1,400**

'Original Bizarre', a Bizarre vase, shape no.358, painted with bands of diamonds in shades of orange and black between orange bands, printed factory marks, 20cm. high. *(Christie's)* **£632 $1,030**

'Inspiration Lily', a Bizarre vase, shape no.386, painted in colours on a turquoise ground, printed and painted marks, 30cm. high. *(Christie's)* **£1,610 $2,625**

'Clouvre Butterfly', a Bizarre Isis vase, painted in colours on a deep blue ground, printed and painted marks, 25cm. high. *(Christie's)* **£2,070 $3,375**

'Appliqué Palermo', a shape no.362 vase, painted in colours between yellow, red and black bands, printed factory marks, 20cm. high. *(Christie's)* **£1,495 $2,450**

A Bizarre hexagonal baluster vase decorated in the 'Sunray' pattern, painted in colours between multibanded borders, 15in. high. *(Christie's)* **£2,300 $3,680**

A Clarice Cliff Bizarre vase, shape no. 342, decorated in the 'Sliced Circles' pattern, painted in orange, green and black, 7¾in. high. *(Christie's)* **£625 $1,000**

An Appliqué Bizarre Isis vase decorated in the 'Blue Lucerne' pattern, painted in colours, 25cm. high. *(Christie's)* **£3,850 $5,891**

'Floreat', a Fantasque Bizarre vase, shape no.360, painted in colours between yellow and orange bands, printed factory marks, 20.5cm. high. *(Christie's)* **£690 $1,125**

'Gibraltar', a Fantasque Bizarre vase, shape no.362, painted in colours between yellow, pink and blue bands, printed factory marks, 20cm. high. *(Christie's)* **£2,530 $4,125**

'Tulip', a Bizarre vase, shape no.362, painted in colours between blue, pink and green bands, printed factory marks, 21cm. high. *(Christie's)* **£747 $1,210**

'Autumn' a Bizarre vase, shape no.386, painted in colours between orange, yellow and green bands, printed factory marks, 31cm. high. *(Christie's)* **£1,380 $2,250**

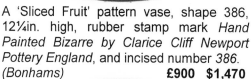

A 'Sliced Fruit' pattern vase, shape 386, 12¼in. high, rubber stamp mark *Hand Painted Bizarre by Clarice Cliff Newport Pottery England*, and incised number *386*. (Bonhams) **£900 $1,470**

'Yellow Roof Cottage', a Fantasque Bizarre' vase, shape no.264, painted in colours between yellow, green and orange bands, printed factory marks, 20cm. high.

This design is known in two colourways, orange and the rarer pink. This example with the yellow roof shows Clarice contemplated a third colourway. It is intriguing as it is clearly not a sample as the enamelling is so casually executed, something her paintresses would not have been allowed to do. We may postulate that a paintress did the outline and Clarice then filled in different colours as an experiment, wandering from bench to bench using the girl's colours as we know she did. (Christie's) **£1,150 $1,875**

'Original Bizarre', a Bizarre Archaic vase, shape no.373, painted with arrowhead motif in shades of blue and red, below yellow triangles, outlined in black between red and blue bands, printed factory marks, 17.5cm. high. (Christie's) **£1,265 $2,060**

A 'Windbells' pattern vase, shape 362, 7¾in. high, lithograph mark Hand Painted Bizarre by Clarice Cliff Newport Pottery England. (Bonhams) **£700 $1,140**

A 'Marigold' pattern Isis vase, 10in. high, rubber stamp mark *Hand Painted Bizarre by Clarice Cliff Newport Pottery England*, hand painted *Marigold* and impressed *Isis*. (Bonhams) **£1,500 $2,450**

'Inspiration Persian', a Bizarre Yo Yo vase, painted in shades of blue, pink, purple and ochre, printed and painted marks, 23.5cm. high. *(Christie's)* **£3,910 $6,375**

A 'Cubist' pattern Archaic series vase, shape 373, 7in. high, rubber stamp mark Fantasque Republica Temple Luxor Thebes captial of the large columns 1250 B.C, and printed gilt retailer's mark for Lawleys. *(Bonhams)* **£1,800 £2,930**

A Fantasque Archaic vase, painted with blue centred orange flowers on a black ground, between blue and orange banding, 7in. high. *(Christie's)* **£880 $1,450**

A 'Patina Country' pattern Isis vase, 9¾in. high, lithograph mark Hand Painted Bizarre by Clarice Cliff Newport Pottery England *(Bonhams)* **£360 $470**

A 'Broth' pattern Archaic series vase, shape 375, 10in. high, small rubber stamp mark *Fantasque Hand Painted Bizarre by Clarice Cliff Newport Pottery England.* *(Bonhams)* **£1,700 $2,770**

A 'Sunrise pattern Isis vase, 9¾in. high, large rubber stamp mark *Fantasque Hand Painted Bizarre by Clarice Cliff Newport Pottery England.(Bonhams)* **£1,100 $1,800**

'Broth', a Bizarre vase, shape no.249, painted in colours between orange and yellow bands, printed factory marks, 20cm. high.
(Christie's) **£276 $450**

'My Garden' vase from the Bizarre range by Clarice Cliff, 5½in. high.
(Muir Hewitt) **£135 $202**

'Melon', a Fantasque Bizarre vase, shape no.205, painted in colours between orange bands, printed factory marks, 21cm. high.
(Christie's) **£862 $1,400**

A 'Blue Autumn' pattern, shape 358, 7¾in. high, lithograph mark *Fantasque Hand Painted Bizarre by Clarice Cliff Newport England*, and relief moulded number *358*.
(Bonhams) **£800 $1,300**

An 'Inspiration' Persian design vase, shape 264, 6¹/₈in. high, blue rubber stamp marks *Hand Painted Bizarre by Clarice Cliff Newport Pottery England*, and brown painted mark *Persian*.
(Bonhams) **£480 $780**

A 'Clouvre' Marigold vase, shape 200, 7½in. high, rubber stamp mark *Hand Painted Bizarre by Clarice Cliff Newport Pottery England,* and hand painted mark *Clouvre*.
(Bonhams) **£600 $975**

'Orange Trees and House', a Fantasque Bizarre vase, shape no.362, painted in colours between orange bands, printed factory marks, 20.5cm. high.
(Christie's) **£1,380 $2,250**

A 'Blue Autumn' pattern vase, shape 365, 8in. high, rubber stamp mark *Bizarre Hand Painted Fantasque by Clarice Cliff, Wilkinson Pottery England.*
(Bonhams) **£800 $1,300**

An 'Orange Gardenia' pattern vase, shape 265, 6in. high, rubber stamp mark *Bizarre Hand Painted Fantasque by Clarice Cliff, Wilkinson Ltd. England*
(Bonhams) **£460 $750**

An early 'Persian' design vase, shape 264, 7¾in. high, green hand painted mark *Persian by Clarice Cliff Newport Pottery Burslem.*
(Bonhams) **£850 $1,385**

An 'Inspiration Bouquet' rare miniature vase, 2¾in. high, hand painted in brown *Inspiration* and stamped *Wilkinson Ltd. England.*
(Bonhams) **£460 $750**

An 'Inspiration Delphinium' Abstract Floral design vase, shape 369, 8in. high, indistinct brown painted mark.
(Bonhams) **£550 $900**

A 'Sunray' pattern vase, shape 186, 5½in. high, rubber stamp mark *Hand Painted Newport Pottery England Bizarre by Clarice Cliff.*
(Bonhams) **£800 $1,300**

A 'Melon' pattern globe vase, shape 370, 5¾in. high, rubber stamp mark Fantasque *Hand Painted Bizarre by Clarice Cliff Newport Pottery England.*
(Bonhams) **£2,100 $3,420**

A 'Football' pattern vase, shape 363, 6½in. high, small rubber stamp mark *Hand Painted Bizarre by Clarice Cliff Newport Pottery England.*
(Bonhams) **£1,400 $2,280**

A 'Rudyard' pattern, vase, shape 451, 6in. high, lithograph mark *Hand Painted Bizarre by Clarice Cliff Newport Pottery England.*
(Bonhams) **£950 $1,550**

An 'Inspiration' Persian Isnik vase, shape 376, 7in. high, brown painted mark *Inspiration Bizarre by Clarice Cliff Newport Burslem England.*
(Bonhams) **£550 $900**

A 'Blue Autumn' pattern vase, shape 361, 8¼in. high, small rubber stamp mark *Hand Painted Bizarre by Clarice Cliff Newport Pottery England.*
(Bonhams) **£500 $815**

'Original Bizarre', a compressed vase, shape no.356, painted with a band of triangles in shades of blue, orange, purple and green outlined in black between purple, blue, orange and green bands, printed factory marks, 17cm. high.
(Christie's) **£920 $1,500**

'Comets', a Fantasque Bizarre Archaic vase, shape no.373, painted in colours between orange and green bands, printed factory marks, 18cm. high.
(Christie's) **£1,955 $3,185**

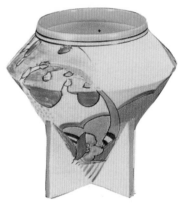

'Moonlight', a Fantasque Bizarre conical vase on four square feet, painted in colours, printed factory marks, 15cm. high.
(Christie's) **£1,092 $1,780**

Clarice Cliff lotus flower vase, 1930s.
(Muir Hewitt) **£150 $245**

'Caprice', a Bizarre vase, shape no.358, painted in colours on a pale blue glaze, printed factory marks, 21cm. high.
(Christie's) **£805 $1,310**

'Double V', a Bizarre vase, shape no.358, painted in colours between blue bands, printed factory marks, 20cm. high.
(Christie's) **£600 $975**

'Original Bizarre', an ovoid vase with collar rim, painted with band of triangles and eye motif, in shades of red, blue and yellow, outlined in green before blue and red bands, printed factory marks, 12cm. high. *(Christie's)* **£402 $655**

A Patina Bizarre spherical vase painted with red tree bearing blue and green foliage, under blue spattered slip, 6in. high. *(Christie's)* **£875 $1,400**

A Fantasque Bizarre globular vase, decorated in the 'Honolulu' pattern, painted in colours, 16cm. high. *(Christie's)* **£1,870 $2,861**

'Melon', a Fantasque Bizarre vase, shape no.370, painted in colours between black and orange bands, printed factory marks, 15cm. high. *(Christie's)* **£1,000 $1,600**

'Broth', a Fantasque Bizarre vase, shape no.358, painted in colours between orange and purple bands, printed factory marks, 21cm. high. *(Christie's)* **£862 $1,400**

A Bizarre ribbed waisted cylindrical vase, decorated in the 'Coral Firs' pattern, painted in colours, 24cm. high. *(Christie's)* **£275 $421**

'Red Roofs', a Fantasque Bizarre vase, shape no.342, painted in colours above green, yellow, orange and black bands, printed factory marks, 20cm. high. *(Christie's)* **£1,035 $1,685**

'Appliqué Avignon', a Bizarre vase, shape no.358, painted in colours between orange and black bands, printed and painted marks, 20cm. high. *(Christie's)* **£2,070 $3,353**

'Farmhouse', a Bizarre Isis vase, painted in colours between yellow, orange and brown bands, printed and painted marks, 25cm high. *(Christie's)* **£1,265 $2,060**

'Inspiration Lily', a Bizarre vase, shape no.386, painted in colours on a turquoise ground, printed and painted marks, 30cm. high. *(Christie's)* **£2,500 $4,075**

An 'Inspiration' Clouvre Tulip vase, 11¾in. high, rubber stamp mark *Hand Painted Bizarre by Clarice Cliff Newport Pottery England,* and hand painted *Inspiration.* *(Bonhams)* **£1,300 $2,120**

A 'Honolulu' pattern vase, shape 452, 8¼in. high, lithograph mark Fantasque *Hand Painted Bizarre by Clarice Cliff Newport Pottery England.* *(Bonhams)* **£1,100 $1,800**

'Solitude' a Fantasque Bizarre globe vase, shape no.370, painted in colours between yellow bands, printed factory marks, 16cm. high.

This piece was probably a sample as the design repeats the tree and bridge elements twice each. On production pieces there are two trees but the mystical bridge is stretched to fill the reverse.
(Christie's) **£3,450 $5,625**

An 'Inspiration' Clouvre Tulip vase, shape 386, 12in. high, blue printed marks and brown painted mark *Clouvre.*
(Bonhams) **£1,300 $2,120**

A 'Rudyard' pattern Daffodil vase, shape 450, 13¼in. long, lithograph mark Hand *Painted by Clarice Cliff Newport England.*
(Bonhams) **£900 $1,470**

'Inspiration Persian', a Bizarre Yo Yo vase, painted in shades of blue, pink, purple and ochre, printed and painted marks, 23.5cm. high.

Clarice's 'Inspiration' ware was the most expensive range issued by Newport Pottery in the late Twenties, and was mainly confined to her simple bowls, vases and plaques. This example on a 'Yo Yo' vase is an unusual combination of a very Art Deco shape with a classical 'Persian' style decoration, executed in the advanced 'Inspiration' glazes. The factory found these too expensive and technically difficult to make so by 1931 they had been phased out. The style was revived briefly with 'Opalesque' ware of the mid-Thirties.
(Christie's) **£2,500 $4,075**

An Appliqué 'Orange Lugano' vase, shape 358, 8in. high, hand painted *Appliqué* and rubber stamp mark *Hand Painted Bizarre by Clarice Cliff Newport Pottery England* and impressed shape number *358.*
(Bonhams) **£3,000 $4,890**

'Rudyard', a Bizarre vase, shape no.720, painted in colours, printed factory marks, 26cm. high. *(Christie's)* **£690 £1,125**

'Orange Trees and House', a Fantasque Bizarre vase, shape no.342, painted in colours, printed factory marks, 20cm. *(Christie's)* **£977 $1,590**

'Appliqué Orange Lugano' vase, shape no.207, painted in colours, printed and painted marks, 21cm. high. *(Christie's)* **£1,500 $2,445**

'Summerhouse', a Fantasque Bizarre vase, shape no.358, painted in colours under an orange band, printed factory marks, 20cm. high. *(Christie's)* **£1,035 $1,685**

'Red Trees and House', a Fantasque Bizarre vase, shape no. 342, painted in colours between red bands, printed factory marks, 20cm. high. *(Christie's)* **£747 $1,210**

'Floreat', a Fantasque Bizarre vase, shape no.358, painted in colours between orange and yellow bands, printed factory marks, 20.5cm. high. *(Christie's)* **£700 $1,140**

'Sungold', a Bizarre Isis vase, painted in colours between yellow and orange bands, printed factory marks, 20cm. high. *(Christie's)* **£460 $750**

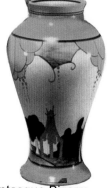

A Fantasque Bizarre baluster vase in the 'Summerhouse' pattern, painted in colours, 31cm. high. *(Christie's)* **£3,080 $4,712**

'Oranges' a Bizarre vase, shape no.365, painted in colours between orange bands, printed factory marks, 21cm. high. (Christie's) **£402 $655**

'Blue Japan', a vase, shape no.362, painted in colours unmarked, 20cm. high.
(Christie's) **£632 $1,092**

A Bizarre vase, decorated in the 'Marigold' pattern, painted with orange flowers on a streaked blue ground, 7¾in. high.
(Christie's) **£400 $640**

Clarice Cliff Bizarre Aurea Isis vase, 8in. high.
(Muir Hewitt) **£400 $650**

'Orange Trees and House' a Fantasque Bizarre vase, shape no.269, painted in colours between orange bands, printed factory marks, 15cm. high.
(Christie's) **£690 $1,125**

'Orange Trees and House', a Fantasque Bizarre vase, shape no.362, painted in colours between orange and black bands, printed factory marks, 20cm. high.
(Christie's) **£920 $1,500**

'Brown Lily', a Fantasque Bizarre vase, shape no.188, painted in colours between yellow, orange and purple bands, printed factory marks, 22cm. high.
(Christie's) **£483 $785**

A Bizarre vase, decorated in the 'Appliqué Lugano' pattern, painted in colours with blue roof and orange sky, 8in. high.
(Christie's) **£1,200 $1,950**

'Café au Lait Autumn', a Bizarre vase, shape no.362, painted in colours on a mottled brown ground, printed factory marks, 20cm. high. *(Christie's)* **£345 $560**

'Comets', a Fantasque Bizarre vase, shape no.358, between green and orange, printed factory marks, 21cm. high.
(Christie's) **£2,070 $3,325**

A Bizarre vase, decorated in the 'Appliqué Lugano' pattern, painted in colours with blue roof and orange sky, 8in. high.
(Christie's) **£1,100 $1,800**

'Inspiration Tibetan', a Bizarre vase, shape no.370, painted with bands in shades of blue and brown, on a turquoise ground, printed and painted marks, 15cm. high.
(Christie's) **£500 $815**

'Inspiration', a Bizarre Yo Yo vase, painted with stylised flowers in shades of blue and ochre on a turquoise ground, printed factory marks, 23cm. high
(Christie's) **£1,150 $1,875**

Clarice Cliff Newport baluster vase, moulded and painted in colours with motifs of parrot perched on a branch, sepia rubber stamp mark, shape no. 844, 8½in.
(G.A. Key) **£90 $145**

'Orange Taormina', a vase, shape no.452, painted in colours, printed factory marks, 22cm. high. *(Christie's)* **£575 $935**

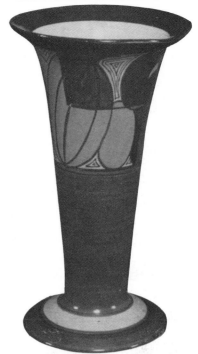

'Melon', a Fantasque Bizarre trumpet vase, shape no.278, painted in colours between blue, orange and purple bands, printed factory marks, 23cm. high. *(Christie's)* **£690 $1,125**

A Fantasque Bizarre squat oviform ribbed vase, shape no. 671, decorated in the 'Pastel Autumn' pattern, 4¼in. high. *(Christie's)* **£350 $575**

Clarice Cliff Newport Bizarre cylindrical vase with collar rim, decorated with abstract pattern of parallel orange, lemon, green and blue bars, black rubber stamp mark, 8in. high. *(G.A. Key)* **£590 $926**

A 'Honolulu' pattern flanged vase, shape 464, 8¹/8in. high, lithograph mark *Fantasque Hand Painted Bizarre by Clarice Cliff Newport Pottery England* and relief moulded mark *464*. *(Bonhams)* **£1,700 $2,770**

Clarice Cliff Inspiration double conical vase with hand written mark.
(Muir Hewitt) **£725 $1,087**

Clarice Cliff Goldstone vase with floral decoration, 7in high, 1930s.
(Muir Hewitt) **£150 $245**

'Clouvre Tulip', a Bizarre Isis vase, painted in shades of red, yellow, green and blue on a deep blue ground, printed and painted marks, 25cm. high.
(Christie's) **£1,380 $2,250**

Clarice Cliff Orange Hydrangea bulbous vase with floral decoration, 8in. high.
(Muir Hewitt) **£550 $900**

A Bizarre Isis vase in the green colourway of the 'Devon' pattern, also known as 'Cornwall', painted in colours, 30cm. high.
(Christie's) **£935 $1,431**

A Fantasque Bizarre vase, shape no.365, decorated in the 'House and Bridge' pattern, painted in colours, 20.5cm. high.
(Christie's) **£385 $589**

'Delecia', a Bizarre globe vase, shape no.370, painted in colours, printed factory marks, 15cm. high.
(Christie's) **£805 $1,300**

A Fantasque mushroom vase, decorated in the 'Sunrise' pattern, painted in orange, green and blue, above orange banding, 5¼in. high. *(Christie's)* **£350 $560**

Clarice Cliff vase in a variation of the Forest Glen design with concentric banding instead of dripware.
(Muir Hewitt) **£600 $975**

Clarice Cliff Patina Brookfields lotus vase, 12in. high. *(Muir Hewitt)* **£650 $1,060**

A Fantasque Bizarre vase, shape no.356, decorated in the 'Blue Autumn' pattern, painted in colours, 20cm. high.
(Christie's) **£1,210 $1,851**

A Fantasque Archaic vase, decorated in the 'Broth' design, painted in green, black and red with corresponding banding, 25cm. high. *(Christie's)* **£1,760 $2,693**

A Clarice Cliff Fantasque vase, shape no. 358, decorated in the 'Trees and House' pattern, painted in colours, 8in. high. *(Christie's)* **£550 $880**

A Clarice Cliff Fantasque Bizarre vase, decorated in the 'Orange House' pattern, painted in colours, 20cm. high. *(Christie's)* **£495 $752**

A Clarice Cliff vase of ovoid form with moulded Greek key frieze, Delecia pattern, 8½in. *(Russell, Baldwin & Bright)* **£260 $398**

A pair of Clarice Cliff Fantasque Bizarre vases, decorated in the 'Autumn' pattern, with bands of orange to rim and base, 9in. high. *(Christie's)* **£2,185 $3,583**

A fine Clarice Cliff Fantasque single handled Isis vase, decorated in the circles and trees pattern with broad orange band, circa 1930, 9½in. high. *(Anderson & Garland)* **£1,400 $2,198**

A 'Latona Red Roses' Isis vase, 9¾in. high, large rubber stamp *Hand Painted Bizarre by Clarice Cliff Newport Pottery England*, hand painted *Latona* and impressed *Isis*. *(Bonhams)* **£2,000 $3,260**

A Clarice Cliff vase in the form of a fish, tinged in light brown on a bed of pink and green weed, 23cm. high.
(Bearne's) **£190 $287**

A Fantasque Archaic vase, decorated in the 'Broth' design, painted in green, black and red with corresponding banding, 25cm. high. *(Christie's)* **£1,760 $2,693**

A Fantasque Bizarre globular vase, decorated in the 'Honolulu' pattern, painted in colours, 16cm. high.
(Christie's) **£1,870 $2,861**

'Kew', a Bizarre vase, shape no.264, painted in colours between green, orange and black bands, printed factory marks, 21cm. high.

This example of the 1931 'Kew' design is on an earlier shape 264 vase which was probably the work of Clarice Cliff before she launched her 'Bizarre' ware.
(Christie's) **£900 $1,465**

A Clarice Cliff twin-handled baluster vase, Bizarre, painted with a sunburst and geometric landscape between two broad orange borders, 11½in. high.
(George Kidner) **£2,000 $3,080**

'Red Tulip', a Fantasque Bizarre globe vase, shape no.370, painted in colours between orange bands, printed factory marks, 15cm. high.
(Christie's) **£3,220 $5,250**

A 'Football' pattern Archaic series vase, 375, 10in. high, large rubber stamp mark *Hand Painted Bizarre by Clarice Cliff Newport Pottery England.*
(Bonhams) **£1,700 $2,770**

'Appliqué Palermo', a Bizarre vase, shape no.280 trumpet form, painted in colours between red and black bands, printed factory marks, 16cm. high.

This is the first example of this landscape from the 'Appliqué' range known on a 362 vase. It demonstrates well how the paintresses were able to construct the full landscape design around pieces with the mountain on one side and the bay with yachts on the other.
(Christie's) **£1,150 $1,875**

A 'Solitude' pattern Isis vase, 10in. high, lithograph mark Hand Painted Bizarre by Clarice Cliff Newport Pottery England.
(Bonhams) **£1,300 $2,120**

'Inspiration', a Bizarre vase, shape no.358, painted in shades of blue, pink and ochre on a turquoise ground, printed factory marks, 20cm. high.
(Christie's) **£575 $935**

A 'Latona Tree' pattern globe shape vase, shape 370, 6in. high, hand painted *Latona* and rubber stamp mark *Hand Painted Bizarre by Clarice Cliff Newport Pottery England.* (Bonhams) **£1,000 $1,600**

'Lorna', a vase, shape no.362, painted in colours, printed factory marks, 21cm. high. (Christie's) **£483 $785**

Clarice Cliff My Garden vase, 7in. high, 1930s. (Muir Hewitt) **£200 $325**

'Sliced Circle', a Bizarre vase, shape no.268, painted in colours between blue bands, printed factory marks, 21cm. high.

The 'Sliced Circle' design first appeared in 1929. Interestingly this example still bears the original retailer's sticker on the base, *Haven's China & Glass Showrooms, Westcliffe on Sea.* The piece dates from around the same time as the window display the store staged for 'Bizarre' ware in December 1929.
(Christie's) **£1,380 $2,250**

'Inspiration Bouquet, a Bizarre vase, shape no.386, painted in turquoise and black on a violet ground, printed and painted marks, 30cm. high. (Christie's) **£517 $840**

A Bizarre vase, shape no.378, in the 'Mondrian' pattern, painted in colours, 20.5cm. high. (Christie's) **£935 $1,431**

'My Garden' vase from the Bizarre range by Clarice Cliff, 7in. high.
(Muir Hewitt) **£210 $319**

'Orange Autumn', a Fantasque Bizarre vase, shape no.451 painted in colours printed factory marks, 16cm. high. *(Christie's)* **£800 $1,300**

A 'Melon' pattern vase, shape 279, rubber stamp Fantasque *Hand Painted Bizarre by Clarice Cliff Newport Pottery England,* 8in. high. *(Bonhams)* **£500 $815**

'Crocus', a pair of miniature vases, ovoid with everted rim, painted in colours between yellow and brown bands, printed factory marks, 7cm. high. *(Christie's)* **£368 $600**

A fine Clarice Cliff Bizarre hexagonal vase decorated in 'The Graduated Football' pattern, 15in. high. *(Anderson & Garland)* **£2,500 $3,925**

A 'Latona Cartoon Flowers' pattern vase, shape 264, 8in. high, large rubber stamp *Hand Painted Bizarre by Clarice Cliff Newport Pottery England* and hand painted *Latona. (Bonhams)* **£500 $815**

A 'Latona Bizarre' stepped circular vase in the 'Red Roses' pattern, painted in red and black, 18in. high. *(Christie's)* **£3,080 $4,859**

Clarice Cliff Fantasque vase of spreading baluster form, decorated with the 'Melon' pattern of stylised fruit in colours, shape no. 365, 8in. high. *(G.A. Key)* **£340 $534**

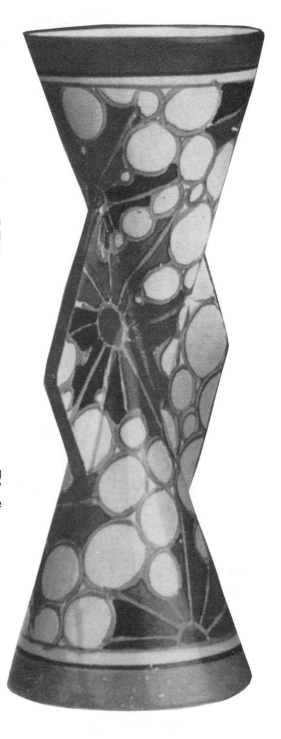

A 'Broth' pattern vase, shape 372, 8in. high, lithograph mark *Fantasque Hand Painted Bizarre by Clarice Cliff Newport Pottery, England* and impressed *372*. *(Bonhams)* **£480 $780**

A 'Broth' pattern Yo Yo vase, shape 379, 9¹/₈in. high, rubber stamp mark *Fantasque Hand painted Bizarre by Clarice Cliff Newport Pottery England* and gilt Lawleys retailer's mark. *(Bonhams)* **£3,700 $6,000**

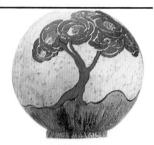

A 'Patina Tree' pattern globe shape vase, shape 370, 5¾in. high, printed mark *Patina* and rubber stamp for provisional patent. *(Bonhams)* **£800 $1,300**

'Rhodanthe', a Bizarre twin-handled Isis vase, painted in colours, printed factory marks, 25cm. high. *(Christie's)* **£600 $975**

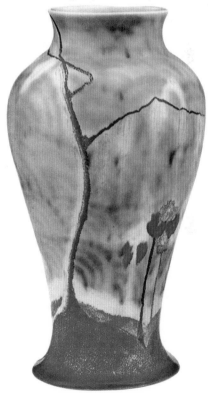

A 'House and Bridge' pattern Meiping Vase, shape 14, 16¼in. high, lithograph mark *Fantasque Hand Painted Bizarre by Clarice Cliff Newport Pottery England.* *(Bonhams)* **£7,500 $12,225**

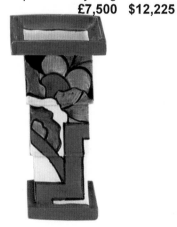

A 'Latona Dahlia' pattern vase, shape 369, 7¾in. high, rubber stamp mark *Hand Painted Bizarre by Clarice Cliff Newport Pottery England* and hand painted *Latona.* *(Bonhams)* **£900 $1,470**

An 'Inspiration Garden' Meiping vase, decorated with a tree amongst flowers and foliage, in shades of blue, brown and yellow on a turquoise ground, 12in. high, hand painted *Inspiration* lithograph mark *Hand Painted Bizarre by Clarice Cliff, Wilkinson Ltd. England.* *(Bonhams)* **£750 $1,225**

Hans Coper (1920-1981) trained as an engineer in his native Germany, but fled to England in the late '30s. During the war, he met another refugee, Lucie Rie, and went to work in her studio. They started making ceramic buttons, then graduated to domestic ware and in the evenings Coper could experiment with his own designs.

His biggest 'break' came when Basil Spence commissioned two candlesticks from him for Coventry Cathedral. His work is now established among the foremost modern pottery with prices to match.

A 'cup and disc' stoneware form by Hans Coper, buff with dark brown disc, impressed HC seal, circa 1965, 4½in. high. *(Bonhams)* **£2,750 $4,400**

A handsome sack form by Hans Coper, with wide brown disc rim on circular neck, the buff body accentuated with brown texturing, circa 1974, 9³/8in. high. *(Bonhams)* **£9,000 $16,515**

A massive stoneware 'Thistle' vase, by Hans Coper, dimpled disc-shaped body with flared rim, on cylindrical foot, circa 1960, 45.6cm. high. *(Christie's)* **£6,325 $9,994**

A small classic example of a bulbous form on a Stem by Hans Coper, buff with dark disc top and triangular design below the trim, impressed *HC* sign, 4¾in. high. *(Bonhams)* **£2,500 $4,000**

A tall stoneware flattened tapering cylinder with spherical belly-form by Hans Coper on drum base, incised with spiral decoration, covered in a bluish-buff slip, circa 1968, 21.2cm. high. *(Christie's)* **£8,000 $12,800**

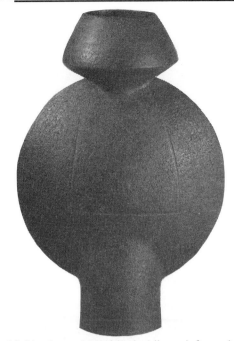

A fine stoneware 'Spade' form by Hans Coper, covered in a buff slip glaze with areas of blue glaze burnished to reveal matt manganese beneath, 31cm. high.
(Christie's) **£3,960 $6,690**

A highly important black 'discus' form by Hans Coper, incised rectangular form on one side, and with a spiral on the other, impressed *HC* seal, circa 1962, 10in. high.
(Bonhams) **£10,000 $16,000**

An early stoneware shallow dish by Hans Coper, covered in a matt manganese glaze, the interior with carved abstract spiralling decoration through to a pitted translucent white glaze, circa 1950, 35.3cm. diameter.
(Christie's) **£5,750 $9,200**

A wonderful oval cup form by Hans Coper, the upper part mottled with dark brown and deep orange, the cup mounted on a cylindrical base which rises to a point, circa 1972, 6¼in. high.
(Bonhams) **£15,000 $27,525**

A rare 'tripot' by Hans Coper, three cylindrical, straight-sided attached pots on narrowing feet decorated with sgraffito lines, circa 1956, 8in. high.
(Bonhams) **£5,000 $8,000**

A rare stoneware bell form pot by Hans Coper, the top third manganese merging into beige, circa 1963, 5in. high. *(Bonhams)* **£4,300 $6,800**

An early stoneware goblet pot by Hans Coper, dark brown over a shiny 'toffee' glaze, the foot unglazed, circa 1952, 6in. high. *(Bonhams)* **£2,500 $4,000**

An early stoneware goblet form by Hans Coper, manganese over a 'toffee' glaze, unglazed foot, impressed *HC* seal, circa 1952, 4¾in. high.*(Bonhams)* **£2,500 $4,000**

A large stoneware bowl by Hans Coper, with horse and rider sgraffito design, impressed *HC* seal, circa 1955, 14¼in. diameter. *(Bonhams)* **£6,000 $9,600**

An outstanding stoneware spade pot by Hans Coper, white with a deep manganese band at the rim merging into a textured surface, impressed *HC* seal, circa 1966, 7¼in. high. *(Bonhams)* **£8,000 $12,500**

A fine stoneware white pot by Hans Coper, the squared form on a drum base, hollowed impressions on both sides, impressed *HC* seal, circa 1975, 5in. high. *(Bonhams)* **£5,250 $8,400**

An important early stoneware 'thistle' form pot by Hans Coper, with diagonal texturing, impressed *HC* seal, circa 1958, 12¼in. high. *(Bonhams)* **£6,750 $10,800**

A stoneware buff cup form by Hans Coper, on a conical base surmounted by a manganese disc, impressed *HC* seal, circa 1970, 6¾in. high. *(Bonhams)* **£1,350 $2,160**

An important early stoneware bottle form by Hans Coper, brown with sgraffito revealing the cream body. This historic pot relates to Coper's discovery of sgraffito together with Lucie Rie, 11in. high. *(Bonhams)* **£5,000 $8,000**

A fine stoneware standing form by Hans Coper, the spherical body surmounted by a flattened oval form, the spherical form has inlaid horizontal lines and the whole surface with orange and brown spots, impressed *HC* seal, circa 1970, 7³/8in. high. *(Bonhams)* **£7,500 $12,000**

A superb stoneware 'egg-in-cup' form by Hans Coper, white with distinctive brown and bluish shading, impressed *HC* seal, circa 1975, 7³/8in. high. *(Bonhams)* **£7,250 $11,600**

A rare cup form stoneware pot by Hans Coper, distinguished by two dark textured panels and two vertical incised lines, impressed *HC* seal, circa 1970, 6¼in. high. *(Bonhams)* **£6,250 $10,000**

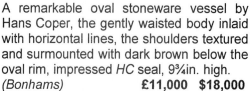

A remarkable oval stoneware vessel by Hans Coper, the gently waisted body inlaid with horizontal lines, the shoulders textured and surmounted with dark brown below the oval rim, impressed *HC* seal, 9¾in. high.
(Bonhams) **£11,000 $18,000**

A stoneware shallow bowl by Hans Coper, the interior covered in a matt manganese glaze, the centre carved with circular band, impressed *HC* seal, 17.5cm. diameter.
(Christie's) **£2,000 $3,200**

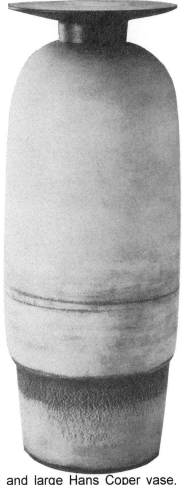

A round stoneware pot by Hans Coper, with a narrow neck and disc top, the body textured to reveal the dark body, the disc top a blend of dark and rust brown, impressed *HC* seal, 6¼in. high.
(Bonhams) **£7,000 $11,400**

A fine and large Hans Coper vase, dated 1972, the cylindrical body rounded at the shoulder and set with a flat disc rim covered in a brown glaze, on a short cylindrical neck, buff glazed with an inlaid brown line and a brown textured glaze around the narrowed base, impressed HC seal, inscribed underneath: *1.X.1972 HC. To Writhlington School. Thank you for Jennea the goat.* Writhlington School, 30¾in. *(Sotheby's)* **£18,400 $29,624**

A stoneware bulbous form on a stem by Hans Coper, surmounted with a two-tone brown disc, circa 1965, 4½in. high. (Bonhams) **£2,200 $4,037**

A stoneware vase form by Hans Coper, buff merging into brown towards the everted rim, with two vertical brown bands, impressed *HC* seal, circa 1958, 8¼in. high. (Bonhams) **£3,500 $5,600**

A stoneware spherical vase, by Hans Coper, with horizontal flange, 1951, 19cm. high. *(Christie's)* **£10,000 $16,000**

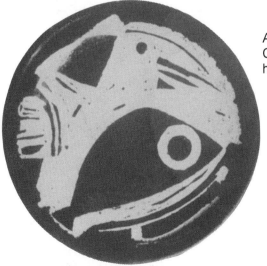

A rare early stoneware shallow dish by Hans Coper, covered in matt manganese glaze, the interior with carved decoration through to a pitted translucent white glaze of abstract design with stylised fish, impressed *HC* seal, circa 1950, 37cm. diameter. *(Christie's)* **£20,900 $37,202**

A fine black stoneware cup form by Hans Coper, made in three pieces, impressed *HC* seal, circa 1965, 6in. high. *(Bonhams)* **£6,250 $10,000**

The greatest name in crested china was Goss but there were some 200 other makers who copied the lead set set by William Henry Goss and his enterprising son Adolphus. The names of their British rivals include Arcadian, Carlton, Foley, Fords China, Grafton China, Macintyre, Melba, Nautilus, Podmore, Savoy, Shelley, Tuscan and Victoria. There were also foreign competitors, notably in Austria, Czechoslovakia and Germany, where even the inmates of German prisons were producing souvenir ware. Rather than compete with their own potteries they chose to flood the British market. From a postcard of a British building they could have the finished article on the market in British shops within a fortnight. Possibly because of this speed and also the language problem, they often misspelt the spelling of the crest or motto which rather adds to the charm.

Crested china boomed as a result of the enthusiasm for day trips and holidays that overtook the British public at the end of the 19th century. Trippers wanted a souvenir of their trip away from home and the perfect solution was a cheap little piece of china with the holiday town's coat of arms on it. Several subjects dominate the china manufacturers' output – the Great War – one of the more unusual items was a figure of Old Bill produced by Shelley; animals and birds; transport; memorials including the Cenotaph; statues; cartoon and comedy characters; sport and musical instruments. A cup and saucer was one of the most common items sold and, as a result today the price for such an item would be considerably less than for an Old Bill or a model of the Cenotaph. The rivals to Goss never took such fastidious care about their products as the trail blazers and their china is never as fine. However when buying crested china it is important to remember that imperfections of manufacture do not affect the price so much as subsequent damage.

While not strictly in the Art Deco style, Crested china flourished throughout the Art Deco period and its kitschiness certainly brings it into the same tradition.

Savoy china, 'Snail', 84mm. long. (Lyle) £35 $55

Carlton fireplace with cauldron in the fireplace, 80mm. wide. (Lyle) £25 $40

Arcadian 'Black cat in a boot', 61mm. high. (Lyle) £60 $100

Arcadian 'Jester on a spade shaped tray', 65mm. wide. *(Lyle)* **£70 $115**

Willow art 'Old Curiosity Shop', 80mm. wide. *(Lyle)* **£160 $250**

Carlton Donkey inscribed *Gee up Neddy*, 110mm. wide. *(Lyle)* **£45 $70**

Carlton 'Owl wearing black mortar board', 75mm. wide. *(Lyle)* **£25 $40**

Arcadian 'Black boy holding pumpkin mustard pot with lid'. *(Lyle)* **£120 $190**

Arcadian 'Policeman holding truncheon', 106mm. high. *(Lyle)* **£70 $115**

Carlton 'Jackie Coogan', 1920s cartoon character inkwell with lid, 73mm. wide. *(Lyle)* **£50 $80**

Arcadian 'Black cat climbing pillar box to post letter', 56mm. high. *(Lyle)* **£70 $115**

Grafton, 'Child kneeling on beach with bucket and spade', 75mm. wide. *(Lyle)* **£130 $210**

Arcadian 'Black boy and girl on log', 80mm. wide. *(Lyle)*   **£85 $135**

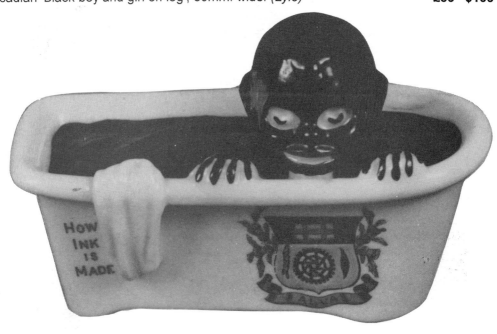

Arcadian black boy in bath of ink, towel hanging at side, inscribed *How ink is made*, with arms of Torquay. *(Crested China Co.)*
                                                        £100 $150

Arcadian black cat on wall with arms of Portsmouth. *(Crested China Co.)* **£75 $120**

Carlton 'Irishman in black hat with yellow pig', 90mm. wide. *(Lyle)* **£160 $250**

Carlton black cat on horseshoe dish. *(Crested China Co.)* **£36 $57**

Gemma recumbent cow creamer, arms of Eastbourne. *(Crested China Co.)* **£36 $57**

Carlton 'Black cat on settee', 80mm. wide. *(Lyle)* **£35 $55**

Arcadian black cat sailing yacht. *(Crested China Co.)* **£125 $200**

Arcadian walking donkey. *(Crested China Co.)* **£75 $120**

Arcadian 'Mr. Pickwick' on horseshoe shaped ashtray base. *(Crested China Co.)* **£95 $152**

Grafton ambulance, arms of Falmouth. *(Crested China Co.)* **£95 $152**

Arcadian 'Drunkard leaning against a statue', 100mm. high. *(Lyle)* **£130 $210**

Grafton airfield tractor, arms of Leamington Spa. *(Crested China Co.)* **£250 $400**

Carlton 'Goose standing on a green base', 85mm. wide. *(Lyle)* **£35 $55**

Arcadian milk basket.
(Goss & Crested China Ltd.)
£20 $30

Arcadian Black Cat radio
operator. *(Goss & Crested
China Ltd)* **£100 $150**

Savoy china fireplace *Keep
the home fires burning*,
94mm. *(Lyle)* **£25 $40**

Grafton Boy with toy yacht.
(Goss & Crested China Ltd.)
£120 $180

Swan china bust of Ally
Sloper.
(Goss & Crested China Ltd.)
£40 $60

Shelley Scottie wearing Tam
O' Shanter.
(Goss & Crested China Ltd.)
£40 $60

Carlton 'Laxey Wheel',
92mm. wide.
(Lyle) **£60 $100**

Carlton cat pepper pot.
(Goss & Crested China Ltd)
£15 $22

Carlton 'Trefoil Dish with five
flags of the Allies'.
(Lyle) **£35 $55**

248

The Crown Devon dynasty was founded by Simon Fielding, who in 1873 invested his savings in the Railway Pottery, Stoke on Trent, with his son Abraham as first apprentice and then partner in the Cresswell Colour Mill.

In 1878, with the Railway Pottery on the edge of bankruptcy, Abraham bought it out and increased its size fivefold by the time his father died in 1906. Abraham was in turn succeeded by his son and grandson. The trade name Crown Devon was introduced in 1913.

The factory was a major producer of items in the Art Deco style, many featuring stylised flowers and fruit set against a rich, dark background. Major ranges include the Mattajade (jade green plates with stylised floral patterns), the Mattatone (matt glazes with Cubist patterns) and Garden ware (decorated with highly coloured flowers on a green, cream or yellow base). Musical novelties were also introduced and, from the 1930s, salad ware and figurines. Many figurines were the work of Kathleen Fisher, and were of an astonishing lightness and delicacy.

Throughout the succeeding decades, the factory moved with the times, continuing to adapt its products to current trends, despite a devastating fire which gutted it in 1951. It continued in business until 1982, when it became an early victim of the recession.

Marks include *FIELDING*, impressed, and *SF & Co* printed with the pattern title.

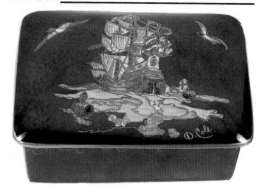

Crown Devon 1930s box and cover designed by D. Cole 5½in. wide.
(Muir Hewitt) **£75 $125**

Crown Devon jug, 1930s, with floral and fruit design, 8in. high.
(Muir Hewitt) **£60 $100**

A Crown Devon octagonal bowl with fluted rim, printed and painted in colours and gilt on a blue ground with a ferocious dragon among flowers, 23cm. diameter.
(Christie's) **£150 $240**

Art Deco cake stand with chromium plate support and Crown Devon floral design plate. *(Muir Hewitt)* **£50 $85**

Crown Devon Dismal Desmond dog in turquoise, 1930s.
(Muir Hewitt) **£40 $65**

Stockholm Crown Devon jampot in red and black, 1950s. *(Muir Hewitt)* **£30 $50**

A Crown Devon baluster vase of footed ovoid form with flaring conical neck, painted with figures in a pagoda landscape, 29cm. high. *(Christie's)* **£250 $400**

A pair of Crown Devon twin-handled vases, ovoid form with fluted base to footrim, collar neck with twin scroll handles, 20cm. high. *(Christie's)* **£600 $975**

A Crown Devon coffeepot and cover painted with a geometric pattern of overlapping circles and diamonds, 19.5cm. high. *(Christie's)* **£77 $117**

Crown Devon lamp base with elaborate enamelled oriental dragon design, 6in. high. *(Muir Hewitt)* **£210 $315**

Crown Devon jug, 1930s, with floral decoration. (Muir Hewitt) **£30 $48**

Crown Devon vase with floral decoration and looped handles, 1930s.
(Muir Hewitt) **£100 $160**

Crown Devon part teaset comprising teapot and cover cup, saucer, plate, cream and sugar, 1930s, teapot 5in. high.
(Muir Hewitt) **£300 $500**

'Mattajade', a Crown Devon single-handled vase, printed and painted in colours and gilt on turquoise ground, printed factory marks, 23cm. high.
(Christie's) **£690 $1,125**

This was a trademark used by A.G. Richardson & Co Ltd, who set up in business at the Gordon Pottery in Tunstall in 1915.

From the outset they produced bright, attractive modern pieces, including their popular Red Tree pattern, which first appeared in 1925, with a stark depiction of black tree silhouettes with bright orange fruit.

In 1931, Charlotte Rhead came to work for them and designed plaques, vases, lamps, tableware and nursery pottery, producing some of her best and most successful designs. Among these were Persian Rose, Byzantine, Rhodian, Wisteria, Indian Tree and, perhaps most popular of all, the ubiquitous Golden Leaves pattern. These would be marked with *C. Rhead* tube lined on the base, with A.G. Richardson's Crown Ducal trademark.

There was such demand for their products that in 1933 Richardson expanded by buying the Britannia Pottery in Cobridge, which they finally sold in 1974 to Wedgwood, and moved to Nottingley in Yorkshire.

Their most common mark is a crown with *Crown Ducal Ware England* below, which came in around 1925. Occasionally one finds an earlier mark, with a crown on an oval belt with *Ducal* on a ribbon across the centre and *A.G.R. & Co. Ltd. England* below.

Crown Ducal pair of vases and matching bowl with fruit design on a lustre background, 1930s.
(Muir Hewitt) **£250 $400**

Crown Ducal dish with stylised tree design, 7in. long. 1930s.
(Muir Hewitt) **£35 $60**

Crown Ducal swell bodied vase, 8in. high, 1930s. *(Muir Hewitt)* **£140 $230**

Crown Ducal three handled vase with floral decoration. *(Muir Hewitt)* **£50 $75**

Crown Ducal tea pot, 1930s, with floral design. *(Muir Hewitt)* **£40 $60**

Crown Ducal wall plaque 14in. diameter, with stylised leaf pattern, circa 1930. *(Muir Hewitt)* **£100 $160**

Charlotte Rhead vase, 1930s, Crown Ducal, 8in. high. *(Muir Hewitt)* **£150 $225**

Crown Ducal vase, 6in. high, 1950s. *(Muir Hewitt)* **£40 $60**

Crown Ducal wall plaque, 1930s 12½in. diameter. *(Muir Hewitt)* **£80 $120**

Charlotte Rhead Crown Ducal Stitch pattern jug, 7in. high.
(Muir Hewitt) **£75 $112**

A Crown Ducal shaped and ribbed two handled cylindrical base decorated with a pattern by Charlotte Rhead, printed factory mark, 5½in. high.*(Christie's)* **£120 $195**

Charlotte Rhead Crown Ducal vase in Persian rose design, 10in. high.
(Muir Hewitt) **£200 $300**

'Byzantine', a Crown Ducal vase, designed by Charlotte Rhead, painted in colours on mottled orange ground, printed marks, 17.5cm. high.
(Christie's) **£200 $325**

1937 Coronation: A Crown Ducal pottery plate decorated in Art Nouveau style in blue, orange and gold. *(Phillips)* **£150 $245**

'Palermo', a Crown Ducal slender ovoid vase, painted in shades of green and turquoise, printed factory marks, 15cm. high.
(Christie's) **£200 $325**

Charlotte Rhead vase, 1930s, Crown Ducal, 8in. high.
(Muir Hewitt) **£210 $315**

Charlotte Rhead baluster jug, decorated with bunches of lemons, fruit and foliage in colours, Crown Ducal printed mark, signed, 8½in. *(G.A. Key)* **£135 $223**

A Charlotte Rhead Crown Ducal pottery vase, of tapering baluster form, decorated with a band of flowerheads and stylised foliage, 10in. high.
(Christie's) **£195 $306**

The 20th century state of Czechoslovakia incorporated Bohemia, which was always noted for its strong ceramic traditions. Until the First World War, too, it had been part of the Austro-Hungarian Empire, and so had been open to new styles coming out of Austria, such as those being produced by the Wiener Werkstätte. Royal Dux is one of the best known names of the period, as is Zsolnay, but there were numerous other smaller firms working with similar designs.

Czechoslovakian 1930s figure of a lady with fan. *(Muir Hewitt)* **£125 $200**

Teplitz pottery vase, Czechoslovakia, early 20th century, swollen form widening towards base, signed *Stillmacher Teplitz* and stamped, 8¼in. high. *(Skinner)* **£400 $650**

Early 20th century Czechoslovakian ceramic wall mask, of a woman's head, naturalistically coloured and wearing an orange cream and yellow head dress, 7½in. *(Peter Wilson)* **£140 $211**

A Czechoslovakian pottery figure modelled as an elegant young woman wearing long orange evening dress, walking with two attendant borzoi, on a lobed oval base, printed mark and impressed numerals, 40cm. high. *(Christie's)* **£345 $560**

Czech Art Deco vase with stitch pattern, Charlotte Rhead used this pattern as a basis for her well known Stitch design, 1930s. *(Muir Hewitt)* **£50 $85**

CZECHOSLOVAKIAN

Czechoslovakian 1930s dancing lady.
(Muir Hewitt) **£140 $230**

1930s coffee service, Czechoslovakian with silver lustre decoration, six cups & saucers, coffee pot, cream and sugar.
(Muir Hewitt) **£200 $325**

Czechoslovakian wall mask, circa 1930, based on Marlene Dietrich.
(Muir Hewitt) **£245 $400**

Czechoslovakian figure of a nude female with red headscarf, 1930s.
(Muir Hewitt) **£200 $325**

Art Deco Czech figure of a dancing lady, 1930s. *(Muir Hewitt)* **£125 $200**

Czechoslovakian face mask of a young lady with flowers in her hair, 1930s. *(Muir Hewitt)* **£150 $245**

Czechoslovakian figure of a girl, 1930s, 10in. high. *(Muir Hewitt)* **£125 $200**

Czechoslovakian figure of a Spanish dancing lady,1930s, 9in. high. *(Muir Hewitt)* **£160 $260**

Czechoslovakian figure of girl with a pair of dogs, 1930s. *(Muir Hewitt)* **£150 $245**

Czechoslovakian painted terracotta wall mask of a lady, circa 1930, 5in. high. *(Muir Hewitt)* **£150 $245**

The Dedham Pottery was established in 1895, following the move of the Chelsea Keramic Art Works to Dedham Mass. under Hugh Robertson, who had succeeded his father as master potter at Chelsea. At Dedham, Robertson produced a crackle glaze on a heavy stoneware decorated with borders of bird and animal designs. Dedham Ware was made in forty eight patterns and proved very popular. Its mark is *Dedham Pottery* over a crouching rabbit.

Dedham Pottery Cat pattern plate, one impressed rabbit, 8½in, diameter.
(Skinner) **£1,225 $2,000**

Large Dedham Pottery high glaze vase, by Hugh Robertson, frothy sea green glaze with hints of red oxide, incised Dedham Pottery, 8½in. high.
(Skinner) **£1,840 $3,000**

Three Dedham Pottery chick pattern items, plate, exhibition sticker, blue stamp, impressed rabbit, 8½in. diameter, bowl and a child's mug, blue stamp.
(Skinner) **£1,150 $1,725**

A crackle ware pottery dinner plate, by Dedham Pottery, the centre painted in blue with a white terrier posed in a landscape, 9¾in. diameter. *(Christie's)* **£652 $1,035**

Dedham Pottery Magnolia pattern plate, blue registered stamp, two impressed rabbits, 7½in. diameter.
(Skinner) **£125 $200**

Dedham Pottery Poppy decoration plate, blue stamp, blue X, one impressed rabbit, 8½in. diameter. *(Skinner)* **£920 $1,500**

Dedham Pottery mushroom pattern pitcher, blue stamp, impressed rabbit, 4¾in. high. *(Skinner)* **£765 $1,150**

Four Dedham Pottery coffee mugs, iris, snowtree, horsechestnut, and magnolia pattern, Dedham mark, 3¼in. high. *(Skinner)* **£437 $690**

Dedham Pottery Crab decorated plate, blue stamp, one impressed rabbit, 10in. diameter. *(Skinner)* **£655 $1,092**

Dedham Pottery Fairbanks House plate, blue registered stamp, two impressed rabbits, 8½in. diameter. *(Skinner)* **£1,035 $1,725**

Dedham Pottery oak block pitcher, unmarked, 6in. high. *(Skinner)* **£575 $863**

Dedham Pottery Elephant pattern covered sugar, blue stamp, 2½in. high, 4¼in. diameter. *(Skinner)* **£920 $1,500**

Dedham Pottery Owl and Lion pattern pitcher, blue stamp, 5½in. wide. *(Skinner)* **£920 $1,500**

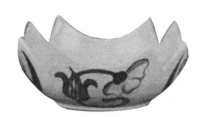

A rare 'elephant' crackle ware pottery paperweight, by Dedham Pottery, modelled as an elephant, painted with features in blue, 4in. high. *(Christie's)* **£4,202 $6,670**

Dedham Pottery Chinese cut bowl with poppy decoration, blue registered stamp, 3½in. high, 8½in. wide. *(Skinner)* **£1,225 $2,000**

A 'Crab' crackle ware pottery serving platter, by Dedham Pottery, decorated in blue with a single large crab and bit of seaweed, 17⅝in. long. *(Christie's)* **£2,028 $3,220**

A 'rabbit' pattern crackle ware pottery No. 1 creamer and No. 1 covered sugar, by Dedham Pottery, decorated in blue in the rabbit pattern, creamer 3½in. high. *(Christie's)* **£544 $863**

Dedham Pottery Polar Bear pattern celery dish, blue stamp, 9¾in. long, 6¼in. wide. *(Skinner)* **£920 $1,500**

Dedham Pottery Snow Tree pattern cup and saucer, blue registered stamp, 2¾in. high, 6in. diameter. *(Skinner)* **£90 $150**

Dedham Pottery Lobster cup, blue registered stamp, 3in. high, 4in. wide. *(Skinner)* **£300 $500**

Dedham Pottery Rabbit pattern salt and pepper, 3in. high, 2½in. diameter. *(Skinner)* **£430 $700**

Dedham Pottery Grape pattern cup and saucer, blue registered stamp, 2¾in. high, 6in. diameter. *(Skinner)* **£90 $150**

Dedham Pottery Turkey pattern cup and saucer, blue registered stamp, 3¼in. high, 6in. diameter. *(Skinner)* **£305 $500**

An 'elephant' pattern crackle ware pottery child's mug, by Dedham Pottery, decorated in blue, 3in. high. *(Christie's)* **£2,536 $4,025**

Dedham Pottery Rabbit pattern bowl, incised *Dedham Pottery* and stamp mark, 4in. high, diameter 9¼in. *(Skinner)* **£430 $700**

Dedham Pottery Turkey pattern covered tureen, blue stamp, 5¾in. high, 9in. diameter. *(Skinner)* **£1,850 $3,000**

Dedham Pottery Rabbit pattern celery tray, blue registered stamp, 9¾in. long, 6¼in. wide. *(Skinner)* **£300 $500**

Dedham Pottery Golden Gate plate, signed *H.C.R.*, blue stamp, M. Shephard, 10in. diameter. *(Skinner)* **£1,587 $2,645**

Dedham Pottery Rabbit Pattern pitcher, blue registered stamp, 6¼in. high x 7in. wide. *(Skinner)* **£345 $575**

Dedham Pottery Rabbit pattern covered tureen, blue stamp, 8in. high, 11in. wide, 7in. deep. *(Skinner)* **£1,530 $2,500**

Dedham Pottery Polar Bear pattern plate, blue stamp, 8½in. diameter. *(Skinner)* **£920 $1,500**

Dedham Pottery Swan pattern charger, blue stamp, initial *A*, 12½in. diameter. *(Skinner)* **£550 $900**

Dedham Pottery Rabbit pattern coffee pot, blue registered stamp, 8¾in. high, 7in. wide. *(Skinner)* **£735 $1,200**

Dedham Pottery Dolphin pattern bowl, blue stamp, one impressed rabbit, 9in. diameter. *(Skinner)* **£550 $900**

Dedham Pottery Oak block pitcher, blue registered stamp, 6in. high, 6¼in. wide. *(Skinner)* **£550 $900**

Three Dedham Pottery Rabbit pattern cups and saucers, blue stamp, 2½in. high, 5¼in. diameter; blue stamp, 2¾in. high, 5¼in. diameter; blue stamp, 2½in. high, 5¼in. diameter. *(Skinner)* **£300 $500**

Dedham Pottery stork pattern plate, raised design, blue stamp, diameter 9in. *(Skinner)* **£3,594 $5,750**

Dedham Pottery Lobster decorated plate, rebus for Maud Davenport, blue stamp, two impressed rabbits, 8½in diameter. *(Skinner)* **£920 $1,500**

Dedham Pottery Owl pattern cup and saucer, blue registered stamp, 2½in. high, 6¼in. diameter. *(Skinner)* **£920 $1,500**

Dedham Pottery Chick pattern bowl, blue registered stamp, 2in. high, 5½in. diameter. *(Skinner)* **£920 $1,500**

Dedham Pottery Swan pattern square dish, blue registered stamp, 2¾in. high, 8¼ x 8¼in. *(Skinner)* **£735 $1,200**

Dedham Pottery Elephant pattern cup and saucer, blue registered stamp, 3½in. high, 6¼in. diameter. *(Skinner)* **£550 $900**

Dedham Pottery Strawberry Pattern plate, raised design, signed Jacob, 6½in. diameter. *(Skinner)* **£920 $1,500**

Dedham Pottery Butterfly with Flower Pattern plate, blue registered mark, two impressed rabbits, 9½in. diameter. *(Skinner)* **£655 $1,092**

Dedham Pottery Dolphin pattern platter, blue registered mark, one impressed rabbit, 13in. long, 8in. wide. *(Skinner)* **£2,145 $3,500**

Dedham Pottery Turkey pattern pickle dish, blue registered stamp, 10in. long. 5in. wide. *(Skinner)* **£370 $600**

Dedham Pottery Rabbit Pattern mug, blue stamp, 5in. high x 5½in. wide. *(Skinner)* **£276 $460**

Dedham Potter Swan pattern creamer, blue registered stamp, 2¼in. high, 5½in. wide. *(Skinner)* **£300 $500**

Dedham Pottery Turtle paperweight, blue registered stamp, 3¼in. long, 2¼in. wide. *(Skinner)* **£920 $1,500**

Dedham Pottery Turtle pattern cup and saucer, blue registered stamp, 3½in. high, 6in. diameter. *(Skinner)* **£920 $1,500**

Dedham Pottery Rabbit pattern bowl, unusual pink glaze, incised *Dedham Pottery*, blue numbering *420*, 3½in. high, 9in. diameter. *(Skinner)* **£1,850 $3,000**

Dedham Pottery Azalea pattern covered tureen, circular form, blue stamp, 5¾in. high, 9½in. diameter. *(Skinner)* **£920 $1,500**

Dedham Pottery Grape pattern plate, raised design, blue stamp, one impressed rabbit, 8½in. diameter. *(Skinner)* **£185 $300**

Dedham Pottery Swan pattern tea tile, blue registered stamp, 5½ x 5½in. *(Skinner)* **£370 $600**

Dedham Pottery Grape pattern pitcher, blue stamp, 4½in. high, 5in. wide. *(Skinner)* **£150 $250**

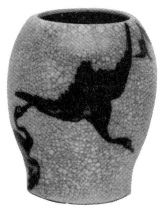

Dedham Pottery Grouse pattern plate, blue stamp, one impressed rabbit, diameter 8¾in. *(Skinner)* **£1,225 $2,000**

Early 20th century Dedham pottery decorated crackleware vase, 7½in. high. *(Skinner)* **£1,200 $1,950**

A 'rabbit' pattern crackle ware pottery No. 3 covered sugar bowl, by Dedham Pottery, the octagonal body moulded with two handles, 6¼in. high. including cover. *(Christie's)* **£471 $748**

Dedham Pottery Horse Chestnut pattern plate, rebus for Maud Davenport, raised design, blue stamp, 8½in. diameter. *(Skinner)* **£86 $143**

Dedham Pottery Turtle and Leaf pattern plate, blue stamp, one impressed rabbit, 10in. diameter. *(Skinner)* **£920 $1,500**

A 'rabbit' pattern crackle ware pottery covered egg cup, by Dedham Pottery, egg-shaped on shallow dish base, 4¼in. high. *(Christie's)* **£796 $1,265**

Dedham Pottery Rabbit pattern teapot, blue registered stamp, 5½in. high., 7in. wide. *(Skinner)* **£735 $1,200**

Dedham Pottery Fish pattern plate, scalloped edge, blue stamp, 9in. diameter. *(Skinner)* **£2,415 $4,025**

A rare crackle ware pottery dish, by Dedham Pottery, modelled with a naked lady reclining, 4½in. long.
(Christie's) **£1,014 $1,610**

Dedham Pottery Lobster decorated plate, blue registered stamp, two impressed rabbits, 10in. diameter.
(Skinner) **£920 $1,500**

Dedham Pottery Stein, Massachusetts, early 20th century, rabbit pattern, impressed and ink stamped marks, 5¼in. *(Skinner)* **£117 $225**

Chelsea Pottery U.S. Clover pattern plate, raised design, impressed *C.P.U.S.* mark, 10in. diameter. *(Skinner)* **£920 $1,500**

A rare crackle ware pottery breakfast plate, by Dedham Pottery, the raised border decorated in blue with long-beaked ibis birds, 9in. diameter.
(Christie's) **£797 $1,265**

A 'rabbit' pattern crackle ware pottery ashtray, by Dedham Pottery, decorated in blue in the rabbit pattern, 3^7/$_8$in. diameter.
(Christie's) **£51 $81**

Dedham Pottery Elephant pattern egg cup, blue stamp, 3in. high.*(Skinner)***£735 $1,200**

Dedham Pottery Moth and Flower plate, blue stamp, H.C.R., exhibition Sticker No. 46, 10in. diameter.
(Skinner) **£1,225 $2,000**

Dedham Pottery Rabbit pattern covered sugar bowl, obscured blue stamp, 4^3/$_4$in. high, 5in. wide. *(Skinner)* **£300 $500**

A 'lion' pattern crackle ware pottery dinner plate, by Dedham Pottery, the border decorated in blue in the tapestry lion pattern, 10^1/$_8$in. *(Christie's)* **£796 $1,265**

Dedham pottery swan pattern dish, oblong form, registered mark, 10in. long, 5½in. wide. *(Skinner)* **£300 $500**

Dedham Pottery Turkey Pattern plate, raised design, blue stamp, one impressed rabbit, 8½in. diameter.
(Skinner) **£370 $600**

A 'lobster' crackle ware pottery breakfast plate, by Dedham Pottery, decorated in blue with two lobsters, 8½in. diameter.
(Christie's) **£544 $863**

Dedham Pottery Grape pattern marmalade jar, blue stamp, 5¼in. high, 4½in. diameter.
(Skinner) **£430 $700**

Dedham Pottery Elephant pattern candlesticks, blue stamp, initials *A.R.*, 2in. high, 4in. diameter.
(Skinner) **£430 $700**

Dedham Pottery Snipe plate, blue stamp, 10in. diameter. *(Skinner)* **£2,932 $4,887**

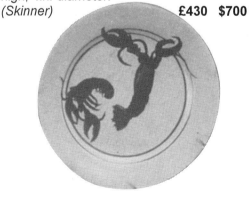

Dedham Pottery Double Lobster plate, blue stamp, one impressed rabbit, 8½in. diameter. *(Skinner)* **£920 $1,500**

Dedham Pottery Night and Morning pitcher, blue stamp, 4¾in. high.
(Skinner) **£150 $230**

Dedham Pottery Grape
pattern marmalade jar, blue
registered mark, 5in. high,
4½in. diameter.
(Skinner)   **£370 $600**

Dedham Pottery Peacock
pattern plate, one impressed
rabbit, 6in. diameter.
(Skinner)   **£920 $1,500**

Dedham Pottery Rabbit
pattern No. 3 covered sugar,
blue registered stamp, 6¼in.
high, 5in. wide.
(Skinner)   **£735 $1,200**

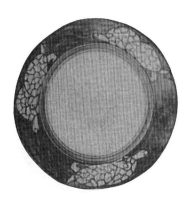

Dedham Pottery Turtle
pattern plate, blue stamp,
one impressed rabbit, 8½in.
diameter.
(Skinner)   **£1,225 $2,000**

Dedham Pottery Swan
pattern boot, blue stamp,
5in. high, 4in. wide, 2in.
deep.
(Skinner)   **£920 $1,500**

Dedham Pottery Pineapple
pattern plate, blue stamp,
8½in. diameter.
(Lyle)   **£920 $1,500**

Dedham Pottery Peacock
pattern plate, one impressed
rabbit, 6in. diameter.
(Skinner)   **£920 $1,500**

Dedham Pottery standing
bunny flower holder, hint of
blue stamp, 6¼in. high,
4¼in. diameter.
(Skinner)   **£920 $1,500**

Dedham Pottery Mushroom
pattern plate, blue stamp,
one impressed rabbit, 6in.
diameter.
(Skinner)   **£360 $600**

Dedham Pottery Wild Rose pattern plate, blue stamp, 6in. diameter.
(Skinner) **£300 $500**

Dedham Pottery Bunny knife rest, blue registered stamp, 2½in. high, 1½in. wide, 3½in. long.
(Skinner) **£550 $900**

Dedham Pottery Poppy plate, blue stamp, 6in. diameter.
(Skinner) **£735 $1,200**

Dedham Pottery pond lily plate with scenic centre, impressed rabbit, signed in centre *HR*, 6in. diameter.
(Skinner) **£650 $978**

A rare crackle ware pottery ashtray, by Dedham Pottery, signed by Charles Davenport, modelled as the figure of a little boy urinating, 4⁷/₈in. high.
(Christie's) **£579 $920**

Dedham Pottery Rabbit pattern child's plate, blue registered stamp, 7½in. diameter.
(Skinner) **£185 $300**

Dedham Pottery Swan pattern marmalade jar, blue registered stamp, 5in. high, 4½in.diameter.
(Skinner) **£735 $1,200**

Dedham Pottery Cherub and Goat pattern, raised design, blue stamp, 9in. diameter.
(Skinner) **£1,380 $2,300**

Dedham Pottery Grape pattern pitcher, blue registered stamp, 4¾in. high, 6¼in. wide.
(Skinner) **£90 $150**

A 'rabbit' pattern crackle ware pottery teapot, by Dedham Pottery, decorated in blue in the rabbit pattern, 5½in. high. *(Christie's)* **£869 $1,380**

A crackle ware pottery coaster, by Dedham Pottery, the small lobed dish painted to resemble a wild rose blossom, 3½in. diameter. *(Christie's)* **£109 $173**

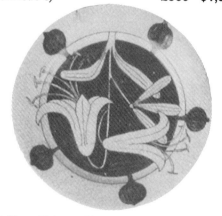

A 'tiger lily' crackle ware pottery bread and butter plate, by Dedham Pottery, the centre decorated with white lilies against blue, 6in. diameter. *(Christie's)* **£1,014 $1,610**

Dedham Pottery day/night pitcher, early 20th century, blue decoration on white craquelure ground, 5in. high. *(Skinner)* **£250 $400**

Dedham Pottery experimental vase, Massachusetts, late 19th/early 20th century, executed by Hugh C. Robertson, 6in. high. *(Skinner)* **£181 $350**

A rare crackle ware pottery dinner plate, by Dedham Pottery, the blue border design of turtles alternating with clover, 10in. diameter. *(Christie's)* **£2,608 $4,140**

Dedham Pottery Wolves and Owls Pattern plate, blue stamp, 12in. diameter. *(Skinner)* **£1,380 $2,300**

Dedham Pottery Mushroom pattern plate, blue stamp, one impressed rabbit, 8½in. diameter. *(Skinner)* **£610 $1,000**

Dedham Pottery Grape pattern charger, blue stamp, one impressed rabbit, 12in. diameter. *(Skinner)* **£345 $575**

Dedham Pottery Moth plate, blue stamp, one impressed rabbit, 8½in. diameter. *(Skinner)* **£920 $1,500**

Dedham Pottery Crab plate, blue stamp, one impressed rabbit, 8½in. diameter. *(Skinner)* **£920 $1,500**

Dedham Pottery Reverse Dolphin in Waves decorated plate, signed H.C.R., J.L.S., blue stamp, 8½in. diameter. *(Skinner)* **£1,850 $3,000**

DELLA ROBBIA

The Della Robbia pottery was established in 1894 at Birkenhead by H. Rathbone and the sculptor Conrad Dressler. It produced vases, bottles, jars, plates and dishes with sgraffito decoration and sometimes elaborate relief modelling with a strong Italian maiolica influence.

The factory closed in 1901, but reopened and continued until 1906. Their mark consists of *Della Robbia* with a ship's device and the decorator's initials.

A Della Robbia dish, with incised and slip decoration of a sea sprite riding a fish, covered with polychrome glaze, dated *1895*, 26.2cm. diameter.
(Christie's) **£375 $610**

A Della Robbia two-handled vase, of bulbous cylindrical form with knopped neck, with incised *Della Robbia* mark and signature, *Enid*, 34.8cm. high.
(Christie's) **£715 $1,165**

A Della Robbia twin-handled vase, decorated by Charles Collis, with eight circular medallions, each with a sea-creature, 35.8cm. high.
(Christie's) **£660 $1,075**

A Della Robbia vase decorated by Charles Collis, with an incised frieze of running hounds against a background, 32.5cm. high.
(Christie's) **£600 $975**

A Della Robbia vase decorated by Liz Wilkins, with slip decoration of frogs, lily-pads, flowers and grasses, 38.8cm. high.
(Christie's) **£1,500 $2,450**

A Della Robbia twin-handled vase decorated by Charles Collis, with a broad decorative frieze of stylised Tudor Roses, 31.6cm. high.
(Christie's) **£660 $1,075**

A Della Robbia vase, with incised and slip decoration of two friezes of equestrian and Ancient Greek figures, 18.4cm. high.
(Christie's) **£165 $270**

A Della Robbia vase of swollen cylindrical shape with flaring cylindrical neck, incised *Della Robbia* mark, 22.2cm. high.
(Christie's) **£150 $240**

A Della Robbia pottery vase by Roseville Pottery, signed with Rozane Ware seal, circa 1906, 8¼in. high.
(Christie's) **£590 $960**

A Della Robbia bottle vase, by Charles Collis, the piped slip decoration of peaches and leaves, 33.5cm. high.
(Christie's) **£330 $535**

A Della Robbia two-handled vase, with incised and slip decoration of foliate designs within large cartouches and borders, 35.2cm. high.
(Christie's) **£300 $490**

A Della Robbia wall charger, the base incised *DR* with a sailing ship and artist monogram, 47.5cm. diameter.
(Christie's) **£380 $620**

A Della Robbia two-handled vase, decorated by Annie Smith, of bulbous cylindrical form with knopped neck, dated *1895*, 37.6cm. high.
(Christie's) **£220 $360**

A Della Robbia vase decorated by Liz Wilkins, with incised and slip decoration of frogs amongst lily-pads and flowers, dated *1903*, 38.5cm. high.
(Christie's) **£715 $1,280**

A Della Robbia pottery vase, with marks of *Chas. Collis*, potter and sgraffito artist and *G. Russell*, paintress, circa 1903/6, 11in. high. **£180 $290**

A Della Robbia twin-handled vase decorated by Liz Wilkins, with incised and slip decoration of daffodils, 40.5cm. high.
(Christie's) **£500 $815**

A Della Robbia vase, decorated by Liza Wilkins, the incised decoration of horses' heads within cartouches, 35.6cm. high. *(Christie's)* **£330 $538**

A Della Robbia jardinière, bulbous shape with incised and slip decoration of a scrolling band between foliate rim, 25.6cm. high. *(Christie's)* **£600 $1,000**

A Della Robbia vase and cover, with incised decoration of yellow tulips against a blue sky, 19.5cm. high. *(Christie's)* **£440 $720**

'The Third Day of Creation', a Della Robbia tile panel after a design by Edward Burne-Jones, 55.5 x 21.5cm.
(Christie's) **£2,860 $4,660**

A large Della Robbia two-handled bottle vase and cover, decoration by Ruth Bare, date *1924*, 63cm. high.
(Christie's) **£385 $630**

A Della Robbia twin-handled terracotta vase by John Shirley, decorated on both sides with confronted peacocks, dated *1898*, 41.5cm. high.
(Christie's) **£935 $1,500**

'Water Avens Tile', a Della Robbia tile panel designed by Conrad Dressler and decorated by E.M. Wood, 51.5 x 34.2cm.
(Christie's) **£605 $1,076**

A Della Robbia terracotta vase, incised with stylised flowers and foliage painted in brown, green and yellow, dated *1896*, 23cm. high.
(Christie's) **£200 $325**

There was scarcely a country in Europe which did not jump on the bandwagon of Art Deco ceramics, and in most cases the output was a mixture of pieces produced by studio potters and industrial manufacturers.

In France, ceramics were designed by the likes of Jean Dufy and Marcel Goupy. Dufy also worked as a designer for the firm of Haviland, who were notable producers of porcelain decorated in the Art Deco style.

Austrian producers followed the styles set by Hoffmann, Powolny and Löffler, while Germany had the Bauhaus, and such companies as Rosenthal were among the commercial Art Deco producers.

Boch Frères, who owned the firm of Keramis in Belgium, employed artists such as Charles Catteau and Jan Windt to transfer their geometric patterns and stylised bird, animal and human figures on to pottery. Their pieces are often characterised by a distinctive crackle glaze, and are highly collectable.

In Italy, we have Lenci and the firm of Ginori, established in Milan by the same family that had established the Doccia factory in 1735.

Eastern Europe, on which the Iron Curtain had not yet been drawn, was also open to Art Deco influences, with companies such as Herend in Hungary and Pacykow in Poland producing pieces which belong firmly in the Art Deco idiom.

A German pottery figure modelled as female dancer wearing short brown dress with green, red and yellow split skirt, stepping forward, on an oval black base, printed marks, 27.5cm. high.
(Christie's) **£368 $600**

A large glazed earthenware vase, designed by Gio Ponti, manufactured by Ginori, circa 1925/30, decorated with a design of household objects, 10½in. high.
(Christie's) **£5,980 $9,747**

German half doll of a young lady with a bonnet, 1920s, no mark.
(Muir Hewitt) **£45 $75**

Stylised Continental wall mask, 8in. high, 1930. *(Christie's)* **£285 $465**

A 1930s Continental vase decorated with a female figure with her voluminous dress enveloping the form, 10in. high. *(Lyle)* **£75 $120**

French stylised boy and girl figures, with pierrot costumes, 1920s. *(Muir Hewitt)* **£65 $105**

Bosse Austrian wall mask of a young lady with a green hat, 1930s. *(Muir Hewitt)* **£300 $500**

Pacykow Polish Art Deco figure of a bear breasted dancer, 17in. high, 1930s. *(Muir Hewitt)* **£1,200 $1,950**

French Art Deco wall mask of a girl with horse, 4½in. high. *(Muir Hewitt)* **£150 $245**

Comical novelty Continental ashtray, 1930s. *(Muir Hewitt)* **£40 $65**

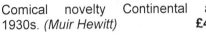

Austrian wall mask of a stylised boy and girl, 1950s. *(Muir Hewitt)* **£120 $195**

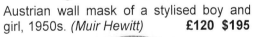

Art Deco German bookends in the form of a young lady and her companion relaxing in easy chairs, 6½in. high. *(Lyle)* **£225 $365**

An earthenware plate decorated to a design by Marcel Goupy, painted in red, black and blue, 12½in. diameter. *(Christie's)* **£120 $195**

J. Martel for Edition Lehmonn, stylised water carrier, 1920s, in cream crackle glazed earthenware heightened with metallic silver glaze, marked *J. Martel,* 29.5cm. (Sotheby's) **£1,265 $2,060**

A large Clément Massier ceramic jardinière. *(Christie's)* **£2,945 $4,800**

A lustre glazed ceramic wall-light, manufactured by Emile Muller, female head, her hair bedecked with flowers, 20in. high, signed *E. Muller.*
(Christie's) **£4,600 $7,500**

A glazed earthenware study of two lovers by Helena Johnova, standing embracing, entwined with garlands and with a putto at their feet, 12in. high, stamped *Helena Johnova*, numbered *206 22 2.*
(Christie's) **£1,500 $2,450**

A lustre glazed earthenware vase, by Clement Massier, delicately lustred with butterflies in flight in shades of red, orange and yellow, 9in. high.
(Christie's) **£1,800 $2,950**

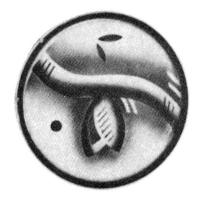

German sailor boy spill holder vase, 1930s.
(Muir Hewitt) **£30 $50**

A Weimar ceramic earthenware cake plate, 22.8cm. diameter.
(Phillips) **£150 $245**

Pincushion with half doll in Continental porcelain.
(Muir Hewitt) **£50 $80**

An Ernst Wahliss Art Nouveau figural jug modelled of an Art relief with the figure of an Art Nouveau maiden, glazed in tones of buff and gilt, 13¾in. high.
(Bonhams) **£210 $340**

A René Buthaud earthenware vase, decorated with floral reserves and bands in turquoise, black and brown, 1920s, 19.8cm. high.
(Christie's) **£750 $1,225**

A French Art Deco porcelain night light, from a model by M. Béver, in the form of a young girl, dressed in pink, rust and blue harlequin costume, 9¼in. high.
(Christie's) **£200 $325**

A Continental figural incense burner, fashioned as a seated clown, in yellow and black costume, 20.5cm. high, marked *Edition Kaza*.
(Phillips) **£150 $245**

A Weimar ceramic porcelain oviform chocolate jug, 19cm. high, printed factory mark *Leuchtenburg*.
(Phillips) **£80 $130**

An Essevi polychrome painted ceramic figure of a naked young boy dressed in drummer's outfit, 12½in. high. *(Christie's)* **£220 $368**

Dutch Art Deco vase in grey with brown and blue decoration, 1930s.
(Muir Hewitt) **£60 $100**

A glazed earthenware figure manufactured by Essevi, circa 1920, modelled as a blushing young girl, her skirts caught by the wind, a cupid at her feet, 13¼in. high, underglazed mark *Essevi Made in Italy Torino-Vento di Primavera-Sandro Vacchetti. (Christie's)* **£2,500 $4,000**

A Soviet porcelain dish, 'The Commissar, Uritskii Square', with underglaze mark of the Imperial Porcelain Factory, period of Alexander III and later, dated 1921, 12in. diameter. *(Christie's)* **£5,520 $8,446**

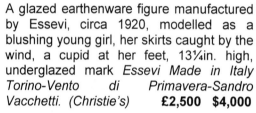

A glazed earthenware figure, manufactured by Essevi, circa 1920, modelled as a young melancholic girl wearing a bonnet and black dress printed with brightly coloured flowers, seated on a low wall, a lizard beside her, 11in. high.
(Christie's) **£1,500 $2,400**

German figurine of a boy with a dog in the style of Mabel Lucie Atwell.
(Muir Hewitt) **£45 $75**

A Soviet porcelain propaganda plate, 'He who does not work does not eat', with underglaze mark of the Imperial Porcelain Factory, dated *1922*, 9⁵/₈in.
(Christie's)   **£2,070 $3,167**

A matched pair of Ernst Wahliss porcelain vases, moulded as squat globular buds opening to reveal long cylindrical trunks, 17¾in. high. printed *Alexander Porcelain Works. (Bonhams)*   **£800 $1,200**

Wassily Kandinsky for the Imperial Russian Porcelain Factory, Petrograd, cup and saucer, 1921, porcelain, polychrome enamel decoration, the underside of the cup with blue enamel maker's mark and dated *1921*, cup 3in. high, saucer 6¼in. diameter.

Surviving examples of porcelain with decoration by Kandinsky are extremely rare. Sketches by Kandinsky in the museum of the Lomonossov Porcelain Manufactory, St Petersburg, show designs for decoration en-suite with this cup and saucer. This is the only recorded example decorated to this design.
(Sotheby's)   **£34,500 $56,235**

A Continental Art Deco figure of a lady, 8in. high. *(Lyle)*   **£60 $100**

'Il Pellegrino Stanco', a ceramic figure designed by Gio Ponti, manufactured by Richard Ginori, circa 1925, melancholic seated figure, head on hand, 10¼in. high.
(Christie's)   **£2,200 $3,580**

A large Continental pottery figure of a butterfly-winged nymph and mirror, standing upon a large snail with actual mother of pearl shell, the young woman with hands clasped against her shoulder, 32½in. high.
(Bonhams)   **£800 $1,300**

A French Art Deco pottery vase, enamelled in blue, black, white and brown with two stylised naked female figures within leafy trees, 31cm. high.
(Christie's)   **£500 $808**

A large lustre glazed plaque, by Clement Massier, *1912*, decorated with a design of moonlit clouds in a rich turquoise/ruby lustre glaze, 24in. diameter.
(Christie's)   **£1,955 $3,185**

Mettlach Pitcher, incised foliate design in colours of blue, yellow, black and cream, 6¾in. high. *(Skinner)* **£163 $258**

Fine Mettlach compote, incised foliate design in colours of blue, yellow, black and cream, impressed mark, 9¼in. high. *(Skinner)* **£730 $1,200**

Mettlach sugar and creamer, incised foliate design in colours of blue, yellow, black and cream, impressed mark, 4in. high. *(Skinner)* **£500 $800**

Fine Gmunder Keramik vase, oviform with black glaze showing through to porcelain body with white slip decoration, blue stamp, Gmunder, G.K., Keramik, made in Austria, 4¼in. high.
(Skinner) **£370 $600**

A pair of earthenware vases, by Arthur Craco, tapering cylindrical shape, the rich ground bubbled with swatches of verdant foliage, 15½in. high.
(Christie's) **£3,000 $4,890**

A Vi Bi polychrome pottery figural group, modelled as a naked young woman struggling in the tentacles of an octopus, 40cm. high. *(Christie's)* **£2,300 $3,750**

A Keramos polychrome pottery wallmask, printed marks and impressed numerals, 25.5cm. high. *(Christie's)* **£175 $285**

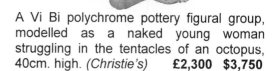

A pair of French Art Deco pottery book ends modelled as Pierrot and Columbine, painted in colours, 19cm. high. *(Christie's)* **£418 $680**

Continental dancing lady figure, 5in. high, 1930s. *(Muir Hewitt)* **£40 $65**

German figurine of a little girl and her puppy in the style of Mabel Lucie Atwell. *(Muir Hewitt)* **£45 $75**

An Italian maiolica bust of a youth in the Della Robbia style, probably representing David, his cuirass painted in blue, yellow and ochre, 20th century, 28cm. high.
(Christie's) **£218 $355**

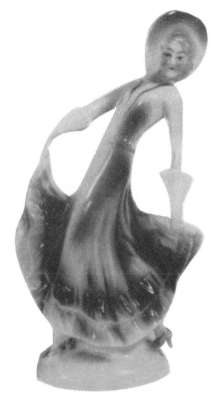

1930s dancing lady figurine, maker unknown, Continental, 5½in. high.
(Muir Hewitt) **£50 $85**

German half doll, 1920, of a Marquise de Pompadour lady. *(Muir Hewitt)* **£50 $85**

A Keramos polychrome pottery figure, from a model by Dakon of a young girl wearing long pink and red tinted evening dress, dancing with shawl around waist, on a domed oval base, impressed and printed factory marks, 30cm. high.
(Christie's) **£600 $975**

A pair of Limoges Art Deco porcelain vases painted in colours and gilt on a yellow ground with stylised palmettes and foliage, 29.5cm. high. *(Christie's)* **£472 $712**

Demetre H. Chiparus porcelain box, Paris, circa 1930, for Etling, semi nude figure with leopard spot skirt, 8¹/₈in. long. *(Skinner)* **£280 $460**

Fornasetti figural cat, white porcelain whimsically decorated with black splotches, circular blue mark on base, 12in. long. *(Skinner)* **£150 $250**

An Essevi ceramic wall mask, modelled as Columbine with a monkey perched on her wrist, 27cm. high. *(Phillips)* **£1,100 $1,800**

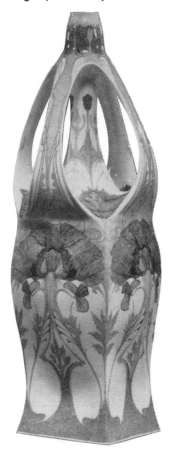

An exceptionally large eggshell vase, manufactured by Rozenburg, decorated by Sam Schellink, 1903, of square baluster form with four handles, painted in purple, green and ochre with formalised flowers and abstracted motifs, 15¹/₈in. high. *(Christie's)* **£7,475 $11,960**

Camille Fauve enamelled vase, black, yellow and cream coloured geometric designs, signed *C. Fauve, Limoges*, 8½in. high. *(Skinner)* **£840 $1,380**

Wedgwood moved with the times during the Art Deco period to produce some pieces a world away from the traditional concept of typical Wedgwood. The fey quality of Daisy Makeig Jones's Fairyland Lustre pieces are a case in point, as are some of the uncompromisingly stylised shapes and designs of the later Art Deco period which were commissioned from artists such as John Skeaping and studio potters like Keith Murray.

Wedgwood porcelain Fairyland lustre footed punch bowl, 1920s, decorated on the exterior with the 'Poplar Trees' pattern of trees before buildings, bridges, and fairies, 11in. diameter.
(Butterfield & Butterfield) **£1,311 $2,200**

Wedgwood Fairyland Lustre punch bowl, designed by Daisy Makeig-Jones, the exterior decorated in the Poplar Trees pattern, the interior with a central mermaid medallion bordered by the Woodland Bridge pattern, monogrammed, printed and enamelled factory marks, 11¼in. diameter.
(Doyle) **£5,500 $9,000**

A rare Wedgwood flame Fairyland lustre 'Fairy Slide' malfrey pot and cover, 7⅛in. high. *(Bonhams)* **£10,000 $14,950**

A Wedgwood Fairyland lustre punch bowl, the interior decorated with The Woodland Bridge pattern, 28.5cm. diamter.
(Bearne's) **£1,730 $2,595**

A rare Wedgwood Fairyland lustre malfrey pot and cover designed by Daisy Makeig-Jones, decorated in the 'Ghostly Wood' pattern, printed and painted in colours and, highlighted in gilt, on original wooden stand printed and painted marks, 38cm.
(Christie's) **£25,300 $40,480**

A good Wedgwood Fairyland lustre bowl, decorated with numerous figures on a waterside, printed mark in brown, circa 1920, 8¾in. diameter.
(Tennants) **£1,250 $2,000**

A Wedgwood Fairyland lustre malfrey pot and cover, designed by Daisy Makeig-Jones, decorated in the Bubbles II pattern, 18cm. high. *(Christie's)* **£12,650 $20,240**

A Wedgwood Fairyland lustre bowl, the exterior decorated with a midnight-blue ground gilt with trees and flowerheads flanking panels of flying fairies against a flame sky, 27cm. *(Phillips)* **£2,937 $4,699**

A pair of Wedgwood Fairyland lustre 'Torches' vases, printed in gold and painted on the exterior in Flame Fairyland tones with 'Torches', 28.5cm. high.
(Phillips) **£2,000 $3,500**

Wedgwood Fairyland Lustre vase, of baluster form, printed and painted with Candlemas pattern, in colours beneath a gilt geometric patterned neck, printed and painted marks, 8in. high.
(Doyle) **£2,450 $4,000**

A Wedgwood Fairyland lustre ovoid vase decorated in purple, green, black, yellow and gilt, with the 'Candlemas' pattern, 18.5cm. *(Phillips)* **£1,750 $2,800**

A rare Wedgwood Fairyland lustre 'White Pagodas' Daventry bowl, designed by Daisy Makeig-Jones, 10¹/₈in. diameter. *(Bonhams)* **£5,000 $7,475**

A Wedgwood Fairyland lustre 'Melba Cup', the ogee bowl externally painted with dancing fairies and goblins, 3in. high. *(Bonhams)* **£600 $1,100**

A pair of Wedgwood Fairyland lustre square vases decorated with panels of the 'Dana' pattern, 19.5cm. *(Phillips)* **£2,750 $4,400**

A Wedgwood Fairyland lustre charger, designed by Daisy Makeig-Jones, in the Ghostly Wood pattern, printed and painted in colours and gilt printed factory marks, 38cm. diameter. *(Christie's)* **£14,625 $23,400**

A Wedgwood Fairyland lustre plate, the centre painted in predominant shades of blue, purple, claret and green and enriched in gilding with goblins crossing a bridge, 1920s, 27.5cm. diameter. *(Christie's)* **£1,045 $1,965**

A fine and rare Wedgwood Fairyland lustre 'Ghostly Wood' ginger jar and cover, designed by Daisy Makeig-Jones, 12¾in. high. *(Bonhams)* **£16,500 $24,667**

A Wedgwood Fairyland lustre octagonal bowl decorated with 'Dana' pattern, the interior with fairies, rainbows and long-tailed birds, 18cm., *Portland Vase* mark and no. *Z5125. (Phillips)* **£900 $1,827**

A Wedgwood Fairyland lustre oviform vase, painted with three panels of fairies, elves and birds before river landscapes, 8½in. high. *(Christie's)* **£770 $1,378**

A Wedgwood Fairyland lustre malfrey pot and cover, designed by Daisy Makeig Jones, printed and painted in colours, highlighted in gilt, in the 'Bubbles II' pattern, 19cm. high.
(Christie's) **£3,000 $4,900**

A Wedgwood Fairyland lustre charger, designed by Daisy Makeig Jones, in the Ghostly Wood pattern, printed and painted in colours and gilt printed factory marks, 38cm. diameter.
(Christie's) **£14,625 $23,400**

A Wedgwood Fairyland lustreware octagonal bowl, the interior decorated with the 'Bird in Hoop' pattern encircling a flaming wheel centre, the exterior with the 'Gargoyles' pattern, 7¼in. diameter.
(Bonhams) **£700 $1,140**

A Wedgwood Fairyland lustre slender baluster vase and cover, the iridescent black ground printed in gold and coloured with three fairies, 1920s, 21.5cm. high.
£2,500 $4,000

A Wedgwood Fairyland lustre octagonal bowl, the 'drake neck green' ground painted in dark blue and gold with Firbolgs, 3¼in. high. (Bonhams) **£300 $550**

Wedgwood Fairyland lustre octagonal bowl, the exterior decorated with panels of river scenes, 10¼in. wide. (Christie's) **£1,000 $1,650**

A Wedgwood Fairyland lustre 'Melba Cup', the ogee bowl externally painted with dancing fairies and goblins, 3in. high. (Bonhams) **£600 $1,100**

A pair of Wedgwood flame Fairyland lustre tapering oviform vases, designed by Daisy Makeig-Jones, decorated with pixies, elves and bats crossing bridges, 1920s, 29.5cm. high. (Christie's) **£4,000 $6,500**

A Wedgwood Fairyland lustreware vase, shape 3149, decorated with the 'Goblins' pattern, 8½in.high. (Bonhams) **£1,200 $1,950**

A Wedgwood flame Fairyland lustre chalice bowl, the interior colour enamelled and gilt with 'Fairy Gondola' pattern, the exterior decorated with the 'Twyford Garlands' pattern, 10½in. diameter. (Bonhams) **£1,500 $2,450**

A Wedgwood butterfly lustre bowl, octagonal, printed in colours and gilt on a pearl lustre ground printed and painted marks, 18cm. diameter.
(Christie's) **£400 $650**

A Wedgwood flame Fairyland lustreware vase, decorated with the 'Willow' pattern in flame lustre, 8in. high.
(Bonhams) **£1,200 $1,950**

A Wedgwood Fairyland lustre bowl, octagonal form, designed by Daisy Makeig Jones, printed and painted the exterior in the 'Castle on the Road' pattern, 23cm. diameter. *(Christie's)* **£1,500 $2,450**

A Wedgwood Fairyland Lustre footed 'Antique Bowl', the exterior enamelled with the Black Fairyland Woodland Bridge pattern, 9in. diameter.
(Bonhams) **£1,500 $2,430**

A Wedgwood Fairyland Lustre footed bowl, enamelled and gilt with fairies, goblins and birds in a fantastic landscape, pattern Z4968, 22.1cm. diameter.
(Bristol) **£1,000 $1,600**

A Wedgwood Fairyland lustre vase decorated with the 'Imps on a Bridge' pattern, with the brown boy and blue Rock bird, 23cm. *(Bearne's)* **£1,500 $2,400**

The name Foley was used by a number of china manufacturers, including Percy Shelley, and it was he who produced hand painted earthenware art pieces which were marketed as Intarsio ware and designed by Frederick Rhead.

While he could use the name for American export pieces, however, he could not register Foley for use in Britain as it had already been registered by E. Brain.

They were noted for the simplicity of their designs, and in the 1930s commissioned work from contemporary artists such as Vanessa Bell, Frank Brangwyn, Dod Proctor, Duncan Grant, Laura Knight and Paul Nash.

A Foley Intarsio ceramic clock, painted in blue, turquoise, green, brown and yellow enamels, 29cm. high.
(Christie's) **£1,500 $2,450**

A Foley Intarsio ware bulbous two-handled vase, printed with a bold pattern of angles below fruit trees, 10½in. high.
(Canterbury) **£230 $370**

A Foley Intarsio circular wall plate, designed by Frederick Rhead, the centre decorated in colours with two classical maidens, 36.8cm.
(Phillips) **£1,000 $1,600**

A Foley Intarsio tapering cylindrical vase with bulbous rim, decorated with stylised trees, 8½in. high.
(Christie's) **£400 $650**

A Foley Intarsio tobacco jar and cover, 14.3cm. high, no. 3458, Rd. no. 364386 (SR).
(Phillips) **£225 $360**

A large Foley Intarsio circular pottery plate painted with sun-flowers, 12½in. diam.*(Christie's)* **£350 $570**

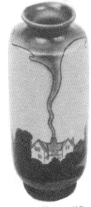

A Foley pastello solifleur, decorated with a cottage in a landscape in shades of blue, purple and yellow, 5in. high. *(Christie's)* **£225 $360**

A Foley Intarsio baluster vase printed and painted in colours with kingfishers, 9in. high.*(Christie's)* **£300 $450**

A Foley Intarsio small oviform jardinière printed and painted in colours, 4½in. high. *(Christie's)* **£230 $345**

A Foley Intarsio vase, printed and painted in colours with panels of seagulls in fiords, 8½in. high.*(Christie's)* **£235 $353**

A Foley Intarsio three-handled vase and cover, with panels depicting the Queen of Hearts, 8in. high. *(Christie's)* **£520 $780**

A Foley bone china teapot and cover, sugar bowl and milk jug, circa 1934, by Freda Beardmore. *(Sotheby's)* **£280 $450**

A Foley Intarsio miniature grandfather clock printed and painted in colours with Father Time, 10in. high. *(Christie's)* **£520 $780**

A Foley Intarsio single-handled spherical vase, printed and painted in colours, 6in. high. *(Christie's)* **£200 $300**

A Foley Intarsio cylindrical biscuit barrel with electro-plate mount and cover, printed and painted in colours, 7¼in. high. *(Christie's)* **£765 $1,147**

A Foley Intarsio twin-handled baluster vase, printed and painted in colours, 9¼in. high. *(Christie's)* **£100 $150**

The Fulper pottery was originally established in 1805 in Flemington New Jersey, to produce drain tiles from local clay. From 1860 onwards it also turned out a range of domestic wares but it was not until 1910 that it turned to art pottery. Early pieces showed much Chinese influence and used colours from the famille rose palette. Lamps with pierced pottery shades were also produced and vases which were characterised by their angular shape. The pottery used a number of glazes including a brownish black intended to resemble dark oak. In 1926 Fulper bought out a pottery in Trenton, NJ, and the operation moved there in 1929, though a showroom was retained in Flemington.

Fulper pottery vase, four buttresses under a butterscotch flambé glaze, vertical mark, 8¼in. high. *(Skinner)* **£140 $230**

Fulper Pottery vase, circular form with two handles under a striated blue and brown glaze with frothy highlights, vertical mark, 9¼in. wide. *(Skinner)* **£125 $200**

Fulper Pottery vase, with intertwining handles under a striated matte green glaze, vertical mark, 4¾in. high. *(Skinner)* **£218 $345**

Fulper Pottery vase, circular form with striated blue, green and cream colour glaze, vertical mark, 5½in. high. *(Skinner)* **£218 $345**

Fulper Pottery vase, tapering form with two handles under a striated green, lavender and pink glaze, vertical mark, 4¼in. high. *(Skinner)* **£145 $230**

Fulper Pottery vase with lamp mount, tapering form with square handles under a mottled blue/green glaze, 6¾in. high. *(Skinner)* **£345 $546**

Fulper Pottery urn, Flemington, New Jersey, circa 1915, cucumber green crystalline glaze, vertical ink mark, 13in. high. *(Skinner)* **£883 $1,700**

Fulper Pottery vase with mottled brown-green glaze flowing over a brown and white speckled body, black vertical ink stamp, 5in. high. *(Skinner)* **£115 $173**

Rare and important Fulper Pottery and leaded glass mushroom table lamp, matt gunmetal glaze over matt olive green glazed and reticulated dome shade, 17in. high. *(Christie's)* **£17,633 $26,450**

Fulper Pottery vase, Flemington, New Jersey, semi-matt glazed in shades of green at rim and ring handles with rose on lower body, 12½in. high. *(Skinner)* **£200 $320**

A Fulper Pottery centrepiece on pedestal base, hammered olive-green on paler green glaze, circa 1915, 10½in. high. *(Skinner)* **£880 $1,400**

Fulper Pottery vase, no. 61, Flemington, New Jersey, matt glazed in blue streak over amethyst drip on rose, 5½in. high. *(Skinner)* **£134 $201**

Fulper Pottery centre bowl, Flemington, New Jersey, gloss flambé glaze in shades of blue, 3½in. high. *(Skinner)* **£96 $144**

Fulper pottery double handled vase, Flemington, New Jersey, circa 1915-25, no. 575, glossy green and eggplant glaze, impressed vertical mark, 6¾in. high. *(Skinner)* **£121 $225**

Exceptional Fulper vase, shape #604, covered with a rich, even silvery mirrored black glaze, raised oval mark, 8½in. high. *(Skinner)* **£385 $575**

Fulper Pottery centre bowl, no. 559, Flemington, New Jersey, gloss interior in pale yellow with caramel and light blue, 3¾in. high. *(Skinner)* **£115 $173**

Fulper Pottery and leaded glass mushroom table lamp, domed shade inset with textured amber slag glass and iridescent green jewels, set into flared cylindrical base with two sockets, grey and light blue flambé glaze over mirrored, lustre gunmetal base stamped with vertical *FULPER* in a box, circular *VASECRAFT* stamp, 20½in. high, shade diameter 17in.
(Skinner) **£13,487 $21,850**

Fulper Pottery copper dust vase with two handles, Flemington, New Jersey, circa 1915, 6in. diameter. *(Skinner)* **£125 $200**

While Emile Gallé (1846-1904) is best known as an artist in glass, he also worked in other media as diverse as furniture and ceramics. He established a small workshop in 1874 at Nancy (Meurthe et Moselle) and there produced earthenware, which was first exhibited in 1890. Later, he experimented with stoneware and porcelain.

His forms were for the most part simple, even a little clumsy, though some of his shapes were borrowed by the Rookwood Pottery in the USA, who acknowledged their debt to him.

His decorative motifs included heraldic themes and scenes which were reminiscent of delft. Perhaps inevitably, too, he used standard Art Nouveau motifs such as plant designs of orchids, chrysanthemums, orchids etc., and his glazes were flowing and opaque, sometimes mingling two or more colours.

Apart from his own distinctive style, he was much influenced by Japanese styles, as reflected in the 'Origami' pieces he produced, the angular shapes of which presage Art Deco themes. Amongst the most charming of his pieces are his cats, which sit, regarding the onlooker with their glass eyes and an expression on their faces which is variously described as 'sweet faced' or a 'silly smile'.

All Gallé's pieces were marked, either with the impressed initials *EG, Em Gallé Faiencerie de Nancy*, or with various versions of his signature.

Emile Gallé crouched nodding cat, circa 1880, pale pink coloured tin glazed earthenware decorated with flowered jacket and a medallion, 15.5cm.
(Sotheby's) **£6, 670 $10,750**

A pair of faience vases by Gallé, of classical form, the cream ground painted with sprays of flowers and a flying butterfly, the details picked out with gilding, 13in. high. *(Christie's)* **£4,025 $6,561**

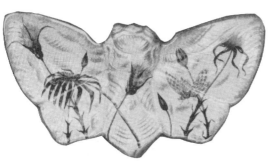

A faience dish by Gallé, circa 1890, formed in the shape of a flying moth, the wings picked out with gilding and the whole enamelled with wild grasses, 17½in. maximum width.
(Christie's) **£6,000 $9,780**

A Gallé pottery vase of dimpled baluster form with everted quatrefoil rim, polychrome decorated with a heraldic lion beneath inscription *Vous Leur Fites Seigneur*, 14.2cm. high.
(Christie's) **£600 $980**

A decorated faience dish, by Gallé modelled in the shape of a basket with tall looping handle, decorated with wild grasses and insects, 11¾in. wide.
(Christie's) **£1,800 $2,934**

Faience jug by Gallé, circa 1885, in the shape of a bearded guitarist sitting on a drum, his hat forming the spout, each boldly decorated, in blue and orange, 16in. high. *(Christie's)* **£3,500 $5,700**

Pair of Mosaic Gallé style models of seated cats with glass eyes, blue detail on a lemon ground, 8in. *(G.A. Key)* **£520 $828**

An earthenware 'Moon' plate by Gallé, with raised border in the shape of the crescent moon, the face decorated with a river landscape, 13½in. diameter.
(Christie's) **£2,300 $3,749**

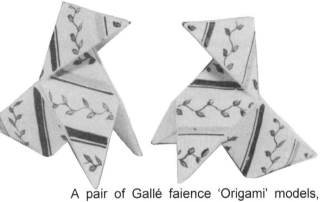

A pair of Gallé faience 'Origami' models, each as an abstract folded creature painted with yellow and blue bands, 8cm. high.
(Phillips) **£500 $800**

A faience bowl by Gallé, circa 1890, gently swollen body in milky white decorated with flitting moths of various size modelled in high relief, the moths sketched with a green glaze and traced with gilding, 8in. high. *(Christie's)* **£4,000 $6,500**

THE Austrian firm of William Goebel is perhaps best known for the their Hummel figures, twee little peasant children in appealing poses. These seem to be particularly popular in America. Goebel also made pieces very much in the Art Deco tradition, wall masks, figures etc., many of which epitomise the kitsch aspect of the style, and are now very collectable.

The firm continues in business today.

Goebel (Wm & Co) Pierrette powder box and cover. *(Muir Hewitt)* **£120 $195**

A pair of pottery book-ends in the form of little girls sitting under sunhats, holding a camera and a rose, 5¾in. high, with the William Goebel crown mark.
(Christie's) **£250 $400**

Goebel container formed as a portly monk, wearing a brown habit; together with two matching graduated jugs, printed and incised marks, 9½in., 6in. and 4in.
(G.A. Key) **£110 $175**

A pottery figure group by Goebels, circa 1930, modelled as three stylised female dancers, 11¼in. high.
(Christie's) **£3,800 $6,156**

Goebel face mask of a young lady with a hat, 1930s. *(Muir Hewitt)* **£280 $450**

It was in 1886 that Friedrich Goldscheider founded his factory in Vienna, After his death in 1897, production continued there under the direction of his widow and brother Alois until, in 1920, the business was taken over by his two sons Marcel and Walter. In 1927, however, Marcel broke away to form the Vereinigte Ateliers für Kunst und Keramik.

While such things as vases were produced, the factory is best known for the figures and wall masks which epitomise the Art Deco style.

Lorenzl for Goldscheider, Butterfly Girl, 1920s, polychrome earthenware, modelled as a young girl in a butterfly dress, 47.5cm. *(Sotheby's)* **£1,955 $3,089**

A pair of Goldscheider pottery figures of negro children, each in a long dress carrying a broad brimmed hat, late 19th century, 25cm. high. *(Bearne's)* **£400 $640**

A Goldscheider Pottery group, by Lorenzl modelled as a naked girl standing in a relaxed pose on a black oval vase with her faithful borzoi behind her, 36.50cm. high. *(Phillips)* **£800 $1,300**

A Goldscheider polychrome pottery figure group, modelled as Little Red Riding Hood and the Wolf, she wears black, white and pink plaid dress and holds a basket, on an oval base, printed factory marks and impressed numerals, applied silver foil label, 22cm. high. *(Christie's)* **£207 $335**

A Goldscheider polychrome pottery wallmask, modelled as a young girl wearing red beret with white pompom and pink spotty scarf, printed factory mark and impressed numerals, applied silver foil label, 24cm. high. *(Christie's)* **£299 $485**

A Goldscheider pottery figure of a dancer, in a floral lilac dress with bonnet, 12in. high, circa 1930. **£350 $560**

A Goldscheider polychrome pottery wallmask of a young woman with stylised features, with brown wavy hair and pink lace scarf at her neck, printed and impressed marks, 30cm. high; and another. *(Christie's)* **£322 $525**

An unusual Goldscheider pottery wallmask modelled as Shirley Temple, painted in colours, 10in. long.
(Christie's) **£475 $712**

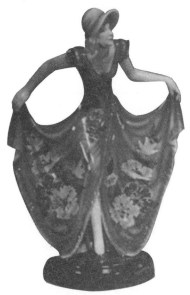

A china Art Deco figure of a woman by Goldscheider, Vienna, 12½in. high.
(Skinner) **£350 $560**

A Goldscheider polychrome pottery figure cast from a model by Dakon, of a young woman wearing blue floral dress and bonnet, stepping forward holding up the hems of her skirt, on a circular black base, printed and impressed factory marks and facsimile signature, impressed numerals *6330 404 16*, 32cm. high.
(Christie's) **£713 $1,160**

A Goldscheider polychrome painted pottery figure of a young female dancer, wearing blue dress painted with bubbles and vines, 15¼in. high. *(Christie's)* **£700 $1,300**

A Goldscheider terracotta wall mask of a female profile painted with turquoise ringlets, orange-banded black hat and yellow scarf, 10in. long. *(Christie's)* **£300 $450**

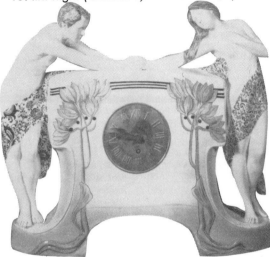

A Goldscheider pottery figural clock, metal dial within shaped rectangular body, flanked at either side with naked female and male figures, reaching towards middle with hands clasped, 41cm. high. *(Christie's)* **£900 $1,460**

A Goldscheider polychrome pottery wallmask, of a young woman wearing a pink, grey and yellow floral spring headscarf, printed factory marks and impressed numerals *8328 2 29*, applied retailers label, 25cm. high. *(Christie's)* **£402 $655**

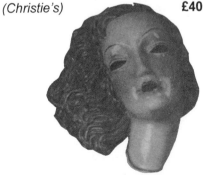

A Goldscheider polychrome pottery wallmask, of a young woman with stylised features, with brown wavy hair and pink lips, printed factory mark and painted numerals *7420*, impressed numerals *2669 6*, 24.2cm. high. *(Christie's)* **£322 $525**

Goldscheider porcelain figure by Lorenzl, 14in. high. *(Muir Hewitt)* **£820 $1,230**

A Goldscheider ceramic wall mask fashioned as the face of a girl with black eyes and orange lips, 28.5cm. high. *(Phillips)* **£450 $735**

A Goldscheider figure, the design by J. Lorenzl, of a striding girl, her head thrown back, and holding her grey dress behind her, 35.4cm. *(Christie's)* **£750 $1,250**

A Goldscheider terracotta wall mask of a young girl with orange curls and green beret holding a Scottie dog to her cheek, 10in. high. *(Christie's)* **£375 $610**

'Suzanne', a Goldscheider figure, the design by J. Lorenzl, the nude figure loosely draped with a patterned grey enamelled robe, 33.6cm. high. *(Christie's)* **£750 $1,250**

A Goldscheider pottery 'Negro' wall mask, 26.5cm. high. *(Phillips)* **£250 $400**

A Goldscheider polychrome-painted pottery figure of a dancer, modelled by Dakon, wearing blue spotted bodice and floral divided skirt, 10½in. high. *(Christie's)* **£800 $1,300**

A Goldscheider figure of a woman standing on tip-toe, holding the skirt of her dress, enamelled in pink, yellow and black, 28.8cm. *(Christie's)* **£750 $1,250**

A Goldscheider polychrome ceramic group modelled by H. Perl, of a Spanish dancing couple, 16¼in. high. *(Christie's)* **£475 $775**

A Goldscheider polychrome painted pottery figure of a Spanish dancer, wearing a short flounced yellow dress, 18in. high. *(Christie's)* **£650 $1,050**

A Goldscheider polychrome painted figure of a young girl in bat costume, printed factory marks, 18½in. high. *(Christie's)* **£950 $1,750**

A Goldscheider terracotta wallmask modelled as the profile of a young woman with orange hair and lips, and green eyes, 11in. long. *(Christie's)* **£375 $610**

A Goldscheider figure of a woman with one hand on her hip, one on her hat, with artist's monogram, 33.5cm. high.
(Christie's) **£1,000 $1,600**

A Goldscheider terracotta wallmask, modelled as a young woman with green coiled hair and orange features, 25cm. high. *(Christie's)* **£315 $500**

A Goldscheider figure, of a girl in a two-piece bathing suit, with elaborate skirt draped across her raised arm, 33cm. high. *(Christie's)* **£800 $1,300**

A Goldscheider terracotta wallmask modelled as the head of a young woman with turquoise ringlets and a yellow tulip at the neck, 10in. long.
(Christie's) **£462 $774**

E. Tell for Goldscheider, Loïe Fuller, circa 1900, earthenware, modelled as the dancer Loïe Fuller with raised arms, 28in.
(Sotheby's) **£2,990 $4,874**

A Goldscheider ceramic wall plaque moulded as the head, neck and hand of a young woman, 7½in. high, printed marks.
(Christie's) **£225 $360**

A Goldscheider polychrome painted pottery table lamp, modelled as a pair of blonde women dancing together, 19in. high.
(Christie's) **£600 $1,110**

307

A Goldscheider polychrome pottery figure cast from a model by Dakon, of a young blonde beauty wearing floral lace dress with green sleeves, 32in. high.
(Christie's) **£632 $1,020**

A Goldscheider pottery figure modelled as Columbine and Pierrot, she stands wearing black and white hat, patterned jacket and wide crinoline skirt, her hands in a large muff, while Pierrot in harlequin costume worships at her feet, 34.5cm. high.
(Christie's) **£322 $525**

A Goldscheider polychrome pottery figure group, modelled as small boy dressed in clown's costume, walking arm in arm with girls dressed in blue spotty knickerbocker costume, 22cm. high.
(Christie's) **£700 $1,140**

A Goldscheider terracotta wall plaque of square form, moulded in low relief with a figure of a skier on the slopes, enclosed in an orange frame, 19cm. diameter.
(Christie's) **£92 $149**

A Goldscheider figural jardinière, glazed earthenware, modelled as a young couple holding up the ends of a voluminous drape to form the body of the vase, 22in. high.
(Sotheby's) **£1,800 $2,935**

A Goldscheider polychrome pottery figure, modelled as three children walking arm in arm, two wearing similar costumes in green and blue of tall a hats and wide trousers, other wearing brown and white plaid trouser suit, 20cm. high.
(Christie's) **£800 $1,300**

A Goldscheider figure of a girl, by Dakon, modelled wearing a green gingham dress and reading a book, 25cm. high.
(Phillips) **£450 $720**

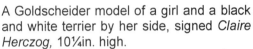

A Goldscheider model of a girl and a black and white terrier by her side, signed *Claire Herczog,* 10¼in. high.
(Anderson & Garland) **£280 $462**

A pair of Goldscheider pottery bookends, in the style of Wiener Werkstätte, each modelled as a kneeling girl with head turned to the side, 8in. high.
(Christie's) **£1,430 $2,531**

A Goldscheider group of a boy and a girl, he wearing a perriot costume, she wearing a tutu, impressed number *8232,* signed *G. Bouret,* 8¾in. high.
(Anderson & Garland) **£310 $512**

A Goldscheider model of 'Mary had a little lamb', the girl wearing dress with red bonnet with a lamb wearing a bell around its neck, on oval base, impressed number *6747,* 7in. high.
(Anderson & Garland) **£220 $363**

Goldscheider ceramic figure, Austria, designed by Dakon, decorated in rose and black on white ground, 8⁷/₈in. high.
(Skinner) **£305 $488**

A Goldscheider earthenware wall mask, 1920s, 17cm. high. **£275 $440**

A Goldscheider polychrome terracotta bust of a young turbanned Arab, signed, late 19th century, 78cm. high.
(Finarte) **£2,392 $3,755**

A Goldscheider Art Nouveau pottery figure of a naked maiden supporting a circular mirror on her thigh, 30in. high.
(Christie's) **£1,120 $1,680**

A Goldscheider terracotta wallmask, in the form of a young woman holding an apple to her throat, impressed *6774*, 19cm. long.
(Christie's) **£320 $508**

A Goldscheider pottery figure modelled by Dakon, of a young woman wearing a sailor's hat, swimsuit and pink trousers, 39cm. high.
(Christie's) **£1,462 $2,207**

A Goldscheider ceramic figure of a negro dandy, dressed in three piece suit, wing collar and tie, with a glass monocle, 20½in. high.
(Christie's) **£2,400 $4,440**

A Goldscheider terracotta wall mask modelled as the head of a young girl holding a fan across her neck, 11in. high. *(Christie's)* **£350 $560**

Hosteas for Goldscheider, dancer with turban, 1920s, modelled as a scantily clad female dancer in mid-step, 44.75cm.
(Sotheby's) **£1,840 $2,907**

A Goldscheider pottery figure of a dancing girl, designed by Lorenzl, 16in. high. *(Lyle)* **£700 $1,210**

A fine Goldscheider terracotta figure of a blackamoor holding a tray, on a shaped square base, 23½in. high. **£2,000 $3,200**

A Goldscheider pottery figure, modelled as a sailor holding a girl, 30cm. high. *(Lyle)* **£375 $600**

Goldscheider painted terracotta bust of a girl wearing a headscarf and shawl, signed, impressed and with seal mark, 16in. high. *(Lawrences)* **£450 $684**

A Goldscheider polychrome painted pottery group from a model by Bouret, of two children walking arm in arm, 9in. high. *(Christie's)* **£495 $876**

A Goldscheider polychrome painted pottery figure of a young girl, wearing pleated sleeveless dress with butterfly patterned split skirt, 23cm. high. *(Christie's)* **£770 $1,170**

A Goldscheider painted plaster bust of a young boy wearing a straw hat, and a scarf tied around his neck, 46cm. high. *(Phillips)* **£440 $669**

A Goldscheider figure of a woman in a long dress and hat, enamelled in shades of mauve, blue and black, 31.3cm. high. *(Christie's)* **£675 $1,080**

A Goldscheider pottery bust of a young woman in the Art Deco style, signed *F. Donatello*, 23½in. high. *(Outhwaite & Litherland)* **£450 $720**

A Goldscheider terracotta wallmask, modelled as the stylised head of a woman with pierced eyes, orange hair and lips, 12in. long. *(Christie's)* **£455 $682**

A 1930s Goldscheider wall plaque of a female face holding a black mask.
(John Maxwell) **£520 $842**

A Goldscheider polychrome-painted pottery figure of a dancer, modelled by Dakon, wearing blue spotted bodice and floral divided skirt, 10½in. high.
(Christie's) **£540 $810**

A Goldscheider polychrome pottery figure, from a model by Lorenzl, of a female dancer wearing red bodice and grey and red spotty skirt, stepping forward holding a cymbal, on a domed oval base, printed factory marks, impressed numerals *6959 128 11*, 19cm. high.
(Christie's) **£350 $570**

A Goldscheider female figure wearing short blue patterned dress and a bonnet standing with a seated alsatian dog on an oval base, number 7219, 8¼in. high.
(Anderson & Garland) **£180 $297**

A Goldscheider terracotta head, of a young woman with pale green combed and curled hair, tin glazed in shades of white, orange and green, 29cm. high.
(Christie's) **£1,462 $2,340**

A Goldscheider nude female child figure and fawn group, on oval base, impressed number *7218*, 6¼in. high.
(Anderson & Garland) **£160 $264**

A pair of Goldscheider pottery figures, modelled as a young peasant boy and girl, he stands with hands in the pockets of his shorts, 48cm. high.
(Christie's) **£138 $223**

A Goldscheider polychrome pottery wallmask, of a young woman with stylised features, with brown curly hair and purple lace scarf, printed factory marks, impressed *652*, 27cm. high.
(Christie's) **£175 $285**

An Austrian bronzed terracotta group of three schoolboys, by Hanniroff, produced by Friedrich Goldscheider, Vienna, late 19th century.

Seated on a brick wall, wearing jacket and shorts, inscribed to the side *Haniroff* and impressed to the back *Friedrich Goldscheider* and with the numbers *35/1190/2061*, 22¼in. high.
(Christie's) **£4,025 $6,600**

A Goldscheider pottery double face wall plaque, the two females in profile, 12in. high. *(Lyle)* **£400 $640**

A Goldscheider terracotta wall hanging, modelled as a female bather standing amongst rushes, with towel draped over right forearm, 15in. long. *(Christie's)* **£675 $1,012**

A Goldscheider polychrome painted pottery figure of a young woman, stepping forward and grasping the hems of her skirt, 34cm. high. *(Christie's)* **£176 $269**

A Goldscheider pottery mask of a girl looking down, marked *Made in Austria*, circa 1925, 23cm. high. *(Lyle)* **£375 $600**

A Goldscheider polychrome pottery figure, from a model by Lorenzl, of a flamenco dancer, standing wearing grey and pink floral dress, standing with one hand on hip, the other holding a blue fan, on a circular black base, printed factory marks, impressed numerals *3232 365 13 12* and faint signature, 35cm. high. *(Christie's)* **£800 $1,304**

A Goldscheider pottery figure of a woman wearing a beaded costume, on a black oval base, 18in. high. *(Christie's)* **£1,850 $3,000**

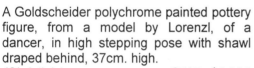

A Goldscheider polychrome painted pottery figure, from a model by Lorenzl, of a dancer, in high stepping pose with shawl draped behind, 37cm. high. *(Christie's)* **£715 $1,094**

A Goldscheider polychrome painted pottery figure, from a model by Dakon, of a young girl, emerging from a blue hat box, 16cm. high. *(Christie's)* **£1,100 $1,683**

A Goldscheider child figure wearing floral patterned coat, bonnet and gloves, holding a packet of sweetmeats with a Scottish terrier looking on, on oval base, impressed number 7663, 9¼in. high. *(Anderson & Garland)* **£150 $248**

Parisienne, a Goldscheider polychrome ceramic figure modelled by H. Liedhoff, printed factory marks, 13¾in. high. *(Christie's)* **£524 $680**

Edward Gray (1871-1959) began his career as a salesman for the pottery wholesaler H.G. Stephenson of Manchester. Believing he could improve on the products he had to sell, he went into the business himself, setting up in 1907 first simply as a wholesaler, but expanding to become a pottery decorating concern.

In 1912 the company moved to larger premises in Mayer Street, Hanley.

Throughout his career, Gray remained dedicated to improving standards of quality and design. This led to an enlightened approach to his apprentices, who were encouraged not only to pursue their studies at evening classes, but were also offered an early form of day release. In this, he cooperated closely with Gordon Forsyth, Head of the Burslem School of Art, and Forsyth, who was himself a brilliant ceramic artist, supplied Grays with designs for their highly successful lustre ware.

Susie Cooper is, of course, the most famous name to be associated with Grays. She joined them in 1922 and remained for seven years, in which time she was promoted to Art Director. She designed a number of floral banded and geometric patterns, many of which can be identified by her name or initials incorporated into the backstamp. Cooper-designed Gloria lustre vases now attract a premium.

In 1933 the firm moved again to larger premises in Stoke, and their work by this time had attracted royal patronage. Their range now included floral tableware, advertising novelties, lustre ware, printed and enamel teaware and commemorative ware. They also made wall pockets, face masks and animal studies, many by Nancy Cato, who worked for Grays as a freelance.

Unlike, for example, Clarice Cliff, Grays allowed their paintresses to sign each piece, so that one often finds such names as Mae or Wyn adorning the jugs and plates from this factory.

Edward Gray retired in 1947 and died in 1959, when the factory was sold to Portmeirion Potteries, though the name continued in use until 1962.

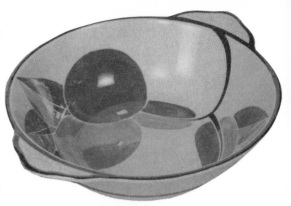

Grays fruit serving dish, 1930s. *(Muir Hewitt)* **£40 $65**

Large Grays plaque with floral decoration, 16in. diameter. *(Muir Hewitt)* **£450 $735**

Grays bowl with shaped rim and floral design, 8in. high. *(Muir Hewitt)* **£70 $115**

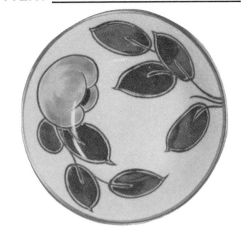

Grays jug 5½in. high. with geometric design pattern, 1930s. *(Muir Hewitt)* **£300 $500**

Grays fruit dish, 1930s, with fruit and leaf decoration. *(Muir Hewitt)* **£25 $40**

Grays floral design plate, 1930s, 10in. diameter. *(Muir Hewitt)* **£200 $325**

Grays Pottery trio, bread and butter plate and cream jug, 1930s. *(Muir Hewitt)* **£70 $115**

Grays Susie Cooper Moon & Mountain Paris jug, 5½in. high, 1930s. *(Muir Hewitt)* **£300 $500**

Grays plate with floral design, 11in. diameter. *(Muir Hewitt)* **£250 $400**

Grays plate with floral decoration, 9in. diameter. *(Muir Hewitt)* **£180 $295**

A pair of Gray's vases of ovoid form with everted rim, painted with flowers and foliage on a powder blue ground, 21cm. high. *(Christie's)* **£350 $575**

Grays 1930s dish with floral design, 7½in. wide. *(Muir Hewitt)* **£75 $125**

A Gray's Pottery bowl designed by Susie Cooper, the well painted with alternating bunches of grapes and vine leaves, 25cm. diameter. *(Christie's)* **£150 $232**

A Gray's Pottery plate, the well painted with stylised flowers in shades of pink, purple and green, 27cm. diameter. *(Christie's)* **£125 $194**

A pair of Gray's Susie Cooper spherical lampbases, painted with golfers and a caddie, 15cm. high. *(Christie's)* **£1,250 $2,000**

Ross's Sparkling Grapefruit by Gray's Pottery, Stoke on Trent, 11cm. high. *(Lyle)* **£150 $245**

'Cubist', a Gray's Pottery coffee set for six, comprising coffeepot and cover, milk jug and sugar basin, six cans and saucers, height of pot 21cm. *(Christie's)* **£2,760 $4,400**

A Gray's Pottery coffee set for six painted in ruby lustre and orange with fruiting vine frieze, coffeepot 19cm. high. *(Christie's)* **£230 $345**

1930s Grays plate with floral decoration, 9in. diameter. *(Muir Hewitt)* **£180 $295**

'Moon and Mountain', a Gray's Pottery Paris jug and twin-handled dish, painted in shades of red, blue, green and black, dish 28cm. wide. *(Christie's)* **£299 $448**

A Gray's Pottery tea for two, painted with floral sprays in blue, green, yellow and orange on a black ground, height of teapot 4½in. high. *(Christie's)* **£430 $645**

A Grays pottery Susie Cooper teaset painted with blue, green, orange and yellow lustre with flowers and foliage, comprising milk jug, sugar bowl and six cups and saucers. (*Christie's*) **£200 $324**

A Grays pottery plate, designed by Susie Cooper, painted with orange and blue flowerheads on a grey trellis radiating from well, 26.5cm. diameter. (*Christie's*) **£175 £283**

Five pieces of Gray's pottery advertising Ross's Soft Drinks, decorated in several colours. (*Lyle*) **£450 $735**

A Grays pottery tea for two, printed and painted with stylised flower spray in shades of blue, yellow and grey, comprising teapot, milk jug, sugar basin, two cups, saucers and a side plate, teapot 10cm. high. (*Christie's*) **£253 $410**

'Festival of Britain', a Grays pottery powder box and cover printed in silver lustre with grape and vine panels, the inside of the cover printed with the Festival of Britain emblem, 13 cm. diameter. (*Christie's*) **£200 $324**

The Grueby Faience Co was formed in 1897 by William H Grueby in East Boston, MA, initially manufacturing tiles, Della-Robbia style plaques and vases. From 1898 matt glazes of opaque enamel were used in shades of blue, brown, yellow and sometimes red. The most characteristic of these, however, is dark green with a veined effect. Vases were hand thrown, some plain, others decorated with geometric patterns or plant forms in low relief. From 1904 glazed paperweights were made in scarab form.

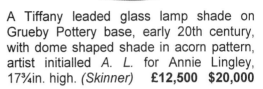

A Tiffany leaded glass lamp shade on Grueby Pottery base, early 20th century, with dome shaped shade in acorn pattern, artist initialled *A. L.* for Annie Lingley, 17¾in. high. *(Skinner)* **£12,500 $20,000**

Late 19th century Grueby Faience Co. bust of 'Laughing Boy', based on a statue by Donatello, 11in. high.
(Skinner) **£990 $1,485**

Impressive Grueby Pottery vase, attributed to Wilhelmina Post, crisp leaves under a mottled green glaze, 11¼in. high.
(Skinner) **£3,066 $4,600**

Exceptional Grueby vase, decorated with moulded crisp leaves, stems and tooled flowers, 4½in. high.
(Skinner) **£15,333 $23,000**

Grueby Pottery two-colour lamp base, Boston, circa 1905, bronze foot signed *Gorham Co.*, 18in. high.
(Skinner) **£10,000 $16,000**

Grueby Pottery vase, circular form bulbous base tapering in toward top, broad and narrow alternating leaf pattern, 4¾in. high. *(Skinner)* **£2,683 $4,025**

Grueby Pottery bowl, Boston, Wilhelmina Post, bisque form with carved and incised overlapping leaves, 8½in. diameter. *(Skinner)* **£550 $825**

Grueby Pottery wide-mouth vase, Boston, circa 1905, with moulded leaf decoration, matte oatmeal glaze exterior, 3½in. high. *(Skinner)* **£195 $375**

Grueby Pottery bowl, Boston, matt green glazed exterior and interior rim, 4in. high. *(Skinner)* **£690 $1,035**

Important Grueby Pottery vase, globular form with rolled rim, seven broad leaf-forms with negative space in relief, exceptional leathery glaze at shoulder transitioning to a smooth glaze at base, circular impressed Grueby mark, incised initials *E.P.*, 11in. high. *(Skinner)* **£15,180 $25,300**

Exceptional Grueby Pottery lamp with Tiffany Studios crocus shade, base with five leaf-forms under a rich, leathery, matte green glaze, original fittings with good patina, shade with unusual shading and glass texture in two colours of green, yellow, opalescent on a deep red background, 20in. high. *(Skinner)* **£22,770 $37,950**

Grueby Pottery lotus bulb vase, heavy walled sphere with seven broad green leaf forms around central light blue matt bottle-top, 8½in. high. *(Skinner)* **£1,636 $3,190**

Grueby Pottery Eros tile, red clay square decorated by raised cupid with bow against matt black background, 6 x 6in. *(Skinner)* **£85 $165**

Grueby Pottery two tile scenic frieze, Boston, circa 1902, depicting four cows in various states of grazing and repose. *(Skinner)* **£3,900 $5,850**

Grueby Pottery vase, Boston, matt green glaze, on high relief wide leaf blade alternating with bud on stem decoration, 4¼in. high. *(Skinner)* **£1,150 $1,725**

Grueby Pottery monumental floor vase, Boston, Massachusetts, circa 1905, the body with repeating broad thumb moulded and ribbed decoration, 21in. high. *(Skinner)* **£2,500 $4,000**

Grueby Pottery two-colour vase leaf-carved jardinière form with textured butterscotch yellow matt glaze decorated by eight white matt enamel flower buds, 7in. high. *(Skinner)* **£2,256 $4,400**

Grueby Pottery vase, Boston, matt dark green glaze, impressed mark, 13in. high.
(Skinner) **£400 $605**

Grueby Pottery vase, Boston, matt green glaze, impressed mark, 12½in. high.
(Skinner) **£1,175 $1,900**

Grueby Pottery vase, matt green glaze, overlapping tooled leaves, impressed marks, 6in. high.
(Skinner) **£575 $860**

A Grueby Pottery two-colour vase, stamped and paper label, circa 1905, 7in. high.
(Skinner) **£500 $800**

Grueby Pottery butterscotch glazed vase, artist's initials *W.P.* for Wilhelmina Post, dated *3/12/06*, 9in. diameter.
(Skinner) **£4,000 $6,500**

A Grueby two-colour pottery vase, circa 1905, 13in. high.
(Skinner) **£4,000 $6,500**

Important Grueby Pottery vase, Boston, attributed to Wilhelmina Post, matt green glaze, 11¼in. high.
(Skinner) **£4,765 $7,150**

Rare Grueby vase, double gourd form, three recessed panels creating a raised stylised flower and leaf pattern, 7¾in. high.
(Skinner) **£1,533 $2,300**

Grueby Pottery vase, Ruth Erickson, circa 1905, impressed mark and incised artist's cipher, 16³⁄₈in. high.
(Skinner) **£19,321 $29,900**

Grueby faience pumpkin vase, squat melon-ribbed organic body with autumn harvest yellow matt glaze, 9in. high. *(Skinner)* **£1,185 $2,310**

Grueby pottery lamp base, Boston, circa 1905, having an elongated neck flaring towards bulbous base, artist signed 'A.L.' for Annie Lingley, 24¼in. high. *(Skinner)* **£3,500 $5,700**

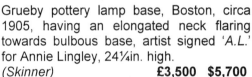

Grueby Faience vase, Boston, modelled by Gertrude Priest, elongated flaring neck on low squat body, decorated with bud on stem alternating with high relief broad, impressed mark and incised artist's cipher, 7³/₈in. high. *(Skinner)* **£1,410 $2,300**

Grueby Pottery vase, Boston, swollen bulbous form, decorated with three broad leaf blades under matte green glaze, unmarked, 7¼in. high. *(Skinner)* **£845 $1,380**

A Grueby pottery lamp with Bigelow & Kennard leaded shade, circa 1905, 17¾in. diameter. *(Skinner)* **£4,000 $6,500**

Rare Grueby Pottery lidded jar, Boston, curdled matt blue glaze with dark blue speckling, 6¾in. high. *(Skinner)* **£1,686 $2,530**

A Grueby Pottery experimental drip glaze vase, Boston, Massachusetts, circa 1905, with wide rolled rim and short neck, 11¼in. high. *(Skinner)* **£2,295 $3,443**

Rare and important Grueby Pottery vase, moulded by Miss Lillian Newman, cucumber green matt body decorated with three hand moulded blossoms arising from spiked leaf clusters, 12¾in.high. *(Skinner)* **£8,000 $12,000**

Rare and important Grueby pottery vase, Boston, circa 1900, designed by George P. Kendrick, modelled by Wilhelmina Post, matt green glaze on high-relief decorated form, 12½in. high. (Skinner) **£20,658 $34,500**

Grueby Pottery vase, Boston, matt green drip glaze, impressed mark, 5¾in. high. *(Skinner)* **£690 $1,035**

Grueby pottery vase, Boston, circa 1905, partial paper label and artist's monogram *JE*, 12in. high. **£1,450 $2,300**

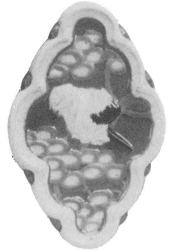

Navy blue Grueby Pottery vase, Boston, circa 1910, impressed and artist initialled, 5½in. high. *(Skinner)* **£1,200 $1,900**

A rare Grueby Pottery fountain tile, decorated with a bird in relief standing on lily pads, glaze combinations of high glaze creamy whites and blue/cobalt blue and matte green, signed *E.M.,* 12½in. high. *(Skinner)* **£3,675 $6,000**

Large Grueby Pottery vase, decorated with seven raised leaves and stems under a rich blue glaze, impressed mark, paper label, artist initials for W. Post, 12½in. high. *(Skinner)* **£5,500 $9,000**

Fine Grueby Pottery lamp, six vertical leaves and buds under a rich, feathered matte green glaze, mounted with a Bigelow and Kennard shade, mounted on teak stand, 23in. high. *(Skinner)* **£9,200 $15,000**

Grueby Pottery vase, Boston, circa 1904, modelled by Marie Seaman, matt-ochre glaze on repeating high-relief foliate decoration, impressed mark, 10½in. high. *(Skinner)* **£1,033 $1,725**

A small early 20th century Grueby pottery vase, Mass., 4¾in. high.
(Skinner) **£360 $585**

Grueby Art pottery vase, Boston, Mass., circa 1900, 21¼in. high.
(Skinner) **£2,500 $4,075**

Fine Grueby Pottery vase, cylindrical form with three broad leaves under a deep matt green glaze, impressed marks, 8in. high.
(Skinner) **£1,237 $1,955**

A Grueby Pottery vase, cylindrical form with leaves in relief under matt green glaze with unusually large glaze skips, impressed mark, 6¼in. high.
(Skinner) **£291 $460**

Green leaded shade on Grueby lamp base, Boston, Mass., circa 1905, 20in. high.
(Skinner) **£4,000 $6,520**

Grueby Pottery vase, bulbous base, alternating leaves and buds under a matt green glaze, 7¼in. high.
(Skinner) **£1,380 $2,070**

Grueby Faience Company vase, Boston, modelled by Wilhelmina Post, leathery matte green glaze on a bulbous form, 5⅞in. high.
(Skinner) **£2,300 $3,737**

Grueby Pottery vase, Boston, circa 1910, designed by George P. Kendrick, 10¾in. high.
(Skinner) **£14,067 $23,000**

Grueby Faience Co. vase, Boston, Massachusetts, circa 1902, with bulbous vase moulded design, matte green glaze, 7in. high.
(Skinner) **£338 $650**

A Grueby Art pottery vase, Mass., the matte green glaze initialled *AVL*, 5½in. high, circa 1905.
(Skinner) **£1,500 $2,450**

Grueby Pottery vase, Boston, circa 1902, designed by George P. Kendrick, modelled by Wilhelmina Post, 16½in. high. *(Skinner)*
£12,395 $20,700

A Grueby Pottery vase, stamped and artist signed, circa 1905, 7⅞in. high.
(Skinner) **£1,000 $1,600**

A Grueby Art pottery vase, Mass., with oatmeal glaze, 3⅝in. high, circa 1905.
(Skinner) **£550 $900**

Early 20th century Grueby Pottery two-colour vase, Massachusetts, 10¼in. high.
(Skinner) **£2,000 $3,250**

Grueby Pottery vase, Boston, Gertrude Stanwood, matt navy blue glaze with incised alternating floral and leaf decoration, 5⁷/₈in. high. *(Skinner)* **£660 $990**

Grueby Pottery vase, Boston, modelled by Wilhelminia Post, cylindrical form swollen at base, decorated with matte yellow glazed buds on elongated stems alternating with elongated leaf blades under matte green glaze, impressed marks and incised artist's cipher, 9⁷/₈in. high, 4¼in. diameter. *(Skinner)* **£3,000 $4,887**

Rare Grueby covered humidor, Boston, curdled matte sea-green glaze, cylindrical form with repeating floral band on rim, fitted disc-shaped lid with central knob, 8in. high. *(Skinner)* **£670 $1,092**

Rare Grueby Faience Company vase, Boston, modelled by Wilhelmina Post, No. 36, decorated with two tiers of overlapping leaf blades and alternating bud on stem, thin matte green glaze, 11¾in. *(Skinner)* **£3,525 $5,750**

A Grueby Pottery two-colour vase, elongated bottle neck on spherical cabbage form, circa 1905, 9¼in. high. *(Skinner)* **£2,800 $4,500**

Sampson Hancock established his pottery at the Gordon Works, Stoke, in 1857. Expansion was rapid, and by his death in 1900 it employed 150 workers. He was joined by his four sons, Sampson, Jabez, Harry and Arthur, and the firm moved to the Corona Pottery in Hanley in 1923, remaining there till its eventual closure in 1937.

Hancocks were one of the first factories to go in for freehand painted art pottery, and their early success was due in no small measure to the work of talented designers such as George Cartlidge, who designed their Morris ware, F.X. Abrahams (Rubens, Woodland and Titian Ware) and Molly Hancock, Jabez' youngest daughter, who produced Cherry Ripe and Cremona ware. Their most overtly Art Deco designs were mainly the work of Edith Gater in the Thirties. Patterns of flowers and fruits in deep, rich colours coexisted alongside brightly coloured cottage plates and dishes, butterfly ware and tableware.

Various marks were used throughout the firm's history, many of which included a crown with *S. Hancock & Sons* on a ribbon below, often also with the range name or designer's name. Later, an artist's palette was also used with the words *Ivory Ware, Hancocks England* on it and *Handpainted* below.

Hancocks Ware floral bowl in brown and orange, 1930s. *(Muir Hewitt)* **£40 $65**

Hancock's Ivory ware Galleon plate with shaped edge. *(Muir Hewitt)* **£50 $80**

Hancock's bowl with floral decoration, 1930s. *(Muir Hewitt)* **£35 $60**

Hancock's ivory ware cottage jug, 1930s, 7in. high. *(Muir Hewitt)* **£45 $70**

Leslie Harradine, who was to become one of Doulton's most prolific and expert modellers, was born in 1887 and joined the company's Lambeth Studios in 1902 as an apprentice modeller. At this time, too he enrolled at the Camberwell School of Art as a part-time student.

In 1912, he suddenly resigned and took himself off to Canada, where, with his brother, he set about farming 4,000 acres of land in Saskatchewan. Here he continued modelling in clay, but was never able to build a kiln to fire his pieces successfully. In the winter, when farm work became restricted, the brothers toured Saskatchewan, giving concerts and puppet shows. They made the marionettes themselves, and Leslie also proved himself as a skilful conjuror. With the outbreak of war in 1914, the brothers joined Lord Strathcona's Horse, and found themselves posted to France. Leslie had two horses shot from under him, and in the second incident badly injured his leg. Thereafter, he spent a good deal of time in hospital, married and started a family. After the war, he decided the wilds of Canada were no place for a wife and young child, so gave up his share of the farm to his brother and endeavoured to set up as an independent artist.

Charles Noke heard he was back in England, and tried his best to persuade him to come to Burslem, but Harradine was adamant. By now he valued his freedom too much to tie himself down once more, and he wanted to open a small studio in London. However, he did agree to work for Doulton on a freelance basis, and thus began one of the most fruitful collaborations in history between a sculptor and a china factory, and one which was to span almost forty years.

'I sent a model a month, sometimes two or three, for almost forty years,' Harradine recalled, shortly before his death in 1965. He had a wonderful eye for depicting movement and expression, and his Top o' the Hill, Autumn Breezes and the Old Balloon Seller are still among Doulton's most popular figures.

Columbine (Style one) HN1296, designed for Doulton by L. Harradine, issued 1928-1938, 6in. high. *(Lyle)* **£650 $1,040**

Rhythm HN1904, designed for Doulton by L. Harradine, issued 1939-1949, colour variation, 6¾in. high. *(Lyle)* **£1,600 $2,560**

Mam'selle HN724, designed for Doulton by L. Harradine, issued 1925-1938, colour variation, 7in. high.
(Lyle) **£1,450 $2,320**

Mask HN1271, designed for Doulton by L. Harradine, issued 1928-1938, colour variation, 6¾in. high.
(Lyle) **£1,600 $2,560**

Bather (Style one) HN1238, designed for Doulton by L. Harradine, issued 1927-1938, colour variation, 7¾in. high. *(Lyle)* **£1,250 $2,000**

Jasmine, HN1862, designed for Doulton by L. Harradine, issued 1938-1949, 7¼in. high.
(Lyle) **£650 $1,040**

Chloe, HN1479, designed for Doulton by L. Harradine, issued 1931-1949, colour variation, 5½in. high.
(Lyle) **£325 $520**

Pamela, HN1469, designed for Doulton by L. Harradine, issued 1931-1938, colour variation, 7½in. high.
(Lyle) **£650 $1,040**

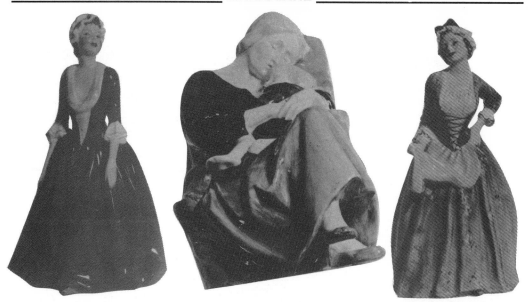

Gwynneth, HN1980, designed for Doulton by L. Harradine, issued 1934-1952, 7in. high.
(Lyle) **£275 $440**

Contentment, HN1323, designed for Doulton by L. Harradine, issued 1929-1938, colour variation, 7¼in. high.
(Lyle) **£1,000 $1,600**

Mary Jane, HN1990, designed for Doulton by L. Harradine, issued 1947-1959, 7½in. high.
(Lyle) **£375 $600**

Carolyn, HN2112, designed for Doulton by L. Harradine, issued 1953-1965, 7in. high.
(Lyle) **£275 $440**

Aileen HN1803, designed for Doulton by L. Harradine, issued 1937-1949, colour variation, 6in. high.
(Lyle) **£650 $1,040**

Biddy, HN1445, designed for Doulton by L. Harradine, issued 1931-1938, 5½in. high. *(Lyle)* **£275 $440**

Margery, HN1413, designed for Doulton by L. Harradine, issued 1930-1949, 11in. high. *(Lyle)* **£325 $520**

Sweet and Twenty, (Style one), HN1298, designed by L. Harradine, issued 1928-1969, 5¾in. high, *(Lyle)* **£325 $520**

Lisette, HN1523, designed for Doulton by L. Harradine, issued 1932-1936, 5¼in. high. *(Lyle)* **£750 $1,200**

Fiona (Style one), HN1924, designed for Doulton by L. Harradine, issued 1940-1949, 5¾in. high. *(Lyle)* **£750 $1,200**

Ermine Coat, HN1981, designed for Doulton by L. Harradine, issued 1945-1967, 6¾in. high. *(Lyle)* **£245 $390**

Butterfly HN1456, designed for Doulton by L. Harradine, issued 1931-1938, 6½in. high. *(Lyle)* **£1,500 $2,400**

Sunshine Girl HN1344, designed for Doulton by L. Harradine, issued 1929-1938, 5in. high. *(Lyle)* **£2,500 $4,000**

Swimmer HN1270, designed for Doulton by L. Harradine, issued 1929-1938, 7¼in. high. *(Lyle)* **£1,400 £2,240**

Iona HN1346, designed for Doulton by L. Harradine, issued 1929-1938, 7½in. high. *(Lyle)* **£2,000 £3,200**

Aileen HN1645, designed for Doulton by L. Harradine, issued 1934-1938, 6in. high. *(Lyle)* **£650 $1,040**

In the Stocks (Style one) HN1474, designed for Doulton by L. Harradine, issued 1931-1938, 5in. high. *(Lyle)* **£1,250 $2,000**

Bather (Style one) HN1708, designed for Doulton by L. Harradine, issued 1935-1938, colour variation, 7¾in. high. *(Lyle)* **£1,250 $2,000**

Lady Jester (Style one) HN1221, designed for Doulton by L. Harradine, issued 1927-1938, 7in. high. *(Lyle)* **£1,500 $2,400**

Negligee HN1219, designed for Doulton by L. Harradine, issued 1927-1938, 5in. high. *(Lyle)* **£850 $1,360**

Pierrette (Style three) HN1391, designed for Doulton by L. Harradine, issued 1930-1938, 8½in. high. *(Lyle)* **£1,750 $2,800**

Babette HN1423, designed for Doulton by L. Harradine, issued 1930-1938, 5in. high. *(Lyle)* **£550 $880**

Charmian, HN1568, designed for Doulton by L. Harradine, issued 1933-1938, 6½in. high. *(Lyle)* **£550 $880**

Mephisto HN723, designed for Doulton by L. Harradine, issued 1925-1938, colour variation, 6½in. high. *(Lyle)* **£1,750 $2,800**

Lady Clown HN1263, also called Clownette, designed for Doulton by L. Harradine, issued 1927-1938, colour variation, 7¼in. high. *(Lyle)* **£2,500 $4,000**

Boy with Turban HN1213, designed for Doulton by L. Harradine, issued 1926-1938, colour variation, 3¾in. high. *(Lyle)* **£550 $880**

Genevieve, HN1962, designed for Doulton by L. Harradine, issued 1941-1975, 7in. high. *(Lyle)* **£225 $360**

Angela (Style one) HN1204, designed for Doulton by L. Harradine, issued 1926-1938, 7¼in. high. *(Lyle)* **£1,250 $2,000**

Carmen (Style one) HN1267, designed for Doulton by L. Harradine, issued 1928-1938, 7in. high. *(Lyle)* **£650 $1,040**

Lady Clown HN717, designed for Doulton by L. Harradine, issued 1925-1938, 7½in. high. *(Lyle)* **£2,500 $4,000**

Bonnie Lassie HN1626, designed for Doulton by L. Harradine, issued 1934-1953, 5¼in. high. *(Lyle)* **£750 $1,200**

Rhythm HN1903, designed for Doulton by L. Harradine, issued 1939-1949, 6¾in. high. *(Lyle)* **£1,250 $2,000**

Bridesmaid (Style one) HN1433, designed for Doulton by L. Harradine, issued 1930-1951, 5¼in. high. *(Lyle)* **£195 $312**

Bather (Style one) HN687, designed for Doulton by L. Harradine, issued 1924-1949, colour variation 7¾in. high. *(Lyle)* **£650 $1,040**

Dawn HN1858, designed for Doulton by L. Harradine, issued 1938-?, 10in. high. *(Lyle)* **£1,500 $2,400**

Dreamland HN1473, designed for Doulton by L. Harradine, issued 1931-1938, 4¾in. high. *(Lyle)* **£2,000 $3,200**

Pierrette (Style three) HN1749, designed for Doulton by L. Harradine, issued 1936-1949, colour variation, 8½in. high. *(Lyle)* **£1,350 $2,160**

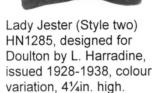

Lady Jester (Style two) HN1285, designed for Doulton by L. Harradine, issued 1928-1938, colour variation, 4¼in. high. *(Lyle)* **£1,500 $2,400**

Clothilde HN1598, designed for Doulton by L. Harradine, issued 1933-1949, 7¼in. high. *(Lyle)* **£600 $960**

Irish Colleen HN766, designed for Doulton by L. Harradine, issued 1925-1938, 6½in. high. *(Lyle)* **£1,750 $2,800**

Belle HN754, designed for Doulton by L. Harradine, issued 1925-1938, 6½in. high. *(Lyle)* **£650 $1,040**

Lambeth Walk HN1880, designed for Doulton by L. Harradine, issued 1938-1949, 10in. high. *(Lyle)* **£1,450 $2,320**

Derrick HN1398, designed for Doulton by L. Harradine, issued 1930-1939, 8in. high. *(Lyle)* **£475 $760**

Mam'selle HN786, designed for Doulton by L. Harradine, issued 1926-1938, colour variation, 7in. high. *(Lyle)* **£1,450 $2,320**

Lido Lady HN1229, designed for Doulton by L. Harradine, issued 1927-1938, colour variation, 6¾in. high. *(Lyle)* **£1,250 £2,000**

Harlequinade HN585, designed for Doulton by L. Harradine, issued 1923-1938, 6½in. high. *(Lyle)* **£650 $1,040**

Harlequinade HN1401, designed for Doulton by L. Harradine, issued 1930-1938, 8½in. high. *(Lyle)* **£1,500 £2,400**

Sylvia, HN1478, designed for Doulton by L. Harradine, issued 1931-1938, 10½in. high. *(Lyle)* **£350 $560**

Pierrette (Style one) HN731, designed for Doulton by L. Harradine, issued 1925-1938, colour variation, 7¼in. *(Lyle)* **£1,450 $2,320**

Bedtime Story, HN2059, designed for Doulton by L. Harradine, issued 1950-1996, 4¾in. high. *(Lyle)* **£195 $312**

Bather (Style two) HN773, designed for Doulton by L. Harradine, issued 1925-1938, 7½in. high. *(Lyle)* **£1,500 $2,400**

Boy with Turban HN662, designed for Doulton by L. Harradine, issued 1924-1938, colour variation, 3¾in. high. *(Lyle)* **£550 $880**

Pierrette (Style one) HN643, designed for Doulton by L. Harradine, issued 1924-1938, colour variation, 7¼in. high. *(Lyle)* **£1,100 $1,760**

Dulcinea HN1343, designed for Doulton by L. Harradine, issued 1929-1938, 5½in. high. *(Lyle)* **£1,500 $2,400**

Scotties HN1349, designed for Doulton by L. Harradine, issued 1929-1949, colour variation, 5¼in. high. *(Lyle)* **£1,250 $2,000**

Carnival HN1260, designed for Doulton by L. Harradine, issued 1927-1938, 8¼in. high. *(Lyle)* **£1,750 $2,800**

Pierrette (Style one) HN644, designed for Doulton by L. Harradine, issued 1924-1938, colour variation, 7¼in. high. *(Lyle)* **£950 $1,520**

Baba HN1247, designed for Doulton by L. Harradine, issued 1927-1938, colour variation, 3¼in. high. *(Lyle)* **£495 $792**

Moira HN1347, designed for Doulton by L. Harradine, issued 1929-1938, 6½in. high. *(Lyle)* **£2,000 $3,200**

Curly Knob HN1627, designed for Doulton by L. Harradine, issued 1934-1949, 6in. high. *(Lyle)* **£650 $1,040**

Harlequinade Masked HN1304, designed for Doulton by L. Harradine, issued 1928-1938, colour variation, 6½in. high. *(Lyle)* **£1,750 $2,800**

Marietta HN1699, designed for Doulton by L. Harradine, issued 1935-1949, 8in. high. *(Lyle)*   **£850 $1,360**

Clothilde HN1599, designed for Doulton by L. Harradine, issued 1933-1949, colour variation, 7¼in. high. *(Lyle)*   **£600 $960**

Gretchen HN1397, designed for Doulton by L. Harradine, issued 1930-1938, 7¾in. high. *(Lyle)*   **£550 $880**

Mephisto HN722, designed for Doulton by L. Harradine, issued 1925-1938, 6½in. high. *(Lyle)* **£1,750 $2,800**

Midinette (Style one) HN1289, designed for Doulton by L. Harradine, issued 1928-1938, 9in. high. *(Lyle)*   **£1,750 $2,800**

Bonjour, HN 1879, designed for Doulton by L. Harradine, issued 1938-1949, 6¾in. high. (Lyle) **£750 $1,200**

Tildy, HN1576, designed for Doulton by L. Harradine, issued 1933-1939, 5in. high. (Lyle) **£750 $1,200**

Rhoda, HN1573, designed for Doulton by L. Harradine, issued 1933-1949, 10¼in. high. (Lyle) **£550 $880**

Sweet Anne, HN1496, designed by L. Harradine, issued 1932-1967, colour variation, 7in. high. (Lyle) **£225 $360**

Autumn Breezes, HN1911, designed for Doulton by L. Harradine, issued 1939-1976, 7½in. high. (Lyle) **£165 $264**

Miss Demure, HN1463, designed for Doulton by L. Harradine, issued 1931-1949, colour variation, 7in. high. (Lyle) **£325 $520**

Hinged Parasol, HN1578, designed for Doulton by L. Harradine, issued 1933-1949, 6½in. high.
(Lyle) **£550 $880**

Gloria, HN1700, designed for Doulton by L. Harradine, issued 1935-1938, colour variation, 7in. high.
(Lyle) **£1,350 $2,160**

Toinette, HN1940, designed for Doulton by L. Harradine, issued 1940-1949, 6¾in. high. (Also called Meryll).
(Lyle) **£875 $1,400**

Patricia, HN1414, designed for Doulton by L. Harradine, issued 1930-1949, 8½in. high. *(Lyle)* **£425 $680**

Lady Charmian, HN1949, designed for Doulton by L. Harradine, issued 1940-1975, colour variation, 8in. high. *(Lyle)* **£225 $360**

Victorian Lady, HN726, designed for Doulton by L. Harradine, issued 1925-1938, 7½in. high.
(Lyle) **£325 $520**

Pantalettes, HN1709, designed for Doulton by L. Harradine, issued 1935-1938, colour variation, 8in. high. *(Lyle)* **£650 $1,040**

Top o' the Hill, HN1833, designed for Doulton by L. Harradine, issued 1937-1971, 7in. high. *(Lyle)* **£165 $264**

Paisley Shawl (Style two), HN1988, designed for Doulton by L. Harradine, issued 1946-1975, colour variation, 6¼in. high. *(Lyle)* **£225 $360**

Priscilla, HN1340, designed for Doulton by L. Harradine, issued 1929-1949, colour variation, 8in. high. *(Lyle)* **£275 $440**

Her Ladyship, HN1977, designed for Doulton by L. Harradine, issued 1945-1959, 7¼in. high. *(Lyle)* **£275 $440**

Phyllis, HN1420, designed for Doulton by L. Harradine, issued 1930-1949, 9in. high. *(Lyle)* **£395 $630**

The firm of Hollinshead & Kirkham was established in the early 1870s in Burslem and in 1876 moved into the old Wedgwood Unicorn Pottery in Tunstall.

In 1915, Clarice Cliff went to them to learn lithography, following a couple of years at Lingard and Webster's. She stayed only a year, however, at which time she received a better offer from Wilkinson's Royal Staffordshire Pottery.

The pottery produced by H & K comprised both table and occasional ware, such as jugs, bowls and dishes in rich deep colours These would be decorated with naturalistically painted flowers such as tulips, pansies and violas as well as fruit, depicted against bright backgrounds in a patchwork of pink, dark blue, brown and beige. They also made use of strong Art Deco shapes, particularly in their table ware.

Hollingshead and Kirkham cup, saucer and plate, 1930s. *(Muir Hewitt)* **£75 $125**

HONITON

The Honiton Art Potteries were established in Devon in 1881 to produce earthenware. Their mark until 1915 was a crest with *G & HH* above and *The Honiton Lace Art Pottery Co* below. Between 1918-47 it became *Collard Honiton England* and from 1947 onwards *The Honiton Pottery Devon.*

Honiton jug designed by Collard. *(Muir Hewitt)* **£75 $120**

Honiton Collard jug with stylised floral decoration, 1930s.
(Muir Hewitt) **£75 $125**

Honiton Art Pottery planter with floral decoration, circa 1950.
(Muir Hewitt) **£40 $65**

Hummel figures are produced by the Austrian firm of William Goebel and are the creation of one of their designers, Berthe Hummel. They are essentially cute/kitsch (depending on your point of view) figures of little boys and girls in peasant costume and in appealing poses. Each is given a name such as 'Just Resting', a little girl sitting on a gate, or 'Little Hiker'.

They were very popular here in the 50s and 60s, and seem to have a great following in America, where whole collections of them appear frequently at auction.

Eventide, No. 99.
(Bearne's)   **£125 $199**

Little Pharmacist, 6in.
(Jackson's) **£135 $220**

Sensitive Hunter, 5½in.
(Jackson's) **£85 $143**

Shepherd's Boy, 5½in.
(Jackson's) **£120 $198**

Little Fiddler, 5¾in.
(Jackson's) **£65 $104**

Coquettes, 5¼in.
(Jackson's) **£95 $145**

Little Hiker, 6in.
(Jackson's) **£80 $132**

Playmates, 4½in.
(Jackson's) **£100** **$165**

Star Gazer, 4¾in.
(Jackson's) **£95** **$154**

Little Bookkeeper, 4½in.
(Jackson's) **£100** **$165**

A Fair Measure, 5⅝in.
(Jackson's) **£80** **$132**

Letter to Santa, 7in.
(Jackson's) **£110** **$181**

Timid Little Sister, 7in.
(Jackson's) **£150** **$247**

Meditation, 5¼in.
(Jackson's) **£70** **$110**

Smiling Through, 4¾in.
(Jackson's) **£100** **$165**

Auf Wiedersehen, 5¼in.
(Jackson's) **£85** **$143**

The Photographer, 4¾in.
(Jackson's) **£100** **$165**

We Congratulate, 3½in.
high. *(Jackson's)* **£40** **$66**

Apple Tree Boy, 4in. high.
(Jackson's) **£50** **$82**

Strolling Along, 4¾in. high.
(Jackson's) **£94** **$154**

Signs of Spring, 5in. high.
(Jackson's) **£80** **$132**

Valentine Joy, 5¾in. high.
(Jackson's) **£114** **$187**

Easter Time, 4in. high.
(Jackson's) **£100** **$165**

*White Angel Holy Water
Font*, 3½in. high.
(Jackson's) **£20** **$33**

Doll Bath, 5¼in. high.
(Jackson's) **£94** **$154**

Wayside Harmony, 5in.
(Jackson's) **£80 $132**

Let's Sing, 3⅞in.
(Jackson's) **£55 $88**

Birthday Serenade, 5¼in.
(Jackson's)   **£95 $154**

Little Tailor, 5½in. high.
(Jackson's)   **£87 $143**

Chicken Licken, 4¾in. high.
(Jackson's)   **£94 $154**

Feeding Time, 5¾in. high.
(Jackson's)   **£117 $192**

Be Patient, 4¼in. high.
(Jackson's)   **£33 $55**

Coffee Break, 4in. high.
(Jackson's)   **£67 $110**

Soloist, 4¾in. high.
(Jackson's)   **£53 $88**

The Thuringian forests have been home to many small porcelain factories in the last few hundred years. Perhaps the best known of these was Kloster Veilsdorf, which in the 18th century was noted for its figure production.

In the 1930s the Katzhütte or Katzenhausen factory continued this tradition, turning out figures, mainly of elegant ladies in striking poses and very much in the Art Deco style, which remind one of the chryselephantine sculptures of Chiparus and Preiss.

Katzhütte or Katzenhausen 1930s figure of a dancing lady, 8½in. high.
(Muir Hewitt)   £280 $450

A Katzhütte Thuringia pottery figure of a young lady with a dog.
(Christie's)   £250 $400

Katzhütte (also known as Katzenhausen) lady figure with fan, 17in. high, 1930s.
(Muir Hewitt)   £1,200 $1,950

A Katzhütte Thuringia ceramic figure of a dancing girl, standing in profile with arms held aloft, printed factory mark, 12¼in. high. (Christie's)   £350 $560

The Lenci pottery was active in Turin during the 1930s and produced three distinctive types of wares. The first, consisting of wall plaques in the form of female heads in scarves, as if going to Mass and figures of the Madonna and Child, were aimed at the domestic market. In stark contrast were the second group, made up of female figures, either nude or clad in contemporary costumes.

The third, and less well-known type, consists of vases and dishes decorated with Cubist-inspired painted scenes.

A Lenci Art Deco ceramic figure with box and cover, moulded as the head, shoulders and torso of a young woman, 21.4cm. high. *(Phillips)* **£1,400 $2,275**

A Lenci polychrome pottery figure group, modelled as a shepherd and shepherdess tending their two sheep, the man leaning against a tree stump gazing at the woman holding a lamb in her arms, 26.5cm. high. *(Christie's)* **£1,200 $1,950**

'Nella', a polychrome painted pottery figure modelled by Helen Konig Scavini for Lenci, circa 1931. *(Christie's)* **£1,900 $3,078**

Lenci, possibly modelled by Adele Jacopi, Europa and the Bull, delicately tinted pink and green, heightened with gilding, marked, circa 1935, 52.5cm. high. *(Sotheby's)* **£3,500 $5,200**

A large figure of a native girl, marked *Lenci, Torino Made in Italy*, 1930s, 55.5cm. high.
(Lyle) **£450 $690**

A large Lenci polychrome painted pottery dish, modelled in the form of an otter trying to catch a salmon in a pond, dated *1938*, 54cm. diameter.
(Christie's) **£660 $1,009**

A Lenci polychrome pottery figure modelled as a young woman wearing a yellow jacket and green trousers, 44.5cm.
(Christie's) **£2,070 $3,208**

A Lenci Art Deco ceramic figure, modelled as a girl wearing an orange hat, black jacket and black, white and grey chequered skirt, 37.5cm. high.
(Phillips) **£2,200 $3,300**

A Lenci earthenware box and cover, cover modelled with a dozing elf, dated 4.2.32, 21cm.
(Lyle) **£345 $517**

A Lenci Pottery model of a young naked girl wearing a black and white chequered tammie, holding a book and with a dog on top of a globe, 19½in. high.
(Christie's) **£4,620 $7,490**

A stylish Lenci pottery figure, modelled as a woman wearing a brown and beige striped dress, 23cm. high.
(Phillips) **£1,100 $1,800**

A Lenci ceramic head of stylised form, the hair and eye sockets painted in shades of blue and green, 14in. high.
(Christie's) **£1,000 $1,500**

A Lenci ceramic figure, the young girl in geometric patterned dress, 9½in. high, painted marks.
(Christie's) **£450 $720**

A fine Lenci female wall face wearing floral head square, 14in. high. *(Anderson & Garland)* **£800 $1,320**

A Lenci figure modelled as a naked girl reclining on a tartan blanket, black painted Lenci marks, 30.7cm. long. *(Christie's)* **£1,000 $1,600**

A Lenci polychrome painted pottery figure of a young woman wearing a blue and black tweed dress, holding her hat, 37cm. high. *(Christie's)* **£4,370 $6,773**

A Lenci polychrome pottery figure of a young girl, wearing a black and white polka dot dress, 39.5cm. *(Christie's)* **£5,520 $8,556**

A rare Lenci pressed felt 'Bersagliere' soldier doll, Italian, circa 1920, with painted face and brown eyes, in original Lenci box. *(Sotheby's)* **£900 $1,450**

A Lenci figure group, of a bare-breasted native woman wearing a patterned wrap-around skirt in yellow, green and black, 44cm. high. *(Phillips)* **£945 $1,417**

A good Lenci ceramic group modelled as a mer-child holding a fish aloft, she kneels on the back of two open-mouthed fish, 51cm. high. *(Phillips)* **£3,150 $4,725**

A Lenci polychrome pottery wall mask, modelled as a young woman wearing a grey top hat, factory marks, 35cm. high. *(Christie's)* **£1,610 $2,495**

A Lenci pottery model of a naked female, dancing with arms outstretched, on a black mound base, 11½in. high. *(Christie's)* **£1,012 $1,811**

A Lenci Pottery box and cover, painted in shades of green with a gingham pattern, 12.5cm. long. *(Christie's)* **£242 $390**

A polychrome ceramic ashtray, the central column as a nude woman holding a vase, factory marks and label, Lenci, circa 1930, 21cm. high. *(Finarte)* **£1,313 $2,127**

A polychrome ceramic head of a young girl, framed by flowers and ears of corn, Lenci, 1930s, 18cm. high. *(Finarte)* **£563 $923**

A polychrome ceramic figure of a little girl in peasant costume holding an urn, factory marks, Lenci, circa 1930, 27cm. high. *(Finarte)* **£874 $1,415**

A Lenci Pottery vase, by Beppe Ferinando, painted in shades of orange, yellow, brown and black with geometric pastoral village scene, dated *1933*, 25.5cm. high. *(Christie's)* **£618 $1,000**

A Lenci polychrome ceramic figure of a mermaid and her baby astride a giant turtle, painted in shades of green and brown, 12¾in. high.
(Christie's)　　　£1,280　$1,920

L Cacio Selle Colombe, a Lenci Pottery figure modelled as a girl sitting with her floral and striped skirts spread out around her, 24.5cm. high. (Phillips)　£600　$900

A pair of Lenci book ends each modelled as a naked young girl with short blond hair, kneeling between a book and a small dog, 23.5cm. high. (Christie's)　£935　$1,431

A glazed earthenware figure manufactured by Lenci, 1930s, modelled as a young woman seated coquettishly on a bookcase, 15¼in. high, painted mark Lenci Made in Italy Torino 9.XI P.
(Christie's)　　　£3,000　$4,800

'Amore Paterno', a Lenci Pottery group, modelled by Sandro Vachetti, of a man clasping a young baby to his lips, painted in colours, dated 1931, 17cm. high.
(Christie's)　　　£780　$1,240

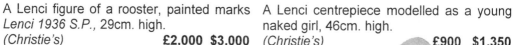

A Lenci figure of a rooster, painted marks *Lenci 1936 S.P.,* 29cm. high.
(Christie's) **£2,000 $3,000**

A Lenci centrepiece modelled as a young naked girl, 46cm. high.
(Christie's) **£900 $1,350**

A Lenci ceramic group, modelled as a seated figure of a girl wearing a black dress, a coloured and patterned cape, and a purple scarf, 34.8cm. high.
(Phillips) **£1,000 $1,500**

A Lenci polychrome pottery figure, by Adele Jacopi, modelled as a young girl with blond hair, wearing floral sprig dress, standing beside small tree and holding two doves on outstretched arms, painted factory marks, impressed signature, 23cm. high. (Christie's) **£517 $840**

A large Lenci female wall mask wearing a brown ground gilt kashmir style scarf, 12in. high, marked, 1937.
(David Lay) **£350 $560**

A Lenci polychrome painted pottery figure of a young woman wearing a short black dress, relaxing with her feet up in a floral patterned armchair, 25cm. high.
(Christie's) **£1,540 $2,356**

The Linthorpe Pottery was established in 1879, near Middlesborough, with Henry Tooth as manager, and, until 1882, Christopher Dresser as art director and designer. Their early wares were designed on simple, flowing lines with equally flowing glazes in two or more rich colours, while later sgraffito or pâte-sur-pâte decoration was introduced. It ceased production in 1890. Pieces are marked with Linthorpe, sometimes over the outline of a squat vase. Some are signed by Dresser, and or initialled with Tooth's monogram.

A Linthorpe teapot, the design attributed to Dr. C. Dresser, 21.3cm. high. *(Christie's)* **£250 $400**

A Linthorpe twin-handled pottery vase designed by Christopher Dresser, the vessel of flattened oviform with bulbous neck, 20.8cm. high. *(Phillips)* **£200 $320**

A Linthorpe earthenware vase moulded on each side with grotesque fish faces, 17.9cm. high. *(Christie's)* **£500 $800**

A Linthorpe Pottery jardinière designed by Dr. Christopher Dresser, the swollen dimpled form, with foliate rim, decorated with double loop handles and alternating rosettes, 13.8cm. high. *(Christie's)* **£400 $640**

A Linthorpe Pottery jug, designed by Dr. Christopher Dresser, with everted rim continuing to form an angled handle, covered in a streaky caramel, crimson and green glaze, 21cm. high. *(Christie's)* **£2,000 $3,200**

A Linthorpe vase, designed by Dr. Christopher Dresser, with frilled lug handles and incised decoration of a bearded face on one side, 22cm. high. *(Christie's)* **£3,000 $4,800**

A Linthorpe vase, designed by Dr. Christopher Dresser, formed as a cluster of five pointed gourd shapes encircling a central funnel-shaped neck, 11cm. high. *(Christie's)* **£1,500 $2,400**

A Linthorpe vase, designed by Dr. Christopher Dresser, decorated with four grotesque heads, each forming a handle, covered in a streaky green glaze, 22.5cm. high. *(Christie's)* **£1,000 $1,600**

A Linthorpe vase, designed by Dr. Christopher Dresser, glazed in streaky pale and dark green, with moulded maze patterns and linear designs, 22.5cm. high. *(Christie's)* **£550 $880**

A large Linthorpe Pottery vase designed by Christopher Dresser, of almost egg shape, covered with a brown, milky green, milky blue and amber glaze, 43.5cm. high. *(Christie's)* **£1,400 $2,250**

A Linthorpe goat's-head vase, designed by Dr. Christopher Dresser, double gourd shape, decorated with four goat's heads, 28cm. high. *(Christie's)* **£3,250 $5,200**

A Linthorpe vase, designed by Dr. Christopher Dresser, the gourd-shaped body with double angular spout and curved carrying-bar, streaked glaze of green and brown. *(Christie's)* **£1,200 $1,900**

A Linthorpe earthenware jug designed by Dr Christopher Dresser, covered in a thick predominantly green and brown glaze, (slight restoration to lip rim) 16.7cm. high. *(Christie's)* **£250 $400**

A Linthorpe vase, designed by Dr. Christopher Dresser, the streaky glaze in tones of green and brown, with incised decoration of a single fern encircling the gourd, 19cm. high.
(Christie's) **£1,100 $1,750**

A Linthorpe face vase, designed by Dr. Christopher Dresser, domed cylindrical shape with double angular spout, decorated with a stylised face on one side, 15.5cm. high. *(Christie's)* **£700 $1,120**

A Linthorpe jug, designed by Dr. Christopher Dresser, humped shape with vertical spout and carved handle, incised geometric pattern, 18cm. high.
(Christie's) **£650 $1,040**

A Linthorpe Pottery vase, designed by Christopher Dresser, decorated with stylised linear patterns, 21cm. high.
(Phillips) **£800 $1,300**

Dame Lucie Rie was born in Vienna in 1902, where her father was a doctor and university professor, and where she studied under Powolny after the First World War.

She married Hans Rie, a business man, and quickly won acclaim in her native land for her work. This consisted mainly of simple, thinly potted stoneware, sometimes polished or covered with rough textured glazes, her style influenced both by functionalist ideals and by Roman pottery. Her mark at this time was *LRG* over *Wien*.

In 1938, as the Nazi menace loomed ever nearer, the Ries fled to Britain. In an amicable separation, Hans moved on to the United States, but Lucie decided to stay. She made contact with Bernard Leach, who was fairly disparaging about her Vienna work, and urged her to make heavier pieces. Desperate to fit in, Lucie attempted to follow his advice, but pottery was a fairly low priority at that stage of the war, and she found work in a lens factory, making ceramic buttons in her spare time. In 1945 she was joined by another German refugee, Hans Coper, and their continuing friendship and mutual support was to be a pivotal influence in both their lives. Coper's encouragement was to do much to restore the self-confidence that Leach had shaken.

After the war, they began making domestic wares as their bread and butter, but also continued with their own pots. Most of Lucie's pieces from this time were either of porcelain decorated with unglazed bands of cross hatched decoration coloured with manganese oxide, or stoneware in elegant, simple shapes.

Lucie used colour sparingly, and developed a number of glazes, notably a yellow one containing uranium. Others were characterised by their rough, uneven texture.

The significance of her work was recognised when she was made a Dame of the British Empire in 1990, shortly after the first of a series of strokes had forced her retirement from active potting. She died in 1995.

A small stoneware cream jug, white glazed interior, bronze exterior feathered rim, rounded body, impressed *LR* seal, circa 1955, 3in. high. *(Bonhams)* **£300 $477**

A stoneware three-piece cruet set, shiny white glaze with inlaid vertical blue lines, impressed *LR* seal, circa 1954, salt 4¼in. high, mustard 2⅛in. high. *(Bonhams)* **£2,200 $3,498**

A porcelain beaker, cream and white running glaze, impressed *LR* seal, circa 1954, 4¼in. high. *(Bonhams)* **£850 $1,352**

A small earthenware bottle with stopper, mustard yellow glaze, cylindrical body, painted *LR*, circa 1942, 3¹/₈in. high. *(Bonhams)* **£450 $716**

An impressive stoneware jardinière by Dame Lucie Rie, yellow and beige pitted glaze, impressed *LR* seal, circa 1960, 8½in. high. *(Bonhams)* **£2,600 $4,771**

A circular mirror, set within a turquoise with brown shading ceramic frame, cloth backing, wire loop for hanging, impressed *LR* seal, circa late 1940s, 6⁵/₈in. diameter. *(Bonhams)* **£1,300 $2,067**

A stoneware bronze cylindrical teapot, white glaze to recessed base, bamboo handle, raised finial to lid, impressed *LR* seal, circa 1955, 5⁵/₈in. high. *(Bonhams)* **£1,600 $2,544**

A stoneware cylindrical white teapot, speckled shiny glaze, brown rim to teapot and feathered brown rim to lid, bamboo handle, impressed *LR* seal, circa 1952, 5½in. high. *(Bonhams)* **£1,500 $2,385**

An outstanding oval vessel by Dame Lucie Rie, the shoulder with a band of impressed hollows heightened turquoise, impressed *LR* seal, 7in. wide. *(Bonhams)* **£9,500 $14,986**

A stoneware pouring vessel by Lucie Rie, white with pulled handle, impressed *LR* seal, circa 1957, 3¼in. high.
(Bonhams) **£425** **$680**

A stoneware beaker by Dame Lucie Rie and Hans Coper, white slightly pitted glaze, impressed *LR* and *HC* seals, circa 1955, 4⁵/₈in. high. *(Bonhams)* **£900** **$1,431**

A small oval stoneware dish, white glaze with ochre speckles and rim, the interior with inlaid blue lines, impressed *LR* seal, circa 1953, 4in. long.
(Bonhams) **£800** **$1,272**

An earthenware straight sided teapot, with sloping concaved top (minus lid), yellow and white glaze, painted *LRG Wien*, circa 1930s, 7³/₈in. long, 3¼in. high.
(Bonhams) **£1,900** **$3,021**

A stoneware cylindrical cigarette box, bronze, the lid with diagonal sgraffito, the interior rims terracotta with diagonal sgraffito, impressed *LR* seal, circa 1967, 4in. high. *(Bonhams)* **£1,700** **$2,703**

A porcelain mustard pot, brown with sgraffito to lower part and interior blue rim, the lid with inset blue circle, impressed *LR* seal, circa 1955, 1¹/₃in. high.
(Bonhams) **£550** **$875**

A white stoneware teapot by Dame Lucie Rie, the lid with brown rim, the tip of spout repaired, circa 1957,9in. wide.
(Bonhams) **£750** **$1,376**

A stoneware cylindrical cigarette box, bronze, the lid with diagonal sgraffito, the interior rims terracotta with diagonal sgraffito, impressed *LR* seal, circa 1967, 4¾in. high. *(Bonhams)* **£1,300** **$2,067**

A stoneware footed bowl, grey/green spiralling glaze with dark brown flecks, impressed *LR* seal, circa 1974, 6in. diameter. *(Bonhams)* **£1,300 $2,067**

A small earthenware white bowl with pale yellow, orange and brown speckling, painted *LRG Wien*, circa 1935, 3¼in. diameter. *(Bonhams)* **£1,500 $2,385**

A rare stoneware 'spinach' bowl by Dame Lucie Rie, covered in a thick cratered glaze with a golden bronze band at the rim, circa 1986, 7in. diameter.
(Bonhams) **£2,200 $4,037**

A fine bronze and white porcelain bowl by Dame Lucie Rie, sgraffito radiating lines inside and contrasting inlaid lines to exterior, circa 1980, 8in. diameter.
(Bonhams) **£3,000 $5,505**

A stoneware salad bowl with pulled lip by Lucie Rie, covered in a finely pitted bluish-white glaze with iron-brown flecks, circa 1954, 14.3cm. high.
(Christie's) **£725 $1,160**

A porcelain bowl by Dame Lucie Rie, covered in a translucent finely crackled yellow glaze and lustrous bronze run and fluxed glaze to rim, circa 1980, 16.6cm. diameter. *(Christie's)* **£1,760 $2,922**

A small stoneware bowl by Lucie Rie, covered in a mirror-black manganese glaze with white rim, circa 1953, 10cm. diameter.
(Christie's) **£500 $800**

A superb porcelain bowl by Lucie Rie, uranium yellow with deep bronze running band at rim, impressed seal, circa 1975, 7in. diameter. *(Bonhams)* **£6,000 $9,600**

An earthenware bowl, shiny black glaze, circa 1944/45, 4in. diameter. *(Bonhams)* **£750 $1,193**

A miniature porcelain footed bowl, bronze, impressed *LR* seal, circa 1974, 3³/₈in. diameter. *(Bonhams)* **£1,200 $1,908**

A stoneware oblong bowl, white with blue/grey shading and brown flecks, impressed *LR* seal, circa 1950, 7¹/₈in. long. *(Bonhams)* **£1,400 $2,226**

An earthenware small bowl, orange glaze, running to the exterior, impressed *LR* seal, circa 1942, 3¾in. diameter. *(Bonhams)* **£380 $604**

A small conical bowl, pale blue/beige interior speckled by blue, the exterior matt beige with inlaid crimson lines, impressed *LR* seal, circa 1960, 3¾in. diameter. *(Bonhams)* **£1,900 $3,021**

A fine porcelain golden bronze bowl by Lucie Rie, the deep terracotta foot and well surrounded by a circular ring of turquoise, circa 1986, 9¼in. diameter. *(Bonhams)* **£4,500 $7,200**

A lime-yellow stoneware bowl by Dame Lucie Rie, with feathered bronzed band, impressed *LR* seal, circa 1975, 5¾in. diameter. *(Bonhams)* **£1,500 $2,753**

A fine stoneware 'knitted' bowl by Lucie Rie, inlaid with concentric dark circles from the well, impressed *LR* seal, circa 1982, 9in. diameter. *(Bonhams)* **£3,000 $4,800**

A small earthenware bowl, lilac with brown underglaze, impressed *LR* seal, circa 1940, 4½in. diameter. *(Bonhams)* **£750 $1,193**

A porcelain miniature bowl, cream glaze, brown feathered rim, slightly squeezed form, impressed *LR* seal, circa 1954, 3in. long. *(Bonhams)* **£480 $763**

A porcelain conical bowl, matt white with bands of inlaid lines near rim and base, impressed *LR* seal, circa 1953, 5⁵⁄₈in. diameter. *(Bonhams)* **£1,800 $2,862**

A porcelain footed bowl by Lucie Rie, 'American' yellow glaze, impressed LR seal, circa 1970, 6¹⁄₈in. diameter. *(Bonhams)* **£1,350 $2,160**

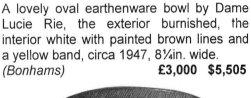

A stoneware footed bowl, by Dame Lucie Rie and Hans Coper, shiny dark brown glaze with inlaid vertical lines to the exterior, impressed *LR* and HC seals, circa 1953, 6in. diameter. *(Bonhams)* **£1,700 $2,703**

A lovely oval earthenware bowl by Dame Lucie Rie, the exterior burnished, the interior white with painted brown lines and a yellow band, circa 1947, 8¼in. wide. *(Bonhams)* **£3,000 $5,505**

A stoneware salad bowl by Lucie Rie, white with speckling and unglazed ring within, circa 1955, 9½in. wide. *(Bonhams)* **£725 $1,160**

A rare porcelain bowl by Lucie Rie, bronze with a sloping white band inlaid with diagonal lines, circa 1958, 4³⁄₈in. diameter. *(Bonhams)* **£1,800 $2,900**

A porcelain bowl, flaring wide rim, pale green with brown shading, impressed *LR* seal, circa 1974, 8¹/₈in. diameter. *(Bonhams)* **£2,800 $4,452**

A porcelain miniature bowl, cream glaze with a brown rim, impressed *LR* seal, circa 1954, 3¹/₈in. diameter. *(Bonhams)* **£380 $604**

A porcelain footed bowl, grey glaze with blue shading to rim, impressed *LR* seal, circa 1960, 6³/₈in. diameter. *(Bonhams)* **£4,200 $6,678**

A small stoneware bowl, pink and white knitted, brown rim, impressed *LR* seal, circa 1965, 5⁵/₈in. diameter. *(Bonhams)* **£1,200 $1,908**

A porcelain conical bowl, pale green with grey shading, feathered bronze rim, impressed *LR* seal, circa 1970, 8⁷/₈in. diameter. *(Bonhams)* **£5,000 $7,950**

A small stoneware bowl, beige and mustard glaze with shades of green, impressed *LR* seal, circa 1954, 3⁵/₈in.. diameter. *(Bonhams)* **£600 $954**

A rare porcelain bowl by Lucie Rie, the white glazed exterior inlaid with small brown circles each with a dot, circa 1968, 5in. diameter. *(Bonhams)* **£4,000 $6,400**

A small porcelain footed bowl, pale cream glaze, with inlaid concentric circles, impressed *LR* seal, circa 1954, 4¼in. diameter. **£1,400 $2,226**

A porcelain bowl, pale green crackled glaze with brown shading darker to interior, the rounded base rising to straight sided rim, impressed *LR* seal, circa 1955, 7¼in. diameter. *(Bonhams)* **£2,200 $3,498**

A stoneware bowl, pale grey with inlaid radiating dark lines, impressed *LR* seal, circa 1980, 9³/₈in. diameter. *(Bonhams)* **£8,500 $13,515**

A stoneware bowl, grey and white pitted glaze with spiral decoration to exterior, impressed *LR* seal, circa 1980, 10¼in. diameter. *(Bonhams)* **£15,000 $23,850**

A stoneware bowl by Dame Lucie Rie, off white, gently curving rim with bronze feathered band, impressed *LR* seal, circa 1954/55, 8¾in. diameter. *(Bonhams)* **£2,600 $4,134**

BOWLS _____ LUCIE RIE _____

A large earthenware bowl, yellow crackled glaze with brown/black shading and rim, embossed *LR* seal, circa 1940, 12¼in. diameter. *(Bonhams)* **£2,500 $3,975**

A dramatic stoneware open bowl by Dame Lucie Rie, the white bowl flecked with dark brown, circa 1960, 12⅝in. diameter. *(Bonhams)* **£4,200 $7,707**

A stoneware blue bowl, a sloping band below the rim to exterior and interior with inlaid criss cross decoration, the lower body sloping to the round base with darker blue running glaze, impressed *LR* seal, circa 1958, 4½in. diameter. *(Bonhams)* **£1,700 $2,703**

A stoneware shallow bowl, shiny white glaze to interior and band below rim, the sloping underside bronze with radiating sgraffito lines, a glazed ring to interior well, impressed *LR* seal, circa 1952, 5¼in. diameter. *(Bonhams)* **£1,500 $2,385**

A footed porcelain bowl, bronze, the interior with radiating sgraffito lines, a blue ring to the well also with radiating sgraffito, impressed *LR* seal, circa 1956, 4⅝in. diameter. *(Bonhams)* **£2,400 $3,816**

A conical stoneware bowl, mottled grey and white glaze, with spiralling sections revealing brown body, impressed *LR* seal, circa 1953, 6in. diameter. *(Bonhams)* **£2,600 $4,134**

A stoneware footed bowl, mottled brown running glaze over beige body, impressed *LR* seal, circa 1957, 5³/₈in. diameter. *(Bonhams)* **£700 $1,113**

A stoneware bowl, oblong shaped to everted rim, beige and pink with brown pitting, impressed *LR* seal, circa 1958, 6½in. long. *(Bonhams)* **£1,400 $2,226**

A stoneware footed bowl, shiny white glaze, exterior with a band of bronze running to the foot, impressed *LR* seal, circa 1955, 4¹/₈in. diameter. *(Bonhams)* **£1,200 $1,908**

A small round stoneware bowl, pale blue and beige interior glaze, the exterior with shiny white glaze, unglazed band to foot and rim, circa 1960, 3⁷/₈in. diameter. *(Bonhams)* **£1,000 $1,590**

A porcelain footed bowl, blue with a ten petalled design in bronze with white echoing inlaid design, impressed *LR* seal, circa 1965, 7⁷/₈in. diameter. *(Bonhams)* **£4,200 $6,678**

A stoneware bowl by Lucie Rie with compressed flared sides, the exterior carved with fluted decoration, impressed *LR* seal, 14cm. high. *(Christie's)* **£2,000 $3,200**

A stoneware oblong bowl, grey, brown and blue speckled glaze, impressed *LR* seal, circa 1950, 9½in. long. *(Bonhams)* **£1,400 $2,226**

An important earthenware shallow bowl, black with a golden bronze interior, painted *LRG Wien*, circa 1936, 9⁷/₈in. diameter. *(Bonhams)* **£15,500 $24,645**

A stoneware bowl, green with mottled brown speckles, inlaid blue horizontal lines to exterior, impressed *LR* seal, circa 1955, 6in. diameter. *(Bonhams)* **£3,500 $5,565**

An earthenware small bowl, reddish brown with an ochre over glaze, incised *LR*, circa 1942, 3⁷⁄₈in. diameter. *(Bonhams)* **£380 $604**

A burnished earthenware bowl with saucer, some slight pitting, signed *LRG Wien*, circa 1930s, 5³⁄₈in. diameter. *(Bonhams)* **£3,200 $5,088**

A stoneware footed bowl, thick running pitted green and brown glaze, impressed *LR* seal, circa 1968, 8⁵⁄₈in. diameter. *(Bonhams)* **£3,000 $4,770**

A fine stoneware bowl by Dame Lucie Rie, on shallow foot, slate-grey ground covered in thick white pitted glaze, circa 1960, 24cm. diameter. *(Christie's)* **£6,050 $10,527**

A stoneware salad bowl, running white glaze over beige, bronze rim, pouring lip, impressed *LR* seal, circa 1966, 10in. long. *(Bonhams)* **£2,500 $3,975**

A stoneware bowl, beige/grey with running mustard/yellow, some brown speckling, impressed *LR* seal, circa 1958, 6¹⁄₈in. diameter. *(Bonhams)* **£700 $1,113**

A small earthenware bowl, yellow glaze with tiny brown flecks, painted *LRG Wien*, circa 1930s, 3½in. diameter. *(Bonhams)* **£1,100 $1,749**

A stoneware shallow bowl, shiny white interior and running band below rim, the sloping underside bronze with radiating sgraffito lines, impressed _LR_ seal, circa 1952, 6½in. diameter.
(Bonhams) **£1,700 $2,703**

A small footed porcelain bowl, shiny white exterior glaze with an unglazed straight sided band to the rim with inlaid vertical lines, the well dark brown matt glaze with sgraffito edged with blue, impressed _LR_ seal, circa 1962, 3in. diameter.
(Bonhams) **£1,000 $1,590**

A porcelain footed conical bowl, interior with a yellow and brown cross meeting in the well dividing a brown grid filled with yellow and green spots, the exterior matt with a yellow cross meeting at a brown circle above the foot, impressed _LR_ seal, circa 1954, 6¼in. high.
(Bonhams) **£6,000 $9,540**

A porcelain manganese bowl, the interior with a band of sgraffito around the well, the exterior with an unglazed band around the foot with inlaid purple lines, similar decoration to recessed foot, manganese drip over the underglaze band, impressed _LR_ seal, circa 1954/56, 6⅛in. diameter.
(Bonhams) **£2,500 $3,975**

A stoneware oval bowl, off white pitted glaze with brown flecks and manganese rim, impressed _LR_ seal, circa 1960, 5⅛in. high. _(Bonhams)_ **£4,200 $6,678**

A stoneware open footed bowl, tones of brown and beige with a green rim, impressed _LR_ seal, circa 1974, 9⅛in. diameter. _(Bonhams)_ **£1,500 $2,385**

A bronze porcelain shallow bowl, the terracotta well with a bronze circle and spot to centre, impressed *LR* seal, circa 1970, 8½in. diameter. *(Bonhams)*   **£8,000 $12,720**

A porcelain footed bowl, white and bronze with parallel horizontal inlaid lines surmounted by three sgraffito circles, the design echoed on the bronze exterior in sgraffito, impressed *LR* seal, circa 1953, 10in. diameter. *(Bonhams)*   **£5,500 $8,745**

A stoneware wide rimmed bowl, the brown interior with blue and white shades, fine inlaid blue lines to the rim, the blue/grey reverse with white inlaid lines and brown flecks, the brown body revealed in places, impressed *LR* seal, circa 1960, 11^{7}/$_{8}$in. diameter. *(Bonhams)* **£5,000 $7,950**

A porcelain footed bowl, by Lucie Rie, white with twelve pointed petal designs inside and out in running golden bronze with inlaid zig zag lines, impressed *LR* seal, circa 1965, 7½in. diameter. *(Bonhams)* **£10,500 $16,695**

A porcelain footed bowl, mixed clay, white with spiral of green, brown and pale pink, impressed *LR* seal, circa 1963/64, 5⅞in. diameter. *(Bonhams)*   **£2,700 $4,293**

A cobalt blue stoneware bowl by Dame Lucie Rie, the rim speckled with a darker blue, impressed *LR* seal, circa 1970, 8¼in. diameter. *(Bonhams)*   **£2,200 $4,037**

A stoneware footed bowl, tones of brown and grey with dark grey flecks over dark brown body, impressed *LR* seal, circa 1964, 7¼in. diameter.
(Bonhams)   **£1,300 $2,067**

A stoneware bowl, straight sided, pale turquoise speckled glaze revealing in places dark brown body, unglazed band to foot, impressed *LR* seal, circa 1954, 4in. diameter.   **£2,000 $3,180**

A small porcelain bowl, white with a deep band of bronze to the exterior with diagonal sgraffito, impressed *LR* seal, circa 1952, 4¼in. diameter.
(Bonhams)   **£1,300 $2,067**

A white porcelain footed bowl, wide flared rim, incised concentric circles to rim and one to well and foot, incised *LR* seal, circa 1960, 5³⁄₈in. diameter.
(Bonhams)   **£2,500 $3,975**

A porcelain white open bowl, shiny glaze footed, impressed *LR* seal, circa 1960, 9¼in. diameter.
(Bonhams)   **£3,500 $5,565**

A Lucie Rie stoneware bowl, with straight sides covered with an off-white glaze having faint brown speckling, 13.5cm. diameter. *(Phillips)*   **£2,000 $3,200**

A large footed conical bowl, by Dame Lucie Rie, matt off white glaze, impressed *LR* seal, circa 1960, 12¾in. diameter. *(Bonhams)* **£12,000 $19,080**

A porcelain white bowl, the circular foot rising to straight sides with raised spots, impressed *LR* seal, circa 1974, 5¼in. diameter. *(Bonhams)* **£9,000 $14,310**

A porcelain footed bowl, shiny white glaze, slightly flaring form, impressed *LR* seal, circa 1975, 6³/₈in. diameter. *(Bonhams)* **£3,500 $5,565**

A large stoneware footed bowl, shiny white glaze, impressed *LR* seal, circa 1962, 12¹/₈in. diameter. *(Bonhams)* **£9,000 $14,310**

A porcelain bowl, white interior and rim, exterior bronze with a band of criss cross sgraffito below the rim, impressed *LR* seal, circa 1953/54, 5¼in. diameter. *(Bonhams)* **£4,800 $7,632**

A stoneware and porcelain bowl, pitted white glaze, unglazed band to exterior and interior and rim revealing brown body, impressed *LR* seal, circa 1977, 9½in. diameter. *(Bonhams)* **£13,000 $20,670**

A smaller stoneware coffee pot, dark brown with vertical sgraffito to cylindrical neck, pulled handle, white glazed interior with slight feathering to neck, impressed *LR* seal, circa 1954, 8½in. high.
(Bonhams)   **£2,600 $4,134**

A stoneware coffeepot by Lucie Rie, brown with cane handle, impressed *LR* seal, circa 1952, 7¼in. high.*(Bonhams)* **£1,400 $2,280**

A stoneware lidded coffee pot, bronze, white glazed interior and band to lid, sloping form from circular base, impressed *LR* seal, circa 1952, 7½in. high.
(Bonhams)   **£1,300 $2,067**

A stoneware coffee pot, shiny black glaze, bamboo handle, the lid with a narrow band of white, impressed *LR* seal, circa 1952, height to top of lid 7¼in.
(Bonhams)   **£1,100 $1,749**

A stoneware coffee pot with pulled handle, straight sided with recessed lid, bronze with white glazed interior, feathering to rim, indented groove to underside of handle, impressed, *LR* seal, circa 1955, 6½in. high.
(Bonhams)   **£2,000 $3,180**

A stoneware lidded coffee pot, dark brown with vertical sgraffito to cylindrical neck, pulled handle, white glazed interior with slight feathering to neck, impressed *LR* seal, circa 1954, 9¾in. high.
(Bonhams)   **£2,600 $4,134**

An important earthenware cup and saucer, shallow cup form, painted *LRG Wien*, circa 1930s, diameter of cup 5¼in.
(Bonhams) **£4,800 $7,632**

An oval stoneware sake cup, pink and grey glaze, brown undulating rim, impressed *LR* seal, circa 1970, 1⅝in. high.
(Bonhams) **£750 $1,193**

A stoneware mug, white glaze to interior, the exterior with running bronze glaze, white glazed rounded base, impressed *LR* seal, circa early 1950s, 3in. high.
(Bonhams) **£420 $668**

A stoneware cup and saucer, shiny white glaze, interior of cup and band to underside of saucer in bronze, conical cup form, impressed *LR* seal, circa early 1950s, 3¼in. high. *(Bonhams)* **£480 $763**

A curved porcelain cup, cream glaze with a light brown rim, impressed *LR* seal, circa 1954, 2¼in. high. *(Bonhams)* **£300 $477**

A small stoneware cup form, interior green and grey, the exterior with shiny white glaze and inlaid circular lines, bronze rim, circa 1952, 2½in. high.
(Bonhams) **£1,100 $1,749**

A stoneware cup and saucer by Dame Lucie Rie and Hans Coper, white with khaki interior and base of cup and interior of saucer foot, impressed *LR* and *HC* seals, circa 1952, 3¼in. high.
(Bonhams) **£550 $875**

A stoneware handled pouring vessel, speckled white interior and recessed base, bronze exterior and handle, handle with three incised lines, impressed *LR* seal, circa 1955, 8in. long.
(Bonhams) **£1,200 $1,920**

A porcelain dish, American yellow glaze with dark brown feathered rim, impressed *LR* seal, circa 1958, 6in. diameter. *(Bonhams)* **£950 $1,511**

A small stoneware dish, pale blue glaze with a faint blush of yellow, brown rim, impressed *LR* seal, circa 1960, 4³/₈in. diameter. *(Bonhams)* **£750 $1,193**

A burnished earthenware small dish, squared form, with gold rim and recessed gold foot, dark beige interior, impressed *LR* seal, circa 1946, 3¾in. diameter. *(Bonhams)* **£900 $1,431**

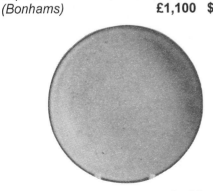

A small stoneware oval dish, brown and pale blue with inlaid white lines to interior, impressed *LR* seal, circa 1953, 4³/₈in. long. *(Bonhams)* **£1,100 $1,749**

An earthenware dish, pale green and brown, incised *LR*, circa 1940-42, 9½in. diameter. *(Bonhams)* **£900 $1,431**

A small stoneware dish, pale blue glaze with a strong blush of yellow, brown rim, impressed *LR* seal, circa 1960, 4½in. high. *(Bonhams)* **£650 $1,034**

A porcelain dish, American yellow glaze with pale brown and white rim, impressed *LR* seal, circa 1958, 6³/₈in. diameter. *(Bonhams)* **£1,050 $1,670**

A stoneware sloping jug, shiny white glaze, brown feathered rim, impressed *LR* seal, circa 1955, 4¼in. high.
(Bonhams) **£600 $954**

A white stoneware milk jug by Dame Lucie Rie, with bronzed feathered rim, impressed *LR* seal, circa 1958, 3⅝in. high.
(Bonhams) **£220 $404**

MIRRORS

A circular mirror, set within a ceramic frame, gold with grooves of inlaid white, short pipe-like attachment, rush backing, wire loop for hanging, circa late 1940s, 6¾in. diameter.
(Bonhams) **£1,600 $2,544**

A circular mirror, set in a white crackle glazed ceramic surround, gold rims, red velvet backing, wire loop for hanging, circa late 1940s, 6⅞in. diameter.
(Bonhams) **£750 $1,193**

PLATES

A stoneware plate, shiny black glaze, white rim, white glazed foot, impressed *LR* seal, circa 1953, 7¼in. diameter.
(Bonhams) **£600 $954**

An earthenware plate, by Dame Lucie Rie and Hans Coper, white crackled glaze, impressed *LR* and *HC* seals, circa 1946, 7⅛in. diameter.
(Bonhams) **£650 $1,034**

A miniature pot, matt buff speckled body, rounded body, oval rim, painted *LR*, 2⅝in. high. *(Bonhams)* **£450 $716**

An earthenware squared pot, white and grey glaze revealing in sections the brown body, round raised rim, incised *LR* seal, circa 1940-42, 5⅛in. high. *(Bonhams)* **£1,300 $2,067**

A porcelain footed 'prune' pot, round foot curving to circular rim, running manganese glaze, impressed *LR* seal, circa 1953, 5¼in. high. *(Bonhams)* **£2,500 $3,975**

A burnished earthenware pot, central cylindrical body, the interior glazed pale green, painted *LR*, circa 1940, 4⅜in. high. *(Bonhams)* **£1,700 $2,703**

An earthenware covered pot, brown and turquoise glaze throughout, recessed lid with hollowed knob finial, impressed *RIE* seal, painted *Made In England*, circa 1942, 5½in. diameter. *(Bonhams)* **£1,300 $2,067**

An earthenware pot, running white glaze with pink and brown shades, interior sections showing dark brown body, painted *LRG Wien*, circa 1930s, 5¾in. high. *(Bonhams)* **£1,700 $2,703**

A small round earthenware pot, squeezed form, the rim almost oblong, shiny yellow glaze with brown rim and flecks, embossed *LR* seal, circa early 1940s, 3in. high. *(Bonhams)* **£950 $1,511**

A porcelain cylindrical cache-pot, white with horizontal inlaid blue lines, slightly flared form, impressed *LR* seal, circa 1965, 5¼in. high. *(Bonhams)* **£900 $1,431**

A tall cylindrical pot, green and brown inlay decoration, impressed *LR* seal, circa 1953, 18¼in. high. *(Bonhams)* **£14,000 $22,260**

A stoneware cream pot by Lucie Rie, covered in an unusual yellow glaze with running bronze rim, circa 1960, 2¾in. high. *(Bonhams)* **£475 $760**

A stoneware miniature pot, matt buff speckled body, rounded body, oval rim, painted *LR*, 2¹/₈in. high.
(Bonhams) **£340 $541**

A round earthenware lidded pot, black glaze, *painted LRG Wien,* circa 1935, 5¼in. diameter, 3¹/₈in. high.
(Bonhams) **£2,500 $4,075**

An earthenware pot, crackled glaze, cream with flecks of blue, green and yellow to exterior, pale yellow interior with darker yellow flecks, painted *LRG Wien*, circa 1930s, 4³/₈in. diameter, 3¼in. high.
(Bonhams) **£2,000 $3,250**

An earthenware pot, pale green glaze with flecks of brighter green, squeezed to form oval rim, painted *LRG Wien*, circa 1930s, 4³/₈in. (Bonhams) **£3,000 $4,770**

A cylindrical earthenware pot, pale yellow glaze flecked and bright green, painted *LRG Wien*, circa 1930s, 4in. high.
(Bonhams) **£2,500 $4,000**

A miniature stoneware pot, the rounded body squeezed to form an oval rim, pale white and pink glaze over brown spiral body, impressed *LR* seal, circa 1945, 2⁷/₈in. high. (Bonhams) **£400 $636**

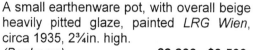

A small earthenware pot, with overall beige heavily pitted glaze, painted *LRG Wien*, circa 1935, 2¾in. high.
(Bonhams) **£2,200 $3,500**

A miniature earthenware pot, pale yellow with brown shading, impressed *LR* seal, circa early 1940s, 2¾in. high.
(Bonhams) **£550 $875**

A white round stoneware pot, with turned in rim, pitted glaze with beige flecks, impressed *LR* seal, circa 1975, 6¾in. high.
(Bonhams) **£4,200 $6,678**

A monumental stoneware covered pot, manganese with vertical sgraffito to upper body, white glazed rim and cover, impressed *LR* seal, circa 1952, 18¼in. high. *(Bonhams)* **£28,000 $44,520**

A tall cylindrical earthenware pot, white with brown and grey shades, incised *LR*, circa 1940, 8¼in. high.
(Bonhams) **£1,200 $1,908**

An earthenware burnished pot with turned in rim, brown and white running glazed interior, painted *LRG Wien*, circa 1930s, 2⁷/₈in. high. *(Bonhams)* **£6,500 $10,335**

A miniature earthenware pot, cream glaze with brown shading, brown feathered rim, impressed *LR* seal, circa 1945, 2¾in. high. *(Bonhams)* **£320 $509**

A miniature earthenware pot, squeezed form, pale pink over brown underglaze, impressed *LR* seal, circa 1945, 2⁷/₈in. high. *(Bonhams)* **£400 $636**

A stoneware green pot, round base sloping to smaller round rim, green with inlaid vertical lines and pitting showing brown body, impressed *LR* seal, circa 1953, 3¾in. high. *(Bonhams)* **£900 $1,431**

A red earthenware covered round pot, with incised Union Jack on cover with glazed blue and white detailing, interior of pot and cover with white glaze, painted *LRG Wien*, circa 1934, 2¾in. high. *(Bonhams)* **£1,900 $3,021**

An early earthenware pot, mottled running green glaze with an ochre splash to one side, circa 1940/42, 7¼in. high. *(Bonhams)* **£4,000 $6,360**

An earthenware pot, pale cream glaze with shades of pale green, blue and yellow, painted *LRG Wien*, circa 1930, 4¾in. high. *(Bonhams)* **£3,000 $4,770**

A tall necked porcelain vase, shiny white glaze, cylindrical foot flaring to rounded body, slender neck flaring to flat topped rim, impressed *LR* seal, circa 1978, 10in. high. *(Bonhams)* **£3,500 $5,565**

A tall necked stoneware vase, rounded central body, beige with brown flecks, impressed *LR* seal, circa 1958, 15¾in. high. *(Bonhams)* **£6,000 $9,540**

A tall necked stoneware vase, conical rim, off white matt crackled glaze, impressed *LR* seal, circa 1954, 15¼in. high. *(Bonhams)* **£2,200 $3,498**

A tall necked speckled vase, stoneware, narrow foot rising to round body and narrowly flared rim, white with brown flecks, impressed *LR* seal, circa 1954, 16in. high. *(Bonhams)* **£6,000 $9,540**

A stoneware porcelain vase, the rounded body rising to long narrow neck and flaring to flattened rim, pale green with shades of pink, brown rim, impressed *LR* seal, circa 1958, 8⁷/₈in. diameter. *(Bonhams)* **£2,900 $4,611**

A fine stoneware vase by Dame Lucie Rie, the body with diagonal fluting, covered by a lightly pitted mustard glaze with a bluish hue, 8in. high. *(Bonhams)* **£2,600 $4,771**

A porcelain composite vase, with disc shaped body rising from oval foot to narrow neck with flared rim, the rim pink and purple with radiating sgraffito and hint of beige, impressed *LR* seal, circa 1956, 7¾in. high. *(Bonhams)* **£4,800 $7,632**

A stoneware oval pitted vase, rounded lower body converging to narrow rim, heavy pitted white glaze with brown flecks, impressed *LR* seal, circa 1965, 8¼in. high. *(Bonhams)* **£2,200 $3,498**

A stoneware vase, heavy pitted white glaze, rounded body rising to flared rim, impressed *LR* seal, circa 1978, 9⁷/₈in. high. *(Bonhams)* **£6,500 $10,335**

A porcelain bottle vase, the rounded body converging from a flattened shoulder to a slender neck which rises to a flared rim, beige lower body, palest blue upper neck and rim, slight crackle, light bronze edge, impressed, *LR* seal, circa 1965, 10½in. high. *(Bonhams)* **£7,000 $11,130**

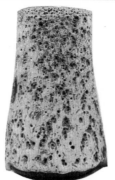

A stoneware oval vase, the form narrowing from brown curved circular base to oval rim, heavy pitted white/beige volcanic glaze, impressed *LR* seal circa 1960, 6½in. high. *(Bonhams)* **£1,700 $2,703**

A stoneware vase, rounded form squeezed to oval rim, pitted green glaze flecked with brown, unglazed sloping base, impressed *LR* seal, circa 1968, 5⅛in. high. *(Bonhams)* **£1,300 $2,067**

A squared stoneware vase, blue and beige pitted glaze revealing brown body, flattened rim, impressed *LR* seal, circa 1958, 8in. high. *(Bonhams)* **£3,000 $4,770**

A stoneware vase, round body rising to curving oval rim, brown and beige pitted glaze, impressed *LR* seal, circa 1962, 7¾in. high. *(Bonhams)* **£4,000 $6,360**

A stoneware oval vase, pitted green glaze with brown flecks, unglazed ring around lower body, impressed *LR* seal, circa 1960, 6in. high. *(Bonhams)* **£1,800 $2,862**

A cylindrical earthenware vase, light blue with shades of brown, incised *LR,* circa early 1940s, 6¾in. high. *(Bonhams)* **£2,500 $3,995**

A stoneware cylindrical vase, blue with beige patches, the exterior with inlaid vertical and diagonal lines, glaze running to foot, impressed *LR* seal, circa 1960, 5¼in. high. *(Bonhams)* **£1,700 $2,703**

A stoneware vase, shades of blue and grey, the exterior with inlaid diagonal blue lines, rounded rim, impressed *LR* seal, circa 1959, 6³/₈in. high. *(Bonhams)* **£2,500 $3,975**

A cylindrical earthenware vase, green and brown running glaze, heavily pitted, slightly upturned rim, painted *LRG Wien*, circa 1930s, 5⁷/₈in. high. *(Bonhams)* **£7,000 $11,130**

A porcelain vase, pale green with bronze feathered rim deeply running in the interior, five bands of embossed criss-cross decoration, impressed *LR* seal, circa 1952, 5¹/₈in. high. *(Bonhams)* **£2,600 $4,134**

A stoneware blue and beige vase, with fine inlaid diagonal lines to exterior, impressed *LR* seal, circa 1957, 7¹/₈in. high. *(Bonhams)* **£2,400 $3,816**

An earthenware straight sided vase, shiny brown glaze, impressed *LR* seal to side, circa 1948, 6½in. high. *(Bonhams)* **£1,100 $1,749**

A small stoneware vase, oval form, pale blue/green with brown flecks, unglazed curving base, impressed *LR* seal, circa 1960, 4in. high. *(Bonhams)* **£800 $1,272**

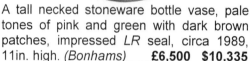

A tall necked stoneware bottle vase, pale tones of pink and green with dark brown patches, impressed *LR* seal, circa 1989, 11in. high. *(Bonhams)* **£6,500 $10,335**

A porcelain conical vase, bronze with a band below the rim, red with two white lines, the cylindrical base flaring to the wide round rim, impressed *LR* seal, circa 1966/67, 7³/₈in. high.
(Bonhams) **£7,500 $11,925**

A tall necked stoneware vase, the oval flattened body rising to flared neck with circular flanged rim, white and beige with brown flecks, impressed *LR* seal, circa 1955, 17¼in. high.
(Bonhams) **£6,000 $9,540**

A small stoneware vase, round sloping base shaped to oval, green/blue with brown flecks, impressed *LR* seal, circa 1965, 3⁷/₈in. high.
(Bonhams) **£750 $1,193**

A porcelain bulbous vase, tones of grey and brown, the rounded middle converging to a round rim, impressed *LR* seal, circa 1972, 5½in. high. *(Bonhams)* **£900 $1,431**

An exquisite white porcelain vase by Dame Lucie Rie, with inlaid lines running around the body, impressed *LR* seal, circa 1980, 7in. high. *(Bonhams)*   **£2,000 $3,670**

A tall necked stoneware vase, spiralling glaze to flared rim and neck, white, green, pink and brown with speckles, impressed *LR* seal, circa 1967/8, 14½in. high. *(Bonhams)*   **£16,000 $25,440**

A porcelain oval bottle vase, shiny bronze running glaze, the unglazed flared rim with radiating inlay decoration to the interior and sgraffito to the exterior, impressed *LR* seal, circa 1960, 8⅛in. high. *(Bonhams)*   **£5,500 $8,745**

A stoneware white pitted vase, the small round base flaring slightly, sloping body to squeezed oval rim, unglazed band to lower body, beige flecks to glaze, impressed *LR* seal, circa 1964, 3⁷/₈in. high.
(Bonhams) **£750 $1,193**

A stoneware bottle vase, narrow neck and slightly flared rim, green pitted glaze on dark body, brown flecks, circa 1960, 7¼in. high.
(Bonhams) **£2,800 $4,452**

A stoneware waisted vase, off white with brown flecks, rounded towards base, impressed *LR* seal, circa 1955, 7½in. high.
(Bonhams) **£1,100 $1,749**

A stoneware bottle vase, grey and beige pitted glaze, the rounded form with a rectangular collar and flared oval rim, impressed *LR* seal, circa 1980, 12in. high.
(Bonhams) **£14,000 $22,260**

An earthenware tall vase, the interior and a deep band at rim of thick running ochre and brown glaze, reddish brown body with incised horizontal lines, painted *LRG Wien*, circa 1935, 9¼in high.
(Bonhams) **£1,700 $2,703**

The Maling Pottery was founded in North Hylton, near Sunderland, in 1762 by the Maling family, in whose possession it remained until the mid 19th century. They produced plain and decorated earthenware.

In 1853 the name was changed to C.T. Maling and the company was bought by the Ford Co. in 1854.

In the early part of the 20th century they produced attractive cream-coloured domestic occasional wares, decorated with bold flower patterns and with a slight lustre effect. Though still relatively inexpensive, these are now increasingly sought after by collectors today.

Maling ginger jar in iridescent green with floral band and lid, 1930s.
(Muir Hewitt)   **£220 $360**

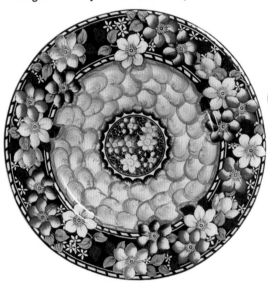

Maling Clematis design plate, 10in. diameter, circa 1948.
(Muir Hewitt)   **£150 $245**

Maling lustre two handled comport with floral decoration, 10in. wide.
(Lyle)   **£100 $160**

Maling lustre bowl with floral decoration, Newcastle on Tyne, 8in. diameter.
(Lyle)   **£140 $230**

A Maling circular plaque with raised floral decoration including tulips on blue ground, 11in. *(Anderson & Garland)* **£240 $396**

A Maling Edward VIII
Coronation plaque,
designed by Lucien
Boullemier, 32cm.
(Tennants) **£1,760 $2,816**

Maling teapot, 1930s, with
grapevine decoration.
(Muir Hewitt) **£40 $60**

Maling plate with floral
decoration, 10in. diameter.
(Muir Hewitt) **£200 $300**

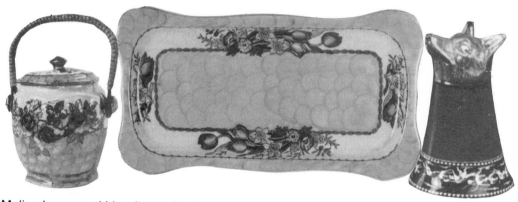

Maling hexagonal biscuit
barrel, decorated with
'Rosine' pattern, circa 1960,
6½in. *(G.A. Key)* **£100 $157**

Maling trinket tray with floral
decoration, 1930s.
(Muir Hewitt) **£75 $125**

A Maling stirrup cup,
modelled as a fox mask with
tapering red body, 15cm.
(Anderson & Garland)
£120 $192

A Maling circular plaque with
raised floral and butterfly
decoration on blue ground,
11¼in. *(Anderson &
Garland)* **£130 $215**

Maling green ground jug
decorated with floral band of
coloured rosettes, 10in.
high, 1930s.
(Muir Hewitt) **£90 $140**

A fine Maling 11in. circular
plaque with raised cottage,
millwheel bridge and floral
decoration. *(Anderson &
Garland)* **£200 $320**

The Marblehead pottery was established in 1905 with the view of providing occupational therapy for patients in a local Massachusetts sanatorium. After a short while, however, it was operating as a separate commercial venture. The pottery produced earthenware vases and bowls, in simple, often straight-sided shapes, and covered in muted matt glazes. Characteristic decoration includes animal and flower motifs and also features of the Massachusetts coast such as seaweed, fish, ships etc. Its produce was sold from 1908 onwards. The Marblehead mark consists of an impressed *M* and the emblem of a sailing ship, with the potter's initials incised.

Important Marblehead Pottery vase, matt blue ground glaze, incised decoration at shoulder consisting of five panels, each with a stalking panther, 7½in. high. (Skinner) **£7,034 $11,500**

A decorated Marblehead pottery four-colour vase, Mass., circa 1910, 6in. high. (Lyle) **£1,320 $1,980**

Pair of Marblehead Pottery sailing ship bookends, Massachusetts, matt glaze decorated in blue, dark blue, light blue, red, black and mustard, 5½in. high. (Skinner) **£307 $460**

Marblehead Pottery decorated vase, Massachusetts, early 20th century, 6³⁄₈in. high. (Skinner) **£623 $1,200**

Marblehead Pottery experimental landscape vase, executed by Arthur E. Baggs, circa 1925, 7¼in. high. (Skinner) **£2,000 $3,200**

Marblehead Pottery decorated vase, Marblehead, Massachusetts, early 20th century, with incised and painted repeating design of flowers, 3¾in. high. (Skinner) **£1,039 $2,000**

Marblehead Pottery decorated vase, Massachusetts, early 20th century, with repeating design of parrots on branches, 7in. high. (Skinner) **£850 $1,275**

The son of the noted designer and china painter Thomas Moorcroft, William Moorcroft (1872-1945) studied at Burslem School of Art and the National Art Training School. He qualified as an art teacher, but in 1896 went to work as a designer for James Macintyre of Burslem. When Macintyre's Art Pottery department closed in 1913, Moorcroft built his own kiln and workshops at Cobridge, where he specialised in floral and landscape designs on deep blue and green grounds, as well as magnificent plain lustre glazes.

Although on the whole his style remained wedded to naturalistic decoration throughout, an Art Deco influence did appear in the late 1920s in bands of geometric motifs and a certain stylisation of his plant forms. He was hugely successful and his products sold worldwide; he was appointed potter to HM Queen Mary in 1928.

Moorcroft struggled to keep his factory going during the war, dying in 1945 just as his son, Walter, arrived back from the forces to take over. Walter retired in 1987, leaving his younger brother, John, in charge. The factory goes from strength to strength today, and Moorcroft pieces are collectable as never before.

A Moorcroft 'Chrysanthemum' pattern two-handled vase, blue-green raised slip decoration of chrysanthemums in amber, yellow, green and purple, 31cm. high. *(Christie's)* **£1,980 $3,544**

'Orchids and Springflowers', a Moorcroft ovoid vase with everted rim, painted in shades of pink, purple, blue, yellow and green on a graduated blue ground, painted blue signature, 16cm. high. *(Christie's)* **£345 $560**

'Dawn', a Moorcroft salt-glaze stoneware vase of shouldered form and everted rim, painted with a landscape band between chevron borders, in shades of blue, pink and cream, painted blue signature, 21cm. high. *(Christie's)* **£1,380 $2,250**

'Claremont', a Moorcroft baluster vase, painted in shades of pink, purple, yellow and blue on a green ground, impressed factory marks, 9.5cm. high. *(Christie's)* **£575 $935**

'Waving Corn', a Moorcroft salt-glaze stoneware plate, painted in shades of blue, impressed factory marks, 22cm. diameter. *(Christie's)* **£402 $655**

An oviform vase decorated with a band of vine leaves and berries, in shades of yellow, pink and green on a deep blue ground, 12in. high. *(Christie's)* **£385 $686**

'Leaf and Berry', a Moorcroft vase, ovoid form with cylindrical neck, painted in shades of yellow, green, pink and purple on a graduated green/blue ground under a partial flambé ground, painted blue signature, original paper label, 30cm. high. *(Christie's)* **£1,725 $2,810**

'Pomegranate', a Moorcroft ovoid jardinière, with everted rim, painted in shades of pink, purple, ochre and blue on a mottled blue ground, painted blue signature, 24cm. high. *(Christie's)* **£1,500 $2,450**

A large twin-handled vase, decorated with a band of plums and foliage, in shades of pink, mauve and green on a dark blue ground, 12½in. high. *(Christie's)* **£1,430 $2,549**

'Claremont', a Moorcroft pottery slender ovoid vase with everted rim, painted in colours under a mottled flambé glaze, painted blue signature, 26cm. high. *(Christie's)* **£2,990 $4,875**

Florian Ware Moorcroft Art Pottery vase, white floral form on cobalt blue ground, 8in. high. *(Skinner)* **£609 $920**

A William Moorcroft Liberty & Co. pewter mounted 'Claremont' jar and cover, 8¼in. high. *(Bonhams)* **£1,000 $1,495**

A Moorcroft Cornflower pattern three handled cylindrical vase, with white piped decoration of cornflowers, covered in a yellow, blue and green glaze against a cream ground, 19cm. high. *(Christie's)* **£1,500 $2,400**

A Moorcroft Chrysanthemum pattern urn shaped vase, the white piped decoration of chrysanthemums amongst scrolling foliage, covered in a puce, green and amber glaze, 1913, 21.6cm. high. *(Christie's)* **£1,750 $2,800**

An attractive Moorcroft Florian Ware vase, slip trailed in white and decorated in shades of blue with a flower pattern. *(Phillips)* **£200 $380**

A Moorcroft 'Liberty & Co.' Florian Ware vase, tube-lined with poppies in blue and green, on a yellow ground, 12.4cm. high. *(Bonhams)* **£500 $807**

A good William Moorcroft Liberty & Co. 'Poppies' flambé biscuit barrel and pewter cover, 6½in. high.
(Bonhams) **£1,000 $1,495**

A pair of Moorcroft Pottery spill vases with 'Pomegranate' pattern on deep blue ground, 12½in. high.
(Andrew Hartley) **£620 $942**

A pair of Moorcroft 'Pomegranate' pattern vases, navy blue background decorated with fruiting pomegranates and green foliage, dated *1919*, 10½in. high.
(Christie's) **£1,322 $2,075**

A Moorcroft 'Hazledene' pattern bowl with incurved rim, decorated in the centre with a large central tree and smaller trees at the side, 24cm. diameter.
(Phillips) **£400 $640**

A Moorcroft 'Willow Tree' vase, footed ovoid, tube-lined with weeping willows in pink and green, 16cm. high.
(Bonhams) **£800 $1,292**

A Moorcroft pair of ovoid vases, the blue/ivory ground divided by green leaves and pink buds, green signature mark, 20.8cm. *(Bristol)* **£720 $1,094**

'Anemone', a pair of Moorcroft candlesticks, painted in shades of pink, purple and green on a blue ground, impressed factory marks, 9cm. high.
(Christie's) **£575 $935**

An ovoid vase with everted rim decorated with a band of frilled orchids, in pastel tones on a cream ground, 8½in. high.
(Christie's) **£300 $480**

'Claremont', a Moorcroft ovoid vase with everted rim, painted in shades of pink, purple, ochre and green on a pale green, painted green signature, 26cm. high.
(Christie's) **£3,450 $5,625**

A pair of cylindrical candlesticks decorated in the 'Pomegranate' pattern, in shades of pink, ochre and green on a mottled green and blue ground, 8in. high.
(Christie's) **£990 $1,765**

A pair of Florian Ware baluster vases decorated with scrolling cartouches of poppies and foliage, in shades of pale and dark blue, 12in. high.
(Christie's) **£1,000 $1,600**

A Macintyre 'Claremont' pattern bowl, streaked blue and green ground with decoration of pink, green and blue mushrooms, circa 1903, 12cm. high.
(Christie's) **£825 $1,477**

An octagonal bowl with everted rim, the interior decorated with alternate panels of peacock feathers and tulips, 10in. wide.
(Christie's)   **£350 $560**

A twin-handled vase, decorated in Florian Ware cartouches of pink roses and green foliage on a blue ground, 8in. high.
(Christie's)   **£3,100 $5,000**

A twin-handled square biscuit barrel and cover, decorated in the 'Pomegranate' pattern, in shades of pink and blue on a sage green ground, 6¼in. high.
(Christie's)   **£475 $760**

'Pomegranate', a Moorcroft shouldered jardinière, painted in shades of pink, purple, ochre and green on a blue ground, painted green signature, 20cm. high.
(Christie's)   **£483 $787**

A Flamminian vase made for Liberty, embossed on the shoulder with three foliate roundels, covered in a rose pink glaze, 6½in. high.
(Christie's)   **£200 $320**

A Florian Ware twin-handled vase, decorated with scrolling cartouches of peacock feathers and flowerheads, in shades of pale and dark blue, 8in. high.
(Christie's)   **£950 $1,500**

Moorcroft Pottery bowl, green/blue ground, decorated with aquilegia, impressed and monogrammed mark, 8in. diameter. *(G.A. Key)* **£85 $123**

A William Moorcroft 'Pansy' vase, tube-lined with purple, yellow, mauve and pink open flowerheads, 5in. high. *(Bonhams)* **£320 $478**

A Moorcroft brown chrysanthemum vase, the twin-handled vessel decorated with red flora against a blue green ground, 9.5cm. high, signed and dated *1913*. *(Phillips)* **£500 $750**

Moorcroft Florian Ware squat oviform three handled vase, decorated in the 'Daisy' pattern in applied raised slipware in shades of yellow, green and blue, 5in. high. *(Peter Wilson)* **£450 $675**

Moorcroft potpourri and cover, England, circa 1905, 'Pomegranate and Pansy' design in green, blue, red and yellow, 5in. high. *(Skinner)* **£550 $880**

A Moorcroft pottery jardinière, decorated with a band of freesias, on a shaded blue and pale green ground, dated *1921*, 9¾in. diameter. *(Christie's)* **£1,265 $1,986**

A Moorcroft twin-handled baluster vase, decorated in the 'Wisteria' pattern, in shades of navy blue, lime green and lilac, 8¼in. high. (Christie's) **£517 $811**

A Moorcroft jug, tube-lined with fish amongst weeds, in grey/blue and brown on a matt cream ground, 13.1cm. high. *(Bonhams)* **£420 $678**

A Moorcroft Pottery 'Claremont' pattern jardinière decorated with mushrooms and coloured in streaked red, blue and yellow glaze against a green ground, 12.5cm. high. *(Phillips)* **£525 $840**

A Moorcroft Pottery fruit bowl of circular form, painted with fish, seaweed and sea anemones in shades of red, blue, yellow and green, 24.5cm. diameter. *(Phillips)* **£525 $840**

A Moorcroft 'Moonlit blue' plate, the obverse tube-lined with trees in a landscape, 21.9cm. diameter. *(Bonhams)* **£380 $614**

A Moorcroft shouldered oviform vase, with a band of leaf and berry design in shades of pink and green on a deep blue ground, 27cm. high. *(Christie's)* **£462 $702**

A twin-handled square biscuit barrel and cover decorated in the 'Hazledene' pattern, in shades of green and blue, 6½in. high. *(Christie's)* **£500 $800**

An oviform powder bowl and cover decorated with pansies, in shades of mauve and green on a deep blue ground, 3½in. high. *(Christie's)* **£300 $480**

A twin-handled tapering cylindrical jardinière, made for Liberty, decorated in the 'Hazledene' pattern, in shades of blue and green, 8¼in. high. *(Christie's)* **£600 $960**

'Leaf and Berry', a Moorcroft shouldered jug, painted in shades of pink, purple, green and yellow on a green ground, painted blue signature, 16.5cm. high. *(Christie's)* **£862 $1,400**

A spherical vase decorated with stylised fish among waterweeds, in shades of red and ochre on a speckled salmon pink ground, the interior blue, 6in.high. *(Christie's)* **£1,250 $2,000**

'Pomegranate', a Moorcroft jardinière with everted rim, painted in shades of pink, purple, ochre and blue on a mottled blue ground, 32cm. high. *(Christie's)* **£1,725 $2,810**

A pierced oval soap dish decorated in the 'Moonlit Blue' pattern, in shades of blue and green, 7¾in. long.
(Christie's) **£350 $560**

A Macintyre Florian 'Poppy' pattern preserve jar on saucer, with domed cover, white ground with raised slip decoration of blue poppies, with brown printed Macintyre stamp, circa 1904, 14cm. diameter.
(Christie's) **£330 $591**

'Moonlit Blue', a Moorcroft shouldered cylindrical vase with everted rim, painted in shades of green and blue on a blue ground, painted green signature, 32cm. high. *(Christie's)* **£1,035 $1,685**

'Pomegranate', an ovoid jug painted with a band between rope borders, painted in shades of pink, purple, blue and green on a blue ground, painted blue signature, 15cm. high. *(Christie's)* **£690 $1,125**

'Pomegranate', a Moorcroft footed bowl, painted in shades of pink, purple, green and blue on a blue ground, painted blue signature, 20cm. diameter.
(Christie's) **£517 $895**

'Leaf and Berry', a large Moorcroft vase, ovoid form with collar rim, painted in colours under a flambé glaze, impressed factory mark, painted blue signature, 31cm. high. *(Christie's)* **£3,450 $5,625**

A small Moorcroft covered jar, 4in. high.
(Dee, Atkinson & Harrison)
£70 $106

Moorcroft Flambé vase, 10in. high, 1930s.
(Muir Hewitt) **£360 $540**

A Moorcroft salt glaze 'Fish' vase with shaped flared body, 7in. high.
(Russell, Baldwin & Bright)
£1,250 $1,900

A William Moorcroft Liberty & Co. 'Pomegranate' pewter mounted trumpet vase, tube-lined with a band of large fruits amongst berries, 6³/8in. high.
(Bonhams) **£340 $508**

A Moorcroft Macintyre Florian ware vase, tube-lined with poppies, in blue and green on a creamed ground, 10cm. high.
(Bonhams) **£190 $307**

A fine Moorcroft 12½in. circular tapered vase, decorated with orchids in blue under flambé glaze, signed in blue.
(Anderson & Garland)
£1,300 $2,041

Baluster vase, decorated with black tulip pattern, circa 1990, signed *Walter Moorcroft*, 7in.
(G. A. Key) **£230 $366**

A Moorcroft Pottery vase, of baluster form with flared rim and with grape leaf design on deep blue ground, 12in. high. *(Andrew Hartley)*
£660 $1,000

A Moorcroft vase, Eagle Owl design on a branch with green/blue ground, 12in. high. *(Russell, Baldwin & Bright)* **£390 $596**

A Moorcroft vase, under salt glaze, Leaves & Berries pattern on a green ground, 11in. high. circa 1920. *(Russell, Baldwin & Bright)* **£820 $1,255**

A Moorcroft large two-handled vase with design of pomegranate, grapes, etc., 14in., green signature. *(Russell, Baldwin & Bright)* **£950 $1,444**

A Moorcroft Pottery shouldered and waisted vase with pansy decoration on pale cream ground, 10½in. wide. *(Andrew Hartley)* **£540 $794**

A Moorcroft Florian Ware vase of squat form with tall neck, decorated in relief with blue forget-me-nots and yellow cornflowers, 13cm. high. *(Phillips)* **£560 $845**

A Moorcroft pottery globular vase decorated with the 'Big poppy' design on a thin blue wash ground, 16.3cm. *(Bearne's)* **£450 $866**

A Moorcroft 'Pansy' pattern vase, white ground with decoration of yellow and purple pansies amid green foliage, circa 1916, 23cm. high. *(Christie's)* **£770 $1,378**

A miniature William Moorcroft vase, tube-lined with pommels of forget-me-nots on a powder-blue ground, 3³/₈in. high. *(Bonhams)* **£220 $329**

A Moorcroft Pottery vase, the ovoid body painted with the 'Anemone' pattern on a red ground, 16.5cm. *(Bearne's)* **£250 $400**

A William Moorcroft 'Pomegranate' tobacco jar and cover, tube-lined with a band of large fruits, berries and foliage, 7½in. high. *(Bonhams)* **£380 $568**

The factory which came to be known as Myotts had operated at Crane Street, Hanley since the beginning of the 19th century and in 1897 it was inherited by Ashley Myott, who became chairman at the tender age of 19, and his elder brother Sydney.

During the next four decades they built up a worldwide trade, allowing them, in 1925, to buy the neighbouring Upper Hanley Pottery and amalgamate the two as the Alexander Pottery.

Myotts were noted for their extreme Art Deco shapes made during the 1920s and 30s, painted in brilliant shades of orange, green, black, brown and yellow, or blue, pink, mauve and green. A fire in 1949 unfortunately destroyed many records and pattern books, so dating and identification of their now highly collectable pieces can be a problem.

Ashley, Sydney and Ashley's son Geoffrey all retired from the business together in the 50s, and the factory was eventually bought by the Arthur Meakin Pottery as Myott Meakin. This in turn was bought in 1982 by Stanley Jackson, and for some years continued to produce on a large scale. In 1991 the company was finally taken over by the Churchill Group.

Up to 1930, the company had some 21 backstamps. The one most often found on Art Deco pieces dates from the mid-1930s and comprises a gold crown above *Myott, Son & Co.* with *England* below.

Myott bowl with stylised flower decoration, 1930s. *(Muir Hewitt)* **£70 $115**

Myott cup saucer and plate, 1930s. *(Muir Hewitt)* **£25 $40**

Myott & Co. planter in orange, cream and brown, 10in. high. *(Muir Hewitt)* **£120 $195**

Myott jug with design in brown, black and orange, 12in. high, (unusually large example of this shaped jug). *(Muir Hewitt)* **£125 $200**

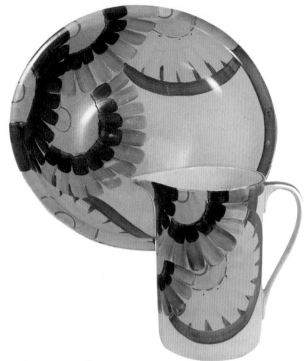

Myott & Son vase by Goldscheider decorated with deer, 11½in. tall. *(Lyle)* **£110 $180**

Myott hand painted jug and basin, 1930s. *(Muir Hewitt)* **£350 $570**

Myott Pierrot vase, 1930s, 8½in. high. *(Muir Hewitt)* **£125 $200**

Myott and Co. Jug in orange, brown and yellow, 1930s. *(Muir Hewitt)* **£50 $85**

This American pottery was set up in 1895 at Newcomb College, New Orleans, a women's section of Tulane University, Louisiana. Essentially, the work of professional potters was bought in to be decorated by the students and the emphasis was on local materials and decorative motifs, such as indigenous trees like magnolia or palms. The products were mainly low fired earthenware painted in underglaze colours, predominantly blue, green and yellow.

Newcomb Pottery vase, New Orleans, circa 1915, Henrietta D. Bailey, matt glazed pale-pink, blue and green on low-relief pine cones and needles, 6⁷⁄₈in. high. *(Skinner)* **£895 $1,495**

Newcomb College Pottery bowl, New Orleans, possibly Sadie Irvine, circa 1920, matt glaze decorated pale blue/green leaves with pale rose berries in low relief, 3in. high. *(Skinner)* **£575 $863**

A Newcomb College Pottery high glaze mug, New Orleans, signed by Ada W. Lonnegan, circa 1901, 4¼in. high. **£960 $1,440**

Newcomb College covered jar, glossy glaze, decorated with blue and green flowers and leaves on white ground, 5½in. wide. *(Skinner)* **£1,000 $1,600**

Newcomb College Pottery low bowl, New Orleans, Henrietta Bailey, circa 1915, matt glazed and decorated at shoulder with low relief stylised bearded irises, 2½in. high. *(Skinner)* **£326 $489**

Newcomb College Pottery scenic vase, New Orleans, Anna Frances Simpson, circa 1915, matt glazed decoration with green/blue mossy trees in low relief, 7¼in. high. *(Skinner)* **£1,457 $2,185**

A Newcomb Pottery floral vase, New Orleans, circa 1928, initialled by Henrietta Bailey, 5¼in. high. *(Skinner)* **£500 $800**

Newcomb Pottery vase, decorated with three trees in Spanish moss with a large moon, 6in. high. *(Skinner)* **£552 $920**

Fine Newcomb College high glaze mug, decorated by Amelie Roman, thrown by Joseph Meyer, depicting five rabbits running and seated in the woods, 4in. high. *(Skinner)* **£2,587 $4,313**

Fine Newcomb Pottery vase, bulbous form with finely carved floral sprays in light green and blue, impressed *CN*, 8¼in. high. *(Skinner)* **£1,410 $2,300**

Newcomb Pottery gloss glaze vase, Marie H. LeBlanc, decorated with cobalt rim over incised band of repeating crocus in cream, yellow, pale blue, blue and blue-green over light blue body, 5½in. diameter. *(Skinner)* **£2,470 $4,025**

Exceptional Newcomb College carved matte vase, decorated by Anna Frances Simpson, thrown by Jonathan Hunt, depicting five live oaks with Spanish moss and a finely detailed landscape, 5¼in. high. *(Skinner)* **£2,760 $4,600**

NEWPORT POTTERY

The Newport pottery was a subsidiary of A J Wilkinson Ltd. operating in the 1930s, and is distinguished by having among its designers the legendary Clarice Cliff.

A 'Blue Autumn' pattern, Dover shape jardinière, 7½in. high, lithograph mark *Fantasque Hand Painted Bizarre by Clarice Cliff Newport Pottery England.*
(Bonhams) **£380 $620**

An 'Autumn' pattern two handled Lotus jug, 11½in. high, rubber stamp mark *Hand Painted Bizarre by Clarice Cliff Newport Pottery England.*
(Bonhams) **£1,300 $2,120**

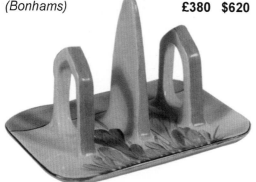

Newport Pottery Co. toastrack by Clarice Cliff in Crocus pattern. *(Lyle)* **£90 $145**

An 'Alton' pattern vase, shape 264, 8in. high, raised shape no. *244* and lithograph mark *Hand Painted Bizarre by Clarice Cliff Newport Pottery England.*
(Bonhams) **£200 $325**

Newport Pottery Nasturtium pattern jug by Clarice Cliff, 11½in. high. *(Lyle)* **£600 $975**

An Appliqué 'Orange Lucerne' beaker, 4½in. high, hand painted *Appliqué* and rubber stamp mark *Hand Painted Bizarre by Clarice Cliff Newport Pottery England.*
(Bonhams) **£850 $1,385**

An 'Original Bizarre' plate, painted with a central radiating star, printed mark *Hand Painted Newport Pottery England*, 8½in. diameter. (Christie's) **£300 $480**

Clarice Cliff Newport three slice toast rack, decorated with the 'Secrets' pattern, of red roofed cottages beside an estuary, 6in. wide. *(G. A. Key)* **£170 $267**

Clarice Cliff Newport Bizarre Fantasque Stamford cream jug and matching sucrier, decorated with the 'Chintz' pattern, both 2½in. *(G.A. Key)* **£310 $511**

A Newport pottery Bizarre charger, 1930s, stylised foliate design in blue, orange and green with blue border, 33.5cm. diameter. *(Muir Hewitt)* **£200 $300**

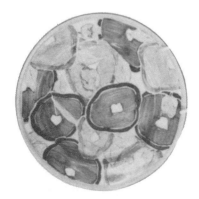

Clarice Cliff Newport Bizarre Fantasque plate, painted in colours with the 'Chintz' pattern of stylised flowers, circa 1932, 9in. *(G.A. Key)* **£280 $448**

An Original Bizarre Athens jug, painted with diamonds and triangles in blue, red and green, stamp *Hand Painted Bizarre by Clarice Cliff Newport Pottery England*, 8½in. diameter. *(Christie's)* **£300 $480**

A large Newport pottery
'Bizarre' vase, 1930s,
36.75cm. high.
(Lyle)   **£3,500 $5,700**

A large Newport pottery
'Bizarre' charger, 1930s,
33.75cm. high.
(Lyle)   **£920 $1,500**

An amusing Newport pottery
model of an owl wearing a
suit, signed *M. Epworth*,
18.5cm.
(Bearne's)   **£120 $180**

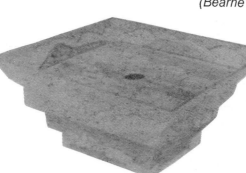

A Clarice Cliff Fantasque
Bizarre Newport pottery
circular tapered biscuit
barrel decorated in the blue
Autumn pattern. *(Anderson
& Garland)*   **£430 $664**

A Clarice Cliff Newport
pottery bough pot, of flared
stepped square, printed
Fantasque and *Bizarre*,
23cm. square. **£650 $1,050**

A large Delecia Lydiat
pattern Yo-Yo vase, by
Clarice Cliff, Newport, shape
no. 379, 18in. high.
(Christie's) **£4,000 $6,400**

A Bizarre single-handled
'Lotus' vase, 29.3cm. high.,
Newport, late 1930s.
              £360 $540

A Forest Glen pattern vase
of footed trumpet form,
marked *Clarice Cliff Newport
Pottery England*, 9in. high.
(Christie's)   **£400 $640**

A large Newport pottery two-
handled vase, 1930s,
29.5cm. high.
(Lyle)   **£2,700 $4,400**

George Ohr (1857-1918) was an American artist potter who was based in Missouri. His work was characterised by being of very thin porcelain, which was then distorted by being squeezed or folded into weird forms with handles then applied. His glazes were notable for their flowing colours, such as green and plum.

George E. Ohr Pottery vase, Biloxi, Mississippi, circa 1904, fluted top on cylindrical form, midnight blue over cobalt glossy glaze, 5in. high. *(Skinner)* **£450 $675**

A 20th century moulded pottery 'steamboat' pitcher, cast after the original by George E. Ohr, 9in. high. **£250 $400**

George Ohr Pottery vase, bulbous base with two curving handles, blue and dark blue mottled glaze incised *G.E. Ohr, Biloxi, Miss.*, 7in. high. *(Skinner)* **£1,650 $2,500**

Fine George Ohr vase with mottled brown and green glaze with hints of iridescent black on an ochre ground, stamped *G.E. Ohr, Biloxi, Miss.*, 6in. high. *(Skinner)* **£1,225 $1,840**

George Ohr Pottery vase, Biloxi, Mississippi, circa 1901, gloss translucent caramel glaze with green and charcoal streaking, 6in. high. *(Skinner)* **£997 $1,495**

George Ohr Pottery vase, cone-shaped over bulbous base with flaring foot, spaghetti handles and twisted neck, 9in. high. *(Skinner)* **£2,500 $3,740**

The Paul Revere pottery was established in the early years of the 20th century in Boston, for the purpose of training girls form poor immigrant backgrounds, the profits to be used for their education in other subjects. It produced earthenware nursery and breakfast bowls and dishes etc. decorated with stylised floral motifs, mottoes etc., with the decoration often confined to the borders. Pieces were marked with initials or with *SEG* for Saturday Evening Girls (q.v.)

Paul Revere Pottery Saturday Evening Girls planter of rectangular form with a decorated frieze of applied flowers, Boston, Mass., 9½in. long. **£500 $800**

Paul Revere Pottery decorated vase, Boston, with incised and painted band of trees, hills and sky, 8½in. high.
(Skinner) **£500 $800**

Paul Revere Pottery vase, Boston, 1926, semi-matt glaze decorated with bands of tulips in yellow and green, 4¼in. high.
(Skinner) **£325 $488**

Paul Revere Pottery decorated vase, Boston, Massachusetts, early 20th century, with incised and painted band of tree design, 8½in. high.
(Skinner) **£2,000 $3,200**

Paul Revere Pottery Saturday Evening Girls tile, incised Boston street scene, coloured pink, blue, brown, white and grey with black outlines, 3¾ x 3¾in.
(Skinner) **£197 $385**

Paul Revere Pottery Saturday Evening Girls decorated pitcher with an incised and painted band of stylised sailing boats, Mass., 1911, 9¾in. high.
(Skinner) **£800 $1,280**

Paul Revere Pottery decorated tea tile, Boston, Massachusetts, early 20th century, with central decoration of a cottage, 5¾in. diameter.
(Skinner) **£195 $375**

Pilkington's Tile and Pottery Co. was set up in 1892 at Clifton Junction Lancashire, to manufacture tiles, but from 1897 the production range was extended to include buttons, vases etc. Shortly afterwards the decoration of bought-in biscuit vases also began.

Opalescent glaze effects were discovered in 1903 and from then on the production of glazed earthenware known as Lancastrian pottery began. These wares, which consisted of vases, bowls, trays etc. were usually simple in shape, but decorated in a wide palette of colours often with a crystalline or opalescent effect.

The company was run by two brothers, William and Joseph Burton, who were both ceramic chemists and who were instrumental in developing the lustre decorated pottery which formed the bulk of the factory's 20th century production. Modelled, moulded or incised decoration appears on these pieces, while the decorator R Joyce modelled animals and birds.

Pilkington's employed many distinguished artists to design for them, and they all had their own marks, as did the potters. Designers such as W.S. Mycock, Gordon Forsyth and Richard Joyce produced designs featuring birds, animals, galleons, flowers and leaves, as well as strong geometric patterns. Those of Joyce in particular showed clearly the influence of Central American Indian art.

In 1928 the Lapis ware range was introduced, featuring a soft, silky, semi-matt surface either left plain or decorated with Art Deco motifs. Self-mottling Cunian glazes were also very popular in the ten years up to the closure of the pottery section in 1938. Production resumed on a small scale ten years later. Royal Lancastrian pottery was sold at Liberty's in London and Tiffany's in New York, as well as in other prestigious stores worldwide, and designs won many exhibition medals.

Until 1904 the mark *P* was sometimes used, followed until 1913 by *P* and *L* and two bees. The Tudor rose was a later mark, and *Royal Lancastrian* is another variation.

A large and important Pilkington Lancastrian lustre vase, painted by Gordon Forsyth to commemorate the Brussels International Exhibition of 1910 where the British and Belgian sections burned, 51cm. high. *(Phillips)* **£11,500 $18,825**

A Pilkington's Royal Lancastrian twin-handled vase decorated by Gordon Forsyth, 1908, 30.2cm. high. **£200 $300**

A Pilkington's Royal Lancastrian lustre footed dish, by Richard Joyce, centrally decorated with a knight on horseback within a broad copper border, circa 1915, 18.5cm. diameter.
(Tennants) **£500 $815**

A Pilkington Royal Lancastrian lustre vase by Richard Joyce, painted in golden lustre 26.5cm. high. *(Phillips)* **£1,000 $1,600**

A Pilkington Lancastrian deep bowl designed by Walter Crane and decorated by Wm. S. Mycock, date code for 1913, 21.6cm. high. **£880 $1,320**

A Pilkington Lancastrian lustre vase and cover decorated by Richard Joyce with a frieze of antelopes and stylised trees, 15.5cm. high. *(Christie's)* **£600 $900**

A Pilkington lustre pottery charger, by W. S. Mycock, with concentrically ribbed interior, with foliate border, dated 1918, 33cm. diameter. *(Bonhams)* **£200 $320**

A Pilkington Royal Lancastrian lustre vase and cover decorated by Gordon Forsyth, with two central reserves each surrounded by laurel leaves and flanked by two lions, 29cm. high. *(Christie's)* **£3,320 $4,980**

A Pilkington Royal Lancastrian lustre charger decorated by William S. Mycock, dated *1924*, 30.6cm. diameter. *(Christie's)* **£360 $540**

A Pilkington Lancastrian pottery vase by Richard Joyce, impressed Bee mark and date code for 1909, 11¾in. high. *(Christie's)* **£650 $1,040**

A Pilkington's Lancastrian lustre moonflask by Walter Crane and Richard Joyce, decorated with the coat of arms of the City of Manchester, 27cm. high. **£1,700 $2,750**

A Pilkington Royal Lancastrian lustre vase decorated by Gordon Forsyth, painted in red and gold lustre with bands of tudor roses, 1915, 8½in. high. *(Christie's)* **£360 $540**

This pottery was established around 1933 in Amicable Street, Burslem, by Edward Thomas Brown Radford (1883-1968). He was the son of another Edward Radford who had had a distinguished career at Pilkington's Royal Lancastrian Pottery. Eddie, as he was known, first went to work at Pilkington's with his father, where he quickly proved himself as a thrower, before becoming a sales representative. In the 1920s he went to work for Wood & Sons, as designer and sales manager.

When he left to set up his own pottery, he found that he could not have sole use of his own name, as Woods were still entitled to use it. In fact they continued to do so until 1980, some 12 years after Radford's death. This complicates the dating of Radford Pottery pieces, and the best indications come from the techniques used.

Radford's early work was mostly thrown by hand and matt-glazed, decorated with flowers which were painted freehand and applied with water based paint under the glaze. Marks on this type of pottery usually consist of simply *E. Radford* or *E. Radford England*. Those from the Woods factory usually have the Woods name added.

During the war the factory was requisitioned as a tyre depot, and at the end of the war Radford and his wife moved away to run a children's holiday home.

Radford 1930s vase with abstract design, 18in. high. *(Muir Hewitt)* **£150 $245**

Radford vase, 1930s stylised foliage design, 12in. high.
(Muir Hewitt) **£175 $285**

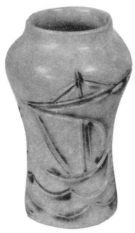

Radford baluster vase with stylised ship design, in grey and green, 1930s.
(Muir Hewitt) **£55 $90**

Radford jug with stylised ship design, in grey and green, 1930s.
(Muir Hewitt) **£60 $100**

Robj was a French dealer who in the 1920s and early 30s commissioned small decorative porcelain items, such as inkwells, ashtrays, preserve pots etc, for sale in his Paris showroom. Lamps, bottles and incense burners often in the form of the human figure were popular as were Cubist inspired statuettes in cream coloured porcelain with a crackle glaze. Robj sponsored annual competitions until 1931, and winning designs were sometimes produced in limited editions at the Sèvres factory.

A Robj porcelain jug, modelled as a rotund lady wearing a plum coloured dress, the spout modelled as an apron, 19.5cm. high, *(Phillips)* **£255 $382**

A Robj porcelain decanter and stopper, the pear shaped decanter modelled as a Scotsman playing bagpipes, printed *Robj, Paris, Made in France,* 27cm. high. *(Bonhams)* **£200 $320**

Robj, twelve polychrome-decorated figural ceramic bottles and stoppers, each representing a different person, marked *Robj Paris,* 26.5cm. high. *(Sotheby's)* **£2,486 $3,755**

A Robj figural nightlight, fashioned as a semi-naked girl in green dress and white cloak, clasping a bunch of flowers, marked *Robj Made in Paris,* 26cm. high. *(Phillips)* **£350 $542**

Robj French porcelain inkwell, figural blackamoor in gold trimmed white turban and costume, 6¼in. high. *(Skinner)* **£155 $275**

A Robj spirit flask and stopper in the form of a Breton girl wearing national dress, 25.7cm. high. *(Phillips)* **£275 $440**

A Robj earthenware bowl and cover, formed as a Red Indian's head, with dark red glazed feather headdress, 20cm. high. *(Christie's)* **£450 $675**

The foundation of the Rookwood pottery in 1880 received enormous publicity because it was established by a Cincinnati society lady, Maria Longworth Nichols. Its initial aim was to produce a better art pottery rather than commercial success, but in 1883 William Taylor, a friend of Mrs Nichols, was appointed manager, and he both extended the range of designs and organised a distribution network on sound commercial lines.

Though some utility wares were made in the early years, the emphasis was mainly on art pottery which was made using various techniques. The results were often characterised by carved, incised or impressed designs in high relief, often with gilt decoration and overglaze painting or slip painting under the glaze. This last, in which rich warm colours were airbrushed to give an evenly blended background, became known as 'Standard' Rookwood.

Tinted glazes and coloured bodies were introduced and in 1884 an aventurine glaze was developed by accident, in which bright gold crystals appeared deep under the surface. This became known as 'Tiger Eye'.

When Mrs Nichols remarried in 1886, her interest in the pottery waned, and in 1889 she transferred the ownership to Taylor. Under his direction, floral decoration on rich brown, orange and yellow backgrounds and on pink and white 'Cameo' pieces predominates. He moved the business to larger premises at Mount Adams, Cincinnati in 1892, and 'Iris' 'Sea Green' and 'Aeriel blue' designs appeared.

Besides floral decoration, Rookwood pieces now were also adorned with portraits of American Indians, Negroes, animals, and figures form Old Master paintings.

The pottery was outward looking in that it sent several of its leading designers to study in Europe. Among these was Artus van Briggle, who came back with the idea of a matt glaze, and this was incorporated into regular production from 1901.

Taylor died in 1913, and the factory continued to live on its reputation for almost thirty years.

Rookwood Pottery sterling silver overlaid standard glaze claret jug, Sallie Toohey, 1896, decorated with stylised leafy twig, 7in. high. *(Skinner)* **£1,303 $1,955**

Rookwood Pottery scenic vellum plaque, Cincinnati, Ohio, 1914, executed by Edward George Diers, (1896-1931), 10¾in. high. *(Skinner)* **£1,200 $1,900**

Large Rookwood Pottery standard glaze pitcher, Cincinnati, Kataro Shirayamadani, 1890, decorated with floral branch in shades of yellow, orange, green and brown 12¾in. high.
(Skinner) **£2,000 $3,000**

Rookwood Pottery standard glaze vase, unusual swirling decoration with green bands and brown flowers on a standard glaze ground, Rookwood logo, 5½in. high. *(Skinner)* **£920 $1,500**

Rookwood Pottery sage green standard glaze bowl and creamer, Cincinnati, Mary A. Taylor, 1886, decorated with chrysanthemum in salmon, cream and beige, 2¾in. high. *(Skinner)* **£249 $374**

Rare Rookwood Pottery ale set, tankard and five mugs, decorated by Sturgis Lawrence in 1898, each with a portrait of a different Native American, 5in. high. *(Skinner)* **£4,312 $6,900**

Pair of Rookwood Pottery matte glaze rook bookends, designed by William McDonald, no. 2275, *1937*, matte ivory glaze, impressed marks and artist's cipher, 5¼in. high. *(Skinner)* **£265 $431**

A Rookwood pottery basket, by artist Artus Van Briggle, decorated in slip underglaze with blossoms, berries and leaves, 6½in. high. *(Skinner)* **£450 $700**

Rookwood bookends, William P. MacDonald, 1922, Art Deco Oriental figural, with black comb highlighted in red, 8in. high. *(Skinner)* **£528 $825**

Rookwood standard glaze three-handled presentation loving cup, painted by William P. McDonald, 1898, painted and slipped with horse chestnut pods, 7in. high.
(Butterfield & Butterfield) **£1,189 $1,840**

Rookwood Pottery vase, decorated by Frederick Sturgis Lawrence, yellowish green shading to brown standard glaze decorated with yellow flowers, Rookwood logo, 10½in. high.
(Skinner) **£1,100 $1,800**

Two Rookwood Pottery tiger eye vases, Kataro Shirayamadani, Cincinnati, Ohio, (1887-1915 and 1925-1948), 14½in. high.
(Skinner) **£1,600 $2,600**

Monumental Rookwood Pottery vase, standard glaze vase decorated with blooms of poppies in red, yellow and deep greens, Rookwood logo, 20in. high.
(Skinner) **£3,000 $5,000**

Rookwood pottery scenic plaque, 'The End of Winter', Cincinnati, Ohio, 1918, original frame, 12¼ x 9¼in.
(Skinner) **£1,700 $2,800**

A Rookwood pottery standard glaze pillow vase, 1889, artist's initials *A R V* for Albert R. Valentien, 14in. high. *(Skinner)* **£1,200** **$1,950**

Rookwood covered jar, by Harriet Wenderoth, dull, putty finish over hammered clay ground, cylindrical neck, broad shoulder tapering to base, deeply incised Virginia Creeper motif, 19in. high. *(Skinner)* **£2,145** **$3,500**

Rookwood Spanish water jug, by Fannie Auckland, dull finish vessel with bands of repeating die-stamped patterns in black and blue around the ovoid-shaped jug, two extending spouts for filling and pouring, 8¾in. high. *(Skinner)* **£1,125** **$1,840**

Rookwood Pottery ewer, decorated with allover oriental designs, images and symbols in rust, blue, yellow, and black, elongated neck on bulbous body, angled handle with a vertical support, 12in. high. *(Skinner)* **£1,840** **$3,000**

A Rookwood pottery scenic vellum loving cup, initialled by Frederick Rothebusch, 1908, 7¼in. high. *(Skinner)* **£1,250** **$2,035**

Rookwood Pottery pitcher, bulbous form, flaring freeform spout, decorated with irises on a peach and cream glazed background, 7in. high. *(Skinner)* **£210 $345**

Two Rookwood candlesticks, by Albert R. Valentien, tan ground with olive green highlights, incised floral and leaf design and grotesque figural handles, 8in. high. *(Skinner)* **£705 $1,150**

Pair of Rookwood crow bookends, 1926, oversize weighted set of mauve moulded rooks in William McDonald's design, 6½in. high. *(Skinner)* **£212 $413**

Rookwood covered egg, dull finish egg with carved and outlined palm-leaf motif, 3¾in.high. *(Skinner)* **£370 $600**

Pair of Rookwood Pottery squirrel bookends, 1928, designed by Sallie Toohey, matte grey-green glaze over squirrel figure holding a nut and standing on a log with leaves in relief, 4¼in. high. *(Skinner)* **£460 $747**

Rookwood Pottery vase, painted by Kataro Shirayamadani, large standard glaze vase decorated with bamboo on a high gloss glaze of mustard, burnt orange, and dark brown, impressed repeating chevron bands on extended neck, 17½in. high. *(Skinner)* **£6,135 $10,000**

Rookwood Pottery bisque finished reversible, lidded pot-pourri jar, Cincinnati, Artus Van Briggle, 1887, decorated with morning-glories, 6¼in. diameter.
(Skinner) **£460 $690**

Rookwood Pottery scenic vellum plaque, Cincinnati, Fred Rothenbusch, 1912, shoreline windmills and landscape in shades of blue and green, 14¼in. wide.
(Skinner) **£5,366 $8,050**

Rookwood pottery vase standard glaze ewer, Cincinnati, Ohio, 1896, by Matthew Daly, underglaze decoration of open petalled white roses against shaded brown green ground, 9¾in. high.
(Skinner) **£250 $400**

Rookwood Pottery standard glaze vase, Cincinnati, Howard Altman, 1903, decorated with poppies, 6¾in. high.
(Skinner) **£345 $518**

Important Rookwood Pottery sea green glaze lamp, 1901, decorated by Kataro Shirayamadani, electroplated copper floral sprays over lotus blossoms on front and back, original shade by Tiffany Studios, unsigned, Rookwood logo, 1901, overall height 17¾in.
(Skinner) **£20,010 $33,350**

Rookwood Pottery standard glaze vase, Cincinnati, Artus Van Briggle, 1891, two-handle form decorated with daisies, 5¾in. diameter. *(Skinner)* **£536 $805**

Three Rookwood Pottery standard glaze mouse plates, Cincinnati, Ohio, circa 1893, each depicting a mischievous mouse, 7in. diameter. *(Skinner)* **£380 $570**

Pair of Rookwood Pottery figural bookends, figure of a seated woman reading a book under a matte blue glaze, 6in. high. *(Skinner)* **£364 $575**

Rookwood Pottery standard glaze vase dated *1892*, initialled by Harriet Strafer, no. 612 W, 6in. high, 6in. wide. *(Skinner)* **£265 $400**

Rookwood Pottery porcelain vase, Cincinnati, Ohio, 1925, executed by Kataro Shirayamadani (1865-1948), 8in. high. *(Skinner)* **£650 $1,000**

Rookwood Pottery tea set, 1900, by Caroline Steinle, yellow and brown pansies with green stems under a green-brown standard glaze. *(Skinner)* **£115 $173**

Rookwood Pottery vase, Cincinnati, Ohio, 1915, with incised line and petal decoration in matte brown glaze, impressed mark, 12½in. high.
(Skinner) **£250 $400**

Rookwood partial tea set, creamer and teapot, light pink, orange peel textured finish, with light green carved flowers, scarab finial on lid, gold highlights.
(Skinner) **£370 $600**

Rookwood Pottery scenic vellum vase, Cincinnati, 1913, decorated with landscape scene in grey blue on shaded yellow to peach background, 13⅝in. high.
(Skinner) **£1,250 $2,000**

Rookwood pitcher in a standard glaze with floral decoration, mark of Albert R. Valentien, 1888, 8in. high.
(Eldreds) **£474 $715**

Rookwood Pottery flower boat, by Albert R. Valentien, standard glaze, decorated with leaves and vines, double opening, impressed *Rookwood* mark, 14¼in. wide. *(Skinner)* **£495 $805**

A Rookwood Pottery ewer, 1903, decorated by Elizabeth Lincoln, standard glaze over floral decoration, 6in. high.
(Skinner) **£144 $230**

A Rookwood Pottery standard glaze portrait vase decorated with a portrait of a black African with a cap, 1897, 12in. high.
(Skinner) **£1,500 $2,400**

A Rookwood Pottery decorated pitcher, artist's initials *M.L.N* for Maria Longworth Nichols, 1882, 6in. high.
(Skinner) **£450 $720**

Rookwood Pottery iris glaze vase, Cincinnati, Ohio, 1906, executed by Charles Schmidt, (1896-1927), 9⅝in. high.*(Skinner)* **£2,400 $3,850**

Rookwood Pottery standard glaze vase, Cincinnati, 1903, decorated with nasturtiums in yellow and green, 8in. high.
(Skinner)   **£345 $518**

Rookwood Elk vase, by Bruce Horsfall, standard glaze pillow vase depicting a bellowing elk, *Rookwood* mark, 8in. high.
(Skinner)   **£1,550 $2,530**

Fine Rookwood Pottery vase, 1932, decorated with wax matte floral decoration in yellow, green and red, 13in. high.
(Skinner)   **£1,310 $2,070**

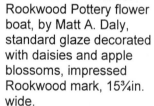

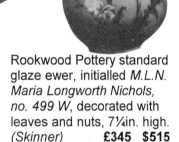

Rookwood large corn jug, Sallie Toohey, 1896, standard glaze with four ears of corn, conforming stopper with cork insert, impressed marks, total height 13in.
(Skinner)   **£621 $1,210**

Rookwood Pottery flower boat, by Matt A. Daly, standard glaze decorated with daisies and apple blossoms, impressed Rookwood mark, 15¾in. wide.
(Skinner)   **£1,720 $2,800**

Rookwood Pottery standard glaze ewer, initialled *M.L.N. Maria Longworth Nichols, no. 499 W*, decorated with leaves and nuts, 7¼in. high.
(Skinner)   **£345 $515**

Rookwood Pottery Spanish water jug, Cincinnati, Ohio, 1882, cobalt blue glaze on strap handled, double spout round pitcher, 10in. high.
(Skinner)   **£275 $440**

Early Rookwood Pottery vase, pinched cylindrical form, irregular opening, with two handles decorated with butterfly, moon and foliate design, 10¾in. high.
(Skinner)   **£691 $1,092**

Rookwood jug, tan bisque finish, flattened round body, sgraffito decoration depicting various scenes of a woman arranging flowers.
(Skinner)   **£1,410 $2,300**

Rookwood butterfly handle goose vase, 1891, standard glaze with three geese in flight, blue green areas, impressed marks, 6½in. high. *(Skinner)* **£423 $825**

A Rookwood pottery jardinière, the oviform creamware body enamelled in black and white with bats flying over fields, dated 1882, 21cm. high. *(Christie's)* **£308 $496**

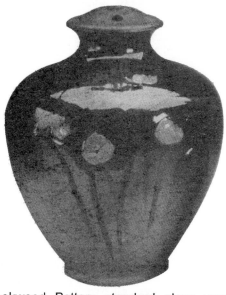

A pair of Rookwood stoneware bookends, modelled as sphinx holding books, light brown glaze, 18cm. high. **£300 $480**

Rookwood Pottery standard glaze vase, decorated by Kataro Shirayamadani, with water lilies in yellow and green, Rookwood logo, 10½in. high.
(Skinner) **£2,750 $4,500**

Rookwood Pottery vellum vase, 1907, by Edward Diers, decorated with white, yellow and pink dogwood on a blue-green ground, 6½in. high. *(Skinner)* **£920 $1,380**

Rookwood pottery scenic vellum plaque, Frederick Rothenbusch, 1915, 'Late Autumn', woodland with light snowfall, 10 x 14in. *(Skinner)* **£1,100 $1,760**

Rookwood scenic vellum plaque, Sara Sax, 1916, 'The Top of the Hill', snow covered landscape, impressed marks, 7³/8 x 9³/8in. *(Skinner)* **£2,087 $4,070**

A Rookwood standard glaze pottery Indian portrait vase, decorated by Grace Young, date cypher for 1905, 30.5cm. high. **£3,250 $5,200**

Rookwood Pottery scenic vellum plaque, Cincinnati, E.T. Hurley, 1913, 'Sunset Through the Birches', dark green foliage against blue/grey foreground, 8¾in. wide. *(Skinner)* **£2,377 $3,656**

Large Rookwood jardinière, by Albert R. Valentien, Limoges-style glaze with branching roses in white and pink on a dark green ground, flattened spherical form with extended neck, 16½in. wide. *(Skinner)* **£2,450 $4,000**

Rookwood Pottery porcelain vase, Cincinnati, Ohio, 1925, executed by Kataro Shirayamadani (1865-1948), 8in. high. *(Skinner)* **£800 $1,300**

Unusual Rookwood Pottery Inkwell, incised deep matte blue decoration on a large bird standing on a leaf form with inkwell cover and insert, 6½in. wide.*(Skinner)* **£655 $1,035**

Rookwood Pottery high glaze jar, Cincinnati, 1946, decorated with low relief medial band of stylised flowers, 6in. high. *(Skinner)* **£153 $230**

Rookwood Pottery scenic vellum plaque, Cincinnati, Carl Schmidt, 'The Trossachs, Loch Katrine', 10¼in. wide. *(Skinner)* **£2,875 $4,312**

Rookwood Pottery scenic vellum plaque, Cincinnati, E.T. Hurley, woodland pond with birches in shades of blue and salmon with ivory and brown, 14½in. high. *(Skinner)* **£5,750 $8,625**

Pair of Rookwood bookends, *1937*, WM.P. McDonald, figural kingfishers in a matte teal glaze, impressed marks, impressed artist's cipher, 5½in. high. *(Skinner)* **£335 $546**

Rookwood Pottery beer tankard for Cincinnati Cooperage Company, raised ribbon mark, no. 1333 S, 7¾in. high. *(Skinner)* **£150 $230**

Rookwood faience grape tile, Cincinnati, high relief grapes on the vine, matt glaze decorated in pale purple, teal green and oatmeal, 6in. wide. *(Skinner)* **£230 $345**

Philip Rosenthal opened his porcelain factory in 1879 in Selb, Bavaria. It was noted from the first for the high quality of its products. He designed three major services, Darmstadt (1905), Donatello (1907) and Isolde (1910) which at first were left undecorated, but later painted under the glaze in various styles.

From the 1920s figures in Art Deco style were also produced, including theatrical characters and subjects in modern dress, many of which were signed by the artist. Philip Rosenthal died in 1937 and was succeeded by his son, also Philip, who appointed independent artists to work in studios in Selb on pieces which were sold in the Rosenthal studio houses. The firm continues in business today.

Marks include a crown over crossed lines and *Rosenthal*, or over crossed roses.

'Fright'. A Rosenthal porcelain bust of a faun by Ferdinand Liebermann, modelled as a young bare-chested faun holding a set of pan pipes, 39.4cm. high.
(Phillips) **£850 $1,350**

A Rosenthal figure of a female tennis player, striding out on an oval base, by Fritz Klimsch, 1936, 51cm. high.
(Kunsthaus am Museum)
£469 $743

A Rosenthal ceramic sculpture by Gerhard Schliepstein, circa 1930, 50.8cm. high.
£1,420 $2,130

A Rosenthal guitar playing pierrot with poodle, seated on a mound, by Rudolf Marcuse, 1913, 33cm. high.
(Kunsthaus am Museum)
£508 $805

A Rosenthal figure of a postilon by T. Kärner, 1920-21. *(Arnold Frankfurt)*
£137 $211

A Rosenthal figure 'Merry March' of a woman in carnival costume, circa 1920, 36cm. high.
(Kunsthaus am Museum)
£472 $746

Rothenthal polychrome figure 'Girl Drinking', signed *Ernst Wenck*, 1865-1929.
(Arnold) **£184 $294**

The Roseville Pottery was established in 1892 in Roseville, Ohio, but moved in 1898 to Zanesville, where the general manager, George F. Young, began making art pottery in 1900.

Their early Rozane ware was characterised by slip painting on a dark ground, finished with a high glaze, and closely resembled other art pottery being made in Zanesville at the time by the Weller and Owens pottery companies. It was renamed Rozane Royal to distinguish it from subsequent styles.

With competitors in such close proximity, however, it was necessary to develop new styles very quickly, and Roseville soon had a wide and rapidly changing range, which tended more and more towards matt glazing over relief modelling.

Roseville Pottery Sunflower vase, cylindrical form with two V-shaped handles at slight shoulder, matte glazed in shades of yellow, green, blue and caramel, unmarked, 6^1/8in. high, 3^1/8in. diameter. *(Skinner)* **£490 $800**

Roseville Pottery hanging basket, freesia pattern, tangerine glaze with white and yellow flowers, two handles, 5in. high, 7½in. diameter. *(Skinner)* **£185 $300**

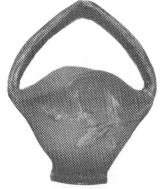

Roseville Pottery silhouette vase, mauve glazed vase, decorated with leaf pattern in relief on squat body with footed base, flaring to rim, raised Roseville mark, *789,* 14½in. high. *(Skinner)* **£490 $800**

Roseville pottery Bittersweet basket, shaded green ground decorated in low relief with bittersweet with orange berries, circa 1951, 8in. high.
(Du Mouchelles) **£55 $85**

Roseville pottery hanging basket, with scalloped edge around the rim, matte, green glaze, early-mid 20th century, 8in. diameter. *(Du Mouchelles)* **£71 $110**

Roseville Pottery Futura vase, *1928*, in matte mauve glaze, sparsely decorated with two long, flowered stems, square rim, rounded square body on square base with four feet, 9in. high.
(Skinner) **£352 $575**

Roseville Magnolia cookie jar, 1943-44, urn form with double handles, tan to green rough ground decorated with white and pink magnolia blossoms, 10½in. high.
(Du Mouchelles) **£90 $140**

Roseville Pottery 'Thornapple' jardinière and stand, circa 1930, cream flowers, brown pods, green leaves in relief on golden yellow, tan and brown ground, 29¼in. high. *(Skinner)* **£920 $1,500**

Roseville pottery ewer, circa 1939-1953, of dusty rose glaze with yellow flowers and teal wash, 10in. high.
(Du Mouchelles) **£135 $200**

Roseville pottery jardinière, circa 1915, Donatello pattern with upper band in orange with green and cream ribs below, 8in. high. *(Du Mouchelles)* **£161 $250**

Cauldon Potteries were born out of Brown, Westhead, Moore & Co. who had been operating at the Cauldon Place Works in Hanley since 1858. From 1904, they traded as Cauldon Ltd., and then, when granted the royal warrant in 1924, they became Royal Cauldon.

Their wide range of products included, during the Art Deco period, several tube-lined types, including their popular Poppy design by Edith Gater, which was used on a number of shapes.

Royal Cauldon ware 'Chang' design wall plaque, 1930s, 17½in. diameter. *(Muir Hewitt)* **£280 $420**

Royal Cauldon Chang jug, 1930s. *(Muir Hewitt)* **£75 $100**

Royal Cauldon Chang dish with wickerwork handle, 1930s. *(Muir Hewitt)* **£50 $85**

Royal Cauldon teaset for one in tray, comprising teapot, sugar, cream and cup, 1930s. *(Muir Hewitt)* **£60 $100**

Royal Cauldon Chang pattern vase, 8in. high. *(Muir Hewitt)* **£55 $85**

This Danish porcelain factory was established in 1775 under the auspices of the Danish royal family, who maintained an interest in it until 1867, when it was bought by Aluminia.

During the 1930s stoneware was used almost exclusively for figure production. One of their leading designers of the period was Jais Nielsen, who had joined them in 1921. He was responsible for vases and bowls, often with a celadon glaze, as well as stoneware figures and groups, many of Biblical inspiration. Another was Knud Kyhn, who designed stoneware figures and porcelain animal figures. Axel Salto was another talented ceramicist who made simple bowls with carved relief decoration in light coloured stoneware.

Royal Copenhagen polychromed porcelain fairytale group, Denmark, marked *April 25, 1955*, 8⁵/₈in. high. *(Skinner)* **£625 $1,000**

A Royal Copenhagen figure, modelled by Carl-Johan Bonnesen, of a clown linking arms with two grey bears who dance alongside him, 29.5cm. high. *(Christie's)* **£977 $1,578**

A Royal Copenhagen silver mounted porcelain vase by Michelsen, Copenhagen 1926, of baluster form, painted with two sailing ships and a steam ship, 12½in. high. *(Christie's)* **£1,265 $1,986**

Royal Copenhagen porcelain group of pigman and sow, decorated mainly in blue and naturalistic colours, 7in. *(G.A. Key)* **£290 $464**

Royal Copenhagen porcelain group of milkmaid feeding a calf from a bucket, 6½in. *(G.A. Key)* **£205 $328**

It was John Doulton's son Henry who set up the firm's famous Art Pottery studios, first at Lambeth and then at Burslem, employing such talented artists as George Tinworth and the Barlows. It was Tinworth who designed the first figurine, although production was not attempted on any scale until Charles Noke joined the firm in 1889. In 1912 a new range was introduced, which proved instantly successful, and the series continued to expand throughout the interwar years. Many of the figures produced at this time have a clear Art Deco style, which makes them very popular with collectors.

Throughout the 30s too, Doulton was producing up-to-date tableware with 'simple, modern lines.' In collaboration with Noke, they also launched Frank Brangwyn's designs in 1930. This was earthenware, each piece hand decorated and different, the signs of modelling left apparent. It was sold very cheaply and was supposed to appeal to those on low incomes. As it turned out, however, it found most favour with the middle classes, who were developing an educated taste for studio pottery.

Bunnykins teapot, in the form of a bunny with ivy handle, painted in shades of brown, black and green, printed factory mark, 12cm. high. *(Christie's)* **£575 $935**

Royal Doulton bowl with geometric decoration, 1930s. *(Muir Hewitt)* **£45 $75**

Royal Doulton plate, in orange, blue and green, 1930s. *(Muir Hewitt)* **£40 $65**

'Farmer Bunnykin' D6003, a Bunnykins figure, painted in colours, printed factory marks, 19cm. high. *(Christie's)* **£800 $1,300**

Doulton figure 'Two Rabbits' HN218, model number 249, introduced 1920, withdrawn 1940s. (Peter Wilson) **£130 $196**

A Royal Doulton Chang bowl by Noke, decorated with green, red, yellow, white and blue glazes on a blue ground, 7in. diameter. (Spencer's) **£750 $1,225**

Pair of Royal Doulton Art Nouveau period slender baluster vases, elaborately decorated with stylised foliage, by Frank Butler, 10in. (G.A. Key) **£900 $1,485**

A Royal Doulton Chang stoneware vase by Charles Noke and Harry Nixon, of shouldered cylindrical form, the short neck applied with a dragon in high relief, on a blue ground with white running crackle glaze under green, yellow and flambé glazes, printed and painted marks, 7¾in. high. (Andrew Hartley) **£2,000 $3,300**

Royal Doulton cup, saucer and plate with angular handle to cup, 1930s. (Muir Hewitt) **£45 $75**

'Billy Bunnykin', D6001, a Bunnykins figure, painted in colours, printed factory marks, 11.4cm. high. (Christie's) **£1,092 $1,775**

A vase with pink swirling panels painted with blue flowers and green leaves, c.m.l. & c., date letter for 1905, 12in. high. **£480 $768**

A pair of Royal Doulton vases, each decorated by Frank Butler and Bessie Newbery, 40.5cm. high. *(Bearne's)* **£1,650 $2,673**

A vase with pink flowers and brown veined white leaves, c.m.l. & c., date letter for 1906, 11½in. high. **£440 $704**

A vase with black and purple designs on a white ground, c.m.l. & c., circa 1920, 8¼in. high. **£165 $264**

A pair of vases, modelled with projecting brown forms growing from a green ground, c.m.l. & c., date letter for 1906, 7in. high. **£540 $864**

A vase painted with pink roses, the stems brown against a pale pink ground, c.m.l. & c., date letter for 1910, 11in. high. **£950 $1,520**

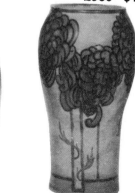

Royal Doulton vase painted by Ethel Beard, 13in. high. **£120 $192**

Pair of Royal Doulton vases with pale green rims, by Florrie Jones, probably circa 1930, 9½in. high. **£180 $288**

A vase painted with stylised yellow chrysanthemums against a mottled pink ground, c.m.l. & c., circa 1912, 9in. high. **£165 $264**

A vase painted with ears of corn in brown, green and purple against a mottled blue ground, circa 1922, 9in. high. **£450 $720**

A pair of vases painted with long-tailed blue birds, c.m.l. & c., date letter for 1916?, 15¾in. high. **£900 $1,440**

A slip-cast vase by William Rowe with green leaves and a black and white chequered design, s.c.m., circa 1920, 9in. high. **£110 $176**

A vase painted with a parrot amongst green tropical foliage, c.m. & l., circa 1922, 10½in. high. **£700 $1,120**

A pair of vases pressed from the inside with pink fruits against green foliage, date letter for 1903, 10¾in. high. **£820 $1,312**

A vase painted with formal purple flowers and green leaves against a white ground, c.m.l. & c., circa 1912, 7¾in. high. **£165 $264**

A large vase with incised green flowering foliage on a mottled blue ground, c.m. & l., circa 1925, 12¾in. high. **£420 $672**

Pair of Royal Doulton Kingsware candlesticks, a hunting scene in low relief, circa 1912, 11in. high. **£195 $312**

A vase after a design by Mark V. Marshall with purple foliage and sepia fruit, c.m. & l., circa 1922, 8¼in. high. **£290 $464**

Royal Dux grew out of the Austrian firm of Royal Vienna, known for its Art Nouveau ornamental ware, and was established in 1860 at Dux, Bohemia, which is now Duchov, in the Czech Republic.

In the Art Deco period, Royal Dux was noted for its attractive figurines of dancers, snake charmers, and stylised animals. The quality of its pottery and porcelain was very good; some pieces were highly glazed in royal blue, white and gilt, others were matt glazed in beige and gilt, while others still were finished in more naturalistic colours. The marks include an *E* (for the proprietor, Eichler), a pink triangle with *Royal Dux* impressed along the sides, accompanied by a double circle of blue lines with *Made in Czechoslovakia*.

Royal Dux wall mask, 7in. high, 1930s. *(Muir Hewitt)* **£200 $300**

A Royal Dux figural dish modelled with a boy and two puppies by a pool, impressed *2106*, 22cm. wide. *(Lyle)* **£200 $320**

A Royal Dux polychrome wall mask of a young woman wearing a blue floral bonnet and gazing at a butterfly, 20cm. high. *(Christie's)* **£230 $356**

A Royal Dux porcelain figure of a young woman standing with hands on hips, with long blue tassel edged scarf draped around her body, on a circular base, applied pink triangle mark impressed *Royal Dux Bohemia*, green printed circular mark *Made in Czechoslovakia*, impressed numerals *3058 10*, blue painted *M*. 35.5cm. high. *(Christie's)* **£300 $490**

A Royal Dux equestrian group, as an elegantly dressed horseman talking to a young peasant girl, impressed pink triangle mark, 16in. high. *(Phillips)* **£820 $1,287**

A Royal Dux pottery figure modelled as a dancing lady, holding up long blue dress to reveal frilly petticoats, painted in shades of blue, white and gold, stamped Royal Dux Czechoslovakia, impressed *222 126 17*, painted *M*, 20cm. high.
(Christie's) **£207 $335**

A Royal Dux group of male and female figures dancing, he wearing a turban, she semi-draped with a flowing blue skirt, 12¼in. high.
(Anderson & Garland) **£380 $627**

A Royal Dux porcelain figure of a standing horse, with green saddle and pink rug, on oblong rustic base, 7½in. wide.
(Andrew Hartley) **£380 $627**

A Royal Dux pottery group modelled as male and female figures in classical garb, 48.5cm. *(Phillips)* **£300 $470**

A Royal Dux Bohemia figure of a young woman in Edwardian dress leaning against a shell, 17.5cm. high. *(Christie's)* **£200 $302**

A Royal Dux Bohemia figure of a young woman in classical dress, standing holding a tambourine, 33cm. high. *(Christie's)* **£184 $278**

A Royal Dux ceramic centrepiece modelled as a young maiden draped on a conch shell, 15in. high. *(Christie's)* **£465 $697**

Royal Dux porcelain figural vase, early 20th century, with two Art Nouveau maidens clinging to the sides, 21½in. high. *(Butterfield & Butterfield)* **£1,207 $1,955**

Royal Dux, Art Nouveau porcelain simulated marble bust of a girl wearing a floral bonnet and dress, with applied pink seal mark, 20in. high. *(Lawrences)* **£1,850 $2,720**

Royal Dux figural compôte, Czechoslovakia, 20th century, bowl mounted to a central tree-form support surrounded by three females, 20¼in. high. *(Skinner)* **£402 $633**

'A Royal Dux figure group, boy in tunic and breeches with setter type dog, on rustic plinth, 13in. wide, pink triangle mark. *(Russell Baldwin & Bright)* **£560 $931**

A Royal Dux bust of a lady dressed in lace trimmed decolleté dress and wearing a ribboned hat, applied pink triangle mark, height 56cm. *(Wintertons)* **£1,650 $2,640**

Royal Dux figural compôte, Czechoslovakia, early 20th century, modelled with female figure atop a shell-form bowl, 14½in. high. *(Skinner)* **£475 $748**

A whimsical Royal Dux porcelain group modelled as a small boy in swimming costume squatting down to fondle his devoted pet dog, 6¼in. high. *(Christie's)* **£115 $172**

A Royal Dux ceramic centrepiece, the base modelled as roots and foliage supporting maiden in flowing robes perched between two shells forming the bowls, 16¼in. high. *(Christie's)* **£890 $1,335**

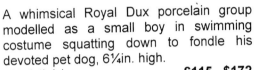

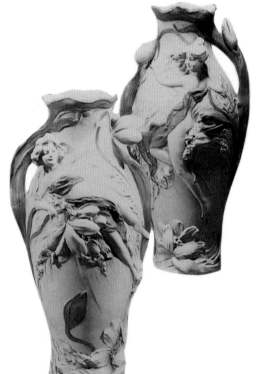

A Royal Dux Bohemia Group, modelled as a Grecian youth riding a horse and leading another, 34.5cm. high. *(Christie's)* **£403 $609**

A pair of Royal Dux pottery vases, of swollen cylindrical form, moulded in relief with blooming foliage and frolicking Art Nouveau maidens, painted in shades of pink, green, sepia and gilt, applied pink triangle impressed *Royal Dux Bohemia E*, one impressed *511* and other *512*, painted mark *43*. *(Christie's)* **£437 $710**

Royal Dux 1930s powder box and cover, 7in. high. *(Muir Hewitt)* **£500 $815**

A Royal Dux porcelain figure of a milkmaid with a cow, in pink, green and ivory colouring, raised on shaped rustic base, 8½in. wide. *(Andrew Hartley)* **£520 $800**

Royal Dux porcelain figure of Marilyn Monroe, designed by V. David, impressed and printed marks, 27cm. high. *(Christie's)* **£125 $205**

A pair of Royal Dux semi-draped female figures, wearing long red dresses, 6in. high. pink tablet marks, No. 3353, printed Czechoslovakia mark. *(Anderson & Garland)* **£190 $290**

'At the Masquerade Ball', a large Royal Dux group, modelled as an elaborately costumed couple dancing, 49cm. high. *(Phillips)* **£600 $960**

A Royal Dux pottery figure group modelled as a running naked girl with dog, painted in shades of green, pink, brown and gilt, impressed numerals *717 7*, stamped mark *9*, painted mark *17*, 36cm. high. *(Christie's)* **£253 $410**

A pair of Royal Dux figures of a lady and a gentleman, each standing holding a large wicker basket, circa 1900-20, 41cm. high. *(Winterton's)* **£1,100 $1,716**

A Royal Dux porcelain figure group of a Roman charioteer, the chariot drawn by two rearing horses, 46cm. overall. *(Phillips)* **£1,000 $1,600**

Royal Dux, Art Nouveau centrepiece, circa 1900, porcelain glazed in shades of green, brown and rust, 13½in. high. *(Sotheby's)* **£805 $1,278**

A pair of Royal Dux book ends in the form of clowns, cream, green and brown designs with gilt work. *(G.A. Key)* **£350 $560**

A pair of Royal Dux figures, one of a goatherd wearing a bear skin over his tunic, his companion feeding a lamb from flowers, 52cm. *(Bearne's)* **£1,000 $1,600**

A Royal Dux group in the form of Pierrot kissing the hand of a young woman wearing a flowing ball gown, after a design by Schaff, 28.5cm. *(Bearne's)* **£600 $950**

451

A Royal Dux pottery jardinière modelled as a scantily clad maiden seated upon a blooming lily pad, beside a large conch shell, painted in shades of pink, sepia and gilt, applied pink triangle impressed *Royal Dux Bohemia E*, stamped *Made in Czechoslovakia*, impressed 2327.
(Christie's)   **£450 $735**

A Royal Dux bust of a fin de siècle lady, dressed in ornate 'Lace' bonnet, in pastel shades of pink, white and blue.
(Phillips)   **£480 $729**

A pair of Royal Dux figures in the form of a shepherd and his companion, 49cm. high.
(Bearne's)   **£1,100 $1,661**

A large Royal Dux group in the form of a scantily clad female welcoming the returning hunter, 70cm. high.
(Bearne's)   **£1,250 $1,888**

A Royal Dux figure of a maiden perched on a large leaf, impressed 855, 24cm. long.
(Lyle) £250 $400

Royal Dux Czechoslovakian wall pocket, with female visage decoration, 1930s.
(Muir Hewitt) £150 $245

A Royal Dux porcelain figure, modelled as a scantily clad female wearing pink and green classical toga dress, a large amphora at her feet, walking forward holding up scarf in one hand, on a shaped circular base, applied pink triangle mark impressed *Royal Dux Bohemia*, printed circular mark *Made in Czechoslovakia*, impressed numerals *1909 4,* 60.6cm. high.
(Christie's) £575 $935

Royal Dux figure, of a snake charmer, printed and impressed marks, 22cm. high.
(Christie's) £125 $205

A pair of Royal Dux figures, in the form of a gardener, his lady companion holding a posy, 40.5cm. high.
(Bearne's) **£720 $1,101**

A Royal Dux pottery group in the form of a brown and white cow, feeding from a bundle of greenery, 46cm. high.
(Bearne's) **£320 $477**

A Royal Dux centrepiece, in the form of a young woman in a sedan chair in conversation with her two attendants, 39cm. high. *(Bearne's)* **£1,350 $2,150**

A pair of Royal Dux bisque porcelain figures of a rustic boy and girl, the young boy wearing a green hat, the girl wearing a décolleté pink blouse, 17in. high.
(Phillips) **£500 $800**

A pair of Royal Dux figures of a near eastern desert dweller and fishergirl, both wearing green and apricot rustic dress, pink triangle pad mark, 20th century, 24¼in. high. *(Christie's)* **£825 $1,425**

A fine Royal Dux group of a carthorse with a boy astride its back, 13¾in. high, bearing initials *A.D.*
(Anderson & Garland) **£540 $847**

A Royal Dux bisque porcelain Art Nouveau style flower holder, as a maiden draped in a brown robe seated upon a rocky outcrop, 27cm. high. *(Phillips)* **£430 $856**

A pair of Royal Dux Bohemia figures of troubadours, in fin de siècle dress, the man with guitar, his companion with mandolin, 80cm. high. *(Christie's)* **£3,220 $4,862**

A Royal Dux Art Nouveau conch shell group with three water nymphs in relief, 17½in. high. **£600 $950**

A pair of Royal Dux figures of water carriers in shades of sepia green and brown, 70cm. high. *(Lyle)* **£750 $1,200**

A Royal Dux centrepiece, the trefoil base with column modelled as three bare breasted girls kneeling and supporting lily-form bowl, 6½in. high. *(Lyle)* **£320 $512**

Royal Dux Czechoslovakian wall mask of a lady, 1930s. *(Muir Hewitt)* **£300 $500**

Royal Dux wall mask of a young girl with bonnet, 8in. high. *(Muir Hewitt)* **£350 $570**

Royal Dux wall mask, of a flaxen haired lady, Czechoslovakian, 1930s. *(Muir Hewitt)* **£300 $500**

Royal Dux wall mask based on Bing Crosby, 1930s. *(Muir Hewitt)* **£275 $450**

Czechoslovakian Royal Dux wall mask of a Spanish señorita, 1930s. *(Muir Hewitt)* **£350 $570**

Czechoslovakian Royal Dux wall mask of a flaxen haired lady, 1930s. *(Muir Hewitt)* **£250 $400**

Royal Dux Czechoslovakian wall mask of a lady, 1930s. *(Muir Hewitt)* **£350 $570**

Czechoslovakian Royal Dux wall mask of a red haired lady, 1930s. *(Muir Hewitt)* **£300 $500**

A Royal Dux vide-poche, circa 1900, the dish modelled as a flower rimmed pool with a female figure in a loosely draped robe kneeling on an overhanging rock as if to gaze into the water, 9⅞in. high. *(Sotheby's)* **£800 $1,300**

'Tango Dancers', a Royal Dux group of two dancers, they both wear blue and gilded costumes, he supports his female companion in a highly stylistic arched pose, 21.50cm. high. *(Phillips)* **£800 $1,300**

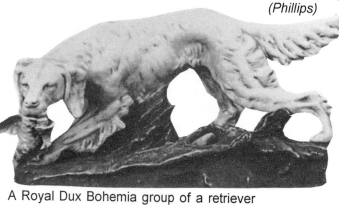

A Royal Dux Bohemia group of a retriever carrying a pheasant, painted in shades of sepia, green and gilt, 41cm. long. *(Christie's)* **£207 $313**

A Royal Dux large figure group, depicting an Arab astride a camel with Moorish attendant carrying baskets on oblong plinth base, stamped and printed marks, 23½in. high. *(Christie's)* **£2,000 $3,250**

A Royal Dux pottery figure of a naked young woman running with a dog, on an oval base, applied pink triangle mark impressed Royal Dux Bohemia, printed mark and impressed numerals 717 46 13, 36cm. high. *(Christie's)* **£125 $205**

The Ruskin Pottery was founded at West Smethwick, Birmingham, in 1898 by William Howson Taylor (1876-1935) who had trained at the Birmingham School of Art. Throughout his career he was constantly experimenting with glazes and it is these which give his work its principal interest.

Initially, he made 'Soufflé' ware, where the predominant colours were blues, greens, purples, greys and celadons with a glaze in a single colour or mottled, clouded or shaded with a harmonising tone.

Lustre wares were also made in a wide range of colours and shades, and a pearl lustre was introduced, sometimes with a blistered texture and often with a kingfisher blue glaze. Flambé glazes with scattered viridian spots derived from the use of copper salts were produced, and after 1929 matt and crystalline glazes were added to the range. Taylor's High Fired wares featured dramatic colour contrasts, for example purple and black streaking on sea green, or black and green on cream.

With regard to the wares produced, many vases were made, some of which could be heavily potted and covered with blue, green, orange or crystalline blue with a frosted effect. The shapes were often based on Chinese styles. Other products included useful tableware, buttons, hatpins and cufflinks, some silver mounted.

Unfortunately Taylor took the secrets of his glazes with him to his grave, determined that his work should not be imitated. Production stopped at the factory in 1933.

A Ruskin high-fired stoneware vase, the oatmeal ground clouded with green and speckled with irregular areas of purple and blue, 1915, 21cm. high.
(Christie's) **£1,100 $2,134**

A Ruskin high-fired stoneware bowl, the exterior glazed in deep red clouding over grey, the interior red speckled with purple and green, 1933, 24.5cm. diameter.
(Christie's) **£900 $1,450**

A Ruskin high-fired egg-shell stoneware bowl, with dark mottled red glaze clouding to green and purple towards the foot, 21cm. diameter.
(Christie's) **£1,100 $2,134**

A Ruskin high-fired stoneware bowl, the oatmeal ground mottled overall in dove-grey overlaid with red and purple clouding, with green speckling, 31cm. diameter.
(Christie's) **£2,000 $3,200**

A Ruskin high fired lamp base, of tapering cylindrical form with bulbous neck, impressed factory marks, 8¼in. high.
(Christie's) **£418 $763**

A Ruskin Pottery high-fired stoneware bowl, the white exterior with mottled grey, impressed *Ruskin England, 1927*, 24.2cm. diameter.
(Christie's) **£770 $1,378**

A Ruskin Pottery high-fired stoneware vase, with tall cylindrical neck, grey ground with mottled liver-red and mauve, 1924, 29cm. high.
(Christie's) **£440 $766**

A Ruskin Pottery high-fired stoneware vase and cover, dove grey ground fragmented with random grey and green 'snake-skin' patterning.
(Christie's) **£5,500 $9,845**

A Ruskin Pottery high-fired eggshell stoneware bowl, the exterior mottled liver red speckled with green, 17cm. diameter.
(Christie's) **£1,540 $2,757**

A Ruskin Pottery high-fired stoneware vase, white ground beneath mottled green with slight red veining, impressed *Ruskin England 1914*, 17.6cm. high.
(Christie's) **£825 $1,477**

A Ruskin Pottery high-fired stoneware vase, white ground beneath liver red and dove grey streaked glaze, 23.6cm. high.
(Christie's) **£1,100 $1,969**

A Ruskin Pottery high-fired stoneware vase, covered in a mottled grey glaze, impressed *Ruskin England 1927*, 9.5cm. high.
(Christie's) **£132 $236**

A Ruskin Pottery high-fired stoneware vase, covered in a mottled dove grey speckled glaze, impressed *Ruskin,* 24cm. high.
(Christie's) **£1,100 $1,969**

A Ruskin high fired stoneware bottle vase, mottled pink glaze 1924, 6½in. high.
(Christie's) **£308 $497**

A Ruskin Pottery high-fired stoneware bowl, grey ground beneath mottled liver red with cloudy purple, 21cm. high.
(Christie's) **£1,100 $1,969**

A Ruskin Pottery high-fired stoneware vase, white ground covered in mottled greenish buff glaze, dated 1922, 22.5cm. high.
(Christie's) **£1,320 $2,363**

A large Ruskin Pottery high-fired stoneware vase on stand, the white ground mottled with liver red, blue and purple 1914, 44.5cm. high.
(Christie's) **£3,520 $6,301**

A Ruskin Pottery high-fired eggshell stoneware bowl, pierced with floral roundels, impressed Ruskin England 1924, 15cm. diameter.
(Christie's) **£770 $1,378**

A rare Ruskin Pottery high-fired stoneware vase, mottled grey ground with areas of cloudy and mottled blue, impressed Ruskin England, 1924, 37cm. high.
(Christie's) **£1,980 $3,544**

A Ruskin Pottery high-fired ginger jar on stand, grey with mottled liver and purple-red and green-black speckling, 11.2cm. high.
(Christie's) **£770 $1,378**

A small Ruskin Pottery high fired bowl, grey ground with mottled liver red and purple glaze speckled with green, 8.6cm. high.
(Christie's) **£440 $788**

A Ruskin Pottery high-fired vase, band of moulded floral decoration, covered in a mottled oatmeal glaze, 27cm. high.
(Christie's) **£330 $591**

This intriguing title (*SEG* is the usual mark) is found on the products of the Paul Revere Pottery, which was set up at the beginning of the 20th century for the purpose of training girls from poor immigrant families in Boston. The profits from the pottery were used to fund the girls' education in other subjects. The output mainly consisted of earthenware, nursery and breakfast bowls and dishes and these were decorated with birds, flowers or mottoes, often around the borders.

Saturday Evening Girls Pottery motto plate, Massachusetts, 1914, signed *S.G.* for Sara Galner, 7½in. diameter. *(Skinner)* **£3,250 $5,200**

Saturday Evening Girl's decorated cream pitcher, Boston, circa 1910, signed *S.E.G., 191-5-10 I.G.*, 3in. high. *(Skinner)* **£800 $1,280**

Decorated Saturday Evening Girls Pottery pitcher and bowl, Boston, 1918, both with rabbit and turtle border. *(Skinner)* **£300 $480**

Saturday Evening Girls Pottery vase, Boston, Massachusetts, 1922, with incised and painted band of tulip decoration, 6¾in. high. *(Skinner)* **£169 $325**

Saturday Evening Girls Pottery decorated motto pitcher, Boston, Massachusetts, early 20th century, 9¾in. high. *(Skinner)* **£1,143 $2,200**

Saturday Evening Girls Pottery bowl, green glazed half-round with sgraffito interior border of yellow nasturtium blossoms, 8½in. diameter. *(Skinner)* **£600 $960**

Early 20th century Saturday Evening Girl's decorated pitcher, Boston, signed *S.E.G. 276-1-10*, 9½in. high. *(Skinner)* **£3,500 $5,600**

Since the 1880s the firm of J.B. Wileman had had as a partner J.B. Shelley, and had also employed his son Percy. In 1896 Percy Shelley built a new factory to produce hand painted earthenware art pieces which were marketed as Intarsio ware and were designed by Frederick Rhead.

Walter Slater became Art Director in 1901. Hitherto the firm had produced mainly for export to America, but high tariffs were making this increasingly difficult and Slater decided to concentrate on the home market. His American export pieces had been marketed as Foley China, but he could not register the name for use in Britain as it had already been registered by E. Brain. The name Shelley China was therefore registered instead, with a marketing campaign to ensure buyers recognised the company's continuing production. The firm's name was finally changed to Shelley Potteries in 1929.

The art ware which Rhead had begun was now developed by the use of glazes which 'ran' together. Thus bright colour combinations could be applied with little hand skill and then the chance element in the firing made each piece unique. The results were considered to typify modern art in their individuality and the quality and immediacy of the colours.

When Percy's son, J.K. Shelley, took over the firm's finances, he persuaded his father to pursue an active marketing policy and to use advertisements to create a market identity for the firm. Such conscious marketing was unheard of at the time. So when Shelley launched their new Vogue shape in early 1931 its name was linked with high fashion and its geometric shape and stylised patterns were advertised as being 'of the modern age'. It was advertised in women's magazines and the national press, while brochures of contemporary graphics were widely distributed at point-of-sale outlets.

The firm's modern approach showed too in their forms and styles, which were considered very advanced for the time.

Shelley were taken over in 1966 by Allied English Potteries, which merged in 1971 with the Doulton Group.

Shelley Art Deco vase with stylised floral decoration. *(Muir Hewitt)* **£55 $85**

A Shelley nursery tea trio designed by Mabel Lucie Attwell, teapot and cover modelled as a duck, jug as a rabbit and sugar bowl as a chicken, teapot 16cm. high. *(Christie's)* **£400 $640**

An early 20th century Shelley china jardinière, decorated with the 'Intarsio' pattern of geese, flower heads and foliage, by Frederick Rhead, about 10in. diameter. *(Riddetts)* **£260 $389**

Shelley Harmony Dripware vase in orange and green, 5in. high.
(Muir Hewitt) **£130 $210**

Shelley Harmony Dripware cake plate with chromium plated handle.
(Muir Hewitt) **£60 $100**

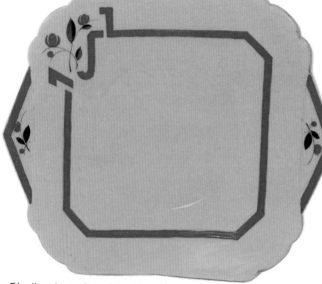

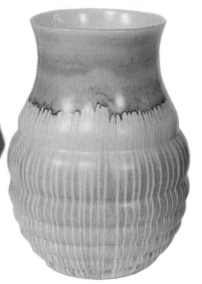

Shelley bread and butter plate with Red J's design. *(Muir Hewitt)* **£40 $65**

Shelley Harmony Dripware vase, 1930s 8½in. high. *Muir Hewitt)* **£125 $200**

Shelley Harmony Dripware waisted vase, 1930s, 6in. high.
(Muir Hewitt) **£70 $115**

'Eve' shape Shelley cup saucer and plate with cottage decoration.
(Muir Hewitt) **£45 $75**

Shelley Harmony Dripware candlestick in orange and green, 1930s.
(Muir Hewitt) **£35 $60**

Shelley milk jug, in red, black and grey, 1930. *(Muir Hewitt)* **£35 $60**

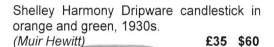

Shelley Harmony Dripware 'Ice Cream Cone' vase, 10in. high.
(Muir Hewitt) **£175 $285**

Shelley Regent shaped tea for two set with globe shaped teapot, 1930s.
(Muir Hewitt) **£120 $195**

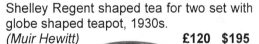

Shelley plate Harmony Ware range in green and cream, 8in. wide.
(Muir Hewitt) **£35 $60**

Shelley Harmony Dripware, spot drip, charger, 13in. diameter.
(Muir Hewitt) **£150 $245**

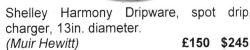

A Shelley Intarsio teapot in the form of a caricature of Austin Chamberlain. *(Lyle)* **£475 $775**

A Shelley ginger jar and cover designed by Walter Slater, painted with a ferocious dragon in shades of blue and green, 23.5cm. high. *(Christie's)* **£400 $640**

Shelley 'Mode' shape part tea service, 1930s. *(Muir Hewitt)* **£125 $188**

Shelley Harmony Dripware jug in orange and green, 13in. high. *(Lyle)* **£100 $160**

Shelley Harmony Dripware conical vase, in red, orange and green, 7in. high. *(Muir Hewitt)* **£180 $295**

Shelley Harmony Dripware preserve pot in orange and grey, 4in. high. *(Muir Hewitt)* **£60 $100**

Shelley dripware vase 1930s, 9in. high.
(Muir Hewitt) **£90 $135**

Shelley Harmony Ware plate, in red and orange. *(Muir Hewitt)* **£35 $60**

Art Deco cup, saucer and plate copying Shelley's Regent shape, 1930s.
(Muir Hewitt) **£20 $32**

Pair of Shelley Art Deco vases with tulip decoration, 7in. high.
(Muir Hewitt) **£125 $188**

Shelley Harmony Dripware ginger jar, in orange, 10in. high.
(Muir Hewitt) **£350 $570**

Shelley Harmony Dripware plate, 8in. wide, 1930s. *(Muir Hewitt)* **£40 $65**

Shelley Harmony Ware juicer, 3½in. high. *(Muir Hewitt)* **£45 $75**

Shelley Harmony Dripware spot drip vase, 1930s. *(Muir Hewitt)* **£120 $195**

Shelley Mode shape cup, saucer and plate, 1930s. *(Muir Hewitt)* **£125 $200**

Shelley Harmony Dripware spot drip vase, 1930s. *(Muir Hewitt)* **£60 $100**

Shelley Harmony Dripware ginger jar and cover, in red and grey 1930s, 8in. high. *(Muir Hewitt)* **£100 $160**

Shelley Harmony Ware cake plate with chromium plate base, 1930s. *(Muir Hewitt)* **£45 $75**

Shelley bread and butter plate from 1930s tea service. *(Muir Hewitt)* **£40 $65**

Shelley Harmony Dripware cone shaped vase, 5in. high. *(Muir Hewitt)* **£100 $160**

Shelley Harmony banded ware jug, 12in. high, 1930s. *(Muir Hewitt)* **£100 $160**

Shelley Queen Anne shape teapot and stand, 1930s. *(Muir Hewitt)* **£170 $275**

Shelley bread and butter plate, 8in. diameter, 1930s.
(Muir Hewitt) **£30 $50**

Shelley Harmony Dripware vase, in orange, green and brown, 1930s, 8in. high. *(Muir Hewitt)* **£140 $225**

Shelley, Mabel Lucie Attwell child's bowl. *(Muir Hewitt)* **£45 $75**

Shelley, Mabel Lucie Attwell baby-plate. *(Muir Hewitt)* **£65 $105**

A Shelley Queen Anne teaset for six, printed in black and yellow with a country sunrise landscape scene, comprising; teapot and cover, milk-jug and sugar basin seven cups, saucers and six side plates, teapot 11cm. high.
(Christie's) **£700 $1,140**

A Shelley bone china 'Tea for Two' service of eight pieces, Eric Slater's 'Mode' shape in orange and black enamels.
(Lyle) **£275 $450**

Shelley Mabel Lucie Attwell baby plate. *(Muir Hewitt)* **£75 $125**

A Shelley nursery teapot by Hilda Cowham, modelled as a marquee and printed with two seated children reading, 5in. high. *(Christie's)* **£400 $650**

Shorter & Son was established by Arthur Shorter, who was the son of the stationmaster at the main railway depot for Stoke-on-Trent at Whitmore. The family were related to the Wilkinsons, and did, therefore, have pottery connections, and when Arthur fell out with his father he went to work as an apprentice at Mintons. He spent some time as a journeyman painter, and then free-lanced for a while as a pottery decorator, before setting up a pottery in partnership with James Boulton. Around 1890, he took over Wilkinson's, while Boulton continued at the original factory.

Arthur had two sons, John and Arthur Colley; the former took over at the Shorter factory on leaving school, while Arthur Colley helped his father at Wilkinsons. Arthur Sr. retired in 1918, leaving his sons in charge of the two factories. Arthur Jr. is distinguished by having employed, and later married, Clarice Cliff, but John also recognised talent and engaged such paintresses as Mabel Leigh at Shorter & Son. On Mabel Leigh's incised ware, her name is included with the factory mark on the base. Shorter's salad and embossed floral ware have a rubber stamp mark reading *Shorter & Son/Stoke on Trent/England* in three lines of block letters. Other ranges have the range name with *Shorter & Son/Stoke on Trent/England* above and below.

Shorter planter in blue, 3½in. high. 1930s. *(Muir Hewitt)* **£45 $75**

Shorter & Co. stylised wall pocket, circa 1930. *(Muir Hewitt)* **£40 $65**

Shorter planter 3½in. high, 1930s. *(Muir Hewitt)* **£45 $75**

Shorter bowl in marbled pink design, 1930s, 8in. wide. *(Muir Hewitt)* **£45 $75**

Susie Cooper was born in Stansfield, near Burslem, in 1902. She attended evening classes at Burslem School of Art and joined A. E. Gray in 1922 to gain the practical experience necessary to qualify for a scholarship at the Royal College of Art. She began as a paintress but became resident designer in 1924. She remained with Gray until 1929 and designed banded ware, nursery ware and hand painted floral and geometric patterns.

In 1929, with the financial backing of her family, she set up on her own as an independent producer. Harry Wood of Wood & Sons offered her facilities to produce new tableware shapes, and in 1931 she settled at the Crown Works in Burslem.

Cooper's avowed policy was to provide well designed, practical pieces at sensible prices, catering for 'professional people with taste and not much money'. To this end, she was quick to adopt new technologies such as lithography.

Factory production ceased for a year following a disastrous fire in 1942, but was back on its feet again by the early Fifties, following participation in the prestigious Festival of Britain in 1951, and bone china was also added to the range. Following another major fire in 1957, Cooper merged with R.H. & S.L. Plant in 1961, and the new company was taken over by Wedgwood in 1966. Cooper, however, continued to design for her own section within the Wedgwood empire for over 20 years. The last surviving 'Pottery Lady', she died in 1994.

Susie Cooper cup and saucer, 1930s, with floral decoration. *(Muir Hewitt)* **£35 $60**

Susie Cooper hand painted coffee service with six cups and saucers, milk jug, sugar bowl and coffeepot. *(Muir Hewitt)* **£550 $900**

Susie Cooper jug, circa 1930, with sgraffito design of flowers. *(Muir Hewitt)* **£100 $160**

Susie Cooper plate, 1930s, of swirl design. *(Muir Hewitt)* **£100 $160**

Susie Cooper two handled green vase, circa 1930, 8in. high.
(Muir Hewitt)
£200 $325

Susie Cooper banded tureen, in fawn, yellow and green, 1930s.
(Muir Hewitt)
£70 $115

Susie Cooper stand circa 1930s, with floral decoration and matching tureen.
(Muir Hewitt)
£150 $245

Susie Cooper jug with sgraffito floral design, 1930s, 5in. high.
(Muir Hewitt)
£75 $125

Susie Cooper vase, circa 1930, with sgraffito decoration of fish.
(Muir Hewitt)
£250 $400

Susie Cooper Homestead cup and saucer, 1930. (Muir Hewitt)
£180 $295

Susie Cooper coffee set with star decoration (coffee pot, sugar bowl, 4 cups and saucers). *(Muir Hewitt)* **£215 $320**

A Gray's Susie Cooper oviform jug, in the 'Cubist' design, painted in colours, 13cm. high. *(Christie's)* **£231 $353**

A Gloria Lustre pedestal bowl, made for the British Empire Exhibition, the interior decorated with putti harvesting fruiting vines, printed British Empire Exhibition marks and Susie Cooper monogram, 23cm. diameter. *(Christie's)* **£385 $589**

A Susie Cooper set in the 'Moon and Mountain' pattern, comprising; coffeepot and cover, milk-jug and sugar bowl, five coffee cans and six saucers, 2nd Galleon mark, height of coffeepot 20cm. *(Christie's)* **£660 $1,010**

Susie Cooper twenty-one piece tea set, all decorated with pale blue comma design on a white ground, 20th century. *(G.A. Key)* **£290 $438**

A Susie Cooper Crown Works plate, painted in silver lustre with stylised tulips, with lime green border, 28cm. diameter. *(Christie's)* **£165 $251**

A pair of Susie Cooper slender ovoid vases in the 'Moon and Mountain' pattern, painted in colours, 22.5cm. high.
(Christie's)   **£1,430 $2,188**

Susie Cooper coffee service, decorated with abstract design of circles with tails, four cups, seven saucers, cream jug and coffee pot. (G.A. Key)   **£70 $109**

A Susie Cooper Kestrel coffee service, decorated with geometric patterning in shades of yellow, black, green and blue, comprising; coffeepot and cover, milk-jug and sugar bowl, five cups and saucers.
(Christie's)   **£1,320 $2,020**

A Gloria lustre pear-shaped vase, with scrolling flowers and foliage in gold, printed factory mark, painted Susie Cooper monogram, 7½in. high.
(Christie's)   **£275 $500**

A cylindrical biscuit barrel and cover in the 'Seagull' pattern, with a stylised gull above blue and green waves, printed facsimile signature, 5¼in. high.
(Christie's)   **£440 $810**

A Susie Cooper coffee set for six, pattern No. E69, painted with an abstract geometric design in blue, black, brown, yellow and green, height of coffee pot 17cm. (Christie's)   **£990 $1,515**

The Shaw & Copestake factory at Longton, Stoke, was founded in 1894 by William Shaw, firstly in a short-lived partnership with William Copestake and thereafter with Richard Hull Sr. It was Hull's son, also Richard, who was to coin the name SylvaC in 1935.

Early Shaw & Copestake products tended to be very ornate in shape and decoration, and consisted of decorative items such as vases, trinket sets and toilet ware. They were marked with a distinctive daisy mark. During the 1920s the company made their name as producers of clock sets in many styles, from Gothic columns to Art Nouveau forms. At this time, too, they produced many highly coloured dressing table sets.

During the 1920s the firm also began to produce a colourful Cellulose Ware. This was cheap and cheerful biscuit ware which was dipped, then hand-painted in vivid colours and left unglazed, though sometimes a light coat of varnish was applied. The content of their range also changed dramatically as they moved to figure production. All sorts of model animals, from rabbits to elephants, were given the cellulose treatment, as were some rather grotesque garden ornaments, mainly gnomes, and human figures such as sailors and dancing ladies.

Concurrently with these developments, matt glazes began to be introduced, and nearly all the items mentioned in the previous paragraph can be found in these, with green by far the most popular colour. Blue, on the other hand, is now the most sought after, as it is the rarest.

When collecting SylvaC ware, one should beware of imitations. The daisy mark, in conjunction, after 1935 with *SylvaC,* continued in use until 1939, and thereafter *SylvaC* was often impressed into the mould, but marking can be haphazard. In 1938 came an added complication when the pottery went into association with Thomas Lawrence's Falcon Pottery, and when the SylvaC factory was requisitioned by the government during the war, Falcon and SylvaC production continued alongside each other at the Falcon Works.

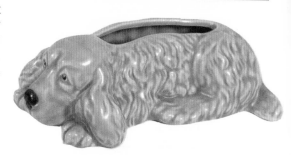

Sylvac brown spaniel posy holder, 1930s. *(Muir Hewitt)* **£40 $65**

A large blue unmarked dog, possibly Sylvac, in seated position, circa 1930. *(Muir Hewitt)* **£150 $245**

Sylvac hare match holder in green, circa 1930. *(Muir Hewitt)* **£45 $75**

Sylvac stylised dog with brown nose, 1950s. *(Muir Hewitt)* **£40 $65**

Brown Sylvac dog with paw in a sling, 1930s. *(Muir Hewitt)* **£45 $75**

Stylised Art Deco style Sylvac jug, 1930s, 7in. high. *(Muir Hewitt)* **£70 $105**

Sylvac hare wall vase, 1950s. *(Muir Hewitt)* **£75 $125**

Sylvac model of a fawn dog with black collar, 1930s. *(Muir Hewitt)* **£40 $65**

Sylvac model of a brown dog with black collar, 1930s. *(Muir Hewitt)* **£40 $65**

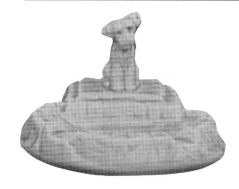

Sylvac dog, 4in. high, 1930s.
(Muir Hewitt) **£30 $45**

Sylvac Pottery ashtray in green, with a brown dog in seated position, *1950*.
(Lyle) **£25 $40**

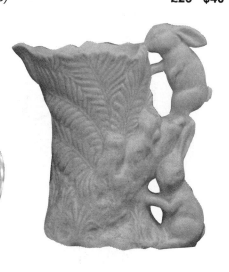

A Sylvac green leaf pottery cream jug with matching saucer, 4in. wide.
(Lyle) **£18 $30**

Sylvac Pottery rabbit jug by Shaw & Copestake, 8½in. high.
(Lyle) **£70 $110**

A North British black Scottie dog advertising figure holding a dimple ball in his mouth by Sylvac, 28cm.
(Phillips) **£440 $830**

A Sylvac Basset hound in naturalistic colour in a seated position.
(Lyle) **£25 $40**

A small Sylvac cat on a top hat ornament, 1930s, 3½in. high. *(Lyle)* **£35 $60**

A Sylvac Basset hound in naturalistic colours in a lying position. *(Lyle)* **£25 $40**

A Sylvac flower vase ornament, 3in. high. *(Lyle)* **£18 $30**

A Sylvac Pottery green jug with squirrel handle, 8½in. high. *(Lyle)* **£70 $110**

Sylvac seated model of a terrier dog, treacle tinted nose and treacle body markings, on a mainly beige ground, 11in. *(G.A. Key)* **£170 $272**

Green Sylvac pot with brown squirrel, 4½in. high. *(Lyle)* **£40 $65**

Sylvac bunny match holder, 4in. high, 1930s. *(Muir Hewitt)* **£30 $45**

Sylvac golfing ashtray in green with white ball, 1950s. *(Muir Hewitt)* **£20 $32**

Brown Sylvac spaniel dog in seated position, 1930s. *(Muir Hewitt)* **£40 $65**

Pair of Sylvac vases with lamb figure, 4in. high. *(Muir Hewitt)* **£75 $120**

Sylvac brown rabbit in seated position, 4in. high. 1930s. *(Muir Hewitt)* **£40 $60**

Sylvac dog in green, in a seated position, 7in. high, 1930s. *(Muir Hewitt)* **£50 $80**

The Teco pottery operated out of Terra Cotta Illinois in the early years of the 20th century. Its output is characterised by matt green glazes which are frequently used on shapes based on natural forms.

Teco Pottery wall pocket, green matt glaze on hanging vase with angular top over moulded roundel, 5¼in. wide. (Skinner) **£220 $385**

A Teco Art Pottery fluted vase, Illinois, circa 1905, 10½in. high.
(Skinner) **£775 $1,250**

Teco Pottery vase with four handles, Terra Cotta, Illinois, circa 1910, squat, impressed twice, 6½in. high.
(Skinner)   **£800 $1,300**

Teco Pottery vase, designed by Fritz Albert, supported on three moulded flaring feet under a green glaze, stamped *Teco 115*, 9in. high.
(Skinner)   **£1,650 $2,500**

Rare and important Teco Pottery vase, Terra Cotta, Illinois, circa 1905, shape 119, designed by Fritz Albert, matt green glaze on ovoid form, 13in. high.
(Skinner) **£9,144 $14,950**

Teco floor vase, Gates Potteries, Terra Cotta, Illinois, circa 1906, green glazed with rolled rim continuing into four squared vertical strap handles, 20⅝in. high.
(Skinner)   **£3,667 $7,150**

Teco Pottery vase, Terra Cotta, Illinois, designed by Hugh M. G. Garden, gloss mottled pale green glaze, 11¼in. high.
(Skinner)   **£383 $575**

Teco Pottery handled vase, decorated by four angular quatriform handles extending to base rim, 13½in. high.
(Skinner)   **£746 $1,320**

A Teco pottery double-handled vase, Illinois, circa 1910, 7in. high.
(Skinner) **£225 $365**

Early 20th century Teco pottery yellow bud vase, Illinois, 4½in. high.
£250 $410

Teco pottery vase, Illinois, early 20th century, flared rim, in matte buff colour glaze, impressed *Teco* mark, 12¼in. high.
(Skinner) **£550 $900**

Teco pottery brown moulded vase, bullet shape on four elongated V feet, Illinois, 1909, 8½in. high.
(Skinner) **£1,500 $2,450**

Teco pottery candlesticks, circular form with square handles under a vibrant blue glaze, impressed *Teco*, 5in. diameter.
(Skinner) **£272 $431**

A Teco pottery four-handled vase, circa 1910, 7¼in. high.
(Skinner) **£400 $650**

Teco pottery matte green vase, Illinois, circa 1908, with four open handles, 6½in. high.
(Skinner) **£750 $1,225**

Rare Teco pottery tile, decorated with an incised frog under matte green, butterscotch and blue glaze, impressed Teco, 8in. square.
(Skinner) **£1,234 $2,000**

A Teco pottery moulded lotus flower vase, Chicago, circa 1905, designed by F. Moreau, 11½in. high.
(Skinner) **£1,750 $2,850**

Terracotta is a fired clay, principally associated with sculpture, and terracotta figures feature among the antiquities of China, Greece and Rome. The art was revived during the Renaissance, and in the 18th century France became a leading centre of production. The popularity of the medium lasted well into the Art Nouveau and Art Deco periods. Such designers as Archibald Knox produced pieces for Liberty, while even Chiparus on occasion abandoned his bronze and ivory for terracotta.

A pair of terracotta garden urns, designed by Archibald Knox and manufactured by Liberty & Co., circa 1902, each with incised entrelac design, 14¹/₈in. high.
(Christie's)   £2,530 $4,124

A plaster terracotta-look sculpture of a young girl's smiling face with grapes, signed *Géo Verbanck*, and dated *1921,* 33cm. high. *(Hôtel de Ventes Horta)*
£351 $537

A Goldscheider terracotta table lamp, modelled in relief with Art Nouveau maiden on a grassy mound above a mirrored pool, 50cm. diameter.
(Christie's)   £747 $1,210

An Austrian gilt and patinated terracotta figure entitled Chianti, by Friedrich Goldscheider, Vienna, of a young woman in summer dress and bonnet, helping with the wine harvest, 42¾in. high.
(Christie's)   £3,450 $5,623

Monumental glazed terracotta bust, designed by Haig Patigian, from the Atlantic Richfield Building, Los Angeles, circa 1930, the muscular winged male depicted looking downward, 24in. high. *(Butterfield & Butterfield)* **£2,307 $3,737**

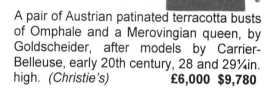

A pair of Austrian patinated terracotta busts of Omphale and a Merovingian queen, by Goldscheider, after models by Carrier-Belleuse, early 20th century, 28 and 29¼in. high. *(Christie's)* **£6,000 $9,780**

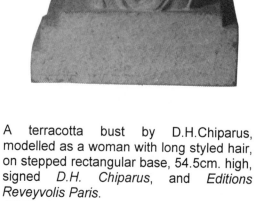

A terracotta garden urn, the design attributed to Archibald Knox, manufactured by Liberty, with four large lug handles, circa 1904, 17in. high. *(Christie's)* **£1,955 $3,167**

A terracotta bust by D.H.Chiparus, modelled as a woman with long styled hair, on stepped rectangular base, 54.5cm. high, signed *D.H. Chiparus*, and *Editions Reveyvolis Paris.* *(Phillips)* **£600 $975**

Artus van Briggle was born in Felicity, Ohio in 1869. He studied painting in Cincinnati, where he also worked as a decorator of dolls' heads and vases. Around 1887 he became Director of the Rookwood Pottery, where he decorated vases with flowers in underglaze colours. It was part of Rookwood's enlightened philosophy to send talented decorators on scholarships abroad, and van Briggle benefited under this scheme with a period at the Académie Julien in Paris in 1893. On his return to Cincinnati he continued at Rookwood, while experimenting at home with the production of Chinese matt glazes.

He fell ill with tuberculosis and moved to Colorado in 1895, where he established the van Briggle Pottery Co. in 1902. There he produced vases and plates decorated with stylised animal and flower forms in the Art Nouveau style. These were often relief decorated and covered in soft-coloured glazes.

Early Van Briggle vase, with incised foliate design, green glaze, incised *AA* logo, *151, Van Briggle*, 1904?, 4½in. high. *(Skinner)* **£946 $1,495**

Van Briggle pottery copper clad vase, Colorado, 5½in. high. **£850 $1,275**

A Van Briggle pottery bowl, the underside formed as a large shell, with the reclining figure of a mermaid to one side, 39cm. diameter. *(Christie's)* **£1,000 $1,550**

Van Briggle Pottery vase, Colorado Springs, circa 1904, with moulded floral design, yellow and ochre semi-matte glaze, 8½in. high. *(Skinner)* **£442 $850**

Early Van Briggle vase, 1904, broad shoulder with two handles under a green glaze, incised *AA, 242, Van Briggle, 1904*, 5in. high. *(Skinner)* **£400 $600**

Van Briggle Pottery vase, caramel glaze with moss green mottling, inscribed mark and *1913*, 6in. high. *(Skinner)* **£299 $467**

A pair of 20th century Van Briggle Pottery vases, Colorado, 5½in. high. *(Skinner)* **£500 $815**

Van Briggle Pottery vase, Colorado Springs, circa 1904, decoration of narcissi, matte green glaze with yellow accents, 9⅝in. high. *(Skinner)* **£364 $700**

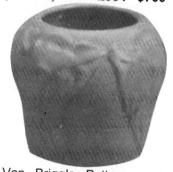

Early Van Briggle vase, with incised foliate design, green glaze, incised *AA* logo, *151, Van Briggle, 1904(?)*, 4½in. high. *(Skinner)* **£946 $1,495**

Van Briggle Pottery vase, Colorado Springs, 1915, semi-matte glazed green at rim and shoulder shading to mottled olive/brown, 7¾in. high. *(Skinner)* **£345 $578**

Van Briggle Pottery vase, 1903 four floral sprays in relief under a speckled matte green-brown glaze, incised logo, *Van Briggle, 20 1903, III*, 4in. high. *(Skinner)* **£1,850 $3,000**

Van Briggle Art Pottery vase, circa 1910, with four large leaves of matt green glaze on a brown ground, 5½in. high. *(Skinner)* **£245 $400**

A pair of Van Briggle Pottery vases, Colorado Springs, Colorado, circa 1909, striated matte glaze, incised marks, 9¾in. high. *(Skinner)* **£475 $775**

Van Briggle Art Pottery vase, circa 1902, decorated with four large moulded leaves of matt yellow-green glaze, 8in. high. *(Skinner)* **£735 $1,200**

Charles Vyse was an English sculptor and potter who studied at Hanley Art School before moving to London where he opened his studio in Chelsea in 1919. With his wife Nell, he experimented with wood ash glazes on stoneware, and also during the 1920s successfully reproduced Chinese Sung vases.

His figure groups, realistically modelled and sometimes coloured, are very sought after. His work is usually marked with initials or a signature. Charles Vyse died in 1968.

'The Balloon Woman', Chelsea pottery figure designed by Charles Vyse, painted in colours, painted factory mark, dated *1922*, 22cm. high. *(Christie's)* **£330 $502**

A stoneware globular vase by Charles Vyse, covered in a lustrous mottled khaki and brown glaze with areas of crimson, incised *CV 1933*, 13cm. high. *(Christie's)* **£490 $800**

A stoneware oviform jar by Charles Vyse, 1928, 17cm. high. *(Christie's)* **£200 $320**

'Mid Day Rest', a Chelsea figure designed by Charles Vyse, 1922, 8½in. high. *(Christopher Matthews)* **£580 $945**

'Fantasy', a Charles Vyse pottery group, of a woman seated cross-legged on a grassy base, scantily clad with a turquoise and mauve robe, 21.5cm. high. *(Phillips)* **£370 $555**

A Charles Vyse figure of
Elizabeth Fry, 17in. high,
circa 1913.
(Lyle) **£2,000 $3,200**

A Charles Vyse figure of a
Shire horse, on rectangular
base, 28.5cm. high.
£310 $465

A Charles Vyse pottery
figure of The Piccadilly Rose
Woman, modelled as a
plump lady, 10in. high.
£560 $840

'The Lavender Girl', a
Chelsea Cheyne pottery
figure by Charles Vyse,
painted in colours, 22cm.
high. *(Christie's)* **£308 $468**

A Charles Vyse stoneware
jug, inscribed *Fishing's a dry
job* in a band around the rim,
above a sceptical fish,
17cm. high.
(Phillips) **£350 $560**

A Charles Vyse group in the
form of Pan kneeling on the
ground, lambs in his arms,
his companion leapfrogging
over his shoulders, 33cm.
(Bearne's) **£1,000 $1,600**

A Charles Vyse figure of a
ribbon seller on a square
plinth, circa 1925, 30.5cm.
high, including plinth.
(Lyle) **£1,000 $1,600**

A Charles Vyse oviform,
stoneware vase decorated
with tenmoku-brown and
yellow-green tree forms,
29cm. high.
(Phillips) **£275 $450**

Flower Seller, a Chelsea
pottery figure by Charles
Vyse, of a woman selling
posies of violets, Chelsea
1926, 29.7cm. high.
(Christie's) **£530 $860**

Louis Wain (1860-1931) was an English illustrator and designer who is best remembered for his illustrations of cats engaged in human pursuits. In the early 1900s he designed a series of postcards, the A-Mewsing Write-away Series, on this theme for Raphael Tuck. These are now highly collectable, as indeed is anything by Wain.

Between 1910-1920 Wain also designed pottery figures of cats. These were very much in the Cubist style, and highly coloured in, for example, green, orange and black. There is a distinct progression which can be noticed in Wain's work. From early, fairly naturalistic portrayals, his style becomes increasingly anguished – no placid, cuddly fireside moggies, these – and some of his latest models are so weird as to be hardly recognisable as cats at all. This reflects the progression of Wain's own psychological decline. He became increasingly eccentric and died in an asylum in 1931.

A Louis Wain porcelain lion vase, decorated in black, yellow, green and russet enamels, 11.8cm. high. *(Christie's)* **£940 $1,410**

A Louis Wain pottery spill holder in the form of a standing bulldog, the yellow body painted with black scrolls, 9cm. high. *(Christie's)* **£330 $502**

A Louis Wain porcelain cat vase, decorated in white, green, russet and black, enamels, with impressed and painted marks, 15.5cm. high. *(Christie's)* **£1,540 $2,602**

A Louis Wain porcelain pig vase, decorated in green, yellow, russet and black enamels, with impressed and painted marks, 12.4cm. high. *(Christie's)* **£1,550 $2,325**

A large Louis Wain pottery vase, modelled as a seated cat, 25.4cm. high. *(Christie's)* **£1,200 $1,800**

'The Lucky Knight Errant Cat And His Meow Meow Notes', a Louis Wain figure, modelled in relief, painted in shades of red, blue, green, yellow and black painted signature, 14.5cm. high. *(Christie's)* **£500 $810**

'Felix the Furturist Cat', an Amphora pottery vase designed by Louis Wain, the body incised with Miaow Miaow notes, 9½in. high. *(Christie's)* **£1,760 $3,115**

A large glazed earthenware cat, designed by Louis Wain, 1920s, modelled with typically formalised features, hollow to form a vase, 10in. high, incised signature *Louis Wain* on the body, impressed mark *Reg. No. 637128*, stamped and stencilled *Made in England*. *(Christie's)* **£2,300 $3,749**

A Louis Wain style 'Haw Haw' cat, the pottery spill holder modelled as a caricature of Lord Haw Haw, 13.5cm. high. *(Christie's)* **£330 $502**

The Walley Pottery flourished around the turn of the century in the town of Sterling, Massachusetts.

Its output consisted mainly of simple forms, vases, mugs etc., designed in equally simple shapes. Decoration was often confined to the glazes, which could be mottled or streaked, and used in combinations of colour such as a green drip on a brown ground. Occasionally pieces were simply moulded with stylised plant and leaf forms. Grotesque mugs with moulded mask faces were also produced.

Fine Walley pottery vase, with a rich speckled green glaze with brown showing through, 7¾in. high. *(Skinner)* **£770 $1,265**

Walley pottery, two-handled vase with frothy green glaze, impressed marks, 6½in. high.
(Skinner) **£175 $288**

Walley pottery vase, bulbous-form under a frothy green speckled glaze with a brown rim, impressed marks, 7in. high.
(Skinner) **£298 $489**

Exceptional Walley pottery vase, reticulated oviform with repeated leaf design under a light brown glaze with green highlights, 6in. diameter.
(Skinner) **£1,050 $1,725**

Walley pottery covered jar, exceptionally frothy speckled green glaze on a brown ground, impressed marks, 6½in. high.
(Skinner) **£105 $173**

Frederick Walrath (c1880-c1920) was an American artist potter who studied under Charles Binns. He also taught at Rochester and Columbia University, New York. His production consisted of earthenware vases and jars decorated with linear motifs and stylised plant forms, covered in matt glazes. He exhibited in 1904 at the St Louis World Fair, and in later life worked for two years at the Newcomb College Pottery (q.v.), New Orleans. His mark consists of *Walrath Pottery*, incised, with a device of four arrows.

Walrath Pottery vase, Rochester, New York, circa 1910, matt glazed with repeating foliate band in pale blue and mustard against blue ground, 4¾in. high. (Skinner) **£610 $920**

Walrath pottery vase, circa 1905, matte green in Grueby manner, 10¾in. high. *(Skinner)* **£750 $1,225**

Unusual Walrath Pottery Sculpture, depicting two fighting lions in mottled green glazes on a green glazes on a green glazed base, incised *Walrath*, 1917, 7¼in. high. *(Skinner)* **£920 $1,500**

A Walrath pottery pitcher and five mugs, circa 1910, pitcher 6½in. high. (Christie's) **£1,000 $1,600**

A Walrath floral decorated vase, circa 1910, 7in. high. *(Skinner)* **£1,500 $2,450**

1930 saw the 200th anniversary of the foundation of the company by Josiah Wedgwood, and it was marked by a decision to enlarge the scope of the firm. This led to the commissioning of a number of leading contemporary designers, such Keith Murray, Eric Ravilious and the sculptor John Skeaping, who produced for them a striking series of stylised animals during the 1930s.

While traditional designs always predominated at Wedgwood, the work of the above ensured an output with a strong Art Deco flavour. Then, too, Daisy Makeig-Jones had been working at the Wedgwood factory from 1915-32, designing and painting bone china with lustre decoration, some showing oriental and others Persian influences.

An Art Deco Wedgwood animal figure, modelled as a fallow deer, designed by J. Skeaping, 21.5cm. high. **£365 $580**

A pair of Wedgwood earthenware book-ends, designed by Keith Murray, rectangular section with ribbed arched supports, covered in a matt green glaze, 15cm. high. *(Christie's)* **£402 $655**

'Sun & Wind', a Wedgwood green and white Jasper plaque designed by Anna Katrina Zinkeisen, 12.5cm. diameter. *(Phillips)* **£400 $650**

A Wedgwood earthenware vase designed by Keith Murray, ribbed spherical form, covered in a matt green glaze, 18cm. high. *(Christie's)* **£460 $690**

A Wedgwood ceramic ewer and basin designed by George Logan, covered in a lilac glaze and decorated with stylised yellow floral designs, height of ewer 29.6cm. *(Christie's)* **£1,000 $1,600**

Samuel Weller (1851-1925) acquired the Lonhuda pottery at Steubenville, Ohio in the early 1890s, and moved production to his own pottery which he had established in 1882 at Zanesville. There, he continued to produce pottery in the Lonhuda style, which was now called Louwelsa. This was very like Rookwood Standard ware in appearance, and Weller continued to imitate subsequent Rookwood innovations.

A French potter, Jacques Sicard, joined the business in 1901 and produced Sicardo ware, on which a lustre decoration was applied to an iridescent ground in shades of purple, green and brown. Later, a variation, Lasa ware, was introduced with landscape decoration.

Weller worked too in imitation of French Art Nouveau styles, with relief decorations of flowers, foliage and female figures. Aurelia ware was introduced by 1904, having a brushed ground, also Jap Birdimal, with stylised natural forms as decoration.

At its height the business employed some 600 workers and by 1925 Weller owned three factories producing art pottery, garden and kitchenwares. He was succeeded by his nephew Herbert, who died in 1932, and the factory finally closed in 1949.

Marks include impressed *Weller* with the name of the style, and incised *Weller Faience*.

Weller Dickensware art pottery mantel clock, housed in elaborate pottery frame decorated with yellow pansies, 10in. high. *(Skinner)* **£249 $440**

Weller Pottery Etna pot, Zanesville, Ohio, high gloss glazed and decorated with low relief flowers in rose, yellow, white and green, 4½in. high. *(Skinner)* **£65 $100**

A Weller Sicard twisted pottery vase, iridescent purples and greens with snails in the design, circa 1907, unsigned, 7½in. high. *(Skinner)* **£400 $640**

Weller silvertone vase, exquisite floral modelling on bulbous body with swirling handles and ruffled rim, 8in. high. *(Skinner)* **£306 $460**

Weller Pottery Sicardo vase, Zanesville, Ohio, circa 1905, iridescent glaze in rose, blue and platinum with stylised peacock feather decoration, 5¾in. high.
(Skinner) **£422 $633**

Weller Pottery vase, six raised leaves under a feathered matte green glaze, unsigned, 14in. high.
(Skinner) **£448 $748**

Exceptional and rare Weller glossy Hudson vase, signed *Timberlake*, decorated with orchids, Weller Pottery half-kiln mark, artist signature, 27in. high.
(Skinner) **£14,550 $21,185**

Weller Sicardo glazed pottery vase, early 20th century, decorated in green, blue, fuchsia and gold iridescence, 6½in. high.
(Butterfield & Butterfield) **£445 $690**

Weller Pottery Turada Lamp, blue glaze with raised slip decoration of yellow, blue, and orange, Bradley & Hubbard oil font, six-panel slag glass shade in colours of green, red, and purple, 24in. high, 15in. diameter. *(Skinner)* **£920 $1,500**

Weller Jap Birdimal vase, decorated by Hattie Ross, decorated with bands of birds in white, green and brown, 5¼in. high. *(Skinner)* **£209 $316**

Important and monumental Weller Pottery vase, decorated by Frank Ferrell, accompanied by the 'Gold Medal' award from the St. Louis Louisiana Purchase Exposition in 1904, large apple tree boughs with leaves and branches in colours of green, reddish-brown, yellow, dark brown, on a standard glaze ground, signed by Frank Ferrell, impressed Weller mark, 5ft.8in. high.

Many problems were encountered in its production, and eight attempts were made before the vase was successfully moulded and fired. The upper portion was moulded in two parts and joined together in a special firing before it was decorated by Frank Ferrell. A special kiln was constructed to accommodate the huge vase; and including labour, materials and expenditures from the seven previous failures, the manufacturing cost was estimated at $2,000.

Weller's perseverance was rewarded; his magnificent entry was selected by the International Jury of Awards to receive the Gold Medal in the Arts Category. *(Skinner)* **£71,202 $112,500**

Weller Sicardo Pottery tile, Zanesville, Ohio, Henri Gellee, circa 1905, iridescent green, glazed cross and border with incised outline, 7½in. wide. *(Skinner)* **£400 $600**

Weller Pottery Louwelsa ewer, Zanesville, Ohio, circa 1905, decorated with an oak twig in shades of green with brown and beige. *(Skinner)* **£65 $100**

WIENER WERKSTÄTTE

The Wiener Werkstätte or Vienna Workshops, were, as the name suggests, an association of Austrian artists and craftsmen after the style of C.R. Ashbee's Guild of Handicraft. Their commercial director was F. Warndörfer, and such notables as Koloman Moser and Josef Hoffmann were the first art directors. The aim of the association was to apply artistic principles and designs to the widest possible range of items, from textiles to architecture, and they became, in the succeeding decades, a driving force in European design.

Their ceramics are notable for their stark simplicity of design. Many of their designs were produced by the Wiener Keramik workshop, which was established in 1905 under Michael Powolny and Bertold Löffler. One of their most characteristic items was black and white majolica, painted with geometric patterns in the Cubist style. Powolny and Löffler also modelled figures.

The Wiener Werkstätte themselves finally closed in 1932, mainly because of their inability to compete commercially with mass production.

A Gmunder Keramik covered box, designed by Dagobert Peche for the Wiener Werkstätte in 1912, of octagonal section with domed lid, 16cm. high.
(Phillips) **£300 $584**

A Wiener Werkstätte terracotta figurative mirror, by Vally Wieselthier, square, the frame with three masks and assorted stylised fruit in high relief, 1928, 40 x 28cm.
(Christie's) **£5,750 $8,754**

'Spring', glazed ceramic figure of a putto, designed by Michael Powolny, manufactured by Wiener Keramik, 1907, standing holding a garland of colourful flowers, 15in. high, impressed designer's monogram and Wiener Keramik mark.
(Christie's) **£7,475 $12,184**

A Wiener Werkstätte terracotta polo player by Gudrun Baudisch, on rectangular base, polychrome glazes, 1927, 18.5cm. high. *(Christie's)* **£747 $1,137**

Phyllis, a female terracotta head by Vally Wieselthier, of a young girl with blushing cheeks and wearing a hat decorated with flowers, with painted Wiener Werkstätte monogram, 1919, 35.5cm. high. *(Christie's)* **£6,670 $10,155**

Wiener Werkstätte ceramic figurine, oriental figure with horse in colours of yellow, blue, black, and green on a white ground, 8in. wide. *(Skinner)* **£552 $920**

A Wiener Keramik ceramic wall-mask, moulded as a girl's head with a hat, painted in polychrome glazes, 24cm. high. *(Christie's)* **£700 $1,120**

A Wiener Werkstätte terracotta lamp base by Vally Wieselthier, of abstract design, the double square section foot on rectangular plinth base, polychrome glazes, 1928-29, 34cm. high. *(Christie's)* **£1,955 $2,976**

This Staffordshire pottery firm operated several factories in the Burslem area from the late 19th century. In 1894, Arthur Wilkinson's brother-in-law, Arthur Shorter, took over, keeping the name of Royal Staffordshire Pottery. His son, John took charge of the family's other pottery, Shorter & Son, while his other son Colley remained with his father.

Wilkinson's had produced many Art Nouveau pieces in the early years of the century, such as Oriflamme and Rubaiyat, but demand for these was waning in the early 1920s. In 1920 they bought the adjoining Newport Pottery, and it was here that they employed Clarice Cliff and allowed her to experiment on some undecorated shapes in the works. At this time she was also attending evening classes at Burslem under Gordon Forsyth. Forsyth did not approve of her work, believing it represented the superficial use of aspects of what he called 'modern art', without any understanding of the principles.

Her experiments attracted more favourable attention from Colley Shorter, who decided to try them on the market. Her Bizarre and Crocus ranges met with such acclaim that the whole factory was soon turned over to producing her designs. The rest, as they say, is history, with Colley Shorter marrying Clarice Cliff in 1940.

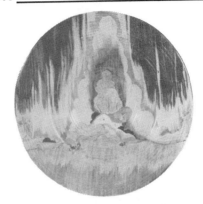

A Wilkinson Bizarre pottery circular charger, by Clarice Cliff, 18¼in. diameter. *(Andrew Hartley)* **£1,600 $2,500**

A Wilkinson Pottery wall mask from the Bizarre series by Clarice Cliff, printed factory marks, 8in. high. 1930s. *(Muir Hewitt)* **£455 $690**

A 'Circus' pattern sugar bowl, designed by Dame Laura Knight, raised upon a short foot with flared rim, the centre well enamelled and gilt with a clown holding open puce drapes before a starlit sky, puce printed marks *Designed by Laura Knight A.R.A. Produced in Bizarre by Clarice Cliff Wilkinson Ltd. England. Copyright Reserved First Edition 1934.* *(Bonhams)* **£440 $720**

Frank Brangwyn for Wilkinson Ltd, painted by Clarice Cliff, painted plaque, 1932-3, 17½in. diameter. *(Sotheby's)* **£1,320 $2,138**

A Wilkinson Ltd matchstriker, formed as a seated dog with painted yellow, black and purple patches, the base titled *Do Scratch my Back*, 12.5cm. long.
(Bristol Auction Rooms) **£85 $125**

A Wilkinson Ltd. toby jug of Winston Churchill modelled by Clarice Cliff, seated on a bulldog draped with a Union Jack, 30.5cm. *(Phillips)* **£625 $1,000**

A 'Circus' pattern milk jug, designed by Dame Laura Knight, with swollen body moulded in full relief with a female acrobat with body arched, the bowl decorated with yellow chevron beneath purple swags outlined in gilt, puce printed marks *Designed by Laura Knight A.R.A. Produced in Bizarre by Clarice Cliff Wilkinson Ltd. England. Copyright Reserved First Edition 1934.* (Bonhams) **£320 $520**

A 'Circus' pattern teapot and cover, designed by Dame Laura Knight, the handle decorated in relief with the figure of a female acrobat arched backwards, the cover knop modelled in the form of two clown's heads, the teapot raised upon four clown style feet, the body decorated with a border of faces, 7¼in. high, puce printed marks *Designed by Laura Knight A.R.A. Produced in Bizarre by Clarice Cliff Wilkinson Ltd. England. Copyright Reserved First Edition 1934.* (Bonhams) **£1,100 $1,800**

Clarice Cliff Wilkinson Bizarre Biarritz plate, decorated with the 'Tralee' pattern of sinuous grey stemmed tree with shaded green foliage, 10½in. high.
(G.A. Key) **£200 $314**